Race, Police, and the Making
of a Political Identity

LATINOS IN AMERICAN SOCIETY AND CULTURE

Mario T. García, Editor

Race, Police, and the Making of a Political Identity

Mexican Americans and the Los Angeles Police Department, 1900–1945

Edward J. Escobar

UNIVERSITY OF CALIFORNIA PRESS

Berkeley • *Los Angeles* • *London*

University of California Press
Berkeley and Los Angeles, California

University of California Press, Ltd.
London, England

© 1999 by the
Regents of the University of California

Library of Congress Cataloging-in-Publication Data

Escobar, Edward J.

    Race, police, and the making of a political
identity : Mexican Americans and the Los
Angeles Police Department, 1900–1945 / Edward
J. Escobar.
        p. cm.—(Latinos in American society and
culture)
    Includes bibliographic references and index.
    ISBN 978-0-520-21335-7 (pbk.: alk. paper)

    1. Police—California—Los Angeles—History—
20th century. 2. Los Angeles (Calif.). Police Dept.—
History—20th century. 3. Police—community
relations—California—Los Angeles—History—
20th century. 4. Mexican Americans—California—
Los Angeles—History—20th century. I.
Title. II. Series. HV8148.L55E73 1999
  365'.9794'93—dc21   98-23322

Manufactured in the United States of America
16 15 14 13 12 11 10
10 9 8 7 6 5 4 3

To my parents,
Steve Escobar (1902–1984)
and
Carmen Bernal Escobar,
for their love and support and the
example of their courage

Contents

Tables

Acknowledgments

As one might expect for a project that took so long to complete, I owe a debt of gratitude to many people who assisted me through the years. First and foremost I wish to thank my wife, Gayle Gullett, whose love, patience, support, and gentle prodding enabled me to continue when my own courage failed. More important, as a noted historian herself, Gayle's intellectual contributions, her numerous reviews and edits of the manuscript, her insightful critiques of the analysis, her sharing of sources, and finally, our ongoing discussion on the nature of historical inquiry greatly enhanced the overall quality of this work.

Numerous other scholars read all or portions of the manuscript and assisted me in inestimable ways. Carlos E. Cortés, in directing the dissertation from which this study evolved, set a standard for historical writing that I hope I approximated here. His passion for precision in both method and analysis, his incisive and demanding critiques, and his faith that I had the ability to become a real historian not only made this book possible but serve as a model for the way to support graduate students. I am deeply indebted to my friend and mentor. I also wish to thank Vicki Ruiz and Mario T. García, who read the entirety of the manuscript. Their insightful comments and queries sharpened my analysis in crucial portions of the text. Rodolfo Acuña, Albert Camarillo, Candy Candelaria, Ronald Cohen, Lewis Erenberg, Juan García, Susan E. Hirsch, James Lane, George Lipsitz, F. Arturo Rosales, Rudy Torres, Lynne Withey, and several anonymous readers read segments of the manuscript and provided insights, commentary, and encouragement along the way. Special thanks also go to the editorial staff at the University of California Press, in particular to Lynne Withey, Monica McCormick, Jan Spauschus Johnson, and Bonita Hurd. All of them contributed to the quality of the final product; any mistakes are my responsibility.

My family has been a constant source of inspiration and support. My parents, the late Steve Escobar and Carmen Bernal Escobar, supported my prolonged education both financially and emotionally. More important, through their hard work, their courage, and their stories of their own struggles to create a labor movement in Los Angeles, they instilled in me a love of history and a dedication to social justice. It is with love, gratitude, and admiration that I dedicate this book to them. My brother and sister, Alfred Escobar and Rebecca Escobar, have helped me in ways I can never repay. Finally, I wish to thank Bill and Pat Gullett not only for their consistent support but also for their daughter.

Many institutions and individuals assisted me in conducting the research for this project. Thanks go to the professional staffs of the Huntington Library, the Southern California Library for Social Studies and Research, the Special Collections sections at the University Research Library at the University of California, Los Angeles, and Green Library at Stanford University. Gayle Gullett, Ruth Needleman, and F. Arturo Rosales generously shared their own research with me. Jaime Aguila, Luisa Bonillas, Steve Ammerman, Teresa Delgadillo, José Maldonado, Pánfilo Márquez, Laura Muñoz, and Nick Tapia provided important research assistance along the way. Judith Steele, former staff historian for the Los Angeles Police Department, gave me access to the department's library and archives and provided invaluable advice on how to maneuver the LAPD bureaucracy to find other sources of information. William G. Cowdin, Secretary to the Board of Police Commissioners, furnished facilities for my review of police commission minutes. The Los Angeles Board of Police Commissioners gave me access to internal and previously confidential LAPD documents, and the staff of the Los Angeles City Records Center/Los Angeles City Archives provided both the facility and the hospitality for my review of those documents. Finally, I owe a particular debt of gratitude to the memory of Lewis Unger, Deputy Los Angeles City Attorney, who personally reviewed all the internal LAPD documents to ensure that privacy and other confidentiality laws and policies were not violated by the documents' release.

I am also grateful to several other institutions and individuals who supported this project in important ways. Stanford University Graduate

Deans W. Bliss Carnochan and Gerald J. Lieberman gave me leave from my administrative duties to begin writing this study. Albert Camarillo and Armando Vásquez allowed me use of the facilities of the Stanford Center for Chicano Research for writing those initial drafts. The Ford Foundation and the National Research Council provided the opportunity to conduct the research through a Ford Foundation Postdoctoral Fellowship for Minorities. I also received financial assistance through the Indiana University Northwest Faculty Summer Fellowship and Faculty Grant-in-Aid programs. Special thanks go to IUN's Chancellor Peggy Elliot, who provided help at a crucial point in the development of this project.

Various other people supported and inspired me throughout my career. Rudy Acuña was the first Chicano professor I ever met; he taught my first Chicano history class, encouraged me to go to graduate school, helped me get my first full-time teaching job, steadfastly encouraged the completion of this book, and most important, impressed me with the importance of incorporating political activism with academic life. Hal Bridges, Leon Campbell, Alice Clement, Robert Hine, and of course, Carlos Cortés have in different times and different ways been mentors, models, and friends. I owe a special debt of gratitude for their friendship and support to David Gutiérrez, Rick Olguín, George Sánchez, Louise Año Nuevo Kerr, F. Arturo Rosales, and my colleagues at Indiana University Northwest, Martín Becerra, Jack Bloom, Fred Chary, Ronald Cohen, Tanice Foltz, Charles Gallmeier, Earl Jones, Paul Kern, Angeline Komenich, James Lane, Inma Minoves-Myers, Ruth Needleman, Rhiman Rotz, and Dorothy Williamson Ige. The National Association for Chicana and Chicano Studies through the years provided a forum to present my research and both inspired and provoked me to new levels of analysis. It is my hope that this organization will continue to provide the same opportunity for emerging scholars.

The community of scholars involved in various ways with Chicana/o Studies at Arizona State University has served as a source of inspiration for the last four and a half years. While my role in leading the effort to create a Department of Chicana/o Studies certainly delayed the completion of this book, the opportunity to succeed in that endeavor and to interact with such a group of dedicated and committed intellectuals improved the final product in innumerable ways. Equally important have been my colleagues in ASU's History Department, especially former department chair Retha Warnicke. Their collegiality and support for the completion of both this project and my work in Chicana and Chicano

Studies helped me to successfully make the transition to a large research university. Among the people I have come to know at ASU, none deserves more of my thanks than Susan Alameda, whose integrity, professionalism, and, most of all, friendship sustained me through the most difficult times.

Finally, I wish to acknowledge my children, Marcos and Cristina. They do not remember a time when this project was not in progress. I apologize to them for the times I've been away, for the times I've chased them out of the study, and for the times I've been in a foul mood because the writing was not going well. I also thank them for their smiling faces, their laughter, their tears, and, yes, even for their interruptions. Marcos and Cristina put this book in its proper perspective: they are a daily reminder of why we engage in the work we do.

CHAPTER I

Introduction

Race and Criminal Justice

Between June 3 and June 10, 1943, the city of Los Angeles was wrenched by the worst rioting it had seen in the twentieth century. Incited by sensational newspaper stories and the statements of public officials, scores of white servicemen, sometimes joined by civilians and even police officers, roamed the streets of the city in search of Mexican American young men and boys wearing a distinctive style of dress called a zoot suit. When they found the zoot suiters, the servicemen attacked and beat the youths, tearing off their clothes and leaving them naked and bleeding in the gutters.[1]

The riots threw a harsh light upon the deteriorating relationship between the Los Angeles Mexican American community and the Los Angeles Police Department (LAPD) in the early 1940s. During the riots, the LAPD enforced the law selectively. Officers allowed servicemen to beat and strip the zoot suiters; only after the servicemen left the scene did police take action—arresting the Mexican American youths for disturbing the peace. Police arrested only a handful of servicemen during the riots but incarcerated over six hundred Mexican Americans.[2] With the passivity of the police, the level of violence escalated. Servicemen entered bars, theaters, dance halls, restaurants, and even private homes in search of victims. Toward the end of the rioting, the servicemen expanded their attacks to include all Mexican Americans, whether they wore zoot suits or not, and African Americans too.

At first, the Mexican American community did not respond directly to the attacks. In the initial days of the riots, neither the zoot-suit "gangs" (as the police and press had dubbed the loosely organized youth groups that had developed in Mexican American neighborhoods) nor Mexican American middle-class organizations took steps to stop the disorder. As the rioting continued and, in particular, as it became evident that the police were not protecting the community, zoot suiters began to defend themselves. According to the local press, bands of youngsters fought pitched battles with servicemen, civilians, and police in various parts of the city. The middle-class organizations also protested the increasing violence, albeit more cautiously. The rioting did not subside until the United States War Department concluded that local law-enforcement agencies could not or would not control the situation and declared parts of Los Angeles "out of bounds" to military personnel.

The Zoot Suit riots exposed a festering wound that infected the body politic of the city of Los Angeles. At its core lay a virulent anti-Mexican racism and the resultant alienation among a growing segment of Mexican American youth. The racism manifested itself as discrimination in employment, education, housing, and public accommodations. Without a doubt, however, the intertwined issues of the zoot-suit phenomenon and police misconduct received the greatest publicity and aroused the most intense passions.

The zoot-suit style and the youth subculture that accompanied it emerged from the anti-Mexican racism and its local manifestations. Much like youth subcultures in other societies, the zoot suiters were reacting to the unkept promises of mid-twentieth-century American society.[3] Educated in public schools to expect that through hard work and determination anything could be accomplished, these young people instead found their way to success barred by racial discrimination. They responded not through direct political action—a practical impossibility for them anyway—but through the symbolic rebellion of wearing an outlandish style of clothing that they knew would provoke an intense reaction from authority figures.

The reaction, however, was more dramatic than these youths anticipated and certainly greater than they wanted. Fueled by rabid and sensational newspaper coverage of juvenile crime, a public hysteria developed over an alleged zoot-suiter crime wave. One manifestation of this hysteria was the infamous Sleepy Lagoon trial that ended in January 1943. Seventeen young Mexican American men were convicted of murder without the prosecution's having presented any evidence that any of the defendants had so much as assaulted the victim. Within the context of this hysteria, police officials announced that they believed that Mexican Americans were biologically inclined toward criminality and that law-enforcement authorities needed to use harsh measures to keep the youths under control.

Because of the attitude of those in law enforcement and the resulting police practices, Mexican Americans in turn reached some harsh conclusions about the LAPD. Many believed that police regularly violated Mexican Americans' rights, that they were inclined toward chronic abuse of the community, and that the community would have to organize itself politically to combat police misconduct. They formed organizations, such as the Sleepy Lagoon Defense Committee, which sought to remedy some of the worst injustices by publicizing the anti-Mexican bias that seemed to pervade the criminal justice system. Their efforts and the often defensive response of the police and government officials contributed to the hostility and animosity that defined the relationship between much of the Mexican American community and the LAPD in the period after World War II.

Writing from the perspective of the late twentieth century, it is hard to imagine a time when conflict was not the underlying theme in the relationship between Chicanos and the LAPD and, more broadly, in the relationship between racial minorities and police.[4] The truth is, however, that the nature and level of this conflict are phenomena of the first half of the century. While relations between the minority communities and urban police have never been "good," the fundamental assumptions upon which the current animosity is based have existed only since the end of World War II. These assumptions are the institutionalized belief within the law-enforcement community that Chicanos and other minority groups are criminally inclined and minority people's understanding that they must protect themselves from police misconduct through strident political activism. The purpose of this study is to examine how these two assumptions developed.

The need for this study stems from the lack of rigorous and in-depth historical analysis of the relationship between Chicanos and big city police departments. Despite the seemingly chronic nature of the poor relations between the two groups, there is no published historical study on relations between Mexican Americans (or, for that matter, any other minority group) and an urban police department. Much of the literature that does exist comes from the social sciences, and to the extent that historical analysis is even attempted it is essentially static, showing little if any change over time. Even the historians who have addressed the

issue have written primarily institutional histories of either the criminal
justice system or urban police departments. To the extent that historians
and other social scientists have addressed police–minority group relations, they have pictured police as the active agents and Chicanos and
other minority groups as the passive and unwitting victims of police
aggression. Besides this obvious essentialization, historians have neglected to investigate the impact of changes in policing on minority communities or how the presence of minority communities has affected the
police. The present study seeks to remedy this situation.[5]

The state of the scholarly literature on police–minority community
relations resulted from the crisis situation from which much of it
emerged. The urban uprisings of the mid-1960s—almost all of which
were sparked by violent encounters between police and minority citizens—provoked a plethora of governmental reports and scholarly studies on the relationship between the Chicano, Puerto Rican, and African
American communities and American law-enforcement agencies. While
these reports and studies lacked historical analysis, they became the accepted interpretation of police–minority community relations throughout the rest of the century. The studies of the 1960s and 1970s generally
concluded that an adversarial relationship existed between minority
groups and law enforcement and that the cause for this state of affairs
lay with what the National Advisory Committee on Civil Disorders (also
known as the Kerner Commission after commission chairman Otto Kerner) called "abrasive" police practices.[6]

A March 1970 report by the United States Civil Rights Commission
entitled *Mexican Americans and the Administration of Justice in the
Southwest* illustrated officials' and scholars' definition of abrasive police
practices. The commission found "evidence of widespread . . . police
misconduct against Mexican Americans." Examples included "excessive
police violence," "discriminatory treatment of juveniles," "excessive use
of arrests for 'investigation' and of 'stop and frisk,' " and interference
with Mexican American political organizations.[7]

While the various studies generally conceded that a hostile relationship existed between police and the minority communities, they disagreed on the nature of and causes for these abrasive practices and the
resulting mutual antagonism. Politically charged groups such as the Kerner Commission, which had to allow for the views of the law-
enforcement community, minimized the actual incidence of police misconduct and hinted that blacks were overly sensitive to standard police
practices. In contrast, independent scholars acknowledged a high inci-

dence of police misconduct as the major cause for the hostility and focused on attitudinal and structural factors as causes of abusive police practices. Most blamed racial prejudice among white officers for their egregious actions. Sociologist Jerome Skolnick stated that "anyone who has spent any time observing police, with any degree of depth, would have to agree that as a group the police are highly antagonistic to Negroes." Scholars believed that this attitude resulted primarily from broader social assumptions about race and ethnicity. Skolnick, for example, agreed with the notion that the average officer "is probably no more prejudiced than his fellow citizens who lead lives isolated from Negroes." In the case of police officers, however, racial prejudice had broader societal implications because it resulted in different standards of police conduct toward minority citizens.[8]

Combining with racial prejudice are the two structural factors that scholars have most often identified as leading to police misconduct—namely, police professionalism and a related police work culture. Initially developed by progressive reformers at the turn of the century and later refined by theorists from within the law-enforcement community itself, the professionalism model alleged that policing demanded as high a level of expertise as other professions. Advocates of the model argued that as professionals, police officers deserved the same level of respect and autonomy as doctors and lawyers. Professionalism also demanded that police develop more efficient methods in the "war against crime." By midcentury, the professionalism model had become the standard by which modern urban police departments judged themselves.

Scholars who subsequently studied this model believed that several of its aspects led to poor relations between police and minority groups. The model called for personnel deployment strategies that placed more officers per capita in minority communities than in white communities and for aggressive preventive patrol tactics that demanded that officers make an increasing number of field interrogations in those communities. These practices led to increased unsatisfactory contact between police and minority citizens and hence to more complaints of police misconduct. Moreover, police control over their own disciplinary process—the most fundamental element of the professionalism model—and an occupational culture that made officers hostile to any outside criticism made it more difficult for minority citizens to lodge successful complaints about police misconduct.[9]

Government commissions and independent scholars alike pointed to the increasing incidence of complaints from minority citizens and the

equally decreasing responsiveness of police departments to those complaints as being among the principal factors that led to the hostility
between the minority communities and the police and to the urban unrest of the 1960s. In an almost prescient analysis, the United States Civil
Rights Commission issued a scathing report in March 1970 detailing
antagonism between the Chicano community and the police, just five
months before major rioting broke out between the two in Los Angeles.
The commission found that in reaction to chronic police misconduct,
"the attitude of Mexican Americans toward . . . police . . . is distrustful,
fearful, and hostile. Police departments, courts, the law itself are viewed
as Anglo institutions in which Mexican Americans have no stake and
from which they do not expect fair treatment."[10]

The basic problem with the prevailing line of analysis that emerged
from the 1960s studies, and even from some more recent reports, is not
so much that it is wrong, but that it is incomplete.[11] To make the analysis
more complete and robust, we must go beyond simplistic and static
notions of racism, professionalism, and work culture and take into account the historical process by which these factors, and other equally
important ones, have evolved. For example, societal racism has infected
not just individual police officers but the police institution itself. Even
more important, evolving police notions linking race and criminality
have infiltrated the wider culture and have altered the way in which
society defines race and racial characteristics. Society has come to equate
minority communities, and especially minority youth, with violent
crime. Not surprisingly, these perceptions have led to popular support
for increased police budgets and autonomy, thus helping to implement
the professionalism model. Finally, contrary to the victimization model
employed by many liberal scholars, the minority communities, through
their political activism and other forms of resistance, have themselves
played a vital role in shaping their relationship with the police.

This book seeks to expand on these concepts by studying the changing nature of the relationship between the Los Angeles Police Department—arguably the most important American urban police department
of the second half of the twentieth century—and that city's largest racial
minority group, Mexican Americans, during the years 1900–1945. This
study's primary finding is that during the years in question the relationship between the two groups changed from one in which neither side
had a particular view of the other to one in which both sides viewed the
other with deep suspicion and hostility. From the interactions between
Mexican Americans and the police, the LAPD concluded that Mexican

Americans, especially Mexican American youths, were a criminally inclined group that needed to be dealt with harshly. The same interactions taught many Mexican Americans that police regularly violated their rights, that they were inclined toward chronic abuse of the Mexican American community, and that the community would have to organize itself politically to combat police misconduct. Informing this narrative are the following three factors: the dynamic nature of race in American society; the role and development of the American police institution—in particular, the LAPD; and the development of the Los Angeles Mexican American community. I will now discuss each of these factors in more detail.

Race is today generally understood, if not by the general public then at least by scholars, as a socially constructed concept. Geneticists and other biological scientists agree that the relationship between genetic structure and morphology is at best haphazard, that no one race possesses a gene or set of genes not possessed by other races, that "one's race is not determined by a single gene or gene cluster," and that there is greater genetic variation within a given race than there is between the races. Thus, there is no scientific basis for the racial categories we typically employ in everyday life.[12]

Rather, race is a socially defined and constructed concept that distinguishes among groups within a population, usually by phenotype but through other mechanisms too, for the purposes of subordination and exploitation.[13] As a socially constructed concept, race is dynamic by definition. What attributes constitute a race, which groups are defined as separate races, and how those races are treated change over time and may even vary from one race to another at any given historical moment. Thus, American society has at times viewed certain European immigrants—the Irish, Jews, and other Eastern Europeans—as separate races and other times as white. Similarly, during the nineteenth century white Americans viewed Mexicans, American Indians, and blacks as different races, but for different reasons and with the consequences of racialization differing for each group. Moreover, even when society has maintained a group in a racialized status over a long period, the basis of that racialization (the social assumptions about the group that maintain it as racially "other") changes over time.

The history of people of Mexican descent living in the United States provides an excellent example of the process of racialization. Mexicans were first racialized during the mid-nineteenth century through the rhetoric of Manifest Destiny, by which Americans sought to justify the Mexican-American War. The United States fought the war to acquire Mexico's northern territories of Texas, New Mexico, and California. American notions of fairness and international justice, however, precluded the United States from waging war against a weaker nation simply for territorial aggrandizement. The rhetoric of Manifest Destiny sought to alleviate these notions by alleging that the inherent superiority of the Anglo-Saxon race and its political, social, and economic institutions gave the United States the right, if not the responsibility, to bring under its control as much of the North American continent as possible. The racial component of this argument resulted in the dehumanization of Mexicans.[14]

Nineteenth-century American racial ideology was based on a biological essentialism that placed whites at the top of the racial hierarchy and Mexicans, along with Indians and blacks, at the bottom. Proponents of expansion justified aggression against Mexico by claiming that the Mexican people were an inherently inferior, "mongrel race" that deserved death and annihilation if they stood in the way of Anglo-Saxon expansion.

The racialization of Mexican people continued during the second half of the nineteenth century despite the fact that the United States had won the Mexican-American War. The historian Arnaldo De León has detailed the fundamental elements of American racial ideology as it applied to Mexican Americans and has concluded that whites considered Mexicans "a species of humanity different from (and inferior to) Anglos." Racial rhetoric tended to become particularly explicit whenever Mexicans and whites competed for control of vital economic resources such as land or labor. Mexicans, however, also engaged in the process of racial formation. According to the historian David Gutiérrez, nineteenth-century Mexican Americans adopted the term "la Raza" (literally, the race) to counter "the stigmatized status many Americans sought to impose on Mexicans." While Mexican Americans have consistently attempted to explain that la Raza has a connotation different from that of the English term *race,* that very effort shows the impact of its usage in American society.[15]

The biological essentialism of nineteenth-century American racial ideology carried over into the first three decades of the twentieth century. Spurred by the massive influx of Mexican immigrants into the United States, opponents of immigration used classic biological determinism to bolster their calls for restriction of Mexican immigration. Restrictionists took for granted the racial inferiority of the Mexican people and feared that continued immigration and Mexican fecundity would overrun the Southwest; many spoke of the negative "race value" of the Mexican population. In particular they feared that miscegenation between Mexicans and whites—which they labeled "mongrelization"—would lead to "the most insidious and general mixture of white, Indian, and negro blood strains ever produced in America." No wonder, then, that the Vanderbilt University economist Roy Garis argued that continued Mexican immigration to the Southwest would result in "the creation of a race problem that will dwarf the negro problem in the South" and in "the practical destruction, at least for centuries, of all that is worthwhile in our white civilization." Significantly, at least for the purposes of this study, Garis supported his argument with criminological studies that claimed that Mexicans were inherently inclined toward criminality.[16]

Proponents of continued Mexican immigration also bolstered the process of racialization, but put a positive spin on it. Employers in agriculture and other areas that profited from cheap immigrant labor generally conceded the racial inferiority of the Mexican population but attempted to use the restrictionists' argument to their own advantage. These antirestrictionists argued that the immigrants did not pose a permanent threat to white demographic dominance because Mexicans possessed a natural "homing instinct" that lured them back to Mexico. Miscegenation, they claimed, was not a problem because Mexican men did not desire white women. They did not pose other social problems because Mexicans were by nature "a very docile people." According to the Texas congressman and future vice president John Nance Garner, Mexicans "can be imposed on, the sheriff can go out and make them do anything. That is the way they are. So far as the laws of our state are concerned, they do not violate them." Finally, the antirestrictionists argued that the restrictionists' fears flew in the face of the generally accepted racial hierarchy. "Have you ever heard," asked an Arizona agricultural spokesman, "in the history of the United States, or in the history of the human race, of the white race being overrun by a class of people of the mentality of the Mexicans?"[17]

Around the turn of the twentieth century, academicians began to question the concept of race as a biological construct and to replace it with cultural and sociological definitions. This new understanding of race was most fully articulated by Robert E. Park and his Chicago school of sociology during the 1930s and 1940s. For Park and his disciples, race was a function of ethnicity, and they equated ethnicity with the experiences of European immigrants in the United States. Like the European immigrants, racial minorities were expected to achieve social mobility and eventual assimilation into mainstream American society. To the extent that racial groups did not readily assimilate, ethnicity theorists saw their cultures as flawed. By World War II these notions of ethnicity and race had gained theoretical dominance and begun to enter popular consciousness and to influence public policy.[18]

While the abandonment of biological theories of race was a welcome circumstance, the ascendancy of ethnicity theory continued the racialization process for Mexican Americans. In equating racial groups' experiences with those of white European immigrants, ethnicity theory failed to consider the fact that the racialized status of Mexican Americans placed them in a chronically subordinated position in American society. Social scientists persisted in looking for flaws in Mexican American culture to explain the lack of social mobility or assimilation of Mexican Americans. According to such thinking, poor performance in school resulted from a present, rather than a future, orientation; low income came from a poor work ethic; and lack of political representation resulted from an inability to organize. Ethnicity theory was therefore every bit as deterministic as biological theories of race, and it served to reinforce negative attitudes among white public officials and the general public toward Mexican Americans.

Nowhere was the impact of ethnicity theory more evident or more significant than in the linkage of race and criminality. At the beginning of the century, while Mexicans were certainly seen by whites as an inferior race, they were not generally regarded by government and law-enforcement officials as inherently criminal. Even the LAPD articulated no such view. During the subsequent half century, however, the deterioration of the relationship between Mexican Americans and the LAPD, and especially the hysteria during World War II over juvenile delinquency, thrust Mexican American youth into the national consciousness as a criminal element in society. Henceforth, the youth "gang" became the metaphor through which much of white society viewed Mexican Americans. While many of the old ideas of Mexicans as lazy and stupid persisted, they eventually faded into the background, only to be replaced with the image of the vicious and treacherous gang member. This was a major reconstitution of the attributes that defined Mexican Americans as a separate race. Moreover, because the crisis achieved national and even international attention, the new definition of Mexican Americans as a criminally inclined racial group became embedded in the national consciousness. While social scientists clamored that race, as a biological construct, was no longer valid, most people, including law-enforcement officials, continued to distinguish on the basis of race. Mexican Americans had become a criminal element within the society and had to be dealt with accordingly.

At the same time, and somewhat ironically, the redefinition of Mexican Americans' racial status also had some salutary effects. The Zoot Suit riots of June 1943 and the efforts of the Mexican American groups to overcome racial injustice highlighted the dire economic conditions under which Mexican Americans lived, the hostility they faced from their white neighbors, and the discrimination—or, at best, indifference—they endured from police, school, and other governmental officials. Thus, the new definition included Mexican Americans as an oppressed and disadvantaged "minority" group whose problems had to be addressed in order to achieve civic harmony. Local business and government leaders established the Los Angeles County Human Relations Commission, whose function was to deal with the problems of racial minority groups. The designation of Mexican Americans as a racial minority elevated their political status, and they dominated the Los Angeles civil rights agenda from the 1940s until the early 1960s.

The function of police in American society has also contributed to the historically antagonistic relationship between Chicanos and the police. As agents of social control, police have historically played a conservative role. Urban elites created the first police departments during the mid-nineteenth century to control the burgeoning working class in industrializing northeastern cities. As the police institution spread and evolved throughout the rest of the nineteenth century and into the first decades of the twentieth century, it continued to concentrate its efforts on maintaining order in the working-class sections of urban America. Police patrolled city streets picking up drunks, jailing vagrants, and if not suppressing vice, at least making it invisible to ensure that the refuse of industrialized society did not disrupt the lives of the more genteel classes. On a more sinister level, police acted as the willing pawns of factory owners and chambers of commerce in suppressing labor unions, radical political organizations, and other expressions of working-class sentiment. As the legal scholar Lawrence Friedman has noted, throughout the nineteenth century and much of the twentieth century, the police functioned as "the army of the status quo."[19]

Law enforcement's essential conservatism is not an accident of history; rather, it stems from the nature of the police function. Maintaining order is a concept that can be taken either literally or metaphorically.

On a literal level, police are taught to be suspicious of anything out of the ordinary. At midcentury, it became a policy for police departments to act on their suspicions. In a 1963 article in *Police* magazine on the issue of field interrogations, the author advised officers to "look for the unusual"—specifically, to be on watch for "persons who do not 'belong' where they are observed [and] automobiles which do not 'look right.' " While courts have since ruled this practice (called profiling in police parlance) unconstitutional, it still continues informally, especially in more affluent areas.[20]

On a broader level the police also enforce the existing social and economic order. Law enforcement functions as the coercive arm of the state, the role of police in any society regardless of its social or economic system. In a capitalist society with inherent class inequalities and equally apparent race distinctions that approximate class distinctions, the police play an important role in maintaining racial inequality. During the first half of the twentieth century, when racial inequality was codified through Jim Crow laws, this role for the police was explicit and overt. But even when a given action does not violate the law, police often enforce racial restrictions as part of their normal mandate to maintain order. Thus, when officers conduct a field interrogation of Chicano youth in a white neighborhood simply because they do not "belong," police not so subtly reinforce the idea that Mexicans should stay in their place. The role of the police in supporting the racial hierarchy becomes overt again when, in the name of maintaining order, they undermine the protest activities of minority groups.[21]

Modern police departments, however, are not simply the pawns of capital. As part of the state apparatus, law enforcement today often plots for itself a course that is at least seemingly independent from, and sometimes even at odds with, capitalist interests. This independent course stems from the professionalism model's major dictum of autonomy from political control. When police departments began adopting professionalism during the middle third of the century, they also began developing agendas that promoted their own bureaucratic interests while—and this is most important—still performing their essential function of supporting the capitalist economic order. Particularly in controlling minority groups, law enforcement has been extraordinarily successful in conflating both agendas. Through the concept of the "thin blue line," police function in the late twentieth century as what author Mike Davis has called the "space police," protecting the enclaves of the rich and powerful from the frustrated and therefore dangerous minority communities.

In return, elites have generally supported law enforcement's arguments for augmented budgets and increased independence.[22]

The history of the LAPD in the first half of the twentieth century demonstrates the impact of professionalization not only on everyday police practices but also on the department's relationship with the white working class and with the minority communities. Prior to 1938, the LAPD functioned as the rather crude instrument by which local business associations maintained Los Angeles as the "citadel of the open shop." Throughout this period, but especially during the 1920s and 1930s, LAPD officers infiltrated labor unions and other "radical" organizations, sabotaged their efforts, violently broke up their meetings and picket lines, and generally harassed and intimidated organized labor and other leftist organizations in Los Angeles. Two sets of consequences resulted from these actions. First, as long as the LAPD successfully performed these functions, it could count on employer groups to support its ongoing demands for additional municipal funding. This vital support came despite the LAPD's reputation as one of the most corrupt police departments in the country. Second, while the experiences of Mexican American workers probably did not differ greatly from those of other Los Angeles unionists and radicals, police repression did help maintain Mexican workers in a subordinated status and it engendered hostility between the Mexican community and the LAPD.

Toward the end of the Depression decade, however, several phenomena converged to change the nature of the relationship between the LAPD and the community it served. First, the department adopted professionalism as its model for reform after a 1938 recall election and the subsequent dismissal of the corrupt chief of police. While the LAPD did not become fully professionalized until the 1950s, the initial efforts of the new reform administration were both controversial and costly and therefore demanded broad political support. The traditional sources of support became more problematic, however, when a general rapprochement occurred between organized labor and business groups that resulted in the LAPD losing employers' automatic backing for its budgetary requests. In order to expand its political base, the LAPD shifted its emphasis from union busting to another aspect of the professionalism model—that of conducting a "war on crime."

The LAPD's declaration of war against the city's "criminal elements" coincided with the department's linking of race and criminality. This association resulted partly from the literature in the emerging field of criminology and the way in which the department interpreted arrest

statistics. In addition, the early 1940s saw the emergence of a rebellious
Mexican American youth culture. This culture was most prominently
characterized by young Mexican American males wearing an outlandish
outfit called a zoot suit, speaking in a special argot called Caló, and
assuming a definitely rebellious, if not hostile, public attitude toward
authority. While a majority of Mexican American youths wore some
part of the zoot suit, only a small number, the so-called pachucos, consistently engaged in pathological, antisocial behavior. Nevertheless,
enough youth crime existed for the police and the press to attribute all
such offenses to zoot-suit gangs. By the end of the war both police and
public equated Mexican American youth with the zoot suit and the zoot
suit with gangsterism.

Government officials and the public reacted with horror and con-
sternation at this unprecedented outbreak of racial and generational defiance. They saw the zoot-suit phenomenon as a sign of the inherent
social deviance in the Mexican American "race" and the pathological
nature of Mexican culture. This analysis led directly to the development
of a broad consensus that Mexican Americans were either biologically
or sociologically inclined toward criminality. On the basis of that conclusion Los Angeles government officials, with the firm backing of the
city's white majority population, gave the LAPD plentiful resources and
broad latitude to institute harsh measures to deal with what the department defined as the criminal elements within the community.[23]

The LAPD, however, did not dictate its relationship with the Mexican
American community. As a public entity, the department had to react
to the political activism that emanated even from this largely disenfranchised minority group. While the essence of that political activism consisted of Mexican Americans' efforts to overcome their chronically subordinated status in American society, the form that the activism took
changed as the Mexican American community developed.[24]

In the nineteenth century, Mexican political activity resulted from the
lingering effects of the Mexican-American War (1846–1848). As noted
earlier, the United States had initiated and prosecuted the war in order
to acquire Mexico's northern provinces, especially California. The
Treaty of Guadalupe Hidalgo ended the war, confirmed that acquisition,
and guaranteed the rights of the approximately one hundred thousand
Mexicans living in those territories. But the Mexicans who remained in
this area, which became known as the American Southwest, never
achieved equality. Indeed, as a result of the enduring effects of the racist
rhetoric of Manifest Destiny that Americans had used to justify the war,

Mexicans found themselves relegated to the position of a politically disenfranchised, economically subordinated, and socially ostracized racial
group. They responded to their generalized subordination by developing
a relatively cohesive ethnic identity and generating a series of defense
mechanisms to protect themselves from the worst aspects of American
racism. In addition, throughout the nineteenth century, some Mexicans,
with at least the tacit support of a large part of the community, engaged
in social banditry to protest their subordinated status.[25]

The arrival of as many as 1.5 million Mexican immigrants between
1890 and 1930 fundamentally altered the nature of the Mexican American community in the United States. By greatly enlarging the Mexican
neighborhoods, or barrios, these newcomers reinforced the presence of
Mexican culture in the Southwest. This influx did not, however, alter
the low status assigned to Mexican Americans, that of an inferior racial
group. This status was manifested in a number of ways, but undoubtedly
the most important was in the continued economic exploitation of Mexican workers. As new workers came into the labor market they were
allowed to compete only for the most menial and lowest-paying jobs.
Thus, many Mexican Americans living in rural areas became migrant
farmworkers and as such were the mainstay of Southwestern agribusiness. In urban areas, including Los Angeles, the overwhelming majority
of Mexican Americans found jobs only in unskilled, blue-collar occupations. The resulting low income meant that Mexican American families lived in conditions that were among the most destitute of any ethnic
group in the country. Mexicans also suffered from overt discrimination
in many other areas, including education, housing, and public accommodations.

Throughout the twentieth century Mexican Americans have used a
variety of strategies to overcome these disadvantages. In the early part
of the century their efforts went largely into the economic arena, with
workers in particular industries either forming overtly nationalistic
Mexican labor unions or joining white-led unions. As community institutions developed, Mexican Americans turned their attention to fighting
other forms of discrimination. In both cases, the resulting protest was
explicit and narrowly focused, as in the work of the labor unions and
the efforts of civil rights groups like the League of United Latin American
Citizens (LULAC). Often, however, the protest was more symbolic and
ill-defined and manifested itself through such phenomena as the zoot
suit. The struggle for equality has defined much of the Chicano experience in the twentieth century.

The relationship between the Mexican American community and the LAPD developed within this context of struggle. At the turn of the century, Los Angeles Mexicans had not yet developed a clear perception of the LAPD. Early-twentieth-century Mexican immigrants concentrated their efforts on day-to-day survival, building community institutions, and demanding social and economic justice. They were not averse to protesting police misconduct when the occasion warranted it, but they did so only in specific incidents, and, in the years before World War II, the police only periodically became a significant issue for the community. Any generalizations about the LAPD drawn by Mexicans at this time resulted from police repression of radical groups such as Ricardo Flores Magón's Partido Liberal Mexicano and from the department's constant persecution of Mexican labor unions.

Chronic conflict with the LAPD, and especially the zoot-suit crisis, transformed this relatively narrow political focus into the community-wide activism—sometimes referred to today as identity politics—that has characterized Mexican American politics since the 1940s. Crucial to the formation of this new political style was the emergence of institutions that served the Mexican American community. Spanish-language newspapers and volunteer groups such as mutual aid societies gave Mexican Americans the organizational and informational base from which to launch protests against police misconduct. Equally important was the rise of what several authors have called "the Mexican American generation."[26] As primarily the American-born and/or -raised daughters and sons of the previous "immigrant generation," members of this generation used their permanent status within the United States and their advanced education, English skills, and knowledge of American institutions to fight for the rights of Mexicans living in the United States. While this new political orientation took on many organizational forms, one organization, El Congreso de Pueblos que Hablan Español, provided an intellectual and structural bridge between the earlier labor and radical conflicts with the LAPD and the struggles of the zoot-suit era.

The crisis of the zoot-suit hysteria, aimed as it was at Mexican American youth, galvanized these forces into a community-wide effort to fight overt anti-Mexican discrimination. Spurred by official pronouncements of Mexican American criminality, by the daily barrage of newspaper stories regarding zoot-suit crime, by spectacular instances of official injustice such as the Sleepy Lagoon case, and, finally, by the riots themselves, Los Angeles Mexican Americans from a broad range of ideological affiliations engaged in an unprecedented level of political activism to defend their community. They formed organizations ranging from the Communist Party–inspired Sleepy Lagoon Defense Committee to the moderate and accommodationist, yet highly influential, Coordinating Council for Latin American Youth. Building a loose coalition, these groups succeeded to a remarkable degree in forcing white institutions to respond to Mexican American concerns. The police department, local newspapers, business and political leaders, and even the courts all took action and made decisions to accommodate the growing political power of the Mexican American minority. In short, as a result of their political activism during the zoot-suit crisis, Mexican Americans became a force with which local leaders had to reckon.

These changes in Mexican Americans' political clout both resulted from and in turn further stimulated a Mexican American political identity. The issue of identity has been widely studied in the literature on Chicanos. Vigorous debates continue on the nature of that identity and on when and how it emerged. While the origins of an ideology of resistance date back to the post-1848 era, historians have concentrated on the early twentieth century and have pointed to concerns ranging from equal employment opportunities to immigration and the repatriations of the 1930s as the issues that forged a Mexican American identity.[27] All of these matters were important and, in the case of the repatriations, even caused an acute community crisis. None of them, however, moved the Mexican American community to large-scale activism like the twin issues of the zoot-suit hysteria and the police misconduct of the 1940s. While other issues may have forced people to think of themselves as Mexican Americans, no other issue made people act politically *as* Mexican Americans. For them, identity politics began in 1943.

CHAPTER 2

Beginnings

1900–1920

The relationship in the early twentieth century between Mexican Americans and the Los Angeles Police Department evolved in the context of rapid, almost radical, change. The factors that affected the relationship included a rapidly developing local economy, dramatic demographic changes, and a struggle between conservatives and reformers over political control of the city. Added to this volatile mixture were the recent creation of the LAPD as an administrative unit of city government and the influx of Mexican immigrants into the city during the first two decades of the century. As important as these variables were in themselves, they were also influenced by the legacy of the nineteenth-century Mexican experience in the United States, which had assigned to Mexicans the status of an inferior racial group within American society.

NINETEENTH-CENTURY EXPERIENCE

As noted earlier, people of Mexican descent first entered the United States in large numbers as a result of the Treaty of Guadalupe Hidalgo that ended the Mexican-American War (1846–1848). The treaty ceded Mexico's northwestern territories to the United States and guaranteed the civil rights of the Mexicans who chose to remain in the transferred territories. Those guarantees, however, were never honored, and Mexicans found themselves relegated to the role of an economically subordinated, politically disenfranchised, and socially ostracized racial group.[1]

Such an outcome was really not all that surprising, given the reasons why Americans had gone to war and the way they justified their aggression. The United States had fought the war in order to acquire the area's rich economic resources, in particular the land. While a significant minority protested the war, Americans justified their aggression through the racist rhetoric of Manifest Destiny. Manifest Destiny proclaimed the racial superiority of white Anglo-Saxons and the inherent inferiority of Mexicans and any other group that stood in the way of American expansion. Focusing on the mixed ancestry of the Mexican people, proponents of Manifest Destiny declared Mexicans to be a "mongrel race," thus dehumanizing them in the eyes of most white Americans. This dehumanization allowed Americans to brutally prosecute the war and even to consider exterminating Mexicans as a race. Such a sentiment is evident in James Russell Lowell's poetic parody of a Yankee soldier's willingness to kill Mexicans:

> Afore I came away from hum I hed a strong persuasion
> That Mexicans worn't human beans,—an ourang outang nation,
> A sort o' folks a chap could kill an' never dream on't arter.[2]

Equally violent was the *Illinois State Register*'s assertion that Mexicans "are reptiles" who, if they stand in the way of American expansion, "must either crawl or be crushed."[3]

The rhetoric of Manifest Destiny had a profound impact on the relations between whites and Mexicans in the second half of the nineteenth century. When hundreds of thousands of Americans began arriving in the Southwest after the war, they found the best land already in the hands of the local Mexican inhabitants, frustrating the economic goals for which Americans had fought the war. The conquering Americans thus resorted to fraud, violence, and explicitly discriminatory laws, in order to achieve their original war aims. Over the next half century, whites managed to confiscate Mexicans' land, expel them from the political system, and, because Manifest Destiny had already dehumanized them, assign to them the status of racial inferiors. This inferior status had many consequences, of which the most important was that it consigned Mexican workers to the most menial and lowest-paying jobs in the local labor market.

In the decade after the conquest, issues of crime, violence, and the workings of the American criminal justice system supported the subordination of Los Angeles Mexicans. During this period, the small pueblo of Los Angeles was one of the most violent municipalities in the country. Much of the violence was interracial in character, with young Mexican men attacking white settlers and white veterans of the war attacking hapless Mexicans. The elaborate criminal justice system created by the California state legislature quickly proved incapable of stopping the criminal activity. In response, white elites, supported by wealthy Mexican rancheros, turned to vigilantism to halt the violence. Vigilante "justice" proved anything but impartial. All twenty-seven of the Mexicans who faced vigilantes in Los Angeles received corporal punishment; twenty-six of them were executed. In contrast, of the nine whites brought before vigilante tribunals only one was executed and a second received a whipping. The formal criminal justice system also seemed to have an anti-Mexican bias. According to the Spanish-language newspaper *El Clamor Público,* among whites it was "a very common habit to murder or injure Mexicans with impunity." Mexicans thus grew "tired of the many abuses and injustices they had suffered and came to believe that justice could not be applied equally [to] Mexicans and whites in Los Angeles."[4]

Mexicans living in the United States responded to their subordination with a series of defense mechanisms to protect themselves from the worst aspects of American racism. In the nineteenth century, for example, Mexicans began developing a relatively cohesive ethnic identity. As historian David Gutiérrez has noted, "By the 1870s scattered evidence indicates that Mexican Americans in various locales had begun to forge an affirmative sense of themselves as an ethnic minority of a larger society." As a result, Mexicans began ethnically oriented volunteer organizations such as mutual aid societies that, when the situation warranted, also functioned as nascent civil rights organizations. Finally, some Mexicans responded with violence of their own to what they must have seen as the theft of their birthright. Throughout the second half of the nineteenth century, individuals and organizations as colorful as Joaquin Murieta, "Cheno" Cortina, Tiburcio Vásquez, and Las Gorras Blancas violently demonstrated Mexicans' anger and frustration at their new, inferior status. Needless to say, such outbreaks of violence put Mexicans in conflict with American law-enforcement agencies.[5]

THE SETTING: EARLY-TWENTIETH-CENTURY
LOS ANGELES

Beginning in the mid-1880s Los Angeles began the process of evolving from a violent frontier cow town into a modern metropolitan center. Consequently, the early-twentieth-century relationship between the LAPD and the Mexican community evolved within the context of rapid demographic, economic, social, and political changes. These changes included the dramatic population growth that the city experienced and the nature of that growth; the desire of local entrepreneurs to turn Los Angeles into a major economic center; and the highly politicized nature of American urban police, particularly the LAPD, at the turn of the century. Of equal importance was the rapidly growing, opportunistic, and politicized Mexican population of the city.

The most easily observed change was the rise in population. Between 1850 and 1880 Los Angeles remained small, growing from 1,610 people to 11,183. With the arrival of the transcontinental railroad in the 1880s, however, it experienced extraordinary growth. Between 1880 and 1890 the city's population rose by 351 percent, reaching a total of over 50,000 people. In 1900 the city's population exceeded 100,000, and by 1920 it was more than 500,000.[6]

This growth made the demography of Los Angeles unlike that of any other major American city. To begin with, the city had a relatively small foreign-born population. New York, Chicago, Detroit, and San Francisco all had significantly higher foreign-born populations than Los Angeles. The nativity of the Los Angeles foreign-born population also differed. Whereas eastern and southern Europeans formed the largest foreign-born segment in most other large American cities, they comprised only a small part of the Los Angeles population. Instead, before 1910 the largest segment of the city's foreign-born came from northern and western European countries. After 1910 the largest group came from Mexico.[7]

Because of the small foreign-born population, white native-born middle-class Protestant Americans dominated most aspects of community life in Los Angeles during the early twentieth century. The largest segment of whites living in Los Angeles were immigrants with relatively prosperous midwestern backgrounds. Upon arrival in Los Angeles, they set about re-creating the image of a midwestern town. They built Protestant churches, replaced the old Mexican adobe structures with American wooden and brick buildings, and organized civic and religious groups. A new local elite quickly emerged, and by the early twentieth century, members of a half-dozen mainstream Protestant denominations—a mere 17 percent of the population—controlled the economic, political, and social institutions of the city.[8]

The homogeneous community that this elite sought to create, however, never became a reality. Los Angeles had in fact a larger nonwhite population (the term *nonwhite* includes Mexicans) than any other major American city except Baltimore. Also, unlike most other American cities, Los Angeles's population was overwhelmingly composed of migrants from other states in the United States. Between 1900 and the Great Depression, 75 percent of the city's inhabitants consisted of white native-born Americans born outside of California. In the other large cities of the United States, the percentage of the American population born outside the state rarely exceeded 35 percent. After the Depression, nonwhite racial minorities and native-born migrants continued to comprise a large proportion of the city's population.[9]

Adding to this diversity was the city's rapidly increasing population of people of Mexican descent. In 1900, between three thousand and five thousand Mexicans lived in Los Angeles. By 1920, the number had jumped to between thirty thousand and fifty thousand. This population thus grew rapidly, not only in terms of actual numbers but also in comparison with the general population. While the latter grew by 500 percent between 1900 and 1920, the Mexican population grew by 1,000 percent. More than any other factor, the rapid increase in size of this racially different immigrant group upset the efforts of the elite to thoroughly anglicize Los Angeles.[10]

One other factor differentiated Los Angeles from other American urban centers. More so than in most other major American cities outside the South, local capitalists successfully built an antilabor consensus that dominated city government until the last years of the Great Depression. The man most responsible for the success of this antilabor movement was General Harrison Gray Otis, owner of the powerful *Los Angeles Times*. The movement began in 1890 when Otis convinced the owners of three other daily newspapers to reduce wages by 20 percent. *Times* workers belonging to the Typographical Union threatened to strike if the wage reduction went into effect, and rather than let the union take the initiative, Otis locked his workers out before they took a strike vote. "Thus was begun," an official *Times* publication later proclaimed, "the memorable struggle which was to shape the industrial relations of a metropolis and to set an example for a whole country."[11]

Otis was probably less concerned with wages than he was with the degree of control he had over his business. He believed that labor had no legitimate role in the decision-making process of his business. He saw his workers as just another commodity necessary for publishing his newspaper. Otis particularly disliked the closed shop, whereby employers agreed to employ only union members. If all the employees in a given enterprise belonged to unions, Otis reasoned, the employer would have to consider the workers' interests when making business decisions rather than only the invisible hand of the marketplace and the welfare of the company. To an authoritarian such as Otis, this not only constituted bad business, it was philosophically unjustified. Thus, largely because of Otis's efforts, maintaining the open shop became the main goal of Los Angeles employers from the turn of the century to the beginning of World War II.

While Otis might have had a philosophical aversion to unionism, he also fought labor activism for more practical reasons. In 1888, two years before the newspaper strike, Otis convened a group of Los Angeles businessmen to develop strategies to overcome a local but devastating economic downturn. These businessmen concluded that only by securing a sound industrial base could economic stability be maintained. They therefore formed a chamber of commerce with the express purpose of attracting more business and capital to the city. Los Angeles, however, had one great disadvantage in this endeavor: it had to compete with San Francisco and its fine harbor, rich hinterland, and forty-year head start in the accumulation of capital and industry. The only disadvantage San Francisco had was a relatively high wage scale. General Otis and his friends thus came to two conclusions: the only way to compete with the northern city was to undercut its wage scale; and the only way to undercut its wage scale was by eliminating unionism in Los Angeles.[12]

The conservative Republican businessmen who formed the Los Angeles Chamber of Commerce developed several strategies to discourage the growth of labor unions. First, they used the pages of the *Times* to rally public support for the antiunion campaign. For almost seventy years the editorial pages and often even the news pages of the *Times* were filled with unrestrained and violent antilabor rhetoric.[13] The bitterness that ensued between the *Times* and organized labor was so great that in 1911 three members of the Iron Workers Union dynamited the Times Building, killing more than twenty people. This single event, probably more than any other, contributed to the almost complete elimination of organized labor as an economic factor in Los Angeles before the Great Depression.

The second tactic used by capital against labor was the formation of employers' organizations such as the Merchants and Manufacturers Association, which gave aid to businesses faced with labor disputes. This aid took a variety of forms. In some cases, the employers' organizations gave monetary assistance to businesses that faced strikes. In other instances, the associations provided logistical support, such as special guards who protected strikebreakers and helped keep businesses functioning. In still other cases the employers' associations, through the pages of the *Times,* gave Los Angeles employers advice on how to maintain the open shop.[14]

Conservatives such as Otis were not alone in their antipathy toward organized labor. Their main political rivals in Los Angeles, the progressive reformers, shared with conservatives a deep-seated bias against labor unions and against the working class in general. Southern California progressivism mirrored the disparate reform movement that swept the United States during the first two decades of the twentieth century. To a certain extent progressives' activities were reactions to the economic and political domination of the state by an extremely powerful monopoly: since 1865 the Southern Pacific Railroad had ruled the state, effectively controlling the governorship, the state legislature, municipal governments, and the state's delegation to Congress. In Los Angeles, with its burgeoning population and economy, the railroad created a political machine to guard its interests. This machine effectively controlled both the Republican and the Democratic Parties and through the parties controlled city government. The Southern Pacific used this power to maintain its domination of southern California's economy, and it was against this domination that the progressives rebelled.[15]

The progressive movement, however, was more than just a reaction against the excesses of big business. It was also an affirmation of the increasing strength and confidence of the growing American middle class. In Los Angeles, progressives fought the Southern Pacific machine for two reasons that were of great importance to the middle class. First, since the political machine's main function was to protect Southern Pacific's monopoly of the area's transportation system, the power of the machine had to be broken to allow for normal economic development. For the progressives, normal economic growth meant allowing competition rather than political influence determine which business endeavors succeeded. The progressives, with supreme confidence in the ability of the middle class to prosper through competition, sought to destroy the privileged status of the Southern Pacific Railroad. Second, the corruption inherent in the machine's control of municipal government offended progressives because it resulted in governmental inefficiency, which in turn brought about higher taxes. Instead of inefficiency, the progressives promised to bring sound business tactics to city government, thus making it more productive and less costly.

The progressives gained control of Los Angeles city government through three distinct efforts. First, they secured passage of a new city charter that provided for the initiative, referendum, and recall. The progressives believed that such "direct legislation" enabled the citizenry to effectively oversee local government. Second, in order to curtail the influence of special interests on local government, they passed a series of charter amendments that created nonpartisan administrative boards, strengthened the power of the mayor over the city council, established the direct primary, and replaced district elections of the city council with at-large elections. Finally, in the 1906 and 1909 elections, the progressives gained control first of the city council and then of the mayor's office.[16]

Aspects of the progressive movement had a direct impact on relations between police and Mexican immigrants in the early part of the twentieth century. First, the progressives attempted to impose on the rest of Los Angeles white Protestant middle-class values regarding sex, alcohol, and gambling. To this end, in 1902 the electorate passed a charter amendment that forbade prostitution and gambling within the city limits. Similarly, Los Angeles progressives passed a variety of laws restricting and then suppressing the sale of alcoholic beverages. These "sumptuary laws" created difficulties for people whose values and culture differed from the progressives'. In the case of Mexicans, passage of the liquor ordinance, in particular, often placed them in violation of the law. The sumptuary laws also provided a great opportunity for police corruption. Since the demand for illicit sex, liquor, and gambling remained high, purveyors of these services could and did bribe police officers in order to stay in business. Thus, one of the ironies of the progressive movement is that in attempting to perfect society, it brought about conditions that in fact created more corruption.[17]

The progressives' attitude toward the working class also had a long-lasting effect on relations between the police and the Mexican community. George Mowry, in his definitive work on California progressivism, states that the urban reformers' "bias against labor was always greater than against the large corporations." An editorial in the *California Weekly*, a progressive journal, proclaimed that "nearly all the problems which vex society have their sources above or below the middle-class man. From above come the problems of predatory wealth. . . . From below come the problems of poverty and of pigheaded and brutish criminality."[18]

The progressives particularly feared socialism and labor unionism. In 1911 Los Angeles progressives formed an alliance with conservative Republicans—who, only three years earlier, had been their sworn enemies—to defeat Job Harriman, the Socialist Party's candidate for mayor. This alliance, many historians believe, led to the destruction of the progressive movement in Los Angeles. The progressives' decision was explained by Meyer Lissner, one of the principal figures in the Los Angeles reform movement, who said that he preferred to see the end of the progressive movement in California "rather than let Los Angeles be thrown under the . . . tyrannical domination of labor unionism." Thus, when the progressives gained full control of the municipal government of Los Angeles in 1910, they passed a stringent antipicketing ordinance. With this law, which became the model for antipicketing laws throughout the country, the progressives sought to remove the strike as an effective tool of labor unions.[19]

The conservatives and progressives therefore worked hand in hand to use city government as a tool in their fight against organized labor. In fact, the tremendous success of capital against labor would have been impossible without the active support of city government. City officials, often successful businessmen themselves, regularly assisted employers by passing antilabor and antiradical ordinances, awarding contracts to nonunion companies such as the *Times,* prosecuting pickets, and generally giving support to open-shop forces. No city agency, however, took a more aggressive role in protecting employers' interests than the Los Angeles Police Department.

DEVELOPMENT OF THE LAPD

The LAPD, like the city that it served, was still in the process of developing in the early years of the twentieth century. The department was a relatively young agency of city government at the turn of the century. Organized in 1877 just before the large increase in population, in its early years it had the responsibility of bringing some order to what was reputedly the "toughest town" in the West. From the very beginning the department adopted a militaristic structure and character. Officers held military ranks and dressed in military-style uniforms. The LAPD struggled during the first dozen years of its existence, going through sixteen chiefs of police and developing an unsavory reputation for corruption and brutality. In 1889, however, John M. Glass became chief and began developing a "professional" tradition within the LAPD. Like the professionals who would follow, Chief Glass excelled at gaining increased budgets for the department, acquiring the most advanced technology to aid police work (in Glass's case this took the form of a centralized communications system), implementing the latest organizational innovations, and developing for his officers the reputation of being impartial enforcers of the law. In spite of his successes, a power struggle in city government forced Glass's resignation in 1900 and ushered in nearly four decades of police chiefs who had neither the will nor the skills to implement police professionalism.[20]

Thus, in the early years of the twentieth century the LAPD came to resemble police departments in other large urban areas. Perhaps the most prominent feature of many big city police departments during this period was that they were thoroughly controlled not by elected government officials, but by the political machine currently in power in their city. Individual police officers were hired or fired, promoted or demoted, on the basis of their service to the machine. Service to the machine meant helping control elections and allowing "friendly" vice to continue to operate while closing down "unfriendly" vice. It also meant allowing political, ethnic, or even organized crime groups supportive of the machine to go about their business while harassing those groups that the machine saw as enemies.[21]

Since a police officer's status within the department depended more on that officer's service to the machine than on a standard of law, officers with political influence took bribes to protect purveyors of vice and even thieves and murderers; brutalized citizens who were not politically well-connected; extorted money from small businessmen; and committed sundry other offenses without fear of punishment. The notion that the police were but the tool of the political party in power was so ingrained that most "reform" efforts were really attempts by the party out of power to gain control of the police for its own purposes. Or, in the words of the historian Robert M. Fogelson, "At issue . . . was not whether the police department would be operated in someone's interests, a point firmly settled, but in whose interests they would be operated."[22]

The LAPD fit well into this mold of being controlled by the local political machine. Throughout most of the first four decades of the twentieth century, Los Angeles police officers regularly protected friends and punished enemies of the machine in power. They also allowed those proprietors of prostitution, gambling, and drinking establishments who contributed to machine candidates' campaigns to go about their business unmolested. Overall, the LAPD gained the reputation of being one of the most corrupt police forces in the nation.

Ostensibly, various programs proposed by reform politicians included professionalizing the LAPD by removing it from political influence and corruption. For example, by extending civil-service protection to the department and by placing it under the authority of a nonpartisan police commission and a strong chief of police, the reformers of the progressive era hoped to end political control of the police. This would ensure that the police enforced the law rather than the interests of any particular interest group. The progressives, however, meddled in police affairs and used the LAPD for their own partisan political purposes as much as any other political group in Los Angeles. Consequently, the LAPD continued to suffer from the twin maladies of partisan political interference and internal corruption until the late 1930s.[23]

An obvious example of political interference was the LAPD's ongoing suppression of organized labor. Since all ruling factions agreed on the undesirability of labor unions and other "radicals," the LAPD worked to suppress such groups. Its role as a union-busting force fell well within the tradition of the American law-enforcement system. Modern, organized police departments came into existence during the early industrial revolution for the express purpose of protecting the interests of the emerging industrial bourgeoisie. In the early years of the republic, keeping the peace had been a relatively simple task. Urban areas were relatively small and a large segment of city dwellers owned property and thus had an interest in the overall welfare of their community. The watch system that patrolled cities at night functioned as the main peacekeeping agency in these years. Increasing industrialization in the mid-nineteenth century, however, brought about demographic changes that in turn necessitated a change in the nature of law enforcement.

The most important of these demographic changes was the emergence of a large impoverished population that provided cheap labor for the growing factories. The men and women who provided this labor had less of a stake in the community than earlier urban dwellers had. Crime rose and members of the so-called dangerous class often rebelled by rioting against their difficult economic condition. Local manufacturing and commercial elites viewed these riots as challenges to their authority and as threats against their increasing wealth. In response, these elites prevailed upon city governments to organize urban police departments to thwart challenges to capitalist authority from the expanding working class. Thus, protecting the power and property of the bourgeoisie became the very raison d'être for urban police. In the late nineteenth and early twentieth centuries the police continued to protect capitalists when the latter felt threatened by the labor movement.[24]

The LAPD performed several important functions in helping to fight unionism in Los Angeles. At the most elementary level, the police helped employers break strikes by protecting scabs and arresting pickets. In addition, the police broke up public demonstrations that they deemed pro-labor or radical and therefore potentially harmful to employers' interests. The LAPD also infiltrated labor unions, radical organizations, and even liberal civil rights organizations such as the American Civil Liberties Union. Upon doing so, the police obtained access to membership lists, gained prior knowledge of the organizations' activities, and even acted as agents provocateurs. Often the LAPD acted within the letter of the law in performing its pro-open-shop functions. Other times, however, the LAPD brutally and violently broke up picket lines and "subversive" demonstrations and generally violated the civil rights of individuals whom the police saw as threats to the existing economic order. At the beginning of the century, it was in this capacity that the department most often came into conflict with the growing Mexican community of Los Angeles.

MEXICANS IN EARLY-TWENTIETH-CENTURY LOS ANGELES

Like most other immigrants to the United States, the Mexicans who moved to Los Angeles in such great numbers in the early years of the century came in search of economic opportunity. They fled a country that was suffering from vast economic dislocations caused by the economic follies of dictatorship and the ravages of revolution. The Southwest, an area that was enjoying vast economic growth, should have provided abundant opportunities for enterprising workers.[25]

Instead, as a result of a half century of economic subordination and exploitation, Mexican Americans increasingly found themselves relegated to working in menial jobs. In 1900, for example, 57.7 percent of Mexicans worked in unskilled, blue-collar jobs, the lowest level on the employment scale. By 1920 that figure had risen to 71.5 percent, and only 9.5 percent held white-collar jobs. In comparison, in 1920 only 6 percent of whites held blue-collar jobs and 47 percent fell into the white-collar category.[26]

Mexican immigrants thus provided an almost permanently subordinated source of cheap labor, which was a crucial element for the economic growth of Los Angeles and the entire southwestern portion of the United States. In *Chicanos in a Changing Society,* Albert Camarillo asserts, undoubtedly correctly, that this economic subordination of Mexican workers resulted from discriminatory employment patterns set in the nineteenth century. It is also true, however, as the data show, that the patterns of economic discrimination against Mexicans became more firmly established and more universally applied as larger numbers of Mexicans entered the Los Angeles workforce in the early twentieth century.[27]

Economic subordination and racial discrimination resulted in Mexicans suffering from a variety of social maladies. To begin with, Mexicans endured severe housing discrimination. In 1913 the Los Angeles Housing Commission stated that "Mexicans cannot find homes except in a crowded district. They want to move away from the industrial district and the center of the city if restrictions and race feelings were not placed upon every new tract of land where lots were sold." Consequently, throughout the first two decades of the twentieth century, Los Angeles's expanding Mexican population found itself confined to certain sections of the city. Prior to 1920 this meant that Sonoratown, the old Mexican section of the city around the central plaza, had to absorb the growing population.[28]

The dilapidated housing and the density of the population in Sonoratown meant that Mexicans had the worst living conditions of any group in early-twentieth-century Los Angeles. Jacob Riis, the muckraking journalist who made a career of exposing the problems of urban living, said that he had seen larger slums than the Mexican barrio, "but never any which were worse than those of Los Angeles." The Los Angeles Housing Commission described a "Cholo court" in a similar fashion: "Here we found filth and squalor on every hand. Miserably constructed houses, made of scrap sheet iron, old bagging and sections of dry goods boxes, were huddled together without any attempt at proper construction or order. . . . The more Mexicans to the lot, the more money for the owner."[29]

During the 1920s, the expansion of commercial and financial interests into Sonoratown and the influx of immigrants into the city forced most Mexicans out of the central core. Many families moved east of the Los Angeles River and established barrios in the Boyle Heights section of the city and in an adjacent unincorporated section of Los Angeles County called Maravilla. The Mexican American population center formed by these two neighborhoods became known as East Los Angeles. In addition, many of the Mexicans working for the Southern Pacific Railroad or one of the interurban railway companies established settlements close to their work sites, thus founding permanent Mexican colonies in outlying sections of the city such as Watts, Wilmington, and San Pedro. Devices such as restrictive covenants on deeds ensured that Mexicans did not move into nonimmigrant sections of the city.[30]

In an effort to improve their economic situation and escape their harsh living conditions, Mexican workers became involved in labor union activity. In agriculture, segments of the railway industry, the garment industry, and others in which Mexican workers predominated, Mexicans often formed overtly nationalistic unions that appealed to the labor union traditions of Mexico. Furthermore, since the unions affiliated with the conservative American Federation of Labor (AFL) usually refused to organize unskilled workers and opposed Mexican immigration anyway, Mexican workers' nationalistic unions rarely affiliated with the AFL. Instead, they often became involved in more radical labor union activity, which white elites relied upon the LAPD to suppress. While the LAPD probably expended no more effort in suppressing Mexican labor unions than it did in suppressing white unions, this suppression had a greater impact in the Mexican community since it maintained the subordination of Mexican labor and the concomitant miserable living conditions that Mexicans had to endure. Subsequent chapters provide a more in-depth analysis of the LAPD's attempted suppression of Mexican labor activity.

MEXICAN CRIME

While clashes between police and Mexican unionists clearly created animosity on both sides, the relationship between the LAPD and the Mexican community was eventually built on the relatively more mundane, but ultimately more important, issues of police perceptions of Mexican crime and Mexicans' perceptions of police misconduct. In the early part of the century Los Angeles Mexicans and the LAPD most often interacted when someone committed a crime. If one believes the local news-

papers, Mexicans committed at least their share of crimes and the police
certainly tried to apprehend Mexican criminals as best they could. Nevertheless, while popular opinion since the 1850s had depicted Mexicans
as violent, and while the local press occasionally printed sensational
stories of Mexican crimes, there is little indication that the LAPD viewed
the Mexican population as posing a particularly serious crime problem.
Other than hiring a handful of Mexican American officers to patrol the
barrios, the department consequently had no specific policy for handling
Mexican crime.[31]

In the early years of the century, the local press on occasion focused
on lurid stories of violent crimes committed by Mexicans. Newspapers
regularly ran graphically detailed stories with such headlines as "Red
Row in Boxcarville; Shooting, Slashing Riot of Drunken Peons," "Mexicans' Fierce Affray," and "Knives Plied by Ugly Ones." These stories
depicted Mexicans as committing violent crimes against each other, with
the aggression usually resulting from a personal grudge or a drunken
brawl. The story behind the first headline above, for example, told of a
fight that broke out toward the end of a baptismal party given among
the boxcars that housed "the pick and shovel brigade" of the Southern
Pacific Railroad. The proud father supplied plenty of drink, which resulted in everyone getting quite drunk and, according to the Los Angeles
Times, "when some peons get drunk their minds run only to their weapons and the use thereof." One man asked another man's wife to dance,
the husband objected, tempers flared, knives and then guns were drawn,
and a general melee broke out. In the end, one person lay dead and
many others were injured. Although the fight broke out at about 2:00
A.M., the police did not arrive at the scene until after daybreak.[32]

Between 1910 and 1920, the Los Angeles media began paying more
attention to crimes in which Mexicans were the perpetrators and non-
Mexicans the victims. Beginning in 1912, newspapers started publishing
stories about Mexican burglars and robbers who menaced white merchants and pedestrians in the downtown area of the city. Even more
sensational were the newspaper accounts of violent conflict between
Mexicans and the police. While most of these confrontations resulted
from suspects resisting arrest, on several occasions Mexicans fought to
stop police from arresting other Mexicans. In September 1908, for example, the Los Angeles Herald ran a story about two Mexican men who
tried to prevent a police officer from arresting a Mexican woman for
drunkenness. According to the Herald, police arrested José Soría and

Julián Martínez for interfering with an arrest after they allegedly attacked and beat an officer. Sometimes these altercations turned into minor riots. In May 1914, for example, one hundred Mexicans rioted at the Plaza, a traditional gathering place for Los Angeles Mexicans, to prevent one of their countrymen from being arrested. In a more alarming turn of events, a few months earlier, in November 1913, a newspaper reported that local Mexicans had plotted to kill a white officer who patrolled the Mexican section of the city. The *Record* stated that a group of five Mexicans ambushed and tried to kill Officer Albert C. Whaples because of his success at apprehending Mexican criminals. Since local newspapers almost never bothered to interview Mexicans in crime-related stories, we have no knowledge of what specific actions may have prompted the individuals to attack Whaples.[33]

By and large the LAPD reacted to Mexican crime in a routine manner. If someone reported a violation of the law in which a Mexican was either the victim or the suspect, officers investigated the matter and, if possible, made an arrest. No evidence suggests that the LAPD overpoliced the Mexican barrios except during times of international crisis or labor unrest. On the other hand, as the example of the baptismal party demonstrates, the police sometimes responded slowly to crime in the Mexican sections of the city.

While the LAPD paid no special attention to Mexican crime, the department occasionally exploited public fears when doing so suited its interests. In June 1913, for example, Juan Soto, an escapee from a mental institution, brutally killed two young Mexican women and their brother. The savage nature of the murders and the publicity they engendered forced the LAPD to launch a massive manhunt for the killer. After a week, however, it became apparent that Soto had escaped captivity and had probably fled to Mexico. Responding to questions from the press, Captain Paul Flammer, head of the LAPD's detective bureau, blamed Soto's escape on the fact that the LAPD did not have sufficient manpower.[34]

Between 1900 and 1920 the LAPD only rarely indicated concern over the amount of Mexican crime. In August 1907, however, the *Los Angeles Express* printed a story under the headline "Cholo Crimes Alarm Police" in which the police expressed distress over increased numbers of assaults and homicides in the Mexican sections of the city. According to the *Express,* the police were particularly disturbed because they had "been able to get [but] little information about [the crimes] on account of the secretiveness of the cholos." Throughout the century, the LAPD consistently complained about the lack of cooperation from the Mexican community.[35]

POLICE MISCONDUCT

Los Angeles Mexicans had good reason to avoid interactions with the American criminal justice system. Throughout the twentieth century judges, prosecutors, and especially the police often paid little attention to standards of justice in their dealings with Mexican suspects. In January 1903, for example, a judge sentenced Servariano Gonzales to life imprisonment for a murder Gonzales swore he did not commit. The *Los Angeles Times* reported that the prosecution presented no evidence directly linking Gonzales to the killing of Charles Underwood. Gonzales could not defend himself because he did not understand the court proceedings, which were not translated into Spanish. Furthermore, he refused to talk to his court-appointed attorney, W. T. Blakely, because he believed that Blakely was "some kind of a detective trying to wring some damaging confession from him." Blakely, therefore, put up no defense and the jury found Gonzales guilty.[36]

In response to this case and another, in which an LAPD officer shot and killed a Mexican national named Francisco López, the Mexican government began to actively assist Mexicans living in Los Angeles. In the Gonzales case, the Mexican consul in Los Angeles hired a local law firm to appeal the conviction on the grounds that Gonzales did not receive a fair trial because he did not understand the court proceedings. The consul general also asked the United States government to indemnify Francisco López's family for his death. Finally, the Mexican government established a special fund that, according to the *Times,* was "to be used in assisting Mexican subjects, who become involved in difficulty, either through ignorance of the laws of this country or through mistaken arrest or accusation of crimes."[37]

While the intervention of the Mexican government resulted from Mexico's belief that its citizens did not receive equal treatment from local courts, Mexicans in fact had more to fear from arbitrary and often brutal treatment by individual police officers. Throughout the twentieth century, Mexicans have accused LAPD personnel of brutality and other forms of misconduct. In all but a handful of cases, this behavior has gone unpunished. The shooting of Francisco López is but an early example of the use of excessive force against Mexicans by the LAPD that achieved notoriety. In this particular case, Officer Sherman Baker shot and killed López as he tried to escape arrest for allegedly stealing some clothes. López's family claimed that the officer had no cause for shooting, but the district attorney refused to prosecute on the grounds that Baker had sufficient reason to believe that López was an escaping felon.[38]

Late in December 1902 an even more gruesome example occurred of police misconduct against a Mexican, conduct that went unpunished despite much public attention. In this particular case several eyewitnesses stated they saw a prison trusty by the name of James Farley kill Brabonel Sepúlveda in the Los Angeles City Jail. According to the witnesses, all of them prisoners, Farley became enraged when Sepúlveda, in a drunken stupor, began demanding back his shoes, which had been taken from him when he was booked. Farley hit Sepúlveda in the face with his fist, kicked him after he fell down, and repeatedly beat the prisoner over the head with a set of heavy keys. At one point, according to the witnesses, Farley became so enraged that he grabbed Sepúlveda by the ears and pounded his head against the steel bars and the concrete floor of the holding tank. A coroner's autopsy concluded that Sepúlveda died of severe head wounds.[39]

Despite the evidence against Farley, the LAPD went to great lengths to protect him from prosecution. The department set free all but one of the prisoners who occupied the tank with Sepúlveda the night he died, and it tried to intimidate witnesses to keep them from testifying against Farley. Chief of Police C. Elton also refused to remove Farley from his duties until the mayor compelled him to do so. When the case went before the grand jury, department officials, including Chief Elton, testified on Farley's behalf and tried to impeach the testimony of the witnesses against the trusty. In the end, the grand jury refused to indict Farley, claiming they had insufficient evidence to pursue the case.[40]

Examples of the LAPD's use of excessive force against Mexicans continued to occur throughout the first two decades of the century. In February 1912, for example, the Los Angeles Record printed a story under the headline "Burly Cop Beat Him Up, Says Boy; Is Not Punished." According to the Record, Patrolman R. C. Bidy knocked Tony Parra off his bicycle and kicked him as he lay on the ground for the offense of riding the bicycle on the sidewalk. Although several people witnessed the incident, police officials refused to discipline Bidy except by transferring him to another beat. Several years later a man by the name of Francisco Díaz suffered such massive brain damage from a beating he received from police Sergeant Arthur C. Graham that the judge handling a criminal case against Díaz dismissed the charges, stating that Díaz was incapable of defending himself against the charges. Since Díaz had allegedly stabbed Graham, the officer faced no punishment for his actions.[41]

Although they rarely succeeded, Mexicans regularly filed charges of police misconduct before appropriate governmental agencies. During the first two decades of the twentieth century the Board of Police Commissioners accepted and heard citizens' complaints. The commission's minutes give a good indication of the types of complaints Mexicans made against the LAPD and, to a lesser extent, of the level of police malfeasance in the Mexican community. Between 1900 and 1919, seventeen charges of police misconduct were brought before the police commission either by or on behalf of Mexicans. The commission exonerated the accused officer in all but three of the cases. Although the minutes do not always give details of the charges against the officers, it is clear that Mexican complaints addressed the category of excessive use of force by the police more often than any other category. The commission, however, consistently refused to sustain any charges brought by Mexicans or any allegations of police brutality. In cases involving Mexican victims, the commission disciplined officers only on charges brought by the chief of police and only for neglect of duty and conduct unbecoming an officer.[42]

CHAPTER 3

The LAPD and Mexican Workers, 1900-1920

While Mexicans came into conflict with the LAPD most often over matters of crime and in reaction to police misconduct, the most spectacular confrontations in the early part of the century occurred when they acted to improve their economic status. Mexicans often attempted to improve their subordinated economic condition by forming overtly nationalistic labor unions. While these unions had traditional goals—union recognition, higher wages, and improved working conditions—labor organizers used nontraditional methods, such as employing Mexican traditions and cultural symbols, to attract workers. These organizing tactics had conflicting and often self-canceling consequences. The Catholic religion, the use of Spanish-language literature, and symbols such as the Mexican flag did attract Mexican workers to the unions, but their use also allowed the LAPD and other enemies of organized labor to attack the Mexican unions as foreign and helped justify police coercion to suppress the unions.

THE LAPD AND MEXICAN WORKERS: THE 1903 RAILWAY WORKERS' STRIKE

The first twentieth-century confrontation between Mexican workers and the LAPD came in the spring of 1903; when Mexican track layers organized the Unión Federal Mexicanos (UFM) and went on strike at Henry E. Huntington's Pacific Electric Railway Company. Both the company and the union had a great deal at stake in the strike. Huntington had gained control of the Pacific Electric only two years earlier and intended to build a first-class interurban railway system for Los Angeles. Crucial to the development of such a system was the laying of the third track on Main Street before the "Fiesta," a commercial booster event that took place during the first week of May. Local officials placed particular importance on the 1903 Fiesta because President Theodore Roosevelt planned to attend, and they hoped the resulting publicity would boost tourism and increase migration into the city. Furthermore, Huntington was fanatically opposed to labor unions and wanted to break the union in order to maintain his reputation of never losing a strike. Earlier in the year, when car men working for the Pacific Electric had attempted to form a union, he had flatly denied them, saying, "No union or no railway."[1]

The situation of the Mexican strikers demonstrated both their personal desperation and the exploited nature of their status in the labor market. About five weeks earlier the Mexican consul had voiced official concern over the treatment of Mexican workers in Los Angeles. According to the *Times,* he was concerned about "the alleged injustice suffered by several hundred Mexican peons, who are employed in railroad construction in this city." Labor contractors had enticed Mexicans to Los Angeles with "lavish promises of abundant work at high wages in the United States." The contractors had also promised the immigrants free transportation back to Mexico after six months of work. Once they arrived in Los Angeles, however, the Mexican workers and their families were forced by the contractors to live in "unsanitary surroundings" and buy their provisions from company stores. If they did not buy there, they lost their right to a free trip home. Several observers maintained that the Mexicans lived "in a situation not far different from slavery." After the strike started, the union issued a letter stating that the strike had been called to end this situation.[2]

If solidarity had been the only measure of success, the UFM would certainly have won the strike. On its first day, every Mexican worker on the Main Street line walked off the job. Only a handful of whites and African Americans remained at work. Union organizers kept the morale of strikers high through a series of rallies that combined religious ceremony and Mexican patriotic demonstrations. The union organized Catholic Masses and stressed the workers' solidarity by hanging the Mexican flag in the union hall. The UFM also collected six hundred dollars toward a strike fund, and to this were added the resources of the

Los Angeles Labor Council of the American Federation of Labor. Consequently, the Mexican unionists had food and shelter throughout the strike.[3]

The main problem for the union and the principal source of potential conflict between union members and the LAPD was the union's need to prevent strikebreakers from taking over the work. On the first day of the strike, the Pacific Electric began recruiting strikebreakers from outlying areas of Los Angeles County and from as far away as El Paso, Texas. In order to make the work more attractive, the company offered new workers a wage of $2.25 for a ten-hour day—$0.25 a day more than the union had requested.[4]

The union, knowing that police would deal harshly with any attempt by the Mexican workers to stop work on the tracks, used nonconfrontational and innovative means to maintain the strike. For example, male UFM members never picketed the work site. The only time anything resembling large-scale direct action took place came on the second day of the strike, when a group of thirty Mexican women entered the pit where the track was being laid and took tools away from the strikebreakers. Two days later, the legendary "Santa" Teresa Urrea, la Niña de Cabora, visited the Main Street line. According to the *Los Angeles Record*, "Just the sight of the great healer and saint was enough to cause 50 Mexican laborers to lay down their shovels and follow her." Apparently the police were caught off guard by the women's aggressive actions.[5]

The union also attempted to stop the flow of additional workers from Mexico. A. M. Nieto, executive secretary of the UFM, told the *Record* that the two hundred Mexicans whom the Pacific Electric had recruited as strikebreakers in El Paso left the train on which they were traveling to Los Angeles when they learned of the strike. Nieto added, "We have sent word to Mexico to our relatives not to come to this country to work, as there is a strike on." The union also attempted to persuade strikebreakers to stop work. Rumors circulated, for example, that the union planned to conduct some kind of demonstration at the work site. The *Times* reported that "certain unionist agitators were trying to induce the strikers to appear upon the streets in force and endeavor by persuasion or intimidation or force to put a stop to the work."[6] No such demonstration, however, ever took place.

To the LAPD fell the job of ensuring that the union strategy failed. Early on in the strike, Chief of Police C. Elton articulated the department's role in the conflict: "It has been stated that the police force is assisting the company in this matter. If by that is meant that the police force is preventing disorder, the statement is true. . . . The men now at work are simply exercising a right which is guaranteed to them by the law, that of earning an honest living, and we do not propose that any man or set of men shall interfere with them in the exercise of that right. We are prepared for any trouble, should trouble occur we will not take to the woods." Elton also feigned neutrality, maintaining that he did not know the causes of the strike. The next day, however, he betrayed his bias for employers by stating that he was "convinced that the large majority of the strikers would prefer being back at work to being out of a job."[7]

Police officers implemented Chief Elton's policy by intimidating potential picketers through a massive show of force and by arresting anyone the police felt might threaten the scabs. For the most part, however, the LAPD managed to follow Elton's orders without making arrests. The principal police tactic was to station large numbers of officers around the working strikebreakers in order to keep unionists from interfering with the work. On the second day of the strike, a few union members jumped into the pit along with the scabs in an effort to persuade the new workers to stop work. When the police realized what had happened, they moved quickly. According to the *Times*, the "striking Mexicans . . . were taken by the collars and led out on to the sidewalk. They 'sabed' all right," the *Times* commented; they "didn't have to be told what was wanted of them, but 'vamoosed' down into Sonoratown." The swift action of the police against the male strikers stands in contrast to officers' hesitancy in dealing with the UFM's women supporters that same day.[8]

The police also kept the work going by preventing crowds from gathering around the scabs. Early in the strike the *Times* reported that a rumor had spread that the UFM planned to mount a parade around the work site and to persuade strikebreakers to join the union. The LAPD responded with a massive show of force both around the work site and in the Mexican sections of the city. The *Record* also reported that many people "were jostled and insolently commanded to 'move on' " by the police. Thus, according to the *Record,* even "disinterested citizens . . . severely criticized" the LAPD's handling of the strike.[9]

One aspect of the strike that could have led to violence was the inflammatory rhetoric that the *Times* aimed at the strikers and their supporters in the local labor movement. Specifically, the *Times* attempted to use popular stereotypes regarding Mexican crime to arouse sentiment against the strikers. From the beginning of the strike, the *Times* maintained that white labor organizers had duped the "ignorant cholos" into going on strike and that the strike might lead to violence. The white labor organizers, the *Times* editorialized on April 26, "would like nothing better than to infuriate a gang of knife-thrusting cholos, some of whom already have committed crimes, and turn them loose on the business community."[10]

On April 28, under the alarmist headline "THIS SMACKS OF TREASON," the *Times* charged that the organizers planned to establish a camp for the strikers within the city limits—"a camp for their herding and maintenance, a camp where they may eat and sleep and drink Dago red and foster their grievances[,] a camp from which they may go forth to do deeds of violence and work destruction to life and property." The *Times* believed that "the average peon laborer is inoffensive when sober, but under the influence of booze[,] stirred up by disturbers and incendiaries[,] . . . he is a reckless dare devil and utterly irresponsible." As evidence of the dangers of establishing such a camp, the *Times* charged that Mexicans had been responsible for recent murders in the area. "Establish 500 or 1000 of these fellows in a camp with nothing to do but to listen to the insidious prompting of walking delegates and to indulge in limitless libations of red wine," the paper warned, "and the possibilities are not to be contemplated with indifference."[11]

The *Times* also condemned the union's use of Mexican patriotic and religious symbols as a recruitment tool. According to the newspaper, "In the hall where the cholo union holds forth . . . hangs a big Mexican flag (not an American flag, mind you)[,] and when new members are received they are made to swear allegiance to the same, and go through the formality of kissing it." The *Times* also claimed that union leaders used the Bible and the crucifix to appeal to new members and that they called on "peon patriotism" in the conflict with the Huntington railroad.[12]

On May 1 the *Times* even called for a return to vigilantism to rid the city of the hated labor organizers. Specifically, it urged the formation of a "Committee of Safety" to advise the chief of police on how "to drive the agitators from the city as dangerous criminal vagrants." Chief Elton did not take this advice, and within a few days the strike fell apart as white conductors and car men refused to join the strike and scabs finished construction on the railway line.[13]

One of the reasons that the 1903 railway strike did not turn violent was that both the police and the strikers refrained from using confrontational tactics. The strikers never picketed the work site and never really attempted to stop work on the rail line. The police, while determined to allow the construction work to continue, did not disrupt union meetings or impede the organizers' activities. In later years, as the battle between workers and management escalated in Los Angeles, the incidence of violence in labor-related disputes dramatically increased. The most spectacular episode was the bombing on October 1, 1911, of the Times Building. Less spectacular but more consistent and certainly more effective were the violent tactics used by the LAPD to suppress union and other "radical" activity.

THE CHRISTMAS DAY RIOT

While many individual Mexicans belonged to unions affiliated with the American Federation of Labor (AFL), it was the Industrial Workers of the World (IWW) that most actively and most effectively recruited Mexican workers in the Southwest in the early years of this century. The IWW, founded in 1905 as an alternative to the AFL, had an anarcho-syndicalist philosophy. While the AFL mostly restricted itself to organizing workers in skilled trades, the IWW, known as the Wobblies, wished to organize all American workers in order to form "One Big Union." Once constituted, the union would take control of not only the factories but also the machinery of government. IWW philosophy thus foresaw the end of both capitalism and government. Furthermore, Wobblies espoused the concept of "direct action" in order to achieve their goals and demanded the right to defend themselves against the hostile forces of capitalism. The IWW was the only national labor organization to make sustained efforts to organize unskilled workers such as Mexicans during the first three decades of the century. Its efforts had little effect, however, since American capitalists and their allies in government used all the means at their disposal, including violence, to destroy such a dangerous organization. Nevertheless, the IWW rhetoric must have had a familiar and welcome ring for many Mexicans who were acquainted with, and who supported, the anarchist philosophy of such Mexican revolutionaries as Ricardo Flores Magón.

The riot that occurred at the Plaza, a traditional gathering place for Los Angeles Mexicans, on Christmas Day, 1913, provides an example of Mexican Wobbly activity, of the LAPD reaction to it, and of the limits that the American justice system placed on Mexican immigrant radicalism. The riot resulted from police breaking up a Wobbly-sponsored rally protesting unemployment in Los Angeles. The nation as a whole was suffering through a mild depression in the fall and winter of 1913, but Los Angeles suffered more than most cities because the intensive labor-recruitment efforts of the Chamber of Commerce and the railroad industry had flooded the local labor market. The unemployment situation seems to have been particularly difficult for Mexicans. Three days before the riot, a group of 250 gathered in front of LAPD headquarters because, police reported, "some jokers" had told them they could obtain work there. Mexican members of the IWW called the Christmas Day rally to protest the continuing recruitment of new workers into the city and to ask the city government to help the unemployed, both men and women, find jobs.[14]

On a rainy Christmas Day 500 men and women, most of them Mexicans, gathered in the Plaza at 2:00 P.M. to hear the speakers. The rally had been in progress for an hour and a half when the police arrived. What happened next became a matter of much debate. Police Lieutenant Herman W. R. Kreige said the trouble started when he and five other officers attempted to enforce a city ordinance that prohibited speeches in public parks without a permit. In a statement given to the *Times,* Kreige stated that when he arrived at the Plaza, "a man was on the stand addressing the crowd in Spanish. I touched him on the leg and said: 'Say, mister, you're not allowed to speak in the park without a permit.' " According to Kreige, he repeated his statement because the speaker ignored him. "Then," Kreige declared, "I heard someone in the crowd shout something about 'go at 'em boys' and at the same time someone struck me on the back of the head." The police drew their weapons in self-defense, Kreige contended, but the crowd continued to throw stones at them. Officer Alfred Koenigheim stated that at one point he saw Rafael Adames point a "vicious-looking .38" gun at a fellow officer, whereupon Koenigheim shot and killed Adames.[15]

The story told by civilian witnesses differed dramatically from the police version. According to these witnesses, when the police arrived at the Plaza, the main speaker stood on a chair which itself stood on a table. Mrs. E. Tatum stated that Kreige went up to the Mexican speaker, brusquely ordered him to stop his speech, and at the same time pulled the chair out from under him. When a Mexican bystander protested the policeman's actions, Kreige "replied by striking the [man] violently in the forehead with his club, leaving a great triangular gash from which the blood flowed freely." Although police gave no order to disperse, the crowd started leaving the Plaza when the police first arrived. Neverthe-

less, according to several civilian witnesses, after officers attacked the
speaker they proceeded to wade through the scattering crowd, hitting
people with their clubs as they went. Not satisfied with moving people
out of the Plaza, police began chasing people in the streets and beating
them with their clubs.[16]

At first the crowd did not fight back. According to one unidentified
observer, however, people soon began pelting the police with stones.
The police retaliated by attempting to make arrests. Eventually, the
crowd managed to isolate and attack Kreige. According to one observer,
"In almost less time that it takes to tell it, the crowd around Kreige
broke away and he emerged with the blood streaming down both sides
of his face. It was before and after this scrimmage that most of the stone-
throwing by the crowd and shooting by police occurred, and it was said
at the time that one man was killed and carried away."[17] Other witnesses
corroborated this story but added that after the assault on Kreige, the
police started firing indiscriminately into the crowd. The *Los Angeles
Record,* a generally pro-labor paper, accused the LAPD of "cossackism"
for its conduct at the Christmas Day disturbance.[18]

The LAPD's actions after the violence ended demonstrate its determination to suppress the sources of Mexican radicalism. At 8:00 P.M.
police detectives began an invasion of Mexican restaurants, pool halls,
and motion picture theaters, and "every man who appeared disarrayed
in dress, showed indication of having been through the battle or bore
blood marks, cuts or fresh bruises, was jerked from his seat and thrown
into the patrol wagon." In total, police arrested seventy-three men, of
whom fifty-six were Mexican.[19]

Police and city officials responded to the Christmas Day disturbances
by calling for further restrictions on the right of free speech. Without
knowing the content of any of the speeches given at the Plaza, Chief of
Police Charles Sebastian stated, "The time has come when this city must
put a curb on the preaching of direct appeals against law and order. . . .
We propose to curtail these speakers who spread their appeals to the
ignorant and inflame them against law and order. From this time onward we shall use every means within our power to keep these trouble
makers within strict bounds. Any further attempts to arouse their listeners against the law and the men appointed to preserve the peace will
be promptly suppressed. We mean business: *liberty shall not be made
license in Los Angeles*"[20] (my italics).

Acting Mayor Frederick J. Whiffen called upon the city council to
pass a resolution "pledging Chief Sebastian its most hearty support in

ridding the city of these public appeals of the malcontents desirous of stirring up the bitterest strife." Other council members wanted the police to take even harsher measures against the IWW. Councilman M. F. Betkouski stated the "troublemakers . . . should and must be firmly suppressed" and called upon the city council "to back Chief of Police Sebastian in any efforts he may make to rid the city of this disturbing element." Finally, Councilman J. S. Conwell declared that the police should take "a stand to clear out of this city the agitators who have been doing their utmost of late to stir up trouble."[21]

Despite the exhortations of these politicians, the LAPD took no further action against the Mexican Wobblies. Instead, city officials sought to make examples of the people arrested during and after the riot by prosecuting them to the fullest extent of the law. In order to justify this, the public had to be convinced that the Wobblies, not the police, were responsible for the riot, and, of course, the prosecution had to succeed in court. Although city and police officials had the firm support of the *Times* in these efforts, the Los Angeles Labor Council, the local Socialist Party, and the *Los Angeles Record* generally opposed the city's position.

From almost the very beginning, city officials and their supporters claimed that the riot had been caused by organized labor and its allies in the news media. In particular they blamed the *Record* and, to a lesser extent, the *Los Angeles Express*. The *Times* stated that "in reality" the Christmas Day riot was "caused and conducted by loafers, reds, I. W. W.'s and boasted anarchists." Law-enforcement officials also maintained that the IWW had actually planned to incite a riot. The police claimed that the Wobblies had stockpiled rocks around the Plaza to use when the trouble broke out. The LAPD also issued a statement that an unidentified Wobbly had told a "disguised detective" that the IWW started the riot in order to get more publicity. "We've got to get into the newspapers some way," the anarchist allegedly stated, "and if we cannot arouse them to talk about our hall meetings, then we'll have to incite news matter of some sort, no matter what the cost. The doctrine must be spread."[22]

In the days immediately following the riot, the showcase for the city's official position was the investigation conducted by the city council's Public Safety Committee. From the beginning of this investigation, it seemed obvious that the committee would issue a report favorable to the police. On the first day of the hearings, the committee allowed only one civilian, an arrested Mexican member of the IWW, to testify. All the other witnesses were policemen and, according to the *Record,* they all gave exactly the same story. The investigation would have ended after only one day had not the *Record* and city council members who were not on the Public Safety Committee demanded to hear more testimony from nonpolice witnesses. Despite the fact that all the civilian witnesses in varying degrees contradicted the police version of the riot, the Public Safety Committee issued a report, which the entire city council adopted, exonerating the police. The report, which referred only to the testimony from the police witnesses and totally ignored civilian witnesses, stated that "the police department was within its rights in enforcing the provisions of the [public-speaking] ordinance." The only hint of criticism of the LAPD was in the suggestion that the police "might have used a little more discretion and tact in handling the situation as it existed."[23]

The *Record* and organized labor came to a totally different conclusion, blaming the LAPD for the outbreak of violence. The *Record* reported that the civilians who testified before the Public Safety Committee clearly demonstrated that the police had caused the riot. These witnesses stated that plainclothes officers already had their weapons drawn before Lieutenant Kreige arrived at the Plaza; that Kreige and his men, "with drawn clubs and revolvers, knocked the crowd right and left in pushing their way to the speakers' stand"; that the police knocked the speaker off his platform; and "that the police started using their clubs before they were attacked." The *Record* concluded that "the testimony of unbiased and unprejudiced witnesses . . . showed up the cossack methods of the police[,] . . . discredited the police stories of the affair and clearly indicated that the action of the police started the riot [and] that the police acted with unnecessary and unwarranted brutality."[24]

Organized labor tried to shift at least part of the blame onto the labor recruiters who had flooded the local labor market. At a December 27 meeting of the Central Labor Council, City Councilman Fred Wheeler, a Socialist Party member, declared that the railroad companies and other public utility companies were at least partially responsible for the riot because they had imported hundreds of Mexican workers who were now unemployed. The constant theme that emanated from organized labor, however, was an intense hostility toward the LAPD. The *Times* reported that at a meeting at the Labor Temple, "the rioters . . . were eulogized as heroes and martyrs in impassioned addresses[,] and the policemen who courageously enforced the law . . . were hissed, sneered [at] and called 'Cossacks, criminals, fiends' and other pet Socialist names." At the same meeting a resolution was passed condemning the "brutality of the police" and "demanding that the city council impress upon the police department that its duty is not to beat up, but to protect the public and that the police should not use violence in the discharge of their duties except in self-defense." Speakers made similar proclamations at other labor meetings, and for a time, a demonstration to protest unemployment and the activities of the police department was contemplated. This demonstration, however, never took place, probably because the organizers feared that it would result in more police violence.[25]

The criminal prosecutions against the men arrested at the riot revolved around the basic issue of responsibility for the violence that broke out on December 25. The first legal proceedings against the men came on December 29, when forty-four of the seventy-three men originally arrested were arraigned before the police court. All but two of the men arraigned were Mexican. The *Times* reported that the "I.W.W. labor-union-Socialist gangsters" were charged with rioting, for which the maximum penalty was two years in jail and a fine of two thousand dollars. At the arraignment hearing, defense attorneys argued for separate trials for each of the defendants, but the judge ruled against them and set the trial date for January 21, 1914.[26]

The trial began on time, with several hundred Mexican supporters of the defendants being turned away from the courtroom. Job Harriman, the former Socialist candidate for mayor, was the chief defense attorney. His basic strategy was to discredit the testimony of individual policemen and to shift blame for the riot away from the defendants and onto the police. On the first day of testimony, Harriman won a major procedural victory when the judge ruled that police witnesses had to identify individually every man they accused of rioting, rather than have the defendant stand up when the witness called his name. Harriman scored a second point when he forced Sergeant W. L. Hagenbaugh to agree that the riot did not start until the police started chasing people through the streets around the Plaza. "Then why did you not leave the men alone and be content with having prevented the violation of a city ordinance?" Harriman asked the sergeant. "Why did you not remain in the park, instead of continuing on the street?" Hagenbaugh replied that to have stayed in the park would have been to show "the yellow feather."[27]

Harriman's strategy proved to be at least partially successful when, on January 30, the prosecution moved to dismiss charges against twelve of the defendants, including the two whites. The district attorney called for the dismissals either because the defendant had never been identified as having committed a crime or because the testimony against the defendant had successfully been called into question by the defense. The

Record noted with indignation that the district attorney offered "no explanation of his reason for holding the exonerated men in jail for 36 days" and only now admitted he had no evidence against them.[28]

As the trial drew toward a close, Harriman stressed more and more that the police actually caused the violence that had taken place the previous Christmas. On February 2 Harriman presented a witness who, according to the *Record,* testified that the "brutal beating[s] administered by police" to the Mexicans in the Plaza had, in fact, caused the violence and that the attack on Kreige came after the shooting of Rafael Adames. The *Record* also reported that four other witnesses gave similar testimony.[29]

The soundness of Harriman's strategy was demonstrated on the evening of February 6 when the jury returned verdicts of innocent on fifteen of the remaining defendants and guilty on ten; the jury was unable to reach a decision on one. The celebration that probably occurred that night in the Mexican section of the city, however, must have ended quickly the following morning, when Police Judge Thomas White imposed extremely harsh penalties on the ten convicted men. White sentenced two men to the maximum term of two years in prison and five others to one year; Pedro Coría, who had only one leg, was sentenced to nine months in jail, another man received a five-month term, and Leon Ygnacio, whom Judge White considered "the least guilty," was sentenced to three months in jail.[30]

The *Record* reported that in passing sentence, Judge White acknowledged the severity of the sentences and "strongly condemned" the "cowards" who had attacked Lieutenant Kreige and rioted at the Plaza. Then, in a statement remarkable for the clarity with which it reflected the status of Mexicans within the criminal justice system, the judge gave his rationale for the severity of the sentences: "I have given careful consideration to the case and I have taken into account the nationality of the accused. If the men came from a country where they were accustomed to liberty and into a land where the iron heel of oppression was ever present, it would put a different aspect to their actions. But they came from Mexico to the United States and were allowed the full privileges that are accorded our citizens. I am going to impose sentences that will warn all such agitators that they cannot dispute men who have been vested by the people of the land with authority to enforce the laws."[31] Judge White probably did not appreciate the irony of his statement. In upholding the authority of the LAPD against the Mexican "agitators," and by imposing the harsh sentences, he proved that Mexicans did not enjoy the full privileges of American citizenship.

THE LAPD AND MEXICAN AGRICULTURAL WORKERS

Mexican American workers and law-enforcement agencies in California have traditionally come into conflict in the agricultural industry. Beginning with the Oxnard strike of 1903 and continuing through the agricultural strikes in the San Joaquin and Imperial Valleys during the Depression, and even into the efforts of the United Farm Workers in the 1960s and 1970s, attempts by Chicano farm laborers to form labor unions have met with violence and other repressive measures on the part of local police officials. In particular, during the Great Depression, attempts by Mexican agricultural workers to organize labor unions and better their working conditions probably led to more violence than any other aspect of labor relations in California. The San Joaquin Valley cotton strike of 1933 and the 1934 Imperial Valley lettuce strike were only the most infamous of the 140 agricultural strikes that occurred in California during the 1930s.

While Los Angeles was one of the richest agricultural counties in the nation until World War II, most of the labor disturbances occurred beyond the Los Angeles city limits and were therefore out of the jurisdiction of the LAPD. Nevertheless, when Mexican American farm labor activity occurred within the city limits, and often even when it took place outside the city, the LAPD intervened on the side of employers, frequently using methods that exceeded their authority and the letter of the law. In this regard, the LAPD again displayed its antilabor, pro-employer bias and helped maintain Mexicans in a subordinate position within the labor market.

An early example of the LAPD using dubious, if not outright illegal, methods to break a strike by Mexican farmworkers came in August 1917. Earlier that summer, Mexican sugar beet workers in Orange County, south of Los Angeles, had gone on strike, demanding a pay increase from $1.75 per day to $2.75 per day and better housing conditions. In an exposé the *Record* charged that the police department and police court had conspired to force men to work in the strike-affected sugar beet fields or face jail sentences ranging from 30 to 180 days for breaking the vagrancy laws. According to the *Record,* "men who are in hard luck and without jobs, or have jobs that do not quite satisfy police authorities, are being arrested in the open streets and sent as contract laborers to the beet fields, where they are being forced to work at wages against which Mexican laborers there now are striking and under conditions the Mexicans refuse to tolerate." Lieutenant D. L. Adams, the officer in charge of the vagrancy detail, acknowledged that more than sixty men had already been sent to work and that the department was sending more "as rapidly as we can pick them up." "We tell these men they can take these jobs or pound city rock," Adams stated. "Most of them take the beet field jobs and are not booked at the station at all."[32]

According to public defender James H. Pope, however, not all the men arrested and sent to the beet fields were actually vagrants. Pope gave examples of several men who had jobs but were unfortunate enough to be caught in the police dragnet. Frank García, for instance, had a wife, family, and job in San Gabriel and had come to Los Angeles to buy clothes when police arrested him while he had a drink in a bar. When he refused to work as a scab, the police court judge sentenced him to thirty days in jail. Other men were out of work but had enough money to support themselves for several days when the police arrested them. One unnamed Mexican worked in the movie industry and had $400 in the bank when police picked him up. Pope asked, "Why should men who have money enough to wait to get the kind of work they are fitted for be forced by police to accept such work as the ordinary decent American looks on as beneath him?"[33]

City officials outside of the public defender's office responded either by feigning ignorance or by supporting the police action. Judge White, who had been imposing the most severe sentences, denied that men accepted work provided by the municipal employment bureau only in order to escape sentencing. Chief of Police J. Butler stated that he was unaware of any "arrangement" between the department and the beet growers but that he "merely wanted to see these men go to work; where[,] I do not care." For his part, Mayor F. Woodman maintained that the arrested men had to accept work in the beet fields because the growers had stated that they needed workers. Two days later, however, the mayor reversed his position. In a prepared statement, Woodman declared that henceforth police and other city officials could not force men arrested under the "vag" law to work for less than standard wages. The *Record* reported that the mayor also announced that he would launch an investigation into "conditions in the police station which are said to have led to . . . supplying beet growers or others with cheap labor." The *Record* made no mention of whether such an investigation ever took place.[34]

THE NADIR OF THE LABOR MOVEMENT

The period beginning with the entrance of the United States into World War I and ending with the start of the Great Depression was the low point of the American labor movement in general and of the Los Angeles labor movement in particular. State and local officials used American involvement in the European conflict as an excuse to pass laws making it illegal to be a member of an anarcho-syndicalist organization, to utter anarcho-syndicalist ideas, or even to display a red flag. Law-enforcement officials used these Criminal Syndicalism Laws, as they were called, to jail IWW officials and suppress any Wobbly activity. After the war ended, an antiradical hysteria known as the Red Scare gripped the nation, and government officials at all levels violated the civil rights of thousands of American residents. Although the Wobblies made sporadic attempts to revive their organization, the Red Scare was the blow that killed the IWW. During the twenties, employers used a variety of innovative tactics, such as the company union, the "yellow dog" contract, and court injunctions, to seriously weaken even the most conservative unions affiliated with the American Federation of Labor. Thus, by the beginning of the Depression, the American labor movement had all but ceased to be a factor in the nation's economy.[35]

Mexican workers in Los Angeles shared the misfortunes of their fellow workers during the antiradical hysteria that swept the nation during and after World War I. The Wobbly Spanish-language newspaper *Imprenta de el Rebelde* was one of the first publications to be shut down under the Criminal Syndicalism Laws. During the Red Scare the *Los Angeles Express* reported that the federal government would begin the "wholesale deportation of Mexicans accused of anarchistic tendencies." Several Mexicans were also among those prosecuted for being members of the IWW.[36]

The wartime repression and the Red Scare all but destroyed the labor movement in Los Angeles for more than a decade. Mexican workers participated in Anglo-dominated unions, and several strikes broke out during the twenties in industries in which Mexicans comprised a large segment of the workforce. Nevertheless, despite the rapid increase in the size of the Mexican population of Los Angeles during the twenties, there is no evidence that any major conflict occurred between predominantly Mexican labor unions and the LAPD during that decade. It would take the beginning of the Great Depression and the seemingly pro-labor policies of Franklin Delano Roosevelt's New Deal to renew that conflict.

CHAPTER 4

The LAPD and the Revolutionaries

Like its antilabor activities, the LAPD's attempts to suppress political activism that was related to events in Mexico fostered animosity between the department and segments of the Mexican community. During the early part of the century, most political activism by Los Angeles Mexicans was in fact related to events in Mexico—specifically, to the Mexican Revolution (1910–1920). Prior to 1910, most of the activity was aimed at ousting Mexican dictator Porfirio Díaz from office. The leading Mexican dissident at this time was Ricardo Flores Magón, who made Los Angeles a base for many of his operations. During the revolution itself, the leaders and representatives of various political factions within Mexico came to Los Angeles to seek the support of the city's growing Mexican population.

The LAPD responded to political activism related to the revolution in two distinct ways. First, before 1910, police attempted to curb any activity based in Los Angeles that might undermine Díaz. This response reflected the general conservative attitude of the city's white middle-class majority and the more specific interests of local capitalists who had large investments in Mexico. Using illegal tactics and acting as paid agents of the Mexican government, members of the LAPD harassed and intimidated enemies of the Díaz regime in Los Angeles and even in other parts of the United States. In particular, they jailed and illegally held Ricardo Flores Magón and other members of the anti-Díaz Partido Liberal Mexicano (PLM). Despite the LAPD's illegal tactics and the fact that officers working as agents of the Mexican government were in violation of the city charter, city officials never disciplined the policemen involved in these activities. Only the final overthrow of the Díaz government ended their activities on the Mexican dictator's behalf. In engaging in these tactics, however, the department put itself at odds with a significant portion of Los Angeles's Mexican population.

The LAPD's anti-PLM activities did not go unchallenged. Members of the Los Angeles Mexican community protested the alleged injustices suffered by Flores Magón and his followers at the hands of the American criminal justice system. In addition, some of the more moderate PLM members received support from white progressive reformers in their conflicts with police. While these challenges served to mitigate the effects of the LAPD attacks on the anti-Díaz forces in Los Angeles, they also contributed to a lingering animosity between the department and the Mexican community and helped establish a tradition of protest against police misconduct.

Díaz's overthrow in 1910 initiated a decade of violent revolution in Mexico. On several occasions, as a result either of violence spilling over into the United States or of American attempts to intervene in Mexico, war seemed imminent between the two nations. During periods of high tension, Los Angeles whites began to doubt the loyalty of Mexicans living in their midst. For such times, the LAPD developed a set of practices to protect the city from a potential Mexican revolt and to suppress any pro-Mexican demonstration in the city's Mexican community. Elements within the Mexican community responded angrily to what they saw as violations of their civil rights. It was only when the threat of hostilities between the United States and Mexico ceased that these police practices came to an end.

THE LAPD AND THE MAGONISTAS

Ricardo Flores Magón, the radical Mexican revolutionary, migrated to Los Angeles to escape political persecution and police harassment; he did not, however, find a safe haven in that city. He arrived in Los Angeles in 1907, having fled Mexico as a result of his opposition to the Díaz regime. In the United States he and his followers continued to agitate against Díaz, publishing their newspaper, *Regeneración*, and forming a political party, the Partido Liberal Mexicano (PLM). They also continued to face repression, this time by a combination of

Mexican government agents, American officials, and private detective agencies.[1]

Mexican government officials could work so freely in the United States because America enthusiastically supported the Díaz regime. Upon gaining power in 1877, Díaz imposed strict social and political order on Mexico by employing authoritarian and often violent measures. He also sought to modernize and industrialize Mexico by granting special economic incentives to foreign investors. By creating the social order necessary for economic growth, Díaz provided American foreign-policy makers with the perfect conservative model for Latin American economic and political development. In addition, American businessmen who had invested heavily in Mexico and who had close personal and political ties to Republican presidents Theodore Roosevelt and William Howard Taft sought to protect their investments by lobbying the federal government to support the Mexican dictator. Consequently, influential interests within the United States pressured the federal government to assist Díaz and suppress his enemies in the United States.[2]

American officials, in cooperation and coordination with Mexican agents, used a variety of tactics to suppress anti-Díaz agitation in the United States. This included surveillance and monitoring of anti-Díaz elements within the United States, providing the Mexican government with information regarding the movements of its enemies in the United States, and disrupting the revolutionaries' activities through criminal prosecution and other forms of harassment. While federal officials directed the effort at the national level, municipal officials, often under pressure from local businessmen, spearheaded local attempts to quiet Mexican revolutionaries.[3]

Some of the most influential Los Angeles business leaders were among the large investors in Mexico and therefore had an interest in keeping Porfirio Díaz in power. The owners of four of the five major Los Angeles daily newspapers held large tracts of land in Mexico. Harrison Gray Otis, the owner of the *Los Angeles Times,* was the president of a company that controlled 850,000 acres of Mexican land, and the owner of the *Herald,* T. E. Gibbons, held stock in the same company. E. T. Earl, owner of the *Express,* was the director of the Sinaloa Land and Water Company, and William Randolph Hearst, owner of the *Los Angeles Examiner,* also had large landholdings in Mexico.[4] In addition, Edward M. Doheney, the owner of the Mexican Petroleum Company, was a longtime resident of Los Angeles and was active in local civic affairs.

These and other local business magnates demonstrated their esteem for the Díaz government at an elegant banquet hosted by Doheny in honor of Mexican ambassador Enrique Creel a week before the PLM leaders' first encounter with the LAPD.[5]

American officials and business leaders had reason to fear Flores Magón not only because he sought to overthrow the Díaz regime but also because his ideology and rhetoric had the potential to radicalize Mexicans living in the United States. In his early years, Flores Magón had been a liberal nationalist who sought to bring democracy and honest government to Mexico. Realizing that peaceful change was impossible in Mexico, he concluded that the only way to improve Mexican society was to overthrow Díaz. As he stayed longer in the United States he grew more radical, first adopting socialism and then converting to anarcho-communism as a utopian ideal. Flores Magón specifically wanted to build a coalition between Mexicans living in Mexico and those living in the United States. He used the PLM newspaper, *Regeneración,* as his main tool to politicize and radicalize the Mexican masses on both sides of the border. Although Flores Magón did not publicly adopt anarchism until 1911, the local press, and presumably local officials, already viewed him as a dangerous radical when he first arrived in Los Angeles in 1907.[6]

While most of Flores Magón's writings addressed conditions in Mexico, over time he also began to pay attention to issues concerning Mexicans living in the United States. In particular, he attacked the subordinate and exploited status of Mexican workers, the biased nature of the American law-enforcement system, and the violence and racism endured by Mexicans living in the United States. The November 10, 1910, issue of *Regeneración* contains a good example of Flores Magón's defense of Mexicans living in the United States:

> Everyone knows the contempt with which Mexican people in general are treated [in the United States], everyone knows that in Texas Mexicans are treated worse than blacks. In the hotels, restaurants, and other public establishments of Texas, Mexicans are not admitted. Public school doors are closed to our children. Semi-savage North Americans exercise their rights as whites over Mexicans. How many of our men have died because some blond haired savage has gotten the idea to prove his skill with guns by shooting them without there even being a dispute between them! In the so-called courts of justice Mexicans are judged, generally without any [legal] propriety, and they are sentenced to be hanged or to suffer terrible punishments, without there being any proof, but not even the slightest doubt that they committed the crime for which they are made to suffer.

In order to remedy this situation, Flores Magón called upon Mexicans to form labor unions to better their lot as workers and to engage in revolutionary activity to free their homeland from the tyrant Díaz. Such ideological positions and activities served as both the reason and the excuse for the harassment Flores Magón and his followers endured while they based their operations in Los Angeles.[7]

Flores Magón first came in contact with the LAPD on August 23, 1907. He and other leaders of the PLM had established their headquarters in the southern California city in the hope that the support they enjoyed from the Mexican community there would provide a strong base from which to expand their operations. The press reported that three Mexican American police officers, Detectives Felipe Talamantes, Louis Rico, and Thomas Rico, acting under the instructions of the Mexican ambassador to Washington, took up surveillance of Flores Magón and the other PLM leaders. Local sources did not explain why Los Angeles police officers received and followed orders from representatives of a foreign government.[8]

On the evening of August 23, three weeks after Flores Magón had arrived in Los Angeles, the LAPD detectives, along with agents of the Thomas Furlong Secret Service Bureau of St. Louis, swept down on a small house on the outskirts of the downtown area. Flores Magón; Librado Rivera, a high-ranking PLM member; and Antonio Villareal, secretary of the PLM, were working there. After a fierce battle, the police and detectives overpowered the three revolutionaries and stuffed them into waiting carriages. Believing that they were being kidnapped and taken to Mexico, Flores Magón, Villareal, and Rivera continued to struggle and called for assistance from the people in the street as they rode to the jailhouse. No help came, however, and the three men soon found themselves in the city jail. Later that same day, police also arrested Modesto Díaz, editor of *Revolución*, the local PLM organ.[9]

The arrests of Flores Magón and the other PLM leaders were part of a larger scheme to crush Mexican opposition to the Díaz regime in the United States. In the aftermath of the 1906 PLM-initiated strike at Cananea, Sonora, Díaz decided to destroy the PLM. He knew that the PLM had instigated the strike and believed that such incidents posed a serious threat to his regime. According to the historian W. Dirk Raat, Díaz selected Enrique Creel, Mexican ambassador to the United States and a member of one of the wealthiest families in Mexico, to "direct a binational espionage system" composed of Mexican consuls, American federal and local government officials, and private detective agencies to suppress the PLM. At first, the Creel operation attempted to gain its objective by bringing extradition proceedings against the *revoltosos* for political crimes in Mexico. When it became apparent that United States law prohibited extradition for political crimes, Creel and his allies turned to kidnapping. Thus, when the police officers Felipe Talamantes, Louis Rico, and Thomas Rico arrested the PLM leaders, the revolutionaries had good reason to believe that they too were being kidnapped.[10]

Local observers generally agreed that the Díaz government had instigated the arrests. The *Los Angeles Herald,* which endorsed the raid, reported that Ambassador Creel "gave directions for the arrest of every member of the junta to be found in Los Angeles" and that the three policemen acted at the ambassador's "special instance." The *Herald* also reported that the three Mexican American detectives took their orders directly from Antonio Lozano, the Mexican consul in Los Angeles.[11]

The charges of the Mexican government against the PLM officials were unfounded. Mexican consular officials charged Flores Magón with murder and treason for inciting the Cananea strike, although he was actually in Canada at the time and did not communicate with the strikers. They charged Villareal with fleeing from prosecution for political crimes in Mexico, Rivera with desertion, and Modesto Díaz with criminal libel against President Díaz. The Mexican government did not attempt to provide evidence to support these charges.[12]

Local sources also generally acknowledged that the charges against Flores Magón and the other PLM leaders were mere pretexts to extradite them to Mexico. The revolutionaries' lawyer complained that the men were held on "nothing but trumped up charges [designed] to get them back to Mexico." The LAPD inadvertently lent support to this contention by publicly stating that "numerous other complaints will be filed from time to time to make sure of holding [the PLM leaders] until the government has had an opportunity to look into the matter." The press for the most part agreed that the arrests were but a prelude to the magonistas deportation, adding that once extradited "it may be the story of the wall at sunrise, and the sharpshooters."[13]

Throughout their incarceration in Los Angeles the jailed men received a strong show of support from the local Mexican community. PLM agents raised $1,950.00 for the defense effort from Mexican workers in the city, in contributions ranging from $0.10 to $3.00. At the PLM leaders' first court appearance, hundreds of their local supporters jammed the courtroom to bolster the PLM leaders' spirits. The *Times* devoted half of the front page of its city section to a description of the courtroom scene, including a detailed illustration. "As the spectators passed out," the article read, "men and women reached over the rail and seized the hands of the prisoners, or planted kisses on their cheeks. Little babes were held by mothers so that the accused men might pat them on the faces. It was clear that this motley crowd was tied by close bonds to the alleged conspirators." Emotions ran so high, according to the *Times,* that being in the courtroom "appeared like [standing] on a barrel of gunpowder as a fuse sputters its way to the interior."[14]

The size and intensity of the pro-PLM demonstrations raised community leaders' concern about the revolutionaries' radical message. The *Times,* for example, charged that Flores Magón, Villareal, and Rivera were "murderous anarchists" with "cowardly plans" who associated with "Nihilists" and other "notorious anarchists." The *Times* seemed most concerned about the demonstrations of support for Flores Magón, which large numbers of Mexicans attended. The following excerpt of a *Times* description of a pro-PLM rally gives a good indication of the newspaper's rhetoric:

> A wild-eyed anarchist with a smoking bomb in his hand was the only thing needful to complete the picture of last night's mass meeting in Simpson Auditorium. Revolutionists, Socialists, Labor Unionists and others of that ilk were present to give utterance to their protest against the imprisonment of Villareal, Magon and Rivera. . . . The audience was composed mainly of Mexicans and Spanish-Americans—but not of the better class. All present were roused to the highest pitch of fanaticism. Threats against all existing forms of government were made. The Presidents of the United States and Mexico were denounced. Atty.-Gen. Bonaparte was ridiculed and threatened with vague retribution for his enforcement of justice. . . . As the hearers warmed beneath the fiery sentiments emitted by the anarchistic speakers, there was formed an embryo band of partisans which would have stopped at nothing.[15]

The arrest and continued incarceration of Flores Magón and the other PLM leaders worsened the relationship between the Mexican community and the LAPD. The prominent Socialist attorney Job Harriman headed the defense team and chose to defend the PLM leaders by painting them as innocent patriots persecuted by the tyrannical Díaz regime and its mercenaries in the United States. Harriman seemed to take particular delight in addressing sympathetic audiences and denouncing Talamantes and the Ricos, the three Mexican American police officers who had originally arrested the revolutionaries. At the November 12 rally, Harriman told the crowd that instead of Flores Magón, Villareal, and Rivera being in jail, Talamantes and the two Ricos should be incarcer-

ated for their unlawful harassment of the Mexican patriots. Mexicans
in the audience cheered the names of the revolutionaries and jeered the
names of the policemen. According to the *Times,* when someone shouted
that Talamantes was in the audience, "scores of cholos jumped to their
feet and started for the spot where the officer was supposed to be sitting.
If he had been there, nothing could have prevented a vicious assault and
possible bloodshed."[16]

The anger directed at Talamantes and the Ricos resulted from their
role in arresting Flores Magón and from their conduct during his incarceration. To begin with, they arrested the PLM leaders without a formal
warrant and held them in jail on fabricated charges. Even a court sympathetic to the wishes of the Mexican authorities had to have some
evidence to continue to hold the men. Since that evidence did not exist,
Talamantes and the Ricos pressed charges of resisting arrest. According
to the attorney for the Mexican vice consul, "the charges of resisting
arrest were placed against the men merely as a means of holding them."[17]
Talamantes and the Ricos had thus apparently perjured themselves, and
it was to this breach of the law that Job Harriman referred when he
called for the incarceration of the policemen who arrested Flores Magón.

The Mexican community's animosity against Felipe Talamantes,
Louis Rico, and Thomas Rico also resulted from the generally held belief
that the three policemen were paid agents of the Díaz regime. While
neither the Mexican consul nor the police department officially acknowledged this, the three detectives took their orders directly from the
Mexican government. At the time of the arrest the *Herald* had noted
that Talamantes and the Ricos expected to receive a substantial "reward" for the capture of Flores Magón. PLM supporters specifically
charged that the officers in fact drew a salary from the Mexican government. Finally, the allegations against the LAPD officers were not confined to those made by PLM partisans. Even the conservative *Los Angeles Times* alluded to a "special relationship" between the three officers
and the Mexican authorities.[18]

If true, the allegation against Talamantes and the Ricos meant that
they had violated the city charter, which forbade police officers from
taking outside employment. Nevertheless, LAPD officials refused to rep-
rimand the three officers or even to launch an investigation into the
charges. While this inaction was probably due to the intervention of the
Mexican government and its influential friends in Los Angeles, at least
part of the reason may be the fact that the overall strategy worked.
Flores Magón and the other PLM leaders languished in the Los Angeles

city jail for over a year, until federal officials extradited them to Arizona, where the revolutionaries were eventually convicted of violating United States neutrality laws and sentenced to prison terms.

LAZARO GUTIERREZ DE LARA AND THE LAPD

The success that Detectives Felipe Talamantes and Louis and Thomas Rico enjoyed in the Flores Magón case encouraged them to harass other PLM members, most notably Mexican attorney Lázaro Gutiérrez de Lara. Superficially, the two cases have similarities. Like Flores Magón, Gutiérrez de Lara was arrested by Talamantes and the two Rico brothers on trumped-up charges and held on those charges until federal extradition proceedings could begin. Also as in the Flores Magón case, if Gutiérrez de Lara were to be sent back to Mexico, he would be, most contemporary observers believed, jailed and probably murdered. Unlike the Flores Magón case, however, the arrest of Gutiérrez de Lara led to a broad coalition composed of white progressives and socialists, along with segments of the Mexican community. This coalition sought to free Gutiérrez de Lara by bringing into disrepute the three Mexican American officers and, through them, the entire LAPD. The incident further exacerbated relations between the LAPD and the Mexican immigrant community.

The case began on October 10, 1909, when police arrested Gutiérrez de Lara and two other men. Police apprehended Gutiérrez de Lara while he gave a speech at the Plaza attacking Mexican dictator Porfirio Díaz; police arrested the two other men for objecting to the officers' actions. As police led the three men to the station, a crowd of five hundred Mexicans followed, protesting the arrests. In the hope of dispersing the crowd, the police arrested the leader of the protest, Querino Limón. As soon as they had taken Limón away, however, an unidentified Mexican woman reconvened the protest. According to the *Times,* when police saw that "the cholo woman['s] . . . speech . . . was having its effect on the simple-minded men who heard her," the officers stepped in and also dispersed this protest. This pattern of small groups of Mexicans gathering in the Plaza to protest the Gutiérrez de Lara arrest, only to have the gathering broken up by the police, continued throughout the rest of the night. In addition, later that night, two of the arresting officers, Felipe Talamantes and Louis Rico, claimed that they were assaulted as they walked through Sonoratown, the Mexican section of the city.[19]

Lázaro Gutiérrez de Lara was by far the most prominent of the men arrested. He came from a wealthy Mexican family and, before falling out of favor with the Díaz regime, had gained a high position in the Mexican judiciary. Because of his liberal political views, he was forced by the Díaz regime to leave Mexico early in 1906. For a time he flirted with radicalism, joining the PLM and helping to organize workers during the Cananea strike. In the fall of 1907, during the excitement over the Flores Magón case, United States officials arrested him and held him for three months while the Mexican consul searched for evidence that warranted his extradition to Mexico. Such evidence was not forthcoming, however, and he eventually gained his freedom.[20]

In 1908 Gutiérrez de Lara secretly accompanied the American journalist John Kenneth Turner on a fact-finding trip through Mexico. The information they gathered resulted in a series of articles that were highly critical of the Díaz regime; one of these articles was published just prior to the arrest. (In 1911, the articles were gathered into Turner's famous book, *Barbarous Mexico*.) By the time of his arrest, Gutiérrez de Lara had become a well-established resident of Los Angeles, admired by the Mexican community for his outspoken criticism of the Díaz government and respected by the more progressive elements of the white community for his cultured manner and moderate rhetoric.[21]

Talamantes and the Rico brothers arrested Gutiérrez de Lara not because he had committed any particular crime, but because of his strong criticism of the Díaz regime. Talamantes and Louis Rico made the arrest while Gutiérrez de Lara delivered a speech in Spanish in which, the two policemen claimed, he had threatened the lives of both Porfirio Díaz and President Theodore Roosevelt. When the policemen and Gutiérrez de Lara arrived at the jail, however, he was held simply "on suspicion." Although the police had plenty of opportunities to bring him before a magistrate, he languished in the Los Angeles city jail for three days without having formal charges brought against him. During this time, police prohibited him from speaking to his wife or friends. When he finally went before a judge, the police charged him with speaking without a permit. When it became apparent that he had spoken in a "free speech zone" (an area that did not require a speaking permit), Talamantes and the Ricos changed the charge to one of disturbance. When Gutiérrez de Lara demanded a jury trial, the officers dropped this charge also. But by this time, they had wired the secretary of commerce and labor in Washington, D.C., telling him that they had captured a dangerous anarchist who should be deported under the undesirable alien law. The secretary then ordered the immigration inspector in Los Angeles, A. C. Ridgeway, to place Gutiérrez de Lara under arrest on federal charges and hold him for extradition proceedings.[22]

The arrest, imprisonment, and possible deportation of Gutiérrez de Lara became a cause célèbre in Los Angeles. But unlike with Flores Magón, Gutiérrez de Lara's local support came not only from Mexicans but also from white progressives who sought to use the case to discredit the LAPD. These progressives formed a "De Lara Defense Committee," which did not include a single Mexican member but which had broad support among reform groups in Los Angeles. For example, the defense committee chose John D. Works, a progressive politician and a former California state superior court justice, to head Gutiérrez de Lara's defense. The committee received letters of support from forty Protestant ministers (several of whom offered to make the Gutiérrez de Lara case the main topic of their Sunday sermon), from Caroline Severance, a revered leader of the Los Angeles women's movement, and from the Reverend D. M. Gandier, assistant superintendent of the State Anti-Saloon League and the man for whom the California prohibition law would eventually be named. On October 23 the defense committee held a "monster rally" at which Judge Works, Gutiérrez de Lara's white wife, and other speakers appealed for public support for Gutiérrez de Lara and excoriated the police. Finally, and perhaps most important, the progressive newspaper the *Los Angeles Herald* championed the Gutiérrez de Lara cause, keeping it before the public eye for almost a month.[23]

Given the usually permissive attitude that Los Angeles progressives took regarding police suppression of Mexican political activity, it is interesting to contemplate the reasons behind their support for Gutiérrez de Lara. At the time of the confrontation, in the fall of 1909, a new political climate existed in Los Angeles. The progressives had just gained full control of city hall for the first time, having won the mayor's office a year before on the issue of police corruption. A city council election, however, was scheduled for that November, and the conservatives of the old machine had fielded a full slate to challenge progressive control of the council. Since Talamantes and the Ricos were notorious functionaries of the old machine, the progressives may have focused on the three policemen's apparent wrongdoings to remind voters of the previous year's campaign issue. Not coincidentally, Judge John D. Works, Gutiérrez de Lara's chief attorney, was running on the progressive slate for the Los Angeles City Council.[24]

The defense committee developed a dual strategy. First, it hoped to relieve Gutiérrez de Lara of the threat of deportation. Second, the com-

mittee hoped to vilify Talamantes and the Rico brothers and thus remind
voters that remnants of the old machine were still on the force. These
two objectives were related. The only charge for which Immigration
Inspector Ridgeway could deport the Mexican was advocating anarchy.
The only evidence that Gutiérrez de Lara was an anarchist came from
the testimony of Talamantes and the Ricos. If the Mexican revolutionary's good character could be demonstrated and the policemen's testimony impeached, Gutiérrez de Lara would go free and the reputation
of the police department would be sullied. Such a sullying of the LAPD's
image was politically useful for the progressives in the upcoming election
and could also lend public support to their efforts to reform the police
department.

In order to assure the public of Gutiérrez de Lara's good character,
friends, business associates, and his wife all made impassioned statements to the effect that he was not an anarchist. Support for this position
came from the Mexican community. Gutiérrez de Lara's supporters also
sought to help the incarcerated man by verbally attacking Talamantes
and the Ricos and, through them, the LAPD as a whole. As Judge Works
declared at a rally on October 23, 1909, "I want to say to you that there
never was a greater outrage perpetrated in a free republic than this. They
[the police] kept him in jail without charges, and then they trumped up
a misdemeanor charge. It was a fraud. It was done to justify the police
in their action. When he [Gutiérrez de Lara] demanded a jury trial, they
were compelled then to release him, but his imprisonment had served
its purpose of holding him [until federal officials could bring deportation
charges against him]. Detectives have made more crime than they have
ever prevented. The best service . . . commissioner [Ridgeway] could
render the country would be to deport them."[25]

Attacking the LAPD made good sense. As noted earlier, the only real
evidence that Inspector Ridgeway had against Gutiérrez de Lara was in
the form of statements from Felipe Talamantes and Louis and Thomas
Rico, three officers who, as alleged paid agents of the Mexican government, had the responsibility of silencing enemies of the Díaz regime. The
first indication that the three officers could not produce the kind of
evidence necessary to deport Gutiérrez de Lara came at the trial of Querino Limón, who had been arrested with Gutiérrez de Lara. At the trial
the prosecution attempted to convict Limón by associating him with
Gutiérrez de Lara and by attempting to prove that Gutiérrez de Lara
was a dangerous anarchist.[26]

This tactic, however, finally made public the evidence under which

Gutiérrez de Lara was held and demonstrated the incompetence of the three officers. Louis Rico, for example, testified that he had taken notes on Gutiérrez de Lara's speech and when he felt that Gutiérrez de Lara had sufficiently incriminated himself, he had made the arrest. Under cross-examination the detective stated that he no longer had his notes and that he only had a limited command of the Spanish language. When asked for specifics of the speech, Rico stated that at one point Gutiérrez de Lara called on the crowd to "fix Díaz." He later conceded, however, that the Spanish word he had translated as "to fix" actually could have radically different meanings in English. Moreover, according to the *Herald,* several linguists who were in the audience commented that Rico's command of the Spanish language was so poor that his translation of Gutiérrez de Lara's speech could not be used as evidence in a court of law.[27]

As a result of their performance in the Limón trial, Talamantes and the Ricos came under severe attack from Gutiérrez de Lara's supporters. The *Herald,* on the one hand, excoriated the three officers for being paid agents of the Mexican government and, on the other, ridiculed them for doing such a bad job of it. "My conclusion of the showing made yesterday," an unidentified attorney wryly stated to the *Herald,* "is that the Mexican officials are getting poor return for the money they are spending. I mean by that [that the] efforts of the autocracy to get possession of political prisoners might be directed by a more efficient mind than the one now in charge."[28]

The passing of the municipal election (with the progressives maintaining control of city hall) and a guarantee of Gutiérrez de Lara's freedom dampened progressive criticism of the LAPD, but not before the defense committee made one more attack on Talamantes and the Ricos. On November 15 word reached Los Angeles that the federal government had dropped all charges against Gutiérrez de Lara. The defense committee issued a statement that gave an indication as to its real priorities. After perfunctorily indicating its pleasure at Gutiérrez de Lara's release, the committee said that it was "sorry not to have an opportunity to show up certain officers who were implicated in Mr. De Lara's arrest and imprisonment. . . . We want to know how it is that Los Angeles police have been so active in the pursuit of Mexican refugees." The committee also sarcastically wondered why Talamantes and the Ricos were involved in so many recent cases involving Mexican political activists. "The city of Los Angeles pays the salaries of these detectives," the committee stated. "Does it not stand to reason that the people would prefer to have Messrs. Talamantes and Rico out chasing hold-up men that seem to operate so fearlessly than to have them spending time trying to get political refugees into the toils?"[29]

Despite their activities in the Gutiérrez de Lara case and other evidence of wrongdoing on the part of Felipe Talamantes and Louis and Thomas Rico, Los Angeles progressives subsequently seemed to lose interest in attempting to discipline the three policemen.[30] But by the fall of 1910 a new chief of police felt he had sufficient evidence against Talamantes and the Ricos to formally charge them with corruption.

THE TRIAL OF FELIPE TALAMANTES
AND LOUIS AND THOMAS RICO

The attack against the three officers began on August 1, 1910, when the progressive police commission, at the request of Chief of Police A. Galloway, demoted the three officers from detectives to regular patrolmen. The three men protested the police commission's action, and the Civil Service Commission ruled the demotions to be invalid because the chief had not followed due process rules. Galloway, who had recently been named chief of police by the progressive Mayor George Alexander, restored Talamantes and the Ricos to their former rank but immediately suspended them pending a trial by the police commission.[31]

The charges against the three officers resulted from their activities against Los Angeles Mexicans and the animosity those activities generated in that community. Initially, the chief brought only the charge of extortion against Talamantes. At the October 10 meeting of the police commission, a Mexican woman, Apolinar Cuevas, claimed that Talamantes had demanded fifty dollars for the return of her kidnapped thirteen-year-old daughter. On November 7 Galloway, on the basis of information he had received from members of the Mexican community, brought ten additional charges against Talamantes and the Rico brothers. These charges included working as private detectives while being on the city payroll; burglary and larceny; subornation of perjury; perjury; "brutal," "improper," and "cruel" conduct; extortion; assisting defendants for pay; and "divers other instances of conduct unbecoming officers." All but one of the victims specified in the charges were Mexican.[32]

The police commission trial lasted throughout November and into December of 1910. A large number of witnesses testified regarding the three detectives' corruption. On November 10, for example, Mrs. Angelita Alvares testified that she had paid Talamantes ninety dollars to help prosecute a man "who had wronged her daughter." Mrs. F. Elizalde claimed that Talamantes had hit her on the face during an interrogation over the alleged theft of twenty-five cents. At the same hearing, a social worker, Mrs. J. Von Wagner, corroborated the earlier testimony regarding the Cuevas case, and attorney H. H. Apple claimed that Talamantes had suborned perjury during a murder case eight years earlier. At the November 14 session, attorney Guy Eddie claimed that the Mexican consul held receipts proving that Talamantes and the Ricos were employees of the Mexican government. At subsequent police commission hearings PLM members Lázaro Gutiérrez de Lara, Ricardo Flores Magón, and Librado Rivera, together with other Los Angeles Mexicans, corroborated Eddie's claim.[33]

Despite this direct and specific evidence against the three detectives and their inability to directly counter it, on November 21 the commission dismissed all charges against Louis and Thomas Rico. The Ricos had only been charged as accomplices of Talamantes and the evidence against them was weaker. On December 5, in a three-to-two vote, the commissioners elected to dismiss all charges against Talamantes as well. Three weeks later, Chief of Police Galloway resigned in disgrace.[34]

Their activities from the time they arrested Ricardo Flores Magón in 1907 through their trial in 1910 render it difficult to understand how Felipe Talamantes and Louis and Thomas Rico escaped punishment. The lack of official condemnation seems particularly odd given the reformist tendencies of the progressives who gained control of city government during these years. It may have been the case that the machine still had the political strength to protect its functionaries. The *Times,* which regularly voiced the machine's political opinions, vigorously defended the three detectives and ridiculed Chief Galloway for filing charges. Even the progressive newspapers, such as the *Herald,* lost their enthusiasm for the case after the initial revelations. Another possible explanation for Chief Galloway's inability to gain a conviction against the corrupt policemen is that businessmen such as Harrison Gray Otis, William Randolph Hearst, Edward M. Doheney, and others may have used their political power to influence the police commission's decision. Given the precarious state of the Díaz regime in the latter part of 1910, these businessmen, who had a tremendous stake in keeping Díaz in power and who regularly supported the Mexican dictator's interests in the United States, may have tried to prevent his agents from being punished in their hometown. Yet another explanation may be that, if the police commission's decision was indeed politically motivated, the fact that almost all the victims were relatively powerless Mexicans gave the commissioners the opportunity to make the most expedient decision in the knowledge that there would be few adverse consequences.

THE PLM AND THE LAPD

American authorities continued to harass Ricardo Flores Magón and members of the PLM for the next ten years. With the exception of some minor incidents, however, most of the harassment came from federal officials. One significant interaction between the LAPD and magonistas took place in the form of a riot on June 25, 1912. In June the previous year, federal authorities had again arrested Ricardo Flores Magón, his brother Enrique Flores Magón, Librado Rivera, and Anselmo Figueroa in Los Angeles for violating United States neutrality laws. PLM organizers then spent a year trying to gain the support of the local Mexican community for the revolutionary cause. Both female and male PLM members worked effectively in this endeavor, women organizing supporters privately and men making speeches at the Plaza praising Flores Magón and denouncing the Mexican government in general and, in particular, the Mexican consul in Los Angeles, Francisco Martinez Baca. The organizers successfully arranged for large numbers of Mexicans to attend the June 1912 trial.[35]

During the trial the prosecuting attorney, hoping to make a name for himself, intimidated witnesses and suborned perjury to get a conviction. On June 22, 1912, this strategy proved successful, with the four men being convicted. Three days later the judge handed down a twenty-three-month sentence for each man. It was the severity of the penalty that then caused a riot.[36]

On the day of the sentencing, between six hundred and a thousand Mexican and white sympathizers congregated both inside and outside the courthouse. When PLM organizers Francisca Mendoza and Blas Lara told the crowd outside the courthouse of the severity of the sentence, the sympathizers rushed the jailhouse. The police, whom officials had placed around the jail in anticipation of just such an event, called for help and laid into the crowd, swinging their clubs. More police arrived and a riot ensued. Several of the protesters were injured—according to the *Los Angeles Record,* "many heads were cracked and considerable blood was spilled." The police arrested nineteen magonistas—fourteen men and five women.[37]

Originally, authorities charged the alleged rioters with attempting to free the federal prisoners, a federal offense. These charges could not be proven, however, and the defendants were released by federal authorities, only to be immediately rearrested by city officials and charged with rioting.[38] The June 25 clash was the last major confrontation between magonistas and the LAPD.

THE BROWN SCARE

The LAPD's fear of Mexican radicalism engendered by the magonistas turned to a fear of insurrection after the Mexican Revolution erupted in 1910 and brought the United States and Mexico to the brink of war on several occasions. In general, this meant that LAPD officers stopped harassing Mexican opponents of the Díaz regime and instead concentrated on suppressing expressions of Mexican nationalism during times of real or potential conflict between the United States and Mexico. This change came about for a number of reasons. To begin with, the Mexican government was no longer strong enough to recruit men like Talamantes and the Ricos as its agents. The decade following Díaz's demise—the Mexican Revolution—was a period of great violence and turmoil in Mexico. The half-dozen or so men who held the Mexican presidency during this period could not control events in the countryside fifty miles from the presidential palace, much less events in Los Angeles. Capitalists in southern California, however, still held large economic interests in Mexico and therefore often involved themselves in the revolution, usually favoring the most conservative faction.[39]

The relationship between the LAPD and the Mexican community also changed, because whites came to see Mexicans as a threat to the security of the nation. The historian Ricardo Romo has identified three factors that gave rise to apprehensions about the presence of large numbers of Mexicans in Los Angeles and that caused the LAPD to develop strategies for dealing with a Mexican population many perceived as potentially dangerous and subversive. First, many whites feared that revolutionary rhetoric from Mexico would spread to the United States and radicalize Mexicans living in this country. Second, whites also worried that violence associated with the revolution would spill over into the United States. This concern was expressed during periods of tension between Mexico and the United States, when whites feared that Mexicans living in this country might rise in rebellion against American rule. Finally, when the United States entered World War I, many Americans saw Mexico as a potential ally of Germany and called into question the loyalty of Mexicans living in the United States.[40]

Part of the LAPD's role during the years of the Mexican Revolution was to maintain order when opposing revolutionary factions openly clashed in Los Angeles. Police officials, for example, feared an outbreak of violence over the visit of Félix Díaz, the nephew of the ousted dictator, Porfirio Díaz. Félix Díaz, along with the American ambassador Henry Lane Wilson and General Victoriano Huerta, had engineered the plot that overthrew the presidency of the well-meaning but weak Francisco Madero. When Huerta placed himself in the presidency and ordered Madero's execution, a great roar of anti-Huerta public opinion rose both in Mexico and in the United States. Fearing the treachery of his former ally, Huerta effectively exiled Félix Díaz by appointing him ambassador to Japan. On July 31, 1913, en route to Japan, Díaz stopped off in Los Angeles.

Police officials feared that an attempt would be made on Díaz's life during his stay in the city. Accordingly, Chief of Police Charles Sebastian ordered a full squad of mounted policemen and a company of footmen to escort Díaz from the train station to his hotel. This show of force was apparently necessary in view of the crowd that gathered outside the depot yelling "Death to Díaz!" and generally menacing the Mexican ambassador when he arrived in Los Angeles. On Friday, August 1, anti-huertistas held a rally in the Plaza, where they passed resolutions charging Díaz with the murder of Madero and calling on President Woodrow Wilson to deport Díaz and refrain from recognizing the Huerta government. The next day this same group held another rally in the Plaza, but this time violence broke out when a group of pro-huertistas began holding a rally of their own praising the Mexican president. A riot ensued involving several hundred people, and police were called in to disperse them. Over the succeeding months and, in fact, years, several violent incidents occurred in Los Angeles between sympathizers of opposing factions in the Mexican Revolution.[41]

The LAPD performed its proper function of maintaining order and even acted with restraint as long as violence related to the revolution stayed within the Mexican community. On three occasions between 1913 and 1917, however, diplomatic tensions and the threat of war between the United States and Mexico led authorities to question the loyalty of Los Angeles Mexicans. On each occasion the LAPD violated Mexicans' civil rights as the police moved forcibly to protect the white community from a feared Mexican uprising. The resulting period of stress between the white and Mexican communities and the unlawful activities of the LAPD has been labeled by historian Ricardo Romo as the "Brown Scare."[42]

The first period of great tension between the United States and Mexico came in April 1914, when President Wilson ordered American naval forces to occupy the Mexican port of Veracruz. In the fighting that ensued nineteen Americans and over three hundred Mexicans, most of them civilians, died. Tensions ran high on both sides of the border and, for a short time, war seemed imminent. In Mexico most revolutionary factions protested the American intervention and vowed to stop fighting among themselves if the United States occupied further Mexican territory. Americans also responded to the war fever by flocking to the recruiting offices of the armed forces and generally preparing themselves for a struggle against Mexico.[43]

In Los Angeles there was also great excitement about the possibility of war with Mexico. The owners of two major newspapers, the *Los Angeles Times* and the *Los Angeles Examiner,* held large tracts of land in northern Mexico, and their two newspapers had long called for American intervention to protect American interests. As a result, anti-Mexican feelings ran particularly high in Los Angeles. Two factors, however, made the war hysteria in Los Angeles different from that in most other parts of the country. First, the proximity of the border with Mexico made the perceived threat of invasion greater; and second, there was a large Mexican population in the city.

The white community worried particularly about the loyalty of Mexicans living in their midst. The usually moderate *Los Angeles Record,* for example, carried a front-page story with the headline "Mexicans in Los Angeles Patriotically Cry 'Viva Mexico!' " In the story, all the Mexicans interviewed supported Mexico's cause in the conflict, including one Mexican American born in the United States, who categorically stated he would fight with Mexico in the event of war.[44]

Chief of Police Sebastian assured frightened white residents that "the police are ready to act instantly in case of an uprising." In order to ensure that no revolt took place, he increased the number of patrolmen on duty in the barrio, ordered the arbitrary search of "all Mexicans" for concealed weapons, and arrested and held without charge several Mexicans "for fear they might make incendiary speeches." The department also organized a special "Citizens' Police Force" and armed them with sawed-off shotguns to protect the city from "being attacked by the Mexican element."[45] Luckily, the threat of war between the United States and Mexico, and with it the hysteria, ended quickly.

The second event that brought the United States and Mexico to the brink of war and resulted in the violation of Mexicans' civil rights was Pancho Villa's raid on Columbus, New Mexico, on March 9, 1916, in which several Americans died. The local press had previously given wide publicity to other incidents in which revolutionary violence spilled over into the United States. In particular, newspapers gave full and sensational coverage to the violence in Texas associated with the Plan de San Diego.[46] Nothing matched the public furor, however, created by the Columbus raid and the American reaction to it.

Coming in the midst of an intense national debate regarding the United States' role in the world war raging in Europe, Villa's raid put President Wilson in a quandary. On the one hand, he did not want to commit American troops to a major conflict in Mexico while a possibility existed that the United States might be drawn into the war in Europe. On the other hand, American blood had been shed on American soil, and Democrats and Republicans alike called for strong punitive action against Villa.[47]

Wilson responded within a week by ordering General John J. Pershing to cross into Mexico and disperse Villa's forces. Hoping to avoid any incident that might lead to war, Wilson limited the military actions that Pershing could take while in Mexico. On April 12, 1916, however, Pershing's forces engaged Mexican civilians in the southern Chihuahua town of Parral, killing forty Mexicans and losing two American soldiers. For the second time in a little more than a month American newspapers renewed calls for war between the two countries. Then, on June 21, 1916, regular Mexican army forces engaged a patrol of American troopers, killing twelve and capturing twenty-three. Anti-Mexican feeling in the United States ran higher than it had at any time since the Mexican-American War of the 1840s, and war between the two countries seemed inevitable. Cooler heads prevailed, however, and after July the crisis moved fitfully toward resolution. United States forces finally left Mexico for good on February 5, 1917.[48]

Villa's Columbus raid and the American response created another crisis for Los Angeles Mexicans, with tensions between whites and Mexicans running highest when war between the United States and Mexico seemed most likely. Again, whites feared an uprising of local Mexicans. On Tuesday, March 14, Mayor Sebastian announced that he had received a letter stating that the local villista organization planned "to dynamite all federal buildings, courthouses, electric power plants and newspaper plants." Two days later a rumor spread that riots were imminent in Sonoratown, the Mexican section of the city. In April word came that San Diego, to the south, was about to be invaded and that "practically all of the Villa cabinet [were] residents of Los Angeles."[49]

In May the *Los Angeles Record* reported that a federal officer "with years of experience along the border" issued a statement that raised white apprehensions to a fever pitch. Of the forty thousand Mexicans living in southern California, the official asserted, two-thirds "would immediately throw themselves with Mexico in case of war with the United States." He also stated that he had "watched conditions in Los Angeles for years," and warned that "the police and government cannot take too much care. The Mexicans of this city are ripe for an upheaval and will cause all manner of trouble, should they rise."[50]

In late June 1916, during the height of the crisis, newspaper stories abounded about local Mexicans desecrating the American flag, about thousands of Mexicans leaving for Mexico to join Villa, and even about Villa himself hiding in the United States. White paranoia became so great that when bombs exploded at a San Francisco Preparedness Day Parade on July 22, 1916, killing ten people, federal government officials first suspected "Mexican anarchists" working out of Los Angeles.[51] Later, authorities tried and unjustly convicted labor organizer Thomas Mooney for this crime.

Los Angeles police officials responded to this crisis with many of the same tactics used during the Veracruz incident. Immediately after news of Villa's raid reached Los Angeles, Chief of Police Clarence E. Snively stated that "no liquor . . . [can] be sold to Mexicans showing the least sign of intoxication. No guns can be sold to Mexicans, and all dealers who have used guns for window display have been ordered to take them from the windows and to show them to no Mexicans until the embargo is lifted." Snively also organized a "special police force" and tripled the number of patrolmen in Sonoratown. The *Times* praised the chief's actions and stated that the "firebrands—and they are not a few—must be watched and snuffed out: the preachers of insurrection must be sequestered and confined."[52]

As it had done during the previous crisis, the LAPD violated the civil rights of Mexicans living in the city. Mexicans were again subject to arbitrary searches and arrest. Moreover, on March 13 police arrested three PLM members and charged them with carrying a concealed weapon. On March 16 police arrested eighteen more Mexicans, seventeen men and one woman, charging them with suspicion of having violated the neutrality laws. According to the police, the group was on its way to Mexico to join Villa's army.[53]

Sunday, March 26, was a day of particular tension in Los Angeles. A week earlier, policemen had been issued deadly dumdum bullets "for use in emergencies such as riots." The newspapers had also reported that "wholesale deportations" of Mexicans from border states would soon take place and that police feared that radicals would incite trouble at the Plaza that Sunday. Chief Snively consequently organized a special detail of over twenty men, many of them Mexican Americans, under the command of Louis Rico, with orders to "mingle with the Mexican crowd and speakers [and] to see that no overt acts are committed." In an uncharacteristic demonstration of moderation, Snively also warned his officers "not to interfere with public speaking, unless it becomes inflammatory or in the nature of inciting a riot." No incident took place.[54]

Tensions again flared the following month when President Wilson called up and nationalized the California National Guard. Fearing that "Los Angeles will be absolutely defenseless in case of serious trouble," the mayor organized a special "home guard" for protection against the Mexican population of the city. Similarly, Snively, giving as the reason "probable war with Mexico," asked the police commission for immediate certification of eligible applicants to the department and for the appointment of an additional eight hundred men to the "Citizens' Police Force." The chief also issued an official proclamation to "citizens of the city, as well as the Mexican residents," ordering them to, among other things, "refrain from intoxication" and to "stay away from groups or crowds that may tend to incite trouble." "With your cooperation," he stated, "we will avoid local trouble and strife." The situation became so tense that officials felt compelled to issue a separate proclamation to reassure the Mexican population. Written in Spanish, it told local Mexicans that "they need fear no effects of the present Mexican crisis." It also attempted to assure them that their "lives and property" would be protected "as long as they behave themselves."[55]

During the second half of 1916 the threat of war between the United States and Mexico subsided and with it so did interracial tensions in Los Angeles. But the disclosure on February 28, 1917, that Germany had offered Mexico an alliance against the United States again raised the

threat of war between the two countries. As on the two previous occasions, the threat of war brought into question the loyalty of Mexicans
living in Los Angeles. While President Wilson never intended to go to
war with Mexico, the popular press, especially in Los Angeles, made
much of the possible threat from the southern republic.

The LAPD used tactics developed during two earlier crises—the Veracruz incident and the Villa raid—to protect the city from German
saboteurs and their "Mexican sympathizers": the chief of police organized a special police force, more policemen patrolled Sonoratown, and
there was strict police surveillance of speakers in the Plaza. With the
exception of events in May 1917 after the United States had formally
entered World War I, however, the anti-Mexican hysteria at this time
was comparatively mild.[56]

The problems in May 1917 began during the yearly Cinco de Mayo
celebrations and demonstrated the lingering animosity between the
LAPD and at least the more radical elements of the Mexican community.
Alerted by rumors that Mexican radicals would attempt to speak to the
thousands of people attending the festivities in the Plaza, police officials
organized a special detail to keep watch on the events. On the second
day of the three-day celebration, officers arrested PLM members Raúl
Palma and Odeleon Luna when they attempted to address the crowd.
Although local police originally charged the two men only with vagrancy, federal officials rearrested them a week later and charged them
with attempting to "incite revolution and anarchy under the alien enemy
act."[57]

The LAPD's actions aroused hostility in at least one segment of the
Mexican community. On the Sunday following the Cinco de Mayo celebrations, the PLM responded to the police's actions by distributing a
circular charging the department with "a series of abuses . . . against the
Mexican laborers of this city." The circular warned Los Angeles Mexicans that they must "unite, men and women," if they "did not wish to
be victims of greater misbehavior and injustice" at the hands of "the
dogs who call themselves guardians of public order." Specifically, the
circular complained about the Cinco de Mayo arrests, arguing that
"there was no reason for the dogs to stick their noses into our business.
. . . Common people, to remain silent before this new insult is to give
reason to the slaves to continue believing that we are incapable of re-
claiming our rights, to continue believing we are beasts who must be
managed with clubs. They may yet end by assassinating us. Then, let us

unite to defend the prisoners and defend ourselves, our children and our families that are in danger if we permit those ferocious human beasts to continue fattening upon us."[58]

A week later, on Sunday, May 20, another Mexican, Vicente Carrillo, again spoke at the Plaza. According to the *Record,* Carrillo told "a large number of Mexicans" that "Americans were planning to send all Mexicans to the front 'to be killed while they [the Americans] remained safely at home.' " Carrillo also exhorted the crowd to refuse to register for the draft as President Wilson had recently ordered them to do. Los Angeles policemen quickly arrested Carrillo and turned him over to federal officials.[59]

The LAPD's activities during the Brown Scare had important consequences for the future. This was the first time in the twentieth century that a local law-enforcement agency had developed a set of practices for controlling the Mexican American community. The LAPD systematically violated the civil rights of Mexicans simply because they were Mexicans, whom the local press had made out to be a threat to the white community. Although the practices did not outlive the hysteria of the war years, their development did set a precedent for how the police would react during other periods of tension between Mexicans and whites in Los Angeles.

The reaction of at least one segment of the Los Angeles Mexican community also set a precedent. While Mexicans had made official complaints regarding police misconduct in the past, the incidents surrounding the 1917 Cinco de Mayo celebrations represented the first time since the 1850s that they had taken their protests to the streets. For future generations, such protests would become all too commonplace.

CHAPTER 5

The LAPD and Mexican American Workers, 1920-1940

With the fear of a "Mexican uprising" at an end, during the 1920s and 1930s the LAPD continued to try to maintain Mexicans as a source of cheap labor. In performing this function the department operated as the rather crude instrument of local capitalists. The Los Angeles business community wanted a source of cheap and undemanding workers to continue the phenomenal economic growth the city enjoyed during the 1920s. The Mexican immigrants who streamed into Los Angeles during that decade, more than tripling the city's Mexican population, helped fill this need. These immigrants left a war-ravaged Mexico and moved to southern California in the hope of finding well-paying jobs and perhaps even a measure of dignity. In Los Angeles they found employment primarily as unskilled blue-collar workers—doing just the kind of jobs that local employers believed were necessary but that white workers refused to accept.

It fell to the LAPD to ensure that the Mexican workers, and indeed all workers, accepted the dominance of big business and the open shop. In order to perform this role, the department developed a special unit— the Intelligence Bureau, also called the "red squad"—to handle labor unrest. The actions of the red squad and of the LAPD in general initiated a series of intense altercations between officers and Mexican workers that were unprecedented in the history of the relationship between the LAPD and the Mexican community. These altercations continued to lay the foundation for animosity and suspicion between the department and the community.

Ironically, the LAPD played an ambiguous role in the worst official anti-Mexican action of the 1920s and 1930s. During the early years of the Great Depression, federal authorities and local officials attempted to ease unemployment in southern California by launching a massive deportation campaign against Mexican nationals. While local law-enforcement officials agreed to assist federal immigration officers in their efforts to discover and deport "illegal aliens," the LAPD in fact played only a minor role and found excuses to avoid being more aggressive. Nevertheless, the labor conflict and deportations worsened relations between the community and the LAPD and strengthened the sense of ethnic identity among Los Angeles Mexicans.

LOS ANGELES IN THE 1920S AND 1930S

The economic fluctuations that Los Angeles experienced during the 1920s and 1930s had dramatic consequences for the city's development. During the 1920s the economy boomed. According to economist Jacqueline Rorabeck Kasun, "value added by manufacture" increased by almost 300 percent between 1921 and 1929. The growth in manufacturing in turn created a tremendous growth in the labor force. The number of employed workers rose from 266,100 in 1920 to 723,824 in 1929—a growth rate higher than that of the general population. All in all, the growth of the economy meant that Los Angeles's industrial capacity grew faster than that of any other area of the country during the 1920s.[1]

The rapid economic development in turn spurred a remarkable decade of growth in the city's size and population. The geographical size of the city grew from approximately 363 square miles in 1920 to over 440 square miles in 1930. The population grew even faster, increasing from 576,673 at the beginning of the decade to 1,238,048 at the end. Most of this population growth resulted from the massive in-migration of Midwesterners in search of a better climate and better jobs.[2]

The 1920s saw an even larger expansion of the city's Mexican population. Tens of thousands of Mexican immigrants flocked to Los Angeles in search of work and better living conditions. While according to census figures the Mexican population of the city rose from nearly 30,000 in 1920 to over 97,000 in 1930, Chicano scholars have estimated that the increase was even greater, ranging from approximately 50,000 in 1920 to 190,000 in 1930. Given that the total population in 1930 was a little over 1,200,000, Mexicans became highly visible and easily the city's largest racial group. The growth in the population in combination with the development of the civic, commercial, and financial centers necessitated an expansion of the barrio away from the central city and east across the Los Angeles River into Boyle Heights, as well as even further east into the Belvedere section of unincorporated Los Angeles County. By 1930 Mexicans lived throughout what came to be generally known as East Los Angeles, and the city as a whole boasted the second largest Mexican population of any metropolitan area in the world, exceeded only by Mexico City.[3]

The rapid industrial development of Los Angeles during the 1920s did not alter Mexicans' subordinated position in the labor market. In 1920 Mexicans were overrepresented in low-paying blue-collar jobs and underrepresented in higher-paying white-collar jobs. A variety of indicators suggests that this type of economic subordination continued throughout the decade. Contemporary observers readily agreed that employers chose Mexicans only for low-paying jobs. A local industrialist, for example, asserted that Mexicans were hired to do "certain classes of menial labor that must be done if we are going to preserve our economic position in the world." Similarly, a religious leader stated that whites had "imported" Mexicans "for the very purpose" of doing "the common labor." The one limited demographic analysis that does exist not only supports these assertions but suggests just how rigidly Mexicans were subordinated into low-paying, menial jobs. According to the historian Ricardo Romo, between 1920 and 1928 not a single Mexican worker in Los Angeles moved up from a blue-collar job to a white-collar job.[4]

The decade of the 1930s brought dramatic and depressing changes in the fortunes of both Los Angeles and its Mexican population. For the city as a whole the Great Depression brought a decline in economic activity, a decrease in the rate of growth of both the population and the labor force, unemployment rates as high as 20 percent, and wages only 36 percent of what they had been in 1926. As in other American cities, in Los Angeles the jobless soon became homeless and the homeless soon went hungry.[5]

The Depression created even greater hardships for Mexicans living in Los Angeles. In 1930 Mexicans suffered from an unemployment rate of 13.1 percent compared with an average of 7.7 throughout the city. Even African Americans fared better, with an unemployment rate of only 7.9

percent. As the Depression wore on, nativist sentiments made this situation even worse. The California state legislature passed laws prohibiting certain categories of employers from hiring alien workers. Other employers soon adopted this "America for Americans" mentality and started replacing Mexican workers with whites. With growing numbers of Mexicans unemployed and thus on the relief rolls, the federal government and some local officials turned first to deporting and later to repatriating Mexicans as a means of relieving both the unemployment problem and pressure on municipal budgets. Authorities therefore treated Mexicans as a classic buffer group by removing them from the labor market during times of economic dislocation.[6]

The city's political system, and especially the LAPD, failed to keep pace with either the rapid economic development and population growth of the 1920s or the challenges brought on by the Depression. Throughout the period from 1919 to 1938 Los Angeles had one of the most notorious reputations for political corruption of any city in the nation. Over the course of almost two decades every mayor and almost every chief of police left office under a cloud of scandal. Most of the corruption involved police protection of organized vice—liquor during the 1920s and gambling and prostitution throughout the period. The continued support of the LAPD by the *Los Angeles Times,* the Los Angeles Chamber of Commerce, and the Merchants and Manufacturers Association ensured that everyone from the cop on the beat to the chief and even to the mayor could continue to accept bribes with impunity from organized crime figures. Reformers launched endless campaigns to end the police corruption, but the LAPD remained insulated from such movements as long as it continued to act as the tool of big business in keeping the city free of labor unions.[7]

THE LAPD RED SQUAD

While the 1920s was a period of relative quiescence between Mexican workers and the LAPD, the decade of the Great Depression saw an intensification of conflict between the two. One of the reasons was the increased sophistication of the LAPD's antiunion capabilities. An irony of Los Angeles labor relations during the 1920s is that while organized labor was in a period of general decline, the police department greatly augmented its union-fighting apparatus. Prior to the 1919 Red Scare no separate unit had special responsibility for antiunion, antiradical activity. During the height of the antiradical hysteria of 1919, however, the chief of police organized an "Anarchist Bomb Squad" consisting of twenty-five men to protect the city from "radicals, persons making unpatriotic utterances, [and] I.W.W.'s." By the late 1920s the bomb squad had evolved into the Intelligence Bureau or "red squad" of the LAPD.[8]

According to an internal police department document, the red squad's major functions included "investigations, surveillance, arrest and prosecution of illegal activities in connection with ultra-radical . . . [and] labor organizations involving strike disturbances, illegal picketing and sabotage." While the legal rationale for its activities was that it would curb the illegal activities of radical organizations and labor unions, the red squad often went far beyond its mandate, violating people's civil rights and committing outright criminal acts. Red squad commander William "Red" Hynes and his men showed particular enthusiasm for suppressing "radical" demonstrations and meetings. Ernest J. Hopkins, an investigator for President Herbert Hoover's Commission on Law Observance and Enforcement (the Wickersham Commission), described the red squad's attack on a Communist-led "Hunger March" in the spring of 1930 as "an eight hour clubbing party" in which the red squad clubbed demonstrators and news reporters alike.[9]

In 1940, after the Intelligence Bureau had been disbanded, the United States Senate Subcommittee on Violations of Free Speech and the Rights of Labor (otherwise known as the LaFollette Committee) documented more than twenty cases of the red squad breaking up peaceful meetings. Many of these meetings were sponsored by truly radical organizations like the Communist Party or the John Reed Club. The red squad, however, also attacked rallies held in support of leftist political candidates and even meetings of liberal organizations such as the American Civil Liberties Union (ACLU). Several of the meetings that the red squad broke up took place in cities other than Los Angeles and therefore outside the LAPD's official jurisdiction.[10]

The Los Angeles business community supported and encouraged the red squad's attacks on freedom of speech and civil rights in general because many businessmen believed that organizations like the Communist Party might radicalize the general public, thus threatening private property. Even more threatening were the activities of the reemerging labor movement during the 1930s. In response to this threat, the red squad became even more diligent. Captain Hynes's men intervened on the side of management in almost every case of labor strife to hit Los

Angeles in the Depression years prior to 1938. In most cases that intervention was violent and brutal, with pickets being dispersed with tear gas, clubs, and illegal arrests.

Furthermore, the red squad, unsatisfied with merely reacting to labor union initiatives, violated individuals' constitutional guarantees and, in an oblique manner, even called for the assassination of union officials. The most alarming of these activities was the use of undercover operatives to act as agents provocateurs whose explicit orders were to disrupt the activities of lawful labor unions. The LaFollette Committee, for example, published a "Plan of Operation" for two agents working for Captain Hynes. In this plan, Hynes ordered the agents to "concentrate their work to keep the organizing of the men to a minimum . . . and[,] as an ultimate end[,] to disrupt [the labor] movement entirely." The plan called for agents to "block every move of the union which holds any promise of effectiveness." Agents were "to assume leadership and . . . secure the removal of aggressive, efficient organizers." The agents were to give the names of union members to employers and disrupt the flow of information to union members. They were also to encourage "[labor] officials and organizers . . . to dissipate their efforts in fruitless channels, [and] internal quarrels among the members." "Dangerous members and officials," the plan concluded, "will be removed through definite action." Hynes did not specify what he meant by "definite action."[11]

The red squad also took part in antilabor activity outside the Los Angeles city limits and therefore outside the area of the department's legal jurisdiction. Perhaps the most important example of such activity (at least for the purposes of this study) is Captain Hynes's involvement in the 1934 Imperial Valley lettuce strike by Mexican farmworkers. A year before the strike, Hynes had written the Imperial County district attorney warning him about Communist labor organizing activities among agricultural laborers. He also sent the district attorney information on Pat Chambers, a Communist labor organizer, and samples of union literature. Hynes received a response indicating that law-enforcement officials were making plans for "taking care of Mr. Pat Chambers in the proper way." When a strike did indeed break out in the winter of 1934, local, county, and state law-enforcement officers combined with vigilante groups to destroy the Mexican workers' picket lines and break up union meetings. A committee of the National Labor Relations Board established to investigate the disturbances "uncovered sufficient evidence . . . that in more than one instance the law was trampled underfoot . . . by public officials under oath to support the law."

According to Clinton Taft, regional director of the ACLU, Hynes directed the whole antiunion operation in the Imperial Valley. In appreciation for Hynes's efforts, the Imperial Valley Growers Association sent a letter to the chief of police thanking him for the red squad leader's assistance during the strike.[12]

Captain Hynes and the red squad thus worked on behalf and at the behest of the local business establishment. So blatant was this relationship that Hynes kept his principal office in the Los Angeles Chamber of Commerce building rather than at LAPD headquarters in city hall. Employers paid the red squad officers' overtime and supplied them with the tear-gas guns and projectiles used against union members. Evidence also exists that local business interests paid special bonuses to members of the red squad and to Hynes himself for their services. Hynes's efforts on behalf of the business community proved lucrative; observers often saw him lose more than a month's salary in one day at local racetracks.[13]

Despite these apparent unlawful activities, local authorities refused to restrain Hynes and his red squad. Although on a few occasions, local courts found the Intelligence Bureau's activities so flagrantly illegal that they awarded damages to victims of police brutality and issued injunctions restricting the squad's activity, the monetary awards were only nominal, and the injunctions applied only to specific cases and were thus of limited significance. Furthermore, neither the district attorney, the city attorney, the mayor, nor the chief of police placed any restrictions on the red squad's activities.[14]

Even the police commission, which had the responsibility of investigating and acting upon citizens' complaints against the police, dismissed out of hand virtually every charge against the red squad brought before it. From the beginning of the Depression until the abolition of the squad in 1938, citizens filed over fifty complaints with the commission alleging that the red squad had violated their rights and committed illegal acts in breaking up political meetings and demonstrations. In not a single case involving political repression did the commission take any action against the Intelligence Bureau. Similarly, labor unions and their allies repeatedly filed complaints with the police commission charging the red squad with illegally disrupting legitimate labor union activity. In only one such case out of more than thirty filed did the police commission offer the unions any redress. Local governmental officials thus relinquished all responsibility for controlling Captain Hynes and his red squad.[15]

Hynes's red squad was thus the main union-fighting apparatus of the

LAPD during the 1930s. City and police officials rationalized its activities by asserting that the squad only enforced laws such as the Criminal Syndicalism Laws and the Anti-Picketing Ordinance—laws that the courts eventually ruled unconstitutional. But in reality the red squad went far beyond the letter of the law, disrupting otherwise peaceful meetings, violently breaking up lawful picket lines, engaging in covert activity, and asserting its authority outside the area of its jurisdiction. Perhaps the most disturbing aspect of the red squad's activities is the fact that the official bodies that had legal jurisdiction over the police department—the police commission, the mayor, and the courts—virtually refused to curb the squad's activities. It took a major political revolt, resulting in the first recall of a big city mayor and the subsequent shake-up of the police department, to put an end to the Intelligence Bureau of the LAPD.

THE LAPD AND THE DEPRESSION-ERA DEPORTATIONS

The onset of the Great Depression and the massive unemployment it engendered created a crisis for the Los Angeles Mexican community. Prior to the Depression, American public opinion had been divided on the issue of continued Mexican immigration. Agricultural interests and other employer groups from the southwestern states had managed to exclude nations in the Western Hemisphere from the National Origins Act of 1924. With this law Congress had intended to reduce immigration from eastern and southern Europe by limiting future immigration to a percentage of the number of immigrants from a specific country living in the United States in 1890. Since relatively few immigrants from Mexico lived in the United States in 1890, inclusion in the restriction would have greatly reduced legal Mexican immigration. Southwestern agribusiness successfully argued, however, that it needed the continued flow of cheap Mexican labor to maintain the economic expansion it had enjoyed through the first two decades of the century. Thus, Mexican immigration continued unabated and, indeed, increased dramatically during the 1920s, making Mexicans the second largest national group to immigrate into the United States during the period and the largest immigrant group in Los Angeles.

The continued immigration of Mexicans into the country did not go unchallenged. After 1924 opponents of Mexican immigration introduced legislation in Congress on a yearly basis that would have ended the exclusion of Mexico from the provisions of the National Origins

Act. The restrictionists objected to continued Mexican immigration because they considered Mexicans an inferior race that could not be as-
similated into American society. The proponents of unrestricted immigration countered not only by arguing that Mexicans were needed to
mitigate the Southwest's chronic labor shortage, but also by maintaining
that since they rarely became permanent residents, there was no need
for concern about whether they could assimilate into American society.
Mexicans were thus not only an asset, they were an asset to be discarded
when no longer needed. Throughout the 1920s, the proponents of continued immigration used this line of argument to gather sufficient votes
in Congress to consistently defeat measures that sought to restrict Mexican immigration into the United States.[16]

The onset of the Great Depression demonstrated, however, the inherent consequences of this line of argument. As a result of the massive
unemployment, government officials treated Mexican immigrants as
scapegoats to solve their political problem. President Hoover's secretary
of labor, William N. Doak, announced in early 1931 that much of the
nation's unemployment problem resulted from the fact that four hundred thousand "illegal aliens" held jobs that should go to American
citizens. Doak also announced that one hundred thousand aliens were
immediately deportable under the current immigration laws, and that
he would send his immigration agents into the field to ferret out these
undesirables. While Doak did not officially single out any specific racial
or ethnic group, in Los Angeles Mexican immigrants became the immediate target of this deportation campaign and of the "repatriation"
program that followed.[17]

The reason authorities focused on Mexicans was not because they
held so many jobs that could go to American citizens but rather because
deporting Mexicans provided an acceptable and convenient solution for
the area's economic problems. As noted previously, as early as 1930
Mexicans suffered from an unemployment rate that was more than 70
percent higher than the city's average. As the Depression wore on, the
unemployment situation for Mexicans became increasingly dire. The
California state legislature passed a law prohibiting companies that did
business with the state from employing aliens in public jobs. The Mexican consul estimated that in Los Angeles alone this law caused nine
hundred Mexicans to lose their jobs. Private employers followed the
state's example and, as a result, one Mexican resident recalled being
told that "from tomorrow on, there is no work for Mexicans." Moreover, employers did not discriminate only against noncitizens. One

United States–born former serviceman of Mexican descent remembered being continually denied employment because supervisors were ordered to hire only whites and he had dark skin. In addition, relief officials systematically denied Mexicans the various forms of public relief available to whites. Thus, the percentage of people of Mexican descent on relief dropped from 21.5 percent in fiscal 1928–1929 to 15.8 percent in 1929–1930, and to 12.5 percent in 1930–1931.[18]

Without employment, the hope of employment, or even the hope of public assistance, many Mexicans turned to desperate solutions simply to survive. Obtaining food became a major problem. Hundreds of Mexican families congregated around local produce markets and gathered whatever rotten fruits or vegetables grocers discarded. Others sustained themselves by eating food thrown away by local restaurants. Many considered themselves fortunate if they could eat beans for a steady diet. Mexicans also found it increasingly difficult to find adequate housing. One resident remembered it as being common to find Mexicans "sleeping on cold cement floors with newspapers and overcoats." As a consequence of these harsh conditions, thousands of Mexican immigrants began returning to their homeland as early as 1929 and throughout 1930.[19] Nevertheless, despite the fact that Mexicans neither took jobs away from whites nor constituted a relief problem, and despite the fact that an ever-increasing number were returning to Mexico of their own volition, Los Angeles officials launched a campaign to terrorize the city's Mexican population into leaving the area.

George Visel, the director of the city agency charged with creating jobs for unemployed workers, took to heart Secretary Doak's comments regarding alien deportations. Instead of concentrating on developing employment, Visel planned to coordinate a minideportation operation in which the LAPD and the Los Angeles County Sheriff's Department would arrest deportable aliens and turn them over to federal immigration officials who would then expel them from the country. Visel understood that none of the designated law-enforcement agencies had the resources to apprehend the twenty thousand deportable immigrants he estimated lived in Los Angeles. Instead, by giving wide publicity to the deportation of a relatively small number of people, Visel hoped to create a psychological atmosphere that would scare others into leaving. "This apparent activity," Visel stated in a telegram to Doak, "will have [the] tendency to scare many thousand alien deportables out of this district[,] which is the result desired."[20]

Visel began his campaign on January 26, 1931, when newspapers published his press release announcing the deportation. In the press release Visel stated that "trained members of the Immigration Department's Deportation Squad" were coming to Los Angeles to cooperate with local law-enforcement agencies in arresting and deporting immigrants. Visel also announced that the LAPD and the sheriff's department would assist in the deportation campaign by seizing immigrants suspected to be deportable and turning them over to the immigration officers. He stated, for example, that County Sheriff William Traeger had "promised" that his department would "clean up" his area of jurisdiction. Chief of Police R. E. Steckel went even further, committing the LAPD and the dreaded red squad to "rounding up the deportable aliens as fast as the Immigration Service calls for them." While the press release stated that deportable aliens included "Chinese, Japanese, Europeans, Canadians, Mexicans, and in fact peoples of every nation in the world," it also emphasized that the Mexican government wanted its people to return to their home country. Newspapers thus reported that law-enforcement officials planned to stop and question all persons who "looked like Mexicans." Since *La Opinión,* the leading Spanish-language newspaper in Los Angeles, also reported that the deportation campaign was aimed primarily at Mexicans, news of the campaign spread quickly through the Mexican community.[21]

The deportation sweeps began in early February when Supervisor William F. Watkins of the Bureau of Immigration and several other agents arrived in Los Angeles. On February 3, 1931, federal agents, supported by officers from the LAPD and the sheriff's department, stopped those they suspected of being deportable immigrants on the streets and questioned them, and held for deportation hearings those who could not prove their legal status. Although both federal and local officials continuously declared that they had targeted no particular group, practically all the people stopped were racial minorities (Asian or Mexican), with Mexicans comprising the overwhelming majority. By Saturday, February 7, immigration officials had arrested a total of thirty-five people considered deportable by agents.[22]

The deportation raids continued over the next several weeks, with the most dramatic incident occurring on February 26. At about three in the afternoon federal immigration agents supported by police officers raided the Plaza, the traditional gathering place for the Mexican community. According to *La Opinión,* law-enforcement officers literally besieged the area. Units of the LAPD, including the red squad, sealed off all exits while federal officials ordered everyone to be seated and questioned each person regarding his or her status in the United States. Witnesses told *La Opinión* that they saw police officers beat several of the Mexicans held in the Plaza. The combined force held over four hundred people for more than an hour and eventually arrested eighteen for deportation hearings.[23]

Immigration officers detained people whom they should have easily identified as legal residents. *La Opinión* reported that officers stopped Mexican vice consul Ricardo Hill and questioned him until he proved his diplomatic position. Immigration agents also arrested Moisés González even though he showed them his passport proving that he had entered the country legally. González was arrested because one officer, presumably a member of the red squad, believed that he remembered seeing the young Mexican at a Communist demonstration. During his interrogation, immigration officials and LAPD officers quickly determined that González was a legal resident but nevertheless vigorously questioned him about his participation in Communist activities. They held him until they had searched the red squad files for proof of radical associations but found no evidence to support their suspicions.[24]

The deportation campaign terrorized the Mexican community. Because immigration laws had been in an almost constant state of flux since World War I, and practically nonexistent before, many Mexicans were unsure of their legal status. The wide and sensational publicity that the raids received caused many Mexicans to panic, staying in their homes and avoiding public places. Thus, after only a few operations, Immigration Supervisor Watkins reported that his men found the streets of East Los Angeles deserted when they drove through the area. More important, many Mexicans in the Los Angeles area, along with their children born in the United States, began leaving the country and returning to Mexico out of fear of being arrested and deported. According to George Clements of the Los Angeles Chamber of Commerce, these people saw voluntary repatriation as preferable to deportation because the Mexican government gave assistance to voluntary repatriates, whereas deportees were treated as outcasts. These departures did not go unnoticed by George Visel. In late March he wrote to Secretary Doak cheering "the exodus of aliens deportable *and otherwise* who have been scared out of the community"[25] (my italics).

Despite Visel's continued pronouncements regarding law-enforcement support for the deportations, the LAPD played a rather ambiguous role in the campaign. In the early days of the campaign, police officials made statements that indicated a high degree of enthusiasm for the deportations. On February 3, for example, Chief Steckel, contradicting the official statistics generated by his own department, justified the expulsions on the grounds that aliens were responsible for most of the city's crime problems. On that same day Steckel also made a statement that must have sent a shock of terror through the hearts of Los Angeles Mexicans. Claiming that immigrants were responsible for "most of our crime problems," the police chief stated that henceforth, when his officers arrested a suspected deportable immigrant, "attention will be paid not only to the person under arrest, but to all members of the family." Steckel thus did not differentiate between legally deportable immigrants and legal residents or even American citizens of Mexican descent in determining who was subject to deportation.[26]

In reality, though, the LAPD played a much more ambivalent role than Steckel's statements indicated. As early as February 6 Immigration Supervisor Watkins held a meeting with Steckel and Sheriff Traeger to secure the law-enforcement assistance that Visel had promised. Steckel and Traeger stated, however, that they could not undertake a full-fledged deportation campaign because, as Watkins noted in his report on the meeting, their officers were "unqualified to determine the question of deportability of aliens." In addition, the two law-enforcement officials stated that their officers could not simply arrest immigrants and turn them over to immigration officials to determine deportability, because to do so would "have no justification in law" and would make their respective departments "liable for numerous damage suits for false arrest." Thus, the most assistance the LAPD ever gave immigration officials was the logistical support that police officers provided during the February 26 raid on the Plaza. After this initial flurry of activity, the raids ended and were replaced by a campaign aimed at repatriating Mexican immigrants. While the repatriation campaign was also highly coercive, the LAPD played no significant role.[27]

Traeger and Steckel's excuse for not playing a more active role in the expulsions sounds somewhat hollow given the LAPD's, and especially the red squad's, historic disregard for the rule of law. A more credible explanation would be that the Los Angeles Chamber of Commerce genuinely deplored the deportation campaign and used its considerable influence with the department to keep the LAPD's role at a minimum. Those at the chamber disapproved of the expulsions and the voluntary repatriations they provoked because they believed that prosperity would soon return and that a large supply of Mexican workers would again be needed. J. A. H. Kerr, the president of the Los Angeles Chamber of

Commerce, explained the position of employers when he wrote President Pascual Ortiz Rubio of Mexico that it was "a matter of great regret" to local businessmen that many Mexicans were returning to their homeland because "many of these Mexican people are much needed in Southern California in our industrial and economic life." Thus, as early as January 8, 1931, Arthur G. Arnoll, the general manager for the chamber, wrote to Visel that he must "keep from upsetting the whole Mexican population by wholesale raids which are misunderstood by the Mexican." As the deportations began, George Clements, the head of the chamber's Department of Agriculture, repeatedly met with the Mexican general consul, Visel, and immigration officials to tone down the anti-Mexican nature of the campaign. While there is no direct evidence that the chamber ordered the LAPD not to assist the immigration officials, it seems likely that as a result of the long-standing relationship between the chamber and the LAPD, the department may have been less than enthusiastic about deporting Mexican workers.[28]

Nevertheless, the Depression-era deportations and the coercive repatriation campaign that followed had a profound impact on Los Angeles Mexicans. According to the historian George Sánchez, the forced expulsions were the crucible upon which a Mexican *American* identity was forged. Those who survived the trauma became committed to bettering their lives in the United States. From this commitment there developed what Sánchez has called a "politics of opposition." One of the manifestations of this new political orientation was the reemergence of a Mexican American labor movement and the willingness to confront both employers and the LAPD in new ways.[29]

THE ILGWU STRIKE OF 1933

During the 1920s Mexican workers in Los Angeles were active in white-dominated unions and several strikes broke out in industries in which Mexicans comprised a large segment of the workforce. Nevertheless, despite the rapid increase in the Mexican population during the 1920s and despite the formation of nascent labor organizations such as the Confederación de Uniones Obreras Mexicanas, there is no evidence of any conflict between predominantly Mexican labor unions and the LAPD during that decade. It took the beginning of the Great Depression and the seemingly pro-labor policies of Franklin Delano Roosevelt's New Deal to renew that conflict.

While the Depression created great hardship for Mexicans, it also inaugurated a new political atmosphere that helped reinvigorate the labor movement in Los Angeles and throughout the nation. In an effort to gain the cooperation of all sectors of the economy necessary for the president's recovery plan, Congress passed legislation that gave workers the right to collective bargaining. Specifically, Section 7(a) of the National Industrial Recovery Act (NIRA) stated that workers had the right "to organize and bargain collectively through representatives of their own choosing . . . free from the interference, restraint or coercion of employers." Los Angeles labor leaders, encouraged by Section 7(a), began organizing drives in a variety of industries almost as soon as President Roosevelt signed the bill. It was, however, Mexican women dressmakers, organized by the International Ladies Garment Workers Union (ILGWU), who conducted the first large-scale strike in Los Angeles under the National Recovery Administration's (NRA's) banner of the Blue Eagle.

The women who joined the ILGWU strike worked in one of the more exploitative industries in the city. Mexican women comprised 75 percent of the dressmakers in the Los Angeles garment industry. They worked in 175 different factories in the central section of the city under difficult conditions. The standard form of pay for dressmakers was by the piece. Since the workload was sporadic, varying from day to day and even hour to hour, the women spent between thirty-five and forty hours a week in the factory in order to be paid for twenty hours of work. Many workers earned only a fraction of the $16-a-week minimum standard set by the NRA for the garment industry. In addition, foremen often gave the most work to certain favorite workers. In times of heavy volume, employers forced the women to do home work if they wanted continued employment. If workers protested or if employers suspected that they belonged to a union, they were quickly discharged and often blacklisted. In fact, since training of new dressmakers took only a short time, employers encouraged an unusually high turnover rate to keep wages low and discourage union organizing.[30]

In September 1933, the ILGWU headquarters in New York sent one of its top organizers, Rose Pesotta, to Los Angeles to organize the Mexican dressmakers. Pesotta, who wrote a book regarding her activities, immediately began informing the women of their rights under the NRA and of the employers' consistent violation of those rights. The ILGWU printed its newspaper, the *Organizer,* in both Spanish and English, and a Spanish-language radio station broadcast news of union activity each evening. As a result of these efforts, hundreds of Mexican workers joined

the ILGWU, and union officials began making demands of the employers.[31]

On September 27, a large meeting of dressmakers took place at which
members aired their grievances, issued demands to employers, gave the
union leadership full authority to negotiate those demands, and authorized a strike against all dressmaking establishments in the city. The demands included union recognition, acceptance of the NRA minimum-
wage codes, a thirty-five-hour work week, arbitration of disputes, no
home work, and a provision that employees be paid for the time they
spent in the factory rather than just for the time they worked. When
employers responded by firing scores of union members, the strike became inevitable.[32]

The strike, called for October 12, 1933, was an immediate success.
Red Hynes of the red squad, who usually attempted to minimize the
significance of any labor activity, estimated that fourteen hundred out
of the twenty-five hundred dressmakers in the city walked off their jobs.
The strikers set up mass pickets throughout the garment district that
effectively shut down the dressmaking industry in Los Angeles. The
ILGWU provided breakfast, lunch, and a weekly cash benefit for all
strikers and sent food home for the poorest workers. Employers responded by starting a publicity campaign claiming that the only issue in
dispute was the union's demand for a closed shop and, through Hynes,
that Communists dominated the ILGWU. At the same time, Pesotta reported that the previously lenient municipally owned utility company
surrendered to pressure from employer organizations and cut off the
water, electricity, and gas of strikers who fell behind on their payments.
The employers' tactic that created the most conflict between police and
striking women, however, was the use of strikebreakers.[33]

To the LAPD, and specifically to the red squad, fell the task of protecting the scabs. Members of the red squad patrolled the garment district from the first day of the strike. As the strike continued, the number
of police present increased. On October 16 the *Times* reported that police officials had detailed sixty-five men to the red squad for strike duty;
by October 26 the number had grown to nearly one hundred. Throughout the strike, Hynes and other police officials repeatedly made
statements that demonstrated the LAPD's pro-employer bias in the conflict. For example, Captain C. B. Horrall, commander of the metropolitan division (and future chief of police), ordered officers to the strike
detail, stating that their role was "to prevent picketing and molesting of
non-striking employees entering and leaving the building." Police and

other city officials also regularly issued statements regarding increased police activity in the strike area. Toward the end of the strike, Hynes and Maine, the city attorney, issued a joint statement declaring that the police would make mass arrests in order to stop the picketing. "You bring them in by the wagon load," Maine told Hynes, "and we'll issue charges against them and we'll see if this disorder can't be stopped."[34]

As well as words, police actions demonstrated their pro-employer, antilabor bias. To begin with, strikebreakers and "guards" hired by employers seem to have been responsible for much, if not most, of the violence that occurred. According to the historians Louis B. Perry and Richard B. Perry, the minor riots that occurred almost daily resulted from "strikers hurling epithets at nonstrikers and the latter reciprocating with fists, sticks, or any other handy weapon." A somewhat less objective Pesotta charged that employer groups used "hired thugs" to "foment disturbances." Nevertheless, the red squad arrested only pickets. Furthermore, despite the fact that both the *Times* and the police blamed all of the violence on the strikers, almost all of the more than forty union members arrested were charged only with disturbing the peace. In fact, the first arrest for assault and battery did not come until the third week of the strike. In addition, the police made most of their arrests in the afternoon so that the arrested Mexican women could not get a quick court hearing and thus had to post bail, at great cost to the union, or spend the night in jail, which greatly disrupted their home lives.[35]

The LAPD's actions brought it into conflict with the striking Mexican women. The first open confrontation between the red squad and the Mexican women came on Monday, October 16. That day had also seen the introduction of private "guards" hired by employers to protect strikebreakers. The clash occurred when police arrested a striker for yelling out "epithets" at people crossing the picket lines. According to the *Times*, "the rest of the pickets raised a hue and cry at the police" that resulted in several more arrests. The police charged all of those arrested with disturbing the peace. Throughout the rest of the day the red squad continued to patrol the garment district, facing the jeers of the striking Mexican women. On the evening of the first clash the police issued a riot call, but no serious injuries occurred and no arrests were made.[36]

The following day a superior court judge issued a temporary injunction restraining the ILGWU from "intimidating or harassing employees of the Paramount Dress Company by any kind of force or violence." While the judge made it clear that the injunction banned only violence and not peaceful picketing, union leaders realized that the injunction would effectively break the strike and decided to challenge the order through mass picketing. Consequently, on the morning of October 19, over a thousand ILGWU pickets massed in front of the Paramount Dress Company. Later, Rose Pesotta recalled that Hynes "and other members of the 'Red Squad' were powerless against that mass of unionists." The police, for example, had prohibited the pickets from calling out the word "Scab!" The sheer number of protesters, however, meant that "no one could prevent pickets from yelling that epithet in lusty chorus." Efforts by the police and "hired thugs" to silence the pickets resulted in a small riot. Though the injunction applied to all members of the ILGWU, the police arrested only five strikers and then charged them not with violating the court order, but with disorderly conduct. After this confrontation the LAPD declared that it would drop its "kid glove" method of handling the striking Mexican women. Ironically, that same day a group of Protestant ministers issued a statement protesting "police violence in the handling of the strike."[37]

Strike-related "disturbances" continued almost daily for the next two and a half weeks. On October 20 police reported a total of fourteen clashes between pickets on one side and strikebreakers and police officers on the other. The first reported physical attack by pickets on scabs occurred during these incidents. Several ILGWU members reportedly attacked strikebreakers after they left the garment district. On this day, too, the striking women resorted to throwing tacks in the streets of the garment district to prevent police cars from entering the area and disrupting strike activity. The final major clash between the red squad and the striking Mexican women occurred on October 31. In what the *Times* called "the most concerted action . . . thus far," police arrested fourteen picketers, the most in a single day. Less than a week later, an NRA binding arbitration board ordered the dressmakers back to work and the strike ended.[38]

Despite both the rhetoric and the actions of the LAPD, employer groups were dissatisfied with the red squad's performance during the strike, arguing that the police had been too restrained in their tactics. On October 27, the *Times* published an editorial claiming that the tougher police policy announced two days previously forced the ILGWU to accept binding arbitration. "More than two weeks were wasted in vacillation," the *Times* editorialized, "before the police were permitted to make it clear that violence would not be tolerated. Once the strikers clearly understood this the trouble came to an end. It should never have begun."[39]

Nevertheless, the red squad probably did all it could, given the context of the situation. First of all, as the *Times* itself acknowledged, the strike situation was "unparalleled in Los Angeles's industrial relations in years."[40] The strike's unexpected nature also fused with the generally positive public reaction to the NRA and the fact that the strikers were all women, albeit Mexican women. The merging of these factors probably made the police more tentative in dealing with the pickets. The red squad quickly learned, however, that the NRA had no teeth and that employers were more concerned with maintaining the open shop than they were with public opinion. Thus, the red squad and the department as a whole were well prepared to take a more aggressive stand the next time Mexican workers tried to form a labor union.

MEXICAN FARMWORKERS AND THE LAPD

No sector of the economy in which Los Angeles Mexicans worked proved more difficult to organize than agriculture. To a great extent, this situation resulted from the nature of California agriculture. Throughout much of the country the family farm dominated agricultural production. In these relatively small farms (usually no bigger than a few hundred acres) most of the work was done by family members or an occasional hired hand. This type of organization meant there was no need for a permanent agricultural proletariat. In contrast, in the Southwest and particularly in California, huge farms (sometimes exceeding a hundred thousand acres) dominated the countryside. During the nineteenth century the owners of these immense farms tried to grow grains, particularly wheat, but soon discovered that they could not compete with midwestern farmers who, because of the heavier rainfall and their proximity to major urban centers, brought their crop to market at a lower price. As a result, before the turn of the century California agricultural enterprises, collectively known as agribusiness, began turning to growing fruits and vegetables.[41]

The turn to truck farming, the growers contended, required a change from traditional forms of farm labor organization. Specifically, agricultural interests argued that this type of specialization demanded a cheap, seasonal, and relatively captive labor force. Growers contended that the very size of the farms necessitated the existence of an agricultural proletariat. They needed to keep labor costs low because they competed in an international market. Employment was seasonal because of the growing cycle. Finally, the workers somehow had to be held captive because free workers refused to work for the meager wages or under the harsh conditions that agribusiness employers felt were necessary to maintain the industry. Since both slavery and a captive peasantry were illegal in the United States, farm employers set out to find the next best thing: a workforce consisting of people whose relative powerlessness (for whatever reasons) tied them to the industry and made it impossible, or at least most difficult, for them to challenge the labor system.[42]

Growers quickly realized that people from racial minority groups provided the type of labor that agribusiness wanted. Racial minorities were usually poor enough that they accepted whatever wages and working conditions the growers offered. Moreover, the growers understood that racial prejudice inhibited minority workers from entering other segments of the economy and, more important, prevented them from seriously challenging the growers' authority. Thus growers came to see racial minorities, first Chinese, later Japanese, and finally Mexicans, as possessing the appropriate characteristics of being sufficiently desperate, docile, and subordinated to make them the dominant form of agricultural labor in California.[43]

To ensure that this labor system stayed intact, agribusiness formed local, statewide, regional, and national organizations to protect its interests. These organizations successfully lobbied for the exclusion of Mexicans from the national immigration laws that restricted immigration by national origin. They also established cooperative labor bureaus to formulate and enforce common wage agreements. Finally, because growers understood that unions would destroy the social relations necessary for the preservation of the agricultural labor system, their organizations worked to prevent labor organizing in the fields. They blacklisted known labor agitators; they forged strong alliances with local politicians and especially law-enforcement officials to ensure their cooperation in case of trouble; they curried favor with local newspapers to ensure that public opinion supported the growers; and, most important, they established a common policy of resisting with whatever means available any labor union and any strike with which they might be confronted.[44]

Despite the hostility of growers, Mexican farmworkers since the turn of the century had engaged in labor union activity. Agricultural labor unions, like all organized labor, went into a period of decline between World War I and the Great Depression, and there exists no record of conflict between the LAPD and Mexican farmworkers during these years. During the Depression, however, the New Deal and the appointment of a politically progressive Mexican consul general awakened the local Mexican agricultural labor movement. The reemergence of union activity among Mexican farmworkers initiated a period of intense hostility between Mexican agricultural workers and the LAPD.

Mexican consul Ricardo Hill was the central figure in the development of Mexican agricultural labor unions and in the conflict between farmworkers and the LAPD. Hill, the son of the Mexican revolutionary general Benjamin Hill, brought a progressive and aggressive philosophy to his position. According to the historian Francisco Balderrama, "Hill regarded capitalism as an 'outmoded profit system' and sometimes expressed this view to close friends in the Southern California community." Hill also believed that as Mexican consul it was his duty "to protect the interest of [his] nationals and to represent them in any and all controversies in which their human and constitutional rights are at stake." He thus became intimately involved in the union-organizing efforts of Mexican farmworkers. He participated in the convention that founded the Confederación de Unión Campesinos y Obreros Mexicanos (CUCOM) and became an honorary but permanent member of the union's governing board. When the growers refused to even negotiate with the new union, an angry Hill publicly vowed: "If the Mexicans [*sic*] workers of Los Angeles County are not organized now, I'll see that they are before winter is over."[45]

CUCOM gained strength not only from the support it received from the Mexican consul but also from the alliances it built with other ethnically oriented farm labor organizations. It united with the Filipino Federated Workers Union, the American Agricultural Industrial Workers, and the Japanese Farm Workers Union of California to form the Federation of Agricultural Workers Union of America (FAWUA). Invigorated with its newfound strength, on April 6, 1936, CUCOM made its demands to Japanese vegetable growers. These demands included a 90 percent union shop for workers affiliated with FAWUA, a thirty-five-cent-per-hour minimum wage for all workers and a forty-cent minimum wage for celery cutters, time and a half for overtime (more than nine hours) and Sundays and holidays, and equal pay for equal work for women. The growers refused to negotiate or even acknowledge CUCOM's demands, claiming that Communists dominated the union. The workers went on strike and set up picket lines around the celery fields of the Venice section of Los Angeles.[46]

Part of the growers' intransigence resulted from pressure they received from the financial and business community. According to the

Open Forum, a publication of the Southern California Branch of the American Civil Liberties Union, the Bank of America compelled Japanese growers to refuse to negotiate with the Mexican strikers. The bank owned most of the fields leased by the Japanese growers and charged a very high rent. The *Open Forum* claimed that the bank was in fact "[in] back of the attempt to break the strike." Another source of pressure for the growers came from the Los Angeles Chamber of Commerce and from the Associated Farmers of Los Angeles County, an affiliate of the Merchants and Manufacturers Association. These two organizations zealously opposed official recognition of CUCOM, arguing that a successful CUCOM strike would lead "to complete unionization on closed shop principles of all farm labor here and throughout California." The employers' organizations assisted growers by developing a strategy, obtaining information about union leaders, assisting in negotiation, and coordinating law-enforcement activity.[47]

Law enforcement provided a crucial element in the employers' strategy, and the LAPD's red squad was on the front line of efforts to break the strike. As early as March 28, 1936, the red squad gained information that a strike threatened "serious damage to the spring crops of the Japanese market gardeners."[48] Once the celery strike started, Hynes's men used brutal and violent tactics to punish strikers and their supporters.

The strike and the red squad response produced violent clashes unprecedented in the relationship between Mexicans and the LAPD. The first major melee came on April 24, when members of the red squad used tear gas and clubs to disperse three hundred picketers in a West Los Angeles field. A riot ensued in which the strikers reportedly used rocks, clods of dirt, sticks, and vegetable crates in their fight with police. At one point Mexican workers seized a squad car and began to destroy it before police recovered it. The *Times* reported that several workers and four policemen received injuries, but only one person was arrested.[49]

The next day an LAPD spokesman stated that the department was making "special preparations," which included using two-way radios in squad cars and having undercover men pose as union members to stop any further disturbances. "Men who need work and are willing to stay on the job deserve protection," the police spokesman stated, "and they are going to get it." If the strikers interfered, the red squad would step in. "We'll stop them peacefully if we can," he proclaimed, "but we'll stop them."[50]

Captain Hynes and his men, however, never seriously attempted to perform their duty "peacefully." On Saturday, April 25, members of the red squad attacked and seriously injured eight picketers. According to the *Open Forum,* after the union members left the work site and were driving home, red squad officers picked them up, took them to an isolated location, and beat them severely. Injuries ranged from badly bruised limbs to fractured arms and broken ribs. The following day saw the largest pitched battle of the strike between Mexican strikers and the LAPD. According to the consistently antilabor *Times,* the fight started when more than one hundred strikers broke through fences and attempted to force strikebreakers from the field. The police responded with tear gas and billy clubs, resulting in over a dozen injuries.[51]

The *Open Forum* had a much different and more detailed account of the fighting. According to the ACLU publication, the battle began when police attacked a picket line of about eighty-five strikers with fists, clubs, and tear-gas guns. One striker was injured when police shot him in the foot with a tear-gas gun while he stood in the middle of the street. Another CUCOM member, "an old man of 50 or 60 years of age," received a four-to-five-inch gash on his head from a policeman's billy club. Peace officers also attacked the wife of a striker and may have broken her arm.[52]

Félix López sustained the most serious injury of the fracas. First police shot him in the chest with a tear-gas projectile from a distance of only eight to ten feet. His companions attempted to pull the badly burned and temporarily blinded man away from the battle. Police followed López and administered another beating, repeatedly striking him with clubs on his already injured chest. An internal LAPD document stated that López was "slugged by [the] Red Squad [and] is in serious condition and may die." Neither the police files nor the local media recorded whether López survived.[53]

Red squad terrorism continued on an almost daily basis. The *Open Forum* reported that whenever strikers tried to leave their camp in Venice, police vehicles followed them and attempted to drive them off the road. Three strikers' cars were thus ruined when the red squad forced them to crash into telephone poles or other obstacles. On another occasion, police threw a tear-gas bomb at the CUCOM headquarters in Venice as they drove past it. The bomb exploded near six children who reportedly "were drenched with the suffocating fumes and fled terror-stricken." An LAPD document obtained by the LaFollette Committee states that "[CUCOM supporter] Dr. Ward Ridgers, Methodist Minister, was stopped, while returning from the Venice lettuce fields, by the Red Squad, beaten up and left lying in a ditch." The violence continued until May 27, when Consul Hill helped negotiate an agreement that met most of the workers' demands and ended the strike.[54]

The LAPD's activities created sympathy among white liberals for the Mexican strikers. Local ACLU director Clinton Taft sent Los Angeles mayor Frank Shaw a letter protesting the red squad's actions. After reminding the mayor of union members' legal and constitutional rights, Taft asked Shaw to use his executive powers to assist "these terrorized workers." Specifically, the ACLU demanded that Shaw "take a hand in this desperate situation and insist that the lawless Red Squad shall observe the legal rights of these Mexicans and Filipinos." Similarly, the Methodist Preachers' Meeting of Southern California formed a "Committee Investigating the Strike of Vegetable Workers." The committee concluded that "the only violence was by officers sworn to enforce the law and protect citizens" and also filed a protest with the mayor's office.[55]

City government's response to these two protests is indicative of the free rein the red squad enjoyed when protecting employers' interests. Shaw turned both protests over to the police commission, which in turn referred the complaints to the chief of police for investigation. After an appropriate length of time, the chief issued reports exonerating the red squad of all wrongdoing. The police commission accepted the chief's word at face value and ordered both the complaints and the reports simply "filed." No further action was taken by any governmental agency.[56]

In contrast, local business organizations applauded the red squad's violent tactics. Much of the correspondence between the Chamber of Commerce and Associated Farmers and the LAPD spoke glowingly of the "prompt and aggressive action by . . . the 'Red Squad' of the metropolitan police" and of the fact that the police regularly " 'beat up' pickets and strikers" in efforts to protect strikebreakers. In recognition of the LAPD's efforts to break the strike, Arthur E. Clark, executive secretary of the Associated Farmers, sent Chief of Police James E. Davis a letter of thanks. In his letter, Clark expressed the Associated Farmers' "appreciation of the splendid work done by officers of your Department during the recent disturbances fostered by radical agitators." Clark gave special commendation to "Captain William Hynes and the men of his squad . . . for the manner in which they have protected those workers— Mexican, Japanese and American—who elected to take the employment offered them in harvesting the celery crop." Clark noted that strong police action was necessary because "outside agitators [sought] to control all farm workers in Los Angeles County . . . in order to secure 'closed shop' concessions and union recognition." He closed by assuring the chief that he and the LAPD had "the full support of the Associated Farmers of Los Angeles County."[57]

THE REMOVAL OF CONSUL HILL

After the settlement of the celery strike, police officials turned their attention to the person they believed was responsible for their labor problems, Mexican consul Ricardo Hill. Hill had been under attack for his pro-labor activities since before the beginning of the celery strike. Once the strike began, the growers' and employers' organizations claimed that the consul collaborated with known Communists and that CUCOM acted only with his prior approval.[58]

The employers' initiative began with a letter from Arthur E. Clark of the Associated Farmers to Captain Hynes of the red squad. Clark reminded Hynes of Hill's vow to organize all Mexican farmworkers and laid all the blame for the growers' labor problems directly on the Mexican consul. "Without the support of the Mexican consul's office," Clark told Hynes, CUCOM "would never have attempted the costly vegetable and citrus strikes of the past few weeks." Clark was particularly incensed over "the spectacle of Consul Hill inviting Mexican labor union officials to Los Angeles [who] openly urged Mexicans to join the local union . . . and aid the strike." He reminded Hynes that at the meeting where the Mexican labor leaders spoke, "Chief Davis and the Red Squad were attacked for their work in keeping peace in the Venice celery strike" and that Hill was also in attendance. Clark concluded by telling the LAPD's main union buster that "agricultural employers . . . are determined that the consul overstepped his position and feel that in the interests of harmony between themselves and Mexican workers, Hill should be removed."[59]

The police department, however, did not need much urging. Chief of Police James Davis and Lieutenant Peter Delgado, Davis's personal aide and the highest-ranking Mexican American on the force, had for some time been displeased with Hill's involvement with CUCOM. According to Hill, the two had even "threatened [him] with removal . . . on account of [his] labor activities." When an altercation occurred between Consul Hill and Delgado, the two police officials had the excuse they needed to make good their threat.[60]

The incident that brought about Hill's demise began, ironically enough, when the Mexican government sent the Mexico City Police Department Orchestra to Los Angeles as part of a goodwill tour. A disagreement developed between Hill and Delgado over whether the orchestra should give a free concert for the city's Mexican population in Lincoln Park. Delgado became angry, called the consul a "son of a bitch," and attempted to slug him. Only the efforts of other police officers prevented an actual fight from taking place.[61]

Immediately after the altercation, Hill fired off a telegram to Chief Davis with a copy to the Mexican Embassy in Washington, D.C. In the telegram Hill stated that Delgado "insulted me[,] . . . stating that my official capacity was of no concern to him. In the name of the government of Mexico, I protest against your officers' conduct and behavior and demand due satisfaction." Initially, Davis supported his aide, stating that the problem was a personal one between the two men. In his official reply, however, the chief expressed his "sincere regrets for the occurrence" and promised to "discipline those responsible."[62]

While Davis publicly apologized, privately he set out to force Ricardo Hill's removal as Mexican consul in Los Angeles. He collected information from the red squad's already extensive file on Hill and added information from the files of the Associated Farmers of Los Angeles and Orange Counties and from the Los Angeles County sheriff's office. He compiled the information into a report, which was included in an official protest from the statewide Associated Farmers' organization to the United States State Department.[63]

The LAPD's efforts proved successful. In the final analysis, it was not so much the content of Davis's protest but its very existence that brought about Hill's departure. The Mexican secretary of foreign relations, the United States State Department, and even Hill himself acknowledged that "the position of a Mexican consular representative in a locality where he encounters the manifest hostility and antipathy of the police authorities is from all perspectives insupportable." In late October of 1936 the Mexican government removed Ricardo Hill from his position as consul general in Los Angeles.[64]

According to Chamber of Commerce official George Clements, the new consul, Renato Cantú Lara, believed that while it was his and his staff's "duty to take care of their nationals as individuals, they would in no way attempt to do so collectively." Henceforth, the new consul would "adhere strictly to his consular work and join with us [the Chamber of Commerce] in every way possible to bring about a correct understanding between his Nationals and the employer."[65] This "correct understanding" did not include labor unions, and while CUCOM continued to exist for a few more years, it never again seriously challenged growers anywhere in the state. Nevertheless, the bitter nature of the conflict between Mexican workers and police created a sense of mistrust and antagonism toward the LAPD among Mexican American labor activists. That mistrust and antagonism played a role in redefining the relationship between Mexican Americans and the department in the 1940s.

CHAPTER 6

Theories and Statistics of Mexican Criminality

While the conflict between the LAPD and Mexican workers continued unchecked through the 1930s, other aspects of the relationship between Mexican Americans and the department went through subtle but significant changes. To a certain extent these changes resulted from the tremendous growth of the city's Mexican population during the 1920s. During this decade, when the economy boomed and jobs were plentiful, Mexicans flocked to the city by the tens of thousands. While employers welcomed the concentration of cheap labor that the Mexicans represented, the presence of a large number of foreign-born, dark-skinned people alarmed many whites who feared that such people would weaken American society. These fears, along with national concerns over both crime and the nature of criminality, prompted the LAPD for the first time to pay special attention to the issue of Mexican crime. The LAPD's growing preoccupation with the linkage between race and criminality became one of the basic factors defining the relationship between Chicanos and the LAPD.

As applied to Mexicans, the idea that certain racial or ethnic groups were criminally inclined had a variety of antecedents. Attitudes dating back to the Mexican-American War regarding the cruel and vicious nature of the Mexican people undoubtedly persisted in the minds of many police officials. Lurid and sensational newspaper stories publicizing the latest crimes committed by Mexicans contributed to the idea that they committed more than their share of crimes. More important, the emerging discipline of criminology gave scientific credence to the notion that certain racial groups were criminally inclined. While the criminologists disagreed among themselves as to whether this proclivity was biologically or socially determined, the results were the same: society labeled certain racially defined groups of people as being prone to crime.

Government officials took notice. At the national and local level, officials launched studies to determine the extent and nature of criminality among racial and ethnic groups and the proper response of law enforcement. The studies that focused on Mexicans reached some interesting conclusions. For the most part, they agreed that Mexicans were no more criminally inclined than any other segment of the population. They also found, however, widespread mistreatment of Mexicans by local law-enforcement agencies.

The LAPD, with jurisdiction over the largest Mexican population in the United States, became concerned about the extent and nature of Mexican criminality. In 1923 it issued its own study, which, like the other studies, found that Mexicans were not particularly inclined toward criminality. This study also unwittingly showed that the LAPD held many unwarranted and racist attitudes about the Mexican population. After 1923 the LAPD began compiling and annually publishing statistics on the number of people arrested for specific crimes, broken down into specific races. While these statistics presented, at best, a highly ambiguous picture of Mexican criminality, they nevertheless demonstrated the LAPD's interest in finding a linkage between race and crime. This growing preoccupation eventually laid the basis for a fully developed racial theory of crime during the 1940s and for the law-enforcement policies and practices that inevitably followed.

FEAR OF CRIME

A variety of factors helped provoke interest in Mexican crime. Newspaper stories, magazine articles, and to a lesser extent, official government studies created the illusion that Mexicans committed a disproportionate number of crimes. The statistics generated by the official studies clearly indicated that Mexicans were not a particularly dangerous segment of the community. Nevertheless, as a result of all the attention given to the subject, by the late 1930s the idea that Mexicans constituted a serious crime problem began to capture the attention of Los Angeles police officials.

A series of spectacular and highly publicized crimes committed by

Mexicans encouraged this growing attention on Mexican criminality. The murder on July 18, 1921, of LAPD Detective Sergeant John J. Fitzgerald by Philip "Little Phil" Alguin stirred the official anger of the LAPD more than any other crime committed by a Mexican in the early 1920s. Alguin shot and killed Fitzgerald as the former returned to a house that he and a group of men had used as a base of operations for burglaries. He shot the policeman through the stomach at 10:30 P.M. as the two men confronted each other on the front porch of the house. Although mortally wounded, Fitzgerald chased Alguin for about sixty feet before collapsing. The officer died less than two hours later.[1]

Fitzgerald's murder enraged the LAPD not only because a Mexican had killed a white police officer but also because Fitzgerald was so highly regarded within the department. According to the *Times,* Fitzgerald "was one of the best known and most popular officers on the force." A detective sergeant since 1909, he had been involved in some of the most spectacular crime investigations in the decade prior to his death, including that of the 1910 bombing of the Times Building. His funeral, described in the *Times* as "probably the most impressive ceremony ever conducted for a deceased police officer in Los Angeles," attracted such a crowd that nearly a thousand people were unable to enter the church. The *Times* noted that practically every officer in the department attended the service, and that "the hour of the service was the only time since the dramatic death of the police officer that the police have slackened up in efforts to catch the murderer."[2]

Alguin, in contrast, already had a long criminal record by the time he killed Fitzgerald. Born Felipe Holguín in Tucson, Arizona, "Little Phil" was first arrested and convicted in Los Angeles in 1911 at the age of sixteen. Over the next ten years police arrested Alguin four more times, first for burglary and later for robbery, and on each occasion he earned longer sentences in the state penitentiary. At the time of the Fitzgerald killing, Alguin belonged to a gang of professional burglars who targeted some of the wealthier homes in Los Angeles.[3]

Immediately upon news of the killing, the LAPD launched a massive, sometimes brutal, search for Alguin. The *Times* reported that on the night of the killing "every detective and patrolman in the city was called out of bed, deputy sheriffs to the last man had joined in the search for the suspect and constables in all surrounding towns had been informed to watch the roads." Throughout the following week, groups of as many as two hundred officers, many organized into "shotgun squads," arbitrarily stopped citizens on the streets, arrested and vigorously questioned over a dozen known acquaintances of Alguin, and ransacked scores of private homes in their search for the suspected murderer.[4]

From the very beginning it seemed clear that the department and, in particular, Chief of Police Lyle Pendegast were not interested in simply arresting Alguin but wanted to mete out their own justice and kill Fitzgerald's murderer themselves. The department began laying the foundation for this action by planting stories in the press that Alguin would never be taken alive. The *Times* reported that it learned from police sources that Alguin, "buoyed up . . . by an abundance of marajuana [*sic*] and bootleg liquor, . . . is carrying two .45 caliber revolvers and will die fighting rather than be captured by the friends of the officer he is declared to have murdered." The *Times* also noted that Chief Pendegast, in addition to the shotguns, had issued his officers machine guns for their expected shoot-out.[5]

Alguin's capture, in fact, became a personal crusade for the chief. Whenever police received word that Alguin had been sighted, Pendegast personally led the shotgun squads that sought to capture the suspected murderer. As the search continued, the LAPD's official publication, the *Daily Bulletin,* all but incited police officers to assassinate Alguin. On the day after the killing, the *Daily Bulletin* ran a full-page picture and description of Alguin under the headline "Arrest This Man for Murder." By Tuesday, June 21, the headline over the picture simply said "Get Him," and a personal message from Chief Pendegast instructed officers, "Study the face. Never forget it until the slaying of Detective-Sergeant Fitzgerald is avenged." Even in his farewell message to the force, Pendegast stated that the one responsibility he hated turning over to his successor was the capture of Fitzgerald's murderer. He ended his message with the exhortation "Let's get 'Little Phil.' "[6]

The Los Angeles City Council and the police commission made Alguin's capture even more attractive by issuing a five-hundred-dollar reward. The *Daily Bulletin* published the announcement of the reward, indicating that officers were eligible to earn it. Furthermore, according to the *Times,* civilians in various sections of the city armed themselves in the hope of capturing Alguin and claiming the reward. Apparently hoping either to worry Alguin or give his associates some ideas, the department planted a story in the newspapers claiming that the people who helped Alguin elude the police were really holding him until the reward for his capture reached five thousand dollars. They would then turn the fugitive over to the authorities themselves. Nevertheless, despite what the *Times* called "the most systematic [manhunt] ever conducted in the Southwest" and the fact that the reward for Alguin's capture did reach five thousand dollars, "Little Phil" managed to avoid the police and escape to Mexico. About a year later, however, LAPD officials discovered his whereabouts in Mexico, and Chief of Police Louis Oaks personally led the team that was to return him to Los Angeles. According to the official version of what happened, Alguin died in a shoot-out with LAPD officers. Department lore, however, has it that Louis Oaks killed Alguin himself in a fit of vengeance.[7]

The official reaction to the Alguin case gives an indication of how national anxiety was growing over a crime wave that Americans believed was sweeping the country during the 1920s. To a great extent, this anxiety was fueled by prohibition and increasingly organized and violent efforts from within the criminal community to circumvent the liquor laws. Journalists fed the popular fear of rising crime rates with stories describing the latest murder, robbery, or kidnapping in vivid detail. More important, newspapers loudly proclaimed that a crime wave was sweeping America. The *New York Times* published a story on October 4, 1924, entitled "Prisons Cannot Keep Pace with Criminals." Three days later the *Times* printed another story stating that Cook County, Illinois (i.e., Chicago), had averaged more than one murder a day that year. On April 1, 1926, it ran still another story that noted the United States was experiencing the worst murder spree in its history. Alarm over the alleged rise in crime reached such proportions that in 1929 President Hoover created the National Commission on Law Observance and Enforcement to determine the causes of and remedies for this "crime wave."[8]

Despite the best efforts of most Los Angeles newspapers, similar fears of rising crime rates affected that city during the 1920s. Most of the city's newspapers refused to acknowledge the fact that a crime problem existed because their owners also owned large parcels of real estate and they did not want to discourage potential migrants or businesses from settling in the city. The *Los Angeles Record,* however, and a handful of religious reformers kept the crime issue alive. The Community Development Association, an alliance of segments of the business community and volunteer organizations interested in crime and police issues, claimed that crime rose by 300 percent in Los Angeles between 1919 and 1923, while the population grew only by 42 percent. Later in 1923, the esteemed August Vollmer, one of the few police chiefs who could accurately be called a reformer, stated that the city had the highest crime rate in the country, greater even than that of Chicago. Throughout the

1920s, then, crime and the inability of the LAPD to control it remained important issues in Los Angeles.[9]

During the Great Depression of the 1930s, the public's preoccupation with crime became even more acute, with spectacular crimes continuing to command the public's attention. Bandits such as John Dillinger, Pretty Boy Floyd, and Baby Face Nelson gained reputations of almost mythic proportions among the American public. Law enforcement responded by attempting to replace the glorified image of these bandits with an equally glamorized portrait of law enforcement. J. Edgar Hoover, in his effort to make the FBI the dominant law-enforcement agency in the nation, launched a publicity campaign that lionized the crime-fighting exploits of his agents. Newspapers and magazines adopted "the Director's" vision of the FBI, and by the end of the decade Hoover and his "G-Men" had become national heroes. Equally important, the motion-picture industry used the conflict between organized gangsters and incorruptible law-enforcement agents as a major theme in many of its movies. One of the consequences of what came to be known as the "war on crime" was a narrowed definition of the role of police officers as crime fighters.[10]

In Los Angeles during the 1930s sensational crimes, often involving public officials, dominated popular attention. In 1931, for example, a deputy district attorney and candidate for a judicial seat shot and killed C. H. Crawford, a politically influential crime boss, and Herbert Spencer, the editor of a local political magazine. Not only did the killings and the subsequent trial remain headline news for months, the removal of Crawford set the stage for gang wars and killings that rocked the city for years. Throughout the decade, then, spectacular murders, attempted murders, and charges of official corruption continued to make crime an important issue in Los Angeles.[11]

CRIMINOLOGICAL EXPLANATIONS OF CRIME

Not only the fact of crime itself but also the explanations given by criminologists for the rising crime rate initiated public and governmental apprehension over Mexican crime. The key to this apprehension was the perceived linkage between race and criminality. During the 1920s criminology was still a relatively new discipline. While criminal activity had taken place since the beginning of recorded time, as late as the Middle Ages there existed no scientific explanation for its causes. Prior to the Enlightenment, most Western philosophers believed that the devil caused criminal behavior. Enlightenment thinkers, however, developed a new explanation for crime based on hedonistic psychology. According to this theory, people made decisions on the basis of considerations of pleasure and pain. To keep people from committing criminal acts, society must guarantee that the pain proceeding from that act (either directly or indirectly) exceeds the pleasure derived from it.[12]

From the mid-nineteenth century through the 1920s a variety of new criminological theories also attempted to explain the causes of crime. The middle of the nineteenth century, for example, saw the rise of the socialist school, which stressed environmental causes for crime. According to the socialists, the unfair distribution of wealth in a capitalist economy caused crime. Do away with capitalism, they argued, and the causes for crime would disappear.[13]

Around the turn of the century, the typological schools, the Lambrosians, the mental testers, and the psychiatric school were founded on the premise that certain personality traits inherent in human beings predisposed people either toward or against crime. The Lambrosians believed that criminal "types" could be identified by certain physical characteristics, such as an asymmetrical cranium, a long lower jaw, or a flattened nose. Criminologists rejected these theories just before World War I, when an English physician demonstrated that no significant differences in physical characteristics existed between criminals and noncriminals. Thus, by the 1920s, only the mental testers and the psychiatric school remained prominent among the typological theories of crime. The mental testers argued that "feeble-mindedness" caused crime because an individual thus afflicted either did not know right from wrong or did not have sufficient willpower to resist evil. According to the psychiatric school, disorders such as epilepsy, psychoses, and various forms of psychopathy were major causes of criminality.[14]

Around 1915 the last major theory trying to explain the causes of crime appeared. According to the sociological school of criminology, crime is just another social phenomenon, in that it is caused by factors at work throughout the society. Sociologists argued that factors such as culture and generational conflict, social and spatial mobility, population density, and the distribution of wealth all had an effect on the crime rate. The sociologists, therefore, like the socialists, emphasized forces in the society in general, rather than characteristics inherent in individuals, as being the major source of crime. However, like proponents of the typological schools, once the sociologists determined which factors caused crime and to which populations these factors applied, they also believed they could predict which groups of people were predisposed toward criminal behavior. Moreover, unlike the socialists who called for fundamental changes in the economic and social order, the sociologists saw capitalist society as a given that would not or should not change.[15]

During the 1920s, the theories of the typological school helped build a linkage between crime and race, with the mental testers and the psychiatric school dominating criminological thinking. During that decade, the *Journal of Criminal Law and Criminology,* the leading academic journal in the field, published only one article that explicitly promoted sociological or economic interpretations of the causes of crime. This journal emphasized internal flaws within the individual that made him or her unable or unwilling to accept the laws that govern society. Moreover, a corollary to this theory maintained that the internal flaws that caused individuals to commit crimes also affected whole groups of people—groups usually defined along racial and ethnic lines.[16]

Of the typological schools, the mental testers were by far the most important in promoting the idea that certain racial and ethnic groups possessed flaws that made them criminally inclined. The mental testers based their conclusion on only recently developed I.Q. tests, which purported to show that people in prison were mentally inferior to the general population. Using such "evidence," many researchers agreed with the criminologist Amy Hewes "that defective mentality is one of the most common if not the chief factor associated with delinquency." Some even argued that every "feeble-minded" person was at least potentially a criminal.[17]

Using inmates at prisons and other correctional institutions as the statistical basis for their studies, researchers soon discovered that racial and ethnic minorities comprised a much larger proportion of the prison population than they did of the general population. On the basis of this information, the mental testers concluded that minorities actually committed a far greater number of crimes than their relative numbers in the population warranted. Furthermore, the I.Q. tests showed that minority group inmates were even less intelligent than white inmates. A study conducted at the Whittier School for Boys in California, for example, found that 31.5 percent of the institution's white population was feeble-minded, while 42.5 percent of the African Americans fell into this category and 61.3 percent of the "Mexican-Indians" were thus afflicted. This same study also alleged that 77.5 percent of the white inmates, 88 percent of the African Americans, and 100 percent of the Mexican-

Indians had below-average intelligence. On the basis of this information, the mental testers reached two conclusions: first, racial minorities and immigrants (especially those from southern and eastern Europe) must be criminally inclined since they were represented in prisons at a higher rate than in the general population; and second, minority people were criminally inclined because they possessed less inherent intelligence than the average.[18]

Some of the advocates of the racial explanation for crime even adopted a neo-Lambrosian idea that certain racial or ethnic groups were inclined to commit certain types of crimes. Edgar Doll argued that "the relation of type of crime to mental age is influenced by the relation of crime to nationality since mental age is related to nationality." He thus concluded that African Americans committed crimes of assault and "illegal receiving" more often than the general population did, and that Italians committed murder and rape "about three times as frequently as the total percentage of Italians warrants."[19]

The mental testers were not alone among criminologists in postulating the idea that certain racial and ethnic groups were criminally inclined. Even those authors who used some aspects of the sociological approach accepted the notion of the inherent criminality of certain racial and ethnic groups. Anne T. Bingham, a psychiatrist for the New York Probation and Protective Association, found that 75 percent of the delinquent girls she studied had foreign-born parents. From this statistic she concluded "that such home influences as the standards and customs of other lands, as well as the lack of progressive characteristics of illiterate peasant types, are important factors in the causation of delinquency in children."[20]

A more comprehensive example of criminologists' attempts to link criminality and race came in a 1926 article by Boris Brasol. Brasol combined current sociological and psychological theories with traditional racism to postulate a hypothesis regarding the cause of crime in the United States. He began with the assumption that both the orderly functioning of society and, therefore, lawful behavior were based on ethics. Crime, the antithesis of ethical behavior, he argued, had no *direct* relation to physical anomalies or heredity. Instead, crime was a "social phenomenon [that] could not be studied [nor] its nature revealed without taking into consideration the nature of society itself." For Brasol one of the laws of the nature of society—indeed, one of the laws of the nature of humanity—was the natural superiority of some races over others. The basic inequality of the races was important because it involved ethical standards. "Racial differences, which are generic," Brasol maintained, "produce ethical differences so deeply rooted that standard morality [and therefore standard observance of the law] is nothing but a dream."[21]

The inequality of the races had one additional implication for Brasol. "In the life of human societies," he asserted, "friction is a fundamental law." Since racial groups are inherently unequal, he argued, conflict between the superior and the inferior forms of the species becomes unavoidable. This conflict becomes particularly tumultuous when questions of economic reward and "social construction" are considered, because the superior groups in society are attempting to impose stability in order to maintain their well-earned economic advantages while the inferior groups are attempting to foment instability in order to gain undeserved equality.[22]

Carl L. May used this exact line of analysis to explicitly link Mexicans with criminality in his article entitled "Our Anti-Social Mexican Class." Writing a polemic to restrict Mexican immigration, May utilized statistics drawn from his experience working for the Los Angeles County Adult Probation Department to assert that Mexicans had been a source of "constant criminal activity" for twenty years. He cited as evidence the fact that while Mexicans comprised only 11.3 percent of the population of Los Angeles County, they accounted for 16.5 percent of those passing through the criminal courts. May believed that Mexicans committed crime out of frustration. Since Mexicans were "untrained and not properly equipped mentally to do other than common labor," they became frustrated at their inability to afford the many material possessions available in American society. "Members of the present Mexican generation," May explained, "believe they, like others, are entitled to recreation and pleasure; and that if they cannot obtain it legitimately, they will resort to criminal acts to satisfy their desires." He concluded that the best solution to the problem was to restrict immigration of Mexicans into the United States.[23]

During the 1930s, the sociologists totally vanquished the typological school of criminology. They demonstrated the logical fallacies in the typological school's statistical methods and argued successfully that race was a social construction rather than a biological imperative. Since there were no significant biological differences among the races, the sociologists showed, the linkage between intelligence, race, and crime that the mental testers had purported to demonstrate was groundless. The theories that the sociologists developed to explain the causes of crime, however, still defined minority people as criminally inclined. The two main factors that sociologists believed led to this proclivity were that minority people occupied a low place in the social structure and that their culture clashed with that of white America. Since poverty bred crime and minority people were poor, it stood to reason that they were criminally inclined.

The work of the sociologist Emory S. Bogardus of the University of Southern California, who, from the 1920s through the 1940s established a national and regional reputation as an expert on Mexican immigrants, is typical of the sociological literature on Mexican criminality. Like most in the sociological school, Bogardus agreed that Mexicans had no "inherited tendencies" toward criminality. He explained what he believed to be an "abnormal" crime rate among Mexicans on cultural traits. Mexicans' proclivity for stealing, Bogardus argued, resulted from "the peon[s'] . . . little training in the meaning of private property"; their involvement in violent crimes stemmed from Mexicans' "uninhibited emotions"; and Mexican juvenile delinquency developed from a generational conflict between traditional parents and youth trying desperately to fit into modern American society. More generally, Bogardus characterized Mexican crime as "elemental, simple, overt." He claimed that "lack of self-control and of social control in a complex and perplexing environment are major explanations."[24] Variations on the sociological themes and even the earlier theories of the typological school not only continued to be discussed in the criminological and popular literature but, more important, also had a long-term effect on the policies and practices of law-enforcement agencies across the nation.

THE CRIME COMMISSIONS

The idea that racial minorities and immigrants were criminally inclined had an immediate impact on government officials. Indeed, during the 1920s government agencies and individual researchers at the federal, state, and local levels inaugurated a series of studies to determine the causes of crime and the extent to which racial minority groups, including Mexicans, were responsible for crime. While most of these studies were of a general nature, four specifically addressed the issue of relations between Mexicans and law-enforcement agencies.

The most elaborate of these was conducted by the National Commission on Law Observation and Enforcement, popularly known as the Wickersham Commission. This commission issued a multivolume report on a variety of topics related to criminality in the United States, including a report on crime and the foreign born. This report contained a long section entitled "The Mexican Immigrant: The Problem of Crime and Criminal Justice." In 1930 a special fact-finding committee appointed by California's Governor C. C. Young issued a report, *Mexicans in California,* which included a section entitled "Crime and Delinquency among the Mexican Population." Finally, and most important for the present study, is a portion of Chief of Police August Vollmer's annual report entitled "A Brief Study of Arrests of Mexicans in Los Angeles for a Twelve-Month Period." Because all of these reports had different goals, used different methodologies, and are of varying importance to this study, I will analyze each separately.

By far the most wide-ranging, comprehensive, and professionally prepared report was the Wickersham Commission's report on Mexicans and the criminal justice system. The document consisted of a lengthy overview of Mexican crime and the law-enforcement response, as well as in-depth analyses written by separate authors on conditions in individual states or local areas. Together, these documents give a good indication of the scholarly and, in some cases, the public perception of Mexican criminality, the effect of these perceptions on law-enforcement practices, and the response of Mexicans to what they saw as discriminatory treatment at the hands of police.

The statistical evidence contained in these reports resulted in ambiguous and even conflicting conclusions regarding the extent of Mexican criminality. Paul Taylor, in his overview of Mexicans and criminality for the Wickersham Commission, stated that while "the statistical record of law violations presented is on the whole, and in varying degrees, somewhat unfavorable to Mexicans, . . . the use of statistics of arrests or convictions is open to serious criticism because racial antipathies and political and economic helplessness of Mexicans swell figures of their apparent criminality." Specifically, Taylor argued that four factors helped inflate the number of Mexican arrests and convictions: 1) racially prejudiced law-enforcement officers tended to arrest Mexicans more often than they arrested whites; 2) Mexicans and whites had different cultural standards concerning issues such as alcoholic beverages; 3) Mexicans lacked the financial resources necessary to mount adequate trial defenses; and 4) a large percentage of the Mexican population consisted of unattached young men, the very group that could be expected to commit more crimes regardless of nationality or race.[25]

While the other contributors to the Wickersham Commission's report on Mexicans gave similar analyses of crime among Mexicans, many of the authors betrayed some of the negative stereotypes about Mexicans long held among the general population. In his study of Mexicans in Illinois, for example, Paul Livingstone Warnshuis noted that while Mexicans come "from a country where petty larceny is extremely common; where everything that is loose and easily portable will disappear if left unguarded for a moment," he nevertheless concluded that Mexicans were no more criminally inclined "than any other nationality or race." Like Taylor, Warnshuis emphasized racial discrimination among law-enforcement officers and economic and cultural factors to explain Mexican crime.[26]

Max Sylvius Handman reached similarly ambiguous conclusions. He determined that "there is no evidence to show that the Mexicans run afoul of the law any more than anyone else[,] and if the complete facts were known they would most likely show that [Mexicans are] far less delinquent in Texas than the non-Mexican population of the same community." Handman did, however, find a slightly higher percentage of murder and aggravated assault crimes among Mexicans than among whites. He explained this phenomenon by stating that while "the Anglo-Saxon . . . has outgrown fighting, . . . among Mexicans fighting is still a socially approved form of gaining superiority." Handman contended that crimes like aggravated assault were "common among Mexicans, not because they are Mexicans but because they live in a certain cultural stage, where fighting is approved and where the community has not evolved [sic] out of the stage of fighting with a knife to fighting with a gun." He thus found Mexicans to be lower on the cultural evolutionary scale than white Americans. Overall, however, Handman maintained that the crimes that "the Mexican" did commit resulted from "the nomadic life which he is leading and with the dislocation and disorganization which take place within a person who is torn from his village community with its system of control and plunged into a new and strange and, in the main, disorganized environment." He concluded, "The remarkable thing is that he is as well behaved as the community in the midst of which he lives."[27]

While in their analyses of Mexican criminality these reports ranged from ambiguous to sympathetic, they were practically unanimous in their descriptions of anti-Mexican bias among police officers. Some individual law-enforcement officers believed that Mexicans, as a race, were criminally inclined. Warnshuis, for example, stated that one Chicago police sergeant believed that Mexicans were born criminals and that the officer supported this contention by stating that "Indian blood and Negro blood does not mix very well. That is the trouble with the Mexican; he has too much Negro blood." Warnshuis in fact found among Chicago officers a general "impression that the Mexican is a born bandit and not to be trusted. He is a new and 'uncertain' quantity with the officers of the law this far from the border, and the worst is likely to be imputed to him."[28]

While Taylor found similar sentiments regarding Mexican criminality in the Midwest, Colorado, and Texas, he also tried to find explanations for these beliefs. One desk sergeant simply stated that he "hated 'em." Others believed that Mexicans were particularly dangerous. "The men downstairs—policemen—have orders to take no chances whatsoever with a Mexican," one officer reported. "They are quick on the knife and are hot tempered, and do the damage before you know it." Still another officer, this one from Chicago, disclosed what may have been a widely held but rarely voiced opinion: he disliked Mexicans simply because they competed with European immigrants for jobs. "They are taking the places of these respectable, law-abiding, large-familied Lithuanians and Poles," he said. A Mexican living in Chicago echoed this idea, contending that "the average policeman's attitude is still against Mexicans [because] the police are largely Irish and Polish." Taylor agreed, stating that, at least in the Midwest, one reason for the animosity between police officers and Mexicans was that "police in the districts inhabited by Mexicans are often first or second generations of the very nationalities which feel themselves in competition with the Mexicans and frequently have clashed with them physically." Such a situation, Taylor concluded, "naturally [does] not result in more gentle treatment of Mexicans."[29]

The belief that Mexicans were criminally inclined also existed to some extent among the general public. Taylor quotes one American who believed that "Mexicans kill one another about once a week. The Mexicans carry guns and have a bad part of town," this person added. "I would not go down in their part of town after dark for anything." Similarly, Warnshuis knew the wife of a faculty member at a Chicago-area university who found Mexicans frightening simply because of their appearance. "And don't you find that Mexicans are dangerous?" she asked. "They always look so treacherous to me!"[30]

Not everyone agreed, however, that Mexicans were criminally inclined. A Texas law-enforcement official stated that "Mexicans are afraid to violate the law." Taylor reported that "another resident linked their fear to a proud Texan tradition: 'The Mexicans are peaceful. The Mexicans dread the Texas people, dating from the time of Texas independence.' "[31]

Individual officers' belief that Mexicans were criminally inclined and dangerous almost inevitably led police to use discriminatory and violent tactics against them. Warnshuis states that Chicago officers regularly arrested Mexicans for trivial or arbitrary reasons and that Mexicans were also subject to mass arrests when police suspected a Mexican of having committed a crime. He also reported that "because of prejudice against them," police subjected Mexicans to particularly brutal treatment when trying to get a confession. According to Warnshuis one Mexican related that after punching him "about a hundred times," a police officer "stuck a revolver in his mouth and threatened to blow off his head" if he did not confess to a crime. The anonymous Mexican told Warnshuis that he believed the police "were animals to treat me that way." Taylor found similar treatment of Mexicans in other sections of the country. One official, for example, acknowledged that in his area "the Mexican gets no real justice. When they are down on him[,] they handle him as they see fit." In the Indiana Harbor section of East Chicago, Indiana, Mexicans themselves complained about differential treatment from police. "The police are bad to the Mexicans," Taylor quotes one Harbor resident as saying. "They do not wait for an explanation, but catch every Mexican they suspect and hit them over the head."[32]

Taylor in particular commented on the use of excessive force against Mexicans. One police official justified the violence, saying, "A Mexican doesn't respect anything except force." Another officer, this one in Texas, tried to be more reflective regarding his treatment of Mexicans. "I try to treat a Mexican prisoner the same as a white man as long as he will let me," the officer commented, "but if he gets smart, I will probably hit him quicker than I would a white man." Taylor thus concluded that because police simply hated Mexicans or because they felt physically threatened by them, "it is clear that Mexicans in the United States, both aliens and citizens, are frequently subjected to severe and unequal treatment by those who administer the law." While Taylor is undoubtedly correct, it is also true, however, that this unequal treatment came almost always at the hands of individual officers and, with the exception of the arrests, this unequal treatment was almost never institutionalized into the policies and practices of the department.[33]

Nevertheless, Mexicans living in the United States complained bitterly about what they saw as discriminatory treatment from the criminal justice system. In particular they complained that they did not receive equal protection in cases of anti-Mexican violence. "It is *muy duro* in this country," one man living in Texas reported. "There is a law for the Americans [i.e., to protect them], but none for the Mexicans." Another complained that it was "no use" seeking protection from the courts. "You never see them sending an American to the penitentiary for killing a Mexican," he charged. Mexicans also specifically complained about unfair treatment from police. One, for example, stated that "policemen here are hard on Mexicans," while another declared that "Mexicans take a lot of abuse here in this town." Both argued that police arrested Mexicans for offenses that they would have ignored had the offender been white. Mexicans were particularly angered by excessive use of force by officers. A man from East Chicago, Indiana, contended that "just because a Mexican is drunk they [the police] hit him or do anything." Another contended that he carried a gun in order to protect himself from law-enforcement officers. Police, he claimed, "shoot the Mexicans with small provocation. One shot a Mexican who was walking away from him, and laughed as the body was thrown into the patrol wagon."[34]

These types of police actions led Mexicans to publicly protest, sometimes with red-hot rhetoric, what they saw as police brutality. One Spanish-language Chicago newspaper editorialized that "in Chicago the Mexicans have been the victims more than two dozen times at the hands of the police—those abusive half-breeds who take advantage of uniforms and shining badges to perpetrate attacks on our people." The editorial admitted that some Mexicans did cause trouble and deserved punishment. Nevertheless, "when honorable and decent Mexicans are jailed merely at the whim of the police[,] we protest violently. We will not permit such attacks; we will continue to protest, let it cost us what it may."[35]

Mexicans in California, the report of Governor C. C. Young's Special Fact Finding Committee, reached conclusions similar to those of the Wickersham Commission regarding Mexican criminality. The Young committee compared the incidence of crime and delinquency among Mexicans with that among the general population in order to develop "an index of racial or national characteristics and also as an index of the adjustment or lack of adjustment of the Mexican to American customs and standards." Relying primarily on the ethnic makeup of populations in California state prisons and on arrest statistics developed by the Los Angeles County Sheriff's Department and the LAPD, the committee found that Mexicans were indeed arrested and incarcerated at a higher rate than the general population; however, it attributed these higher rates to racial discrimination and to economic and demographic differences.[36]

The committee also found that juvenile delinquency among Mexican youths seemed to be growing. It reported that officials at the two state schools for boys were "sharply concerned . . . by the rapid increase in the number of Mexican boys committed to their care." The committee explained, however, that the large number of Mexican boys in state schools resulted from the policy of private schools rejecting boys of Mexican descent. On the other hand, it presented statistics from the LAPD showing that Mexican youths comprised a disproportionately high and rising percentage of all juveniles arrested and concluded that this "indicates a degree of delinquency or maladjustment [among Mexican youths] exceeding that of the estimated general population." The question of "maladjusted" Mexican American youth would become a major issue in Los Angeles decades later.[37]

Taken together, the various reports on Mexicans issued by the Wickersham Commission and the section on crime and delinquency in *Mexicans in California* paint a rather sympathetic picture of criminality among Mexicans living in the United States. The statistics presented in the reports are, at best, conflicting regarding the extent of Mexican criminality: in some parts of the country Mexicans committed more crimes than the general population; in other parts they committed fewer. Moreover, the analysis of these statistics usually led to the conclusion that factors such as the age and gender makeup of the Mexican population and the financial inability of Mexicans to mount court defenses, not to mention the racism and discriminatory treatment at the hands of law-enforcement officials, all tended to inflate the crime rate among Mexicans. But perhaps the most interesting aspect of these findings is that they stood in such sharp contrast to the beliefs of individual police officers at the local level.

THE LAPD STUDY

The difference between the assessment of Mexican criminality made in the Wickersham and Young reports and the views held by Los Angeles law-enforcement officials was even more clearly, and in some ways more profoundly, revealed in the account on Mexican arrests written for police reformer August Vollmer at the end of his year as LAPD chief of police. Entitled "A Brief Study of Arrests of Mexicans in Los Angeles for a Twelve-Month Period," this report differs from those previously cited in some important ways. To begin with, it was written not by a panel of experts or scholars such as Paul Taylor, but by a rank-and-file officer in the LAPD named S. H. Bowman. Unlike the Wickersham report, the purpose of the study was not to examine the criminal justice system but rather to analyze the extent and variety of Mexican criminality. The sole source of evidence used in this analysis consisted of statistics on the number of Mexicans arrested by the LAPD and estimates of their numbers in the general population. In analyzing this data, the department did not consider the sociological, demographic, and economic factors that the other authors believed inflated the number of Mexicans arrested. The importance of this study results from the fact that, as part of the police chief's annual report, it stood as the LAPD's official view regarding Mexican criminality.

Since this report and much of the rest of this discussion of Mexican criminality rely on crime statistics from official sources, it is important here to note some of the limitations and proper and improper uses of this type of data. To begin with, it must be remembered that LAPD "crime" statistics during this era usually meant arrest statistics, and arrest statistics simply do not accurately reveal the extent of crime in any given area or within any given population subgroup. The criminologists Edwin H. Sutherland and Donald R. Cressey stated the problem succinctly: "The statistics about crime and delinquency are probably the most unreliable and most difficult of all social statistics. It is impossible to determine with accuracy the amount of crime in any given jurisdiction [or for any subgroup in the population, I might add] at any given time. Some behavior is labeled, 'delinquency' or 'crime' by one observer but not by another. Obviously a large proportion of all violations goes undetected. Other crimes are detected but not reported, and still others are reported but not officially recorded." For Sutherland and Cressey, therefore, crime statistics are, at best, an "index" of the crimes actually committed; such an index, however, does "not maintain a constant ratio with the true rate, whatever it may be."[38]

If arrest statistics do not accurately describe the extent of crime in society, of what use are they? According to the criminologist Richard Quinney, while arrest statistics give only an indication of the extent of crime, they also "reflect the policies and behaviors of the agencies administering criminal law." He gives as an example a study dealing with drug arrests that found "that although there were distinct trends and distributions by time and place for the drug offenses, these patterns [of

arrests] were shaped by systematic biases in the operation of police assigned to the narcotics division." Thus, while "the arrest rates reflect in
some way the use and sale of drugs, the rates can be better understood
as the combined behavior of the offenders and agencies of control."
Arrest statistics, Quinney therefore asserts, can best be understood as
reflecting "a mixture of the *incidence of criminality and the administration of criminal law*"[39] (Quinney's emphasis). An arrest, after all, results
directly from an action taken by a police officer, not by the person arrested. Furthermore, under the American system of justice, being arrested establishes neither guilt nor even that a crime has been committed.
Both must be proven in court.

The arrest statistics that I am using are particularly problematic for
measuring the extent of Mexican criminality. Beginning in 1924 the
LAPD annually published statistics on all arrests made each year. The
department cross-tabulated these statistics in a number of ways, including by race, and counted Mexicans as the "Red" race. These statistics
are an excellent source of information, in that they give us the total
number of Mexicans arrested ("the universe," in statistical terminology)
on a yearly basis. Unfortunately, accurate statistics measuring the overall
population of Mexicans living in Los Angeles are all but nonexistent.
For the period prior to 1930, scholars have made estimates based on
census records and city directories. These estimates vary by as much as
300 percent.[40] After 1930, even reliable estimates do not exist. Since
there are no comparable population statistics, it is extremely difficult to
determine whether the rate at which the LAPD arrested Mexicans was
higher or lower than their proportion in the general population. The
crime statistics that I use, therefore, tell us more about the implicit and
explicit assumptions, policies, and practices of the LAPD regarding the
Mexican community than they do about the extent and nature of Mexican criminality.

The 1923 Bowman report clearly illustrates this principle. It was the
first attempt by the LAPD to use statistics to analyze crime within a
specific segment of the population. While the LAPD subsequently published raw statistics of arrests by race, this was one of the few cases in
which the department attempted to analyze those statistics. Thus, the
report serves several purposes: first, it details the types of offenses for
which the LAPD arrested Mexicans; second, it gives some indication of
the number and types of crimes Mexicans committed; and third, it states
explicitly the LAPD's official view regarding Mexicans.

The Bowman report's discussion of the arrest rate of Mexicans demonstrates the LAPD's understanding of the nature of Mexicans' criminality. The report found that while the estimates of Mexicans living in the city ranged from 5.5 percent to 8 percent of the total population, Mexicans accounted for only 4.5 percent of the total arrests made by the LAPD. The report, however, did not stress this overall low arrest rate. Instead, Bowman emphasized the fact that Mexicans constituted 11.84 percent of all persons arrested for felonies in Los Angeles, a rate higher than their estimated representation in the general population. From these figures the LAPD concluded that the Mexican community consisted of a "large population of law-abiding persons, but numbering in their midst is an element distinctly inferior to the average resident of Los Angeles, in its attitude to the laws of the state, and more especially to those [laws] considered of greatest importance with reference to the safety of life and property."[41]

The discussion on the type of crimes for which police arrested Mexicans illustrates what the LAPD believed to be the factors that caused Mexicans to commit crimes. The report showed that of a total of 3,489 Mexicans arrested, 1,049 were arrested for liquor-related offenses and another 558 were arrested on some sort of vagrancy charge. Combined, these two categories of offenses constituted 55.41 percent of all misdemeanors and 47.9 percent of all arrests. To the department, these statistics demonstrated that "it is evident that our Mexican population who are caught in the meshes of the law are very largely in trouble because of weakness of will and lack of initiative." In addition, the more "serious crimes [felonies] are, to be sure a predictable consequence of these character defects, when associated with economic stress and with opportunity, sought and unsought." The report thus concluded that flaws in Mexican culture contributed to Mexican criminality.[42]

The report's analysis of the occupations of those Mexicans arrested generally agreed with the mental-testers' claim that criminality was linked to intelligence and that Mexicans were intellectually inferior. It found "very significant" the fact that over 72 percent of the Mexicans arrested labeled themselves as laborers and that only a small percentage defined themselves as working in an occupation that required "definite training of some sort." These figures suggest, the Bowman report contended, that "training for useful occupations" might act as a "cure for much of the condition leading to petty crime." Nevertheless, Bowman pessimistically concluded that since "the Mexican whom we find in Los Angeles is, as a class, of relatively low mentality[,] he is probably best fitted for work demanding ability of an inferior grade."[43]

The report did not blame Mexican criminality solely upon the Mexicans. It also blamed the fact that American institutions had failed to instill proper American values in the immigrants. The report showed that the average age at which the Mexicans arrested had entered the United States was 9.5 years of age and that they had lived in this country for over 14 years. Bowman found this situation to be "a rather unpleasant reflection upon our attitude as a nation toward these men and women from our sister republic." The report found lamentable the idea that although most had been in the United States during the "formative years of their lives, so many of them have developed into manhood and womanhood with weak initiative, small ambition, and in some instances a disregard for the law." More important, despite the presence of typical negative stereotypes regarding Mexicans, the report did not conclude that Mexicans were inherently inclined toward criminality. Bowman believed that if the department undertook a longitudinal statistical study of crime by race, it would discover a "close correspondence" of criminal activity among the races.[44]

Perhaps because the report did not find Mexicans to be criminally inclined, it made no recommendations for changing the way in which the LAPD policed the Mexican community. The only specific recommendation in the report was the aforementioned call for a longitudinal study of crime by race. The following year, the LAPD began collecting and publishing the type of statistics that Bowman had recommended; but the effect of those reports was exactly the opposite of what Bowman had anticipated.

ANNUAL REPORT STATISTICS

The LAPD's *Annual Reports,* which from 1925 through 1949 listed all the arrests made by the LAPD by charge and race, demonstrate the department's growing interest in linking crime to race. Moreover, the statistical tables in these reports give us an indication of the rate at which the LAPD arrested Mexicans in relation to the rate at which it arrested members of the rest of the community; in addition, the reports provide a clear picture of the types of crimes for which the LAPD arrested Mexicans and some understanding of how the LAPD policed the Mexican community. It seems evident that at least for the years for which we have some reliable statistics regarding the number of Mexicans living in Los Angeles, the LAPD did not arrest Mexicans at a rate much higher than their proportion in the general population. As I have already noted, the

1923 Vollmer report estimated the Mexican population to be between 5.5 and 8 percent of the whole but found that Mexicans comprised only 4.5 percent of all those arrested in the city.[45]

The next year for which somewhat reliable estimates of the Mexican population exist is 1930. These figures range from a low, issued by the Census Bureau, of 97,116, or 7.84 percent of the total population, to a high of 190,000, or 15.35 percent, estimated by several scholars. As a result of the deportation and repatriation campaigns of the Depression, the number of Mexicans living in Los Angeles fluctuated during the early 1930s and did not begin to stabilize until the end of the decade.[46]

The arrest rate for adult Mexicans on all charges between 1925 and 1939 closely mirrored this demographic pattern. The percentage of Mexicans arrested rose steadily in the 1920s, hitting 16.04 percent in 1930—only slightly above the highest estimate for the Mexican population in Los Angeles and more than double the lowest estimate. During the Depression the rate of Mexican arrests dropped off significantly, hitting a low in 1933, and then generally rose again throughout the rest of the 1930s. At the end of the decade the LAPD was arresting Mexicans at a rate that was less than .5 percent higher than the rate in 1925. The arrest rate for Mexican adults charged with violent felonies (homicide, rape, robbery, and felonious assault) reveals a similar pattern.[47]

Beginning in 1927, the LAPD began to publish arrest statistics for juveniles by charge and race. While we do not know what percentage of the juvenile population (people under eighteen years of age) were of Mexican descent, we can assume that as the decade of the thirties wore on, more and more of the children of the large wave of Mexican immigrants that entered the United States earlier in the century reached the age when they were most likely to run afoul of the law. The LAPD statistics do indeed show a steady increase in the percentage of Mexican juveniles arrested. In 1927 Mexican juveniles comprised 15.87 percent of all juveniles arrested; by 1939 they comprised 27.48 percent. The data on Mexican juveniles arrested for violent felonies show an even higher increase. In 1927 Mexican juveniles accounted for only 7.35 percent of all juveniles arrested for such crimes. In only one year that rate jumped to 19.63 percent, and by 1939 Mexicans accounted for almost 38 percent of juveniles arrested for these serious crimes, or almost as high a percentage as that of whites.

The high percentage of Mexican American juveniles arrested demands an explanation. While we do not know what percentage of the juvenile population was of Mexican descent, we can be reasonably certain that it was substantially lower than the percentage of Mexican American youths arrested on all charges or for violent crimes. People of Mexican descent simply did not account for even as much as 20 percent of the population of Los Angeles during the 1930s. Thus, the question that needs to be answered is, to what extent did the arrest statistics represent actual delinquency among Mexican American youth?

Anecdotal evidence demonstrates that since at least the mid-1930s both police officials and community leaders believed that Mexican American youth constituted a particular delinquency problem. For example, since at least 1934 the LAPD carried on youth work in East Los Angeles. Individual officers received commendations from the Los Angeles Board of Parks and Playgrounds for preventive and rehabilitative work with Mexican American youth, which consisted of overnight outings and other recreational activities. According to a letter of commendation, the purpose of these projects was to provide Mexican American youth with "constructive and wholesome activities to take the place of maliciously mischievous ones." The LAPD again demonstrated its ongoing concern with Mexican American juvenile delinquency in 1938 when the department sent Lieutenant E. W. Lester and a "policewoman" to Mexico City to study prevention methods for juvenile delinquency in the hope that they could learn effective methods for dealing with Mexican American youth. Lester went on to be one of the department's experts on Mexican American youth. The fact that the LAPD took these types of actions is evidence that it perceived Mexican American juvenile delinquency as being an issue it had to address.[48]

East Los Angeles civic leaders also believed that Mexican American juvenile delinquency constituted a special problem for their community. The community newspaper the *Belvedere Citizen,* for example, began publishing articles on the issue as early as 1935, and throughout the remainder of the decade it continued to print stories depicting Mexican American juvenile delinquency. Mexican American businessmen's organizations also took note of the problem. The *Citizen* reported in 1936 that the Mexican Chamber of Commerce had initiated a special youth activities program, ostensibly because "the preponderance of the juvenile [delinquents] are of that nationality." Finally, in 1939, the East Los Angeles Property Owners and Businessmen's Association petitioned the police commission, complaining about the removal of Lieutenant Joseph Reed from the LAPD's Hollenbeck Division, which served East Los Angeles. According to the complainants, Reed "thoroughly understands the problems of this district and has made substantial progress in removing juvenile delinquency and in work of crime prevention."[49]

Thus, it seemed that a relatively wide spectrum of the community believed that Mexican American juvenile delinquency constituted a significant problem. On the other hand, the LAPD arrest statistics reveal little about the extent of that problem. The total number of juvenile arrests for the most serious category of crimes, violent felonies, was small and practically insignificant. Throughout this period the total number of arrests in this category for all races never approached two hundred. In comparison, throughout the 1930s the LAPD generally made between three and four thousand adult arrests for this category of crime. Furthermore, the number of juvenile arrests for violent felonies fluctuated wildly from year to year. In 1930 the LAPD made 66 percent fewer arrests of Mexican American juveniles for this category than it made in 1929. Does this mean that Mexican American juveniles committed 66 percent fewer violent felonies in 1930? Probably not; it is more likely that these figures indicate changes in police activities from year to year. In the final analysis, it seems safe to say that a Mexican American juvenile delinquency problem did exist in the 1930s, but that LAPD statistics reveal little about the nature and scope of the problem. These arrest statistics are nevertheless important because they laid the basis for subsequent law-enforcement claims that Mexican juveniles committed an extraordinarily high number of crimes.

While the arrest statistics tell us little about crime in the barrios, they do tell us about police practices. The statistical data are, for example, useful for showing the types of crimes for which the LAPD arrested Mexicans and for seeing if the department arrested them for certain classes of crimes more often than it did for others. The police statistics demonstrate that the LAPD most often arrested Mexicans for violation of sumptuary laws or other "victimless" crimes. Data taken from the 1923 Vollmer report, for example, reveal that over 63 percent of all Mexicans arrested were charged with crimes that had no apparent victim.

During the 1920s and 1930s the LAPD continued to arrest adult Mexicans most often for alleged violations of sumptuary laws. In 1928, for example, arrests for alcohol-related offenses and vagrancy accounted for over 70 percent of all arrests of Mexicans. In the following years, arrests for vagrancy dropped off precipitously but arrests for alcohol-related offenses rose at such a rate that by 1936 more than 76 percent of all Mexicans arrested by the LAPD were apprehended for alleged alcohol-related offenses. In contrast, during the same period, arrests for violent crimes and crimes against property combined never exceeded 15 percent.

While arrest statistics generally need to be handled judiciously, the data on violations of sumptuary laws need to be given even more careful attention. Police exercise a high degree of discretion in many aspects of their work, including in reaching decisions on whether or not to make an arrest. Criminologists agree that officers base their decisions on many variables, among which some of the most important are the demeanor of the suspect and the importance given to a category of offense by the government or police officials, the media, or the general public. Equally consequential factors are the race of the police officer and that of the suspect. Discretion becomes even more important in sumptuary cases, in which there is no victim and therefore no civilian complainant. In such instances, the decision as to whether to make an arrest rests solely with the police officer.[50]

The extremely high percentage of Mexicans arrested on liquor-related charges therefore raises some questions regarding the attitude of individual officers and the methods police used to enforce these laws in the Mexican community. How did police officers know when a person was legally drunk and therefore in need of incarceration and was not, instead, someone who had had just a little too much to drink and was in need of being sent home? Did LAPD officers believe that Mexicans suffered from some inherent "weakness of will," as the 1923 report contended, thus making them more inclined to drink too much liquor? Did police officers therefore expect more drunkenness among Mexicans and, as a result, did they indeed find more Mexican drunks? Did language differences cause problems? Did police arrest Mexicans as drunks more often than they arrested drunks among the general population simply because the officers did not understand Spanish and therefore could not determine whether the suspect was drunk, suffering from some ailment, or maybe even sober? Did the accented English that many Mexicans spoke sound like slurring to police officers? Finally, did officers use their authority to vent anti-Mexican prejudices by arresting Mexicans for violations that they ignored among whites? In other words, do these arrest statistics mean that Mexicans broke the liquor laws significantly more often than the general population, or do they mean that Los Angeles police officers were more likely to arrest Mexicans for violation of the liquor laws than they were to arrest other members of the general population?

While the paucity of data for Los Angeles precludes any definitive answer to these questions, Mexicans in other parts of the country certainly believed that officers enforced the liquor laws against them more stringently than they did against others. One Mexican in East Chicago, Indiana, complained bitterly about differential police enforcement of liquor laws. "The policemen here are hard on the Mexicans," he said. "If they see a Mexican drunk, they run him in, even if he has [only] a breath. If it's a Polillo, they pat him on the back, take him by the hand, and say, 'Go home and sleep it off,' even if they are acting like mad. It costs a Mexican $18 and $20 to drink; not a Pole."[51]

Even if it could be proven that the arrest statistics accurately reflected the degree of liquor-law violation in the Mexican community, it should not be concluded that Mexicans were inherently more criminal. The liquor laws, like other sumptuary laws, criminalized activities that Mexicans considered lawful and part of normal everyday life. Recent Mexican immigrants, who came from a society that did not share the same antiliquor sentiments that produced prohibition, found themselves arrested for behavior that was considered legitimate in Mexico. Thus, in order to understand the arrest statistics we must take into consideration the fact that the single largest category of offenses for which Mexicans were arrested were violations of laws that were practically unique to the United States and that Mexicans were culturally disinclined to obey.

Similarly, the statistics for the category of offenses that produced the second highest number of arrests—violation of vagrancy laws—must also be treated with caution. From the 1920s through the 1930s the rate of Mexicans arrested for vagrancy dropped significantly but averaged well over 10 percent. According to the criminologist Richard Quinney, police have traditionally made arrests on vagrancy charges "to accomplish a multitude of extralegal objectives." Primary among these was the extralegal control of a segment of the population deemed dangerous or a nuisance by police. This seems to have been the practice of the LAPD through at least the late 1920s. For example, the 1923 report on Mexican crime states that in the department "it is very common to 'vag' a man or a woman who has been suspected of some serious offense, but who cannot be convicted for lack of evidence." Moreover, the LAPD sometimes mistakenly "vagged" innocent people. The report recounts how officers arrested one steadily employed Mexican simply because he was in the company of a "roughly dressed" friend late at night. The report concluded that "undoubtedly great injustice is at time done, [*sic*] in this way."[52]

The data for juveniles are similar to the data for adults, in that the LAPD arrested both Mexican American juveniles and juveniles from the general population for analogous categories of crime. Department statistics show that the LAPD most often arrested juveniles of all races for crimes against property; noncriminal detention was the next most common category. Like adults, juveniles were rarely arrested for violent crimes, and Mexican juveniles were arrested for violent crimes at a rate that was only slightly higher than that of youths from the general population. The LAPD, however, arrested a significantly higher percentage of Mexican youth for crimes against property than it arrested in the general population, but detained them considerably less often on noncriminal grounds.

Again, the statistics raise as many questions as they answer. Do they mean that Mexican youths committed more burglaries but were less likely to run away than the general population? Or do they mean that the LAPD monitored Mexican youths more closely for this kind of offense and were more protective of white youths who were on their own? Again, the evidence does not address these questions, but we do know that during the 1920s and 1930s the LAPD instituted practices that greatly increased the possibility that certain segments of the population would be overarrested. Specifically, the department regularly conducted "dragnets" in which they arrested anyone—but especially juveniles—on the street within the vicinity of a crime or anyone who resembled the suspect in a case. These arrests ensnared many innocent people, and most of the people thus arrested were never charged in court or they had the cases against them dismissed. We also know that the LAPD engaged in mass arrests of Mexicans during both World War I and World War II. Thus, it is entirely possible that the arrest statistics reflect as much the conduct, or misconduct, of the LAPD as they do the behavior of Los Angeles Mexicans.[53]

The importance of the LAPD arrest statistics lies not so much in what they tell us about police practices or Mexican criminality; in these two regards, the conclusions that can be drawn are ambiguous and speculative. Rather, the arrest statistics are important because they show that beginning in the 1920s the LAPD began linking race and crime. The very fact that the department kept increasingly detailed and sophisticated statistics of arrests by race shows a growing interest in explaining crime in racial terms. Furthermore, to the extent that the statistics reinforced stereotypes regarding Mexican criminality, they also provided the basis for the fully developed theory of Mexican criminality that dominated relations between the police and Mexican Americans in subsequent decades.

CHAPTER 7

Police Misconduct and Community Protest

The LAPD's increasing focus on a linkage between race and criminality resulted in increased tensions between the department and the Mexican American community. On the one hand, individual officers, believing that Mexicans were somehow inherently inclined toward criminality, began using ever harsher tactics in their interactions with that community. The community responded with increasingly vigorous and effective protests against what many saw as instances of police misconduct. Fueled by some spectacular cases as well as by everyday occurrences, over time many Los Angeles Mexicans came to believe that the LAPD acted in a discriminatory and often brutal manner in its interaction with their community. The emergence of community institutions such as newspapers and volunteer organizations provided the vehicles for the articulation of community discontent. In addition, the 1930s saw the rise of a "Mexican American generation" with a new political sophistication and assertiveness. This new assertiveness coalesced with labor and radical elements within the community to make Mexican Americans increasingly vocal about abusive police practices. The growing perception of the police as violent oppressors of the Mexican community resulted in numerous denunciations of police methods by groups throughout the 1920s and 1930s and eventually contributed to the development of a combative relationship between law enforcement and the Mexican American community.

COMMUNITY INSTITUTIONS

Crucial to the development of this combative relationship was the development of immigrant community institutions. The proliferation in the 1920s of Mexican mutual-aid societies and cultural and professional associations gave the community the organizational base from which to launch protests. Many of these organizations, such as the Comisión Honorífica and the Unión Mexicana, functioned primarily to promote Mexican culture and/or nationalism by sponsoring festivities around Mexican national holidays. Others, such as Cruz Azul, were mainly concerned with providing assistance to Mexican families that had fallen on hard times.[1]

The members of most of these organizations, however, understood well that they had also to protect Mexicans from the effects of racism in general and more specifically from police abuse. Club Independencia, for example, had as one of its goals the "protection of the rights of Mexicanos" who lived in this country. The Sociedad de Madres Mexicanas raised funds to help defend Mexicans who ran afoul of the law. More important, Spanish-language newspapers such as *El Heraldo de México* and, later, *La Opinión* stirred the Mexican population's interest by publishing stories of official abuse and calling on the community to come to the aid of their countrymen.[2]

One fleeting but nevertheless significant example of the organizational and political sophistication of the Los Angeles Mexican community occurred when, on March 23, 1928, a convention of members of Mexican mutual-aid societies formed the Confederación de Uniones Obreras Mexicanas (CUOM; Federation of Mexican Workers). CUOM's membership included many IWW and Communist sympathizers, and the union's bylaws recognized the principle of class struggle. At its height, CUOM comprised twenty-one locals and a membership of as many as three thousand. The union, however, never engaged in aggressive organizing activity, or strikes, and by 1929 its membership had greatly declined. Nevertheless, CUOM continued to have influence in the Mexican community, especially on issues of police misconduct through the early 1930s.[3]

In addition to the community institutions, the Mexican consulate in Los Angeles also addressed police issues. During the period before 1920 the intense rivalries between factions involved in the Mexican Revolution often put the consul in conflict with much of the Mexican population.* After the revolution, however, many of the men whom the Mexican government appointed to the post of Mexican consul general in Los Angeles worked to protect the civil rights of their compatriots. Consequently, throughout the 1920s and 1930s the consulate regularly issued official complaints about the LAPD's treatment of Mexican immigrants and helped raise awareness about the police problem in the Mexican community.[4]

While the 1920s was a decade of relative political quiescence for Los Angeles Mexicans, the 1930s was charged with activism. The historian Mario García has argued that during the 1930s there came of age a "political generation" of Mexican Americans determined to end discriminatory practices against their people. Comprising primarily the American-born and/or -raised sons and daughters of the previous "immigrant generation," members of this "Mexican American generation" used their permanent status within the United States (they could not be deported) and their advanced education, English skills, and knowledge of American institutions to fight for the rights of Mexicans living in the United States. Although during the Depression years Los Angeles Mexican Americans quite naturally concentrated on gaining economic justice, the very idea of fighting for their rights compelled Mexican Americans to question police practices in their community. The fact that police malpractice seemed to be on the rise only made the need for protest more compelling.[5]

COMPLAINTS TO THE POLICE COMMISSION

During the 1920s and 1930s the Los Angeles Board of Police Commissioners was the only semi-autonomous body to which a citizen could bring a complaint regarding police misconduct. Thus, the number of complaints brought to the police commission gives an indication of the discontent in the Los Angeles Mexican community regarding the LAPD. Compared with the previous two decades, between 1920 and 1930 the number of complaints involving Mexicans rose dramatically. To a certain extent, the increase in complaints resulted from the earlier noted growth of the Mexican population. This population increase, in turn, produced a growth in the number of contacts between Mexicans and police and, more important, in the number of arrests. Between 1926 (the first year for which there exist comparable statistics) and 1939, the number of Mexicans arrested by the LAPD rose by close to 79 percent. The increase in arrests almost inevitably led to a growth in the number of complaints of police misconduct. The number of complaints regarding police misconduct against Mexicans, however, far outstripped either the rise in the Mexican population or the rise in arrests. As noted earlier, between 1900 and 1919 seventeen charges of police misconduct were brought before the police commission by or on behalf of Mexicans. Between 1920 and 1939 the number of similar complaints swelled to fifty-six—a rise of over 229 percent.[6]

While the number of complaints to the police commission rose dramatically during the 1920s and 1930s, the reasons for the complaints and the complaints' disposition resembled the trends set in previous decades. As in the period 1900–1920, during the next two decades Mexicans most often complained about officers using unnecessary force against them. Of the forty-six complaints filed by Mexicans or filed for them by third parties (as opposed to those emanating from within the department but involving Mexican victims), twelve were for unnecessary force, followed by five each for discourteous conduct, illegal search, and false arrest. Similarly, the police commission only rarely sustained the complaints filed by Mexicans or by third parties on their behalf. Of the forty-six such complaints over a twenty-year period, the police commission only sustained the complaint on two occasions—once for conduct unbecoming an officer and the second time for illegal search. The case involving illegal search deserves some comment, if only because it stands in sharp contrast to the way in which the commission usually handled Mexicans' complaints.[7]

On June 18, 1929, F. G. Burruel complained to the police commission that "three negro officers" entered his home without a search warrant looking for illegal alcoholic beverages. According to Burruel, his daughter, who was pregnant, became so alarmed by the intrusion that she miscarried her baby. Angered by this pitiful story, the commissioners passed a resolution ordering officers not to enter a private residence in search of liquor without a warrant. That order, in turn, created a major uproar that consumed most of the police commission's time for the next month.[8]

The week after the police commission passed its resolution, Dr. S. T. Montgomery, a member of the Anti-Saloon League and a former police commissioner, addressed the commission, condemning the order. Montgomery argued that the order demanding that an officer obtain a warrant before searching a home critically weakened the police department's ability to enforce the liquor laws and far exceeded the standard for searches set by state statutes or the Constitution. The police commission responded by establishing a committee to investigate the matter and requesting a legal opinion from the city attorney.[9]

In its formal reply, the city attorney's office stated that not only was the original order legally correct, it "is the only proper instruction that could be given the Police Department in regard to such searches without a warrant." Nevertheless, on July 17 the police commission effectively voided the original order by defining a private residence as not meaning "any place where any law is being violated." Presumably, the police commission left it to the police officer's discretion to decide whether such a condition existed. Ironically, Burruel's original complaint got lost in the shuffle. On August 13, 1929, the city attorney reported that Burruel had requested a formal reply to his complaint, to which the police commission responded by sending him a letter "stating that the Search and Seizure order was the direct result of his reporting this matter to the police commission." Burruel received no compensation for his or his daughter's loss, nor was he ever informed of whether the officers involved received any punishment.[10]

The police commission's actions in the Burruel case, were, however, almost unique, and as stated earlier, the police commission generally refused to sustain complaints brought by Mexicans or those brought on their behalf by parties outside the LAPD. The normal procedure was for the police commission to refer such a complaint to the chief of police for investigation and report, and then to simply accept the chief's usual report that the evidence did not support the charge.[11]

A typical example of how the police commission dealt with complaints involving Mexicans, even when those complaints came from highly influential sources, occurred in late 1927 over the LAPD practice of making wholesale arrests of suspected Mexican vagrants. In August 1927, Captain John D. Hubbs reported to the police commission that a previous complaint from the Mexican consul F. A. Pesqueria regarding mass arrests of Mexicans in the Plaza had been satisfactorily settled between consular staff and LAPD officials. Captain Hubbs's assessment of the situation was, however, somewhat premature. The following December the Mexican consul sent another complaint to the police commission regarding the LAPD vagrancy squad making unwarranted arrests of Mexican "workmen who congregate at the Plaza." Specifically, Vice Consul Joel Quiñones charged that the arrested men were "kept for several days in jail and later released without any apparent investigation being made of their cases." Mayor George Cryer entered the fray with a letter forwarding complaints from the Mexican consul and from businessmen's organizations that the LAPD had made "wholesale arrests of unemployed men" in the Plaza district. For his part, the mayor argued that he felt "that the mere fact that a man is unemployed, and found loitering in public places, does not constitute sufficient cause for his arrest and imprisonment, and I believe that such a policy inflicts undue hardship upon the individuals so arrested and upon the business men who are dependent upon them for trade."[12]

Chief of Police James Davis and the police commission felt differently. The chief reported that instead of the two thousand arrests that the businessmen's associations charged that the LAPD had made, his officers had arrested only 452 men for vagrancy. Davis also "assured the Commission there was no discrimination [against Mexicans], inasmuch as there were some 86 white men arrested in this number." Finally, the chief reported that the LAPD did not intend "to work a hardship on these people, but was simply taking a precaution to reduce the criminal activities in this vicinity." The police commission formally accepted the report and sent a copy to the mayor as its response.[13]

In contrast, while the police commission usually dismissed complaints regarding Mexicans when those complaints came from outside the department, it regularly sustained the charges of a police officer's misconduct when those charges emanated from the chief of police. Between 1920 and 1940 the police commission entertained seven such complaints, and in each instance it approved the actions of the chief in bringing disciplinary actions against the officer involved.[14]

AURELIO POMPA AND COMMUNITY PROTEST IN THE 1920S

While complaints to the police commission give an indication of the amount and type of police misconduct to which Los Angeles Mexicans objected, the complaints themselves had little impact on the Mexican community. They usually came from individuals who wanted some satisfaction for wrongs they believed the police had done to them or their loved ones. These complaints rarely received much news coverage. In contrast, a handful of spectacular and highly publicized cases involving injustices against Mexicans helped politicize them regarding the increasingly discriminatory nature of law-enforcement practices in their community. This politicization resulted directly from the collective efforts of the Mexican community to reverse what it saw as obvious cases of official injustice. As Mexicans organized and participated in defense committees, held fund-raising events, and attended rallies, court hearings, and even funerals, they not only became more conscious of LAPD misconduct, but gained more confidence in their own ability to end abusive police practices. Moreover, as more community members read about these activities in Spanish-language newspapers, they became increasingly inclined to doubt the integrity of the LAPD and also more likely to protest police practices.

During the 1920s no other case stirred the Los Angeles Mexican community more than the execution of Aurelio Pompa for the murder of William D. McCue. While the case did not include allegations of misconduct by the LAPD, it did alert the Mexican community to discrimination within the criminal justice system. On October 19, 1922, Pompa shot and killed McCue, his foreman, in an argument over some tools. Earlier that same day, McCue had beaten Pompa with the side of a saw and Pompa had gone home to retrieve his revolver. When Pompa returned to the work place, McCue again accosted him and Pompa drew his revolver and shot McCue twice, once directly through the heart. According to the *Times,* the other workmen would have lynched Pompa had the police not arrived when they did.[15]

From the very beginning, Pompa claimed that he shot McCue in self-defense. His attorney, however, exerted little energy in his defense, and Pompa was arraigned, tried, found guilty, and sentenced to death all in one day. As the date for his execution neared, his mother, the Spanish-language newspaper *El Heraldo de México,* Mexican mutual-aid societies, and even the Mexican government mounted a major effort to save Pompa's life. Mexican community leaders collected over three thousand dollars to fund an appeal, and when that legal tactic failed they solicited close to thirteen thousand signatures on a petition to California's Governor F. W. Richardson to commute the sentence. Community leaders also implored the Mexican government to use its diplomatic resources on behalf of the twenty-two-year-old Mexican citizen. Telegrams flew back and forth between Los Angeles and Mexico City and between Mexico City and Sacramento in the effort to spare Pompa's life. Throughout the campaign, Pompa's supporters claimed that he was a victim of racial discrimination and that he would have received a lighter sentence, or perhaps even an acquittal, had the case not involved a Mexican killing a white. In the end, however, not even the personal entreaties of President Alvaro Obregón of Mexico persuaded Governor Richardson to commute Pompa's sentence. The execution was particularly grisly, with Pompa taking fifteen minutes to die when California authorities hanged him on April 4, 1924.[16]

The Pompa case so aroused Los Angeles Mexicans that they memorialized Pompa's life and death with a *corrido* (ballad) that was recorded and sold in Mexican communities throughout the United States. The corrido attributed the following lines as Pompa's last words:

> Farewell my friends; farewell my people;
> Dear Mother, cry no more.
> Tell my people not to come here;
> For here they will suffer; here there is no pity.[17]

The reaction of the Mexican community to the trial and execution of Aurelio Pompa indicates a growing awareness of discrimination within the criminal justice system. More important, it demonstrates a collective and therefore more sophisticated response to official injustice and a growing commitment to political action. For rather than just responding through individual complaints, the community as a whole made a substantial effort to reverse what people saw as an obvious case of anti-Mexican bias in the courts. Although this collective effort failed, the bitter words of the corrido, as well as its popularity (few corridos were ever recorded at the time), show that Los Angeles Mexicans were beginning to respond politically to some of the more negative aspects of life in the United States.

JUAN REYNA AND COMMUNITY PROTEST IN THE 1930S

Less than eight years later another incident occurred that not only indicated the increasingly poor relations between the LAPD and the Mexican community but also demonstrates how instances of police misconduct politicized the community. On Saturday, June 10, 1930, twenty-nine-year-old Juan Reyna shot and killed the LAPD officer Verne A. Brindley. That evening, after working all day in a foundry and, according to the police, having had something to drink, Reyna got into an automobile accident with a car containing three members of the LAPD vice squad, their informant, and two prostitutes they had arrested. Angered by the accident, the officers dragged Reyna out of his automobile and stuffed him into the police car, handcuffing him to the informant.[18]

What happened next was a matter of considerable contention. According to the official police version, since there was no more room on the back seat of the car, Brindley sat partially on the lap of one of the prostitutes and partially on the informant's lap. Although handcuffed, Reyna somehow managed to reach over the informant, take Brindley's service revolver from the officer's holster, and shoot Brindley in the head and Officer L. E. Williams, who sat in the front seat, in the knee before finally being subdued. During the trial, the police claimed that Reyna made a confession verifying this version of the slaying. They quoted him as saying, "It was that damned liquor. Sometimes it makes me crazy." Los Angeles newspapers also claimed that Reyna was unrepentant for the killing, stating that his only regret was that he had not killed all three officers.[19]

In contrast, Reyna maintained that he acted in self-defense. He stated that Brindley and the other officers cursed him, called him a "dirty Mexican," and beat him over the head with their revolver butts. Out of anger, confusion, and fear for his life, Reyna grabbed Brindley's gun. The two men struggled and the gun went off twice, killing Brindley and injuring Officer Williams. Reyna claimed that he was not legally answerable for Brindley's death since he was only defending himself from obvious police brutality.[20]

Reyna's story hit a responsive chord among Los Angeles Mexicans. As indicated by the complaints brought before the police commission, Mexicans believed themselves to be victims of police brutality and discourteous conduct at the hands of LAPD officers. Reyna's case fell well within this pattern. Officer Brindley had made racial slurs against Reyna and had beaten him viciously simply because he was Mexican. But for the Mexican community Reyna symbolized not only Mexicans as victims, but also Mexicans as belligerents, struggling for justice against the blows and insults of a racist police force. Juan Reyna thus symbolized Mexican pride and determination to resist police abuse. The Spanish-language newspaper La Opinión noted that Reyna gained his strongest support from the Mexican community after police officers publicized his confession in which he allegedly stated that he killed Brindley because the officer had insulted him "as a Mexican, not as a man."[21]

Despite the mitigating circumstances, the Los Angeles district attorney decided to prosecute Reyna for first-degree murder. As the trial date neared, Reyna's friends in the Mexican community established a defense fund of over four thousand dollars to pay his legal expenses. A white defense attorney, C. V. Rude, was hired, and he fought vigorously on his client's behalf. At one point the debate between Rude and the prosecuting attorney, Deputy District Attorney Ugene Blalock, became so heated that after the hearing the two men got into a fist fight. Only the intervention of the court bailiff and the county clerk ended the altercation. The defense's effort paid off, at least initially. Despite an array of prosecution witnesses who tried to sway the jury to return a guilty verdict, Reyna made a credible witness, and on September 10, 1930, the judge declared a mistrial when the jury did not reach a verdict after more than five days of deliberation.[22]

The police department and the district attorney's office, however, refused to relent. They demanded and got another trial set for the end of October. Again, the prosecution paraded its array of witnesses. Again, Reyna's attorneys provided a vigorous defense, using Reyna himself as their star witness. This time the jury, in an apparent attempt to reach some form of compromise and after nearly seventy-two hours of deliberation, found Reyna guilty of manslaughter. The judge, noting the mitigating circumstances of the case, gave Reyna the minimal sentence of from one to ten years in the state penitentiary at San Quentin and recommended that he be considered for parole after his first year in prison.[23]

Had the Reyna case ended with his conviction and sentencing, it would already have had a dramatic impact on the Mexican community. Reyna symbolized resistance to racist police, and Los Angeles Mexicans responded to his plight through a community-wide effort that not only raised money for his defense but also sharpened the perception that the police were a problem for the community. That perception and the Reyna case in general were memorialized in "El Corrido a Juan Reyna," written by an anonymous poet at the time of Reyna's departure for San Quentin. The corrido told the story of Reyna's altercation with the LAPD, his shooting of Officer Brindley in defense of his honor and his life, and his subsequent trials, conviction, and incarceration. Proclaiming that Reyna had only acted in self-defense, the corrido concluded with words reminiscent of the Aurelio Pompa corrido:

I advise you countrymen
To avoid difficulties
With policemen who don't know
How to perform their duties as people of authority.[24]

The Reyna case did not end here, however. On the morning of May 3, 1931, Reyna's mother, Petra G. Vda. de Reyna, received a telegram from James B. Holohan, the warden at San Quentin prison, stating that Reyna was gravely ill from a self-inflicted wound. The next day she received another telegram from Holohan informing her that her son had died and tersely asking if she would claim the body or have her son buried at the state's expense. On May 5 Holohan sent her an official letter informing her that Reyna had died of self-inflicted wounds and stating that he was sending her Reyna's personal belongings, the amount of money left in his prison account, and her son's final letter. In none of his correspondence did Holohan so much as offer his condolences to the grieving mother.[25]

Juan Reyna's death shocked Los Angeles Mexicans. *La Opinión,* the city's main Spanish-language newspaper, reported the news of his death on May 5, a major Mexican holiday, with a front-page banner headline. For several days afterward, stories involving Reyna's death and his upcoming funeral continued to dominate *La Opinión*'s front page. On May 9 news stories and pictures of Reyna's funeral took over practically all of *La Opinión*'s front page as well as several inside pages.[26]

La Opinión's coverage of the Reyna case reflected public interest. Mexican organizations from throughout southern California, led by the remnants of the Confederación de Uniones Obreras Mexicanas and the Watts chapter of the magonista Partido Liberal Mexicano (PLM), held meetings, called press conferences, and made demands for investigations into the cause of Reyna's death. In fact, it was doubts regarding the official version of how Reyna died that created so much interest.

Warden Holohan's official explanation of Reyna's death contended that the young Mexican had committed suicide. The warden stated that Reyna's cell mates were awakened by his moaning early on the morning of May 3 and called prison guards. Recognizing the serious nature of Reyna's wound, prison officials immediately sent him to the prison hospital, where "everything possible was done for him," but he died that afternoon. The initial reports on the death indicate that there was some confusion regarding the type of weapon Reyna used to inflict the mortal wound on himself. The *Times* reported that he had stabbed himself in the heart with a file; the Mexican consul told *La Opinión* that the weapon had been a pallet knife; and the United Press wire service reported that Reyna killed himself with some kind of knife or dagger.[27]

From the very beginning, a large segment of the Mexican community doubted that Reyna had killed himself. To many it seemed more likely that someone in the law-enforcement community had concluded that a Mexican who had killed a white police officer could not go free after only one year in prison. In addition, suicide seemed to be out of character for Reyna. His mother, together with other relatives and friends, stated that Reyna in his letters from prison never demonstrated any depression, not to mention any desire to commit suicide. Instead, his letters were filled with hope for the future and the desire to return home to his four children. Indeed, just three weeks prior to his death he had written his eldest daughter, Sarita, apologizing for missing her eleventh birthday but promising to be on hand for her twelfth. His family in particular emphasized the fact that his suicide made no sense since he would be eligible for parole in only five months. Given the recommendation of the judge presiding at the second trial, Reyna and his family had every reason to believe that he would be home soon. "I expected my boy in five months," his mother cried, "instead I am going to receive his corpse."[28]

Los Angeles Mexicans had other reasons to doubt that Reyna had committed suicide. La Opinión reported that the autopsy performed by a local doctor found that Reyna's heart, lungs, esophagus, and most of his intestines had been removed before prison authorities shipped the body south. The doctor observed that this meant that he must have drunk some type of corrosive agent just before his death. The autopsy also showed that the trajectory of the weapon that allegedly killed Reyna was very odd. The stab wound appeared just to the left of his left nipple and followed a course from left to right into his chest. Since the weapon was not made available to the local pathologist, and since Reyna's heart and lungs were no longer in place, it was impossible to tell whether he actually died of the stabbing. The autopsy detected one other important abnormality. The stab wound that authorities alleged killed Reyna hit him with such force that it caved in one of his ribs. As one of the speakers at Reyna's burial later noted, it was practically impossible for a man, no matter how strong, to give himself such a fatal blow.[29]

The final factor that brought doubt into people's minds was the suicide letter that Reyna allegedly wrote shortly before his death. Warden Holohan's May 5 letter to Mrs. Reyna stated that her son's letter was enclosed. It was not. For the next several days, La Opinión publicly wondered why Reyna's mother had not yet received her son's final letter, noting that Reyna's body would arrive in Los Angeles before his letter. On May 8 La Opinión reported that San Quentin authorities had responded through the Mexican consul that the letter was delayed because the original was being photographed. That evening the Mexican consul received a hand-copied reproduction and shared it with La Opinión, which published it the next day. The Reyna family did not receive the original until the morning of May 9, the day of Reyna's funeral and six days after the alleged suicide. The delay in getting the letter raised the suspicion that Reyna had not written it himself but that officials had had it written to cover up Reyna's murder.[30]

People in the Mexican community continued to doubt the authenticity of the suicide letter once it arrived. Armando Flores of CUOM, for example, called for handwriting experts to examine the letter and determine if it was genuine. A *La Opinión* reporter asked Mrs. Reyna if she recognized her son's handwriting, to which she responded that her eyesight was so poor that she was unable to even read the letter. Although these questions were raised, the sources do not indicate whether anyone ever determined the authenticity of the alleged suicide letter.[31]

As important as the cause of Reyna's death was at the time, equally significant from a historical perspective was the way in which the case mobilized the Mexican community. Specifically, a wide range of community organizations came together to protest Reyna's death. These protests, in turn, raised a new awareness of official injustice against Los Angeles Mexicans and in general helped politicize the community.

One of the reasons for this mobilization was the fact that Reyna himself had belonged to the Watts chapter of the Partido Liberal Mexicano. The PLM in the early 1930s apparently was more of a leftist workingman's organization than the revolutionary movement that Ricardo Flores Magón had founded a quarter of a century earlier. The PLM took it upon itself to organize the community in the wake of its late member's death. The PLM worked closely with the Confederación de Uniones Obreras Mexicanas and other Mexican organizations on two specific projects that helped politicize the Mexican community on the law-enforcement issue: the organization of protest demonstrations showing the Mexican community's outrage over Reyna's death, and the call for investigations into the causes of his death.[32]

The PLM and CUOM were undoubtedly most successful in boosting public interest in the case. Since Reyna had been a PLM member, that organization requested and received permission from his family to hold the wake at the PLM meeting hall in Watts on Thursday, May 7. The PLM sent invitations to all Los Angeles County Mexican workers' organizations, asking them to send an honor guard for the wake. The magonistas also organized a cortege made up of Mexican workers to accompany the body from the Southern Pacific Railroad station in Watts to a mortuary, where the body would be examined, and then to the PLM hall. The PLM asked *La Opinión* to publicize the time and place of the body's arrival, the wake, the funeral services the next day, and the burial in order to maximize the number of people who attended these activities.[33]

As a result of the publicity, the PLM succeeded in drawing large numbers of people to these events. According to *La Opinión,* half the Mexican population of Watts met Reyna's body at the PLM hall when it arrived on May 7, and hundreds, perhaps even thousands, of people viewed the body that night and the following morning before the funeral. In addition, *La Opinión* reported that all the Mexican workers' and social organizations in the city sent representatives to act as honor guards at the wake. A particularly touching moment came when Reyna's mother first saw her son's body and practically threw herself upon it, covering his face with kisses. Another poignant moment occurred when Reyna's four young children first viewed their dead father. Since *La Opinión* faithfully reported all these events in vivid detail, the Mexican community could not help but have experienced anguish over the whole episode.[34]

The funeral itself was a massive affair. People were still lining up to join the procession at the PLM hall when the first cars arrived at the church. Altogether, a throng of over five thousand people converged on the Watts Methodist church where the religious services took place. The funeral procession from the church to the cemetery extended for over four miles. *La Opinión* claimed that the Reyna funeral was the largest funeral ever to take place in the western United States.[35]

Perhaps the most extraordinary aspect of the funeral, apart from the large number of people who attended, was its political nature. After the official service had ended at the cemetery, PLM and CUOM leaders transformed the religious assembly of five thousand people into a community meeting. Armando Flores of CUOM took the rostrum and proceeded to recite the specific facts of the Reyna case, stressing the fact that Reyna had been the victim of police brutality. He stated that LAPD officers had "unjustifiably apprehended" Reyna and that "he had been beaten and insulted with the greatest abuse that could be directed at a man." The police attacked Reyna, Flores explained, for the sole reason that he was a Mexican. "They insulted him as a Mexican," Flores told the crowd; "they berated his people; they taunted him, [touching] one of the most sensitive chords that could be touched on the citizen of any nation."[36]

Most of that afternoon's speeches, however, called on various official bodies to conduct a thorough and honest investigation into the causes of Reyna's death. "There are very powerful reasons," Armando Flores told the crowd, "to doubt that Juan killed himself." These reasons, which Flores went on to list, included the fact that Reyna would have been eligible for parole in only five months; the tone of his letters, which were never despondent but instead always optimistic; the bizarre findings of the local autopsy; and the fact that, even as he was being buried, his mother had not yet received the suicide letter. (Apparently Flores did not know that the letter had arrived that morning.) Flores therefore exhorted the crowd to write to Governor James Rolph and Attorney General W. S. Webb, "asking them to accede to the most just petition that the [Mexican] colony could make." A colony that, he added, as much for the crowd at hand as for the government officials, had furnished "its strength, its intelligence, its entire being for the enrichment of this large and hospitable country." "Let this case be investigated," Flores concluded; "let there be light, and if this was not a suicide, let whoever is responsible [for Reyna's death] be punished." *La Opinión* reported that the crowd responded to Flores's speech with loud applause.[37]

Some of the other speakers that day used the Reyna funeral to make an even more blatantly political statement. Luciano Falcón and his son Luciano Falcón Jr. of the PLM noted that their organization, as demonstrated in the Reyna case, always stood ready to do its duty for the Mexican colony. The PLM spokesmen, however, went beyond simply extolling the achievements of their own organization. They called for harmony and fraternity among all Mexicans living in the United States and for unity of purpose among the diverse Mexican organizations in Los Angeles. Such unity, the father-and-son team exclaimed, "is indispensable for the success and triumph of the [Mexican] colony."[38]

The community meeting that had begun early in the afternoon ended that evening at seven o'clock. Before it concluded, however, the assembly passed a resolution authorizing the PLM and CUOM to send messages to the president of Mexico and various other Mexican officials, to the governor and attorney general of California, and to all other officials who had an interest in the case, calling on them to launch an investigation into Reyna's death to discover whether "it was a suicide, or not." That evening the two organizations sent off their messages. In their telegram to Governor Rolph they stated that they suspected Reyna was in fact murdered out of "cruel vengeance" for the reduced sentence he received for the killing of Officer Brindley. In their telegram to President Pasqual Ortiz Rubio of Mexico, the PLM and CUOM asked him to use his influence with the United States government to have an investigation conducted. They also noted the racial factor involved in the case, stating that Reyna's death was an affront to the dignity of the Mexican people.[39]

Although the PLM and CUOM continued to try to organize the Mexican community around the issue of Reyna's death, American law-enforcement officials successfully avoided making any further investigations into the case. On May 22, 1931, in what he declared would be his last word on the subject, San Quentin warden James Holohan stated that he was surprised that anyone would even suspect that Reyna had died in any way other than by his own hand. Totally ignoring the evidence of Reyna's optimistic letters, Holohan claimed that the young Mexican had been melancholy and despondent, that he rarely smiled, and that he often missed his meals. "In addition," Holohan argued, "there is no reason for anyone to doubt our statements. Reyna sent his family a long goodbye letter explaining his actions." With this statement, Holohan ended the official inquiry into the death of Juan Reyna.[40]

PEDRO J. GONZALEZ AND CONTINUING PROTEST

The Pedro J. González case further politicized the Mexican community on the issue of discriminatory law-enforcement practices. González, unlike Aurelio Pompa and Juan Reyna, was a noted public figure in the Los Angeles Mexican community well before he ran afoul of the law. During the late 1920s he began hosting a popular Spanish-language program on one of the most respected radio stations in the city, KMPC. González formed his own musical group, Los Madrugados, which became a popular source of entertainment at both Mexican and white social functions. According to González, Los Madrugados even became a fashionable attraction at many gatherings of the city's white social and political elite. González, therefore, became well known, if not always well liked, by Los Angeles politicians.[41]

González alarmed government officials both because of his politics and because of his popularity. As a very young man, he had been a soldier in Pancho Villa's army during the Mexican Revolution. He was proud of this experience, and he embraced many of the more radical ideas that emanated from the revolution. Once in the United States, he became angry over the racism and discrimination that his Mexican compatriots faced every day. "I have [sic] very patriotic feelings and very revolutionary feelings when I saw the bad treatment given to Mexicans," González later recalled. Not only was he angered, he used his radio show to protest everything from police repression of Mexican labor unions to the deportation and repatriation campaigns of the Depression years. This political use of the airwaves and González's prominence within the Mexican community apparently frightened Los Angeles officials.[42]

González's popularity stemmed from the fact that he catered to the Mexican working class. During his radio show and at his personal appearances he played *ranchera* music, which was very popular among the poor immigrants who comprised the overwhelming majority of the Mexican population in Los Angeles. Especially during the Depression years, he developed a tremendous following among that segment of the community. So many people listened to González's early-morning show that on one occasion, two hours after he had announced that work was available at a construction site, hundreds of workers carrying picks and shovels arrived at the pickup point. The LAPD, fearing that this was the beginning of a Mexican insurrection, arrested all the workers and sent them off to jail.[43]

City officials' paranoia undoubtedly derived from the blatantly discriminatory employment practices that aimed to replace Mexican workers with American citizens, as well as from the deportation and repatriation drives of the Depression era. This paranoia was so great that local officials chose to interpret this particular incident as proof of González's influence over the Mexican population rather than as a sign of Mexicans' desperate desire to work. District Attorney Buron Fitts was the most vehement in his denunciations of González. Fitts asked the press, "What if this madman, troublesome as he is, and on top of that a Villista, a telegraphist for Villa, what if he starts telling all the Mexicans . . . to rise up with a bottle of gasoline, at a certain hour, and start burning all the Americans' houses. What an incredible conflict could develop just because of this despicable madman."[44]

Given this intense hostility, Fitts, with the cooperation of the LAPD and other government officials, sought to destroy González. First Fitts tried to have González's radio announcer's license revoked on the grounds that González had purposely lied on his application. When González proved this allegation wrong, local officials had him arrested for not sending his thirteen-year-old daughter to school. González's wife had been taken ill and a doctor had ordered her to stay in bed for two weeks. The couple decided to keep their daughter at home in order to help tend to the younger children. Upon hearing the entertainer's explanation, the judge dismissed the case. Local officials then charged González with kidnapping when two teenage girls were reported as missing.

On the day of the preliminary hearing, the two girls emerged and stated that they had gone to San Bernardino for a few days with their boyfriends. The judge angrily dismissed the charges against González. Two weeks later police again arrested González, this time for picking up underage girls and giving them rides in his car. For the third time, González went before the same judge and explained that the only times he had minors in his car were when he took his own daughter to school and they stopped to give some of her friends a ride. The judge again angrily dismissed the charges, stating that he did not want to see any more charges against González in his court.[45]

Having failed to destroy González on trumped-up charges, local officials conspired to frame the popular entertainer for allegedly raping a teenage girl. As a favor to a store owner who paid for commercials on his radio show, González encouraged listeners to vote for the store owner's stepdaughter, Dora Versus, as queen of the yearly Mexican Independence Day festivities. According to González, an embittered former employee of his, Rosa Mason, convinced Versus to go to a hotel room with her to meet some men. Mason also tried to lure González to the room, but he refused to go. Nevertheless, Mason testified that González had gone to the room and had sex with both Mason and the younger girl. Versus, in exchange for leniency from the district attorney's office for previous juvenile offenses, concurred. On the basis of this testimony, the district attorney's office obtained a conviction and a fifty-year prison sentence against González. After the trial, Dora Versus reneged and signed an affidavit stating that she never had sex with González. The judge, however, refused to accept the affidavit and upheld the conviction and sentence.[46]

All along, local authorities seemed more intent on getting González off the air than on sending him to prison. They offered him probation if he agreed to sign a confession that he had indeed had sex with the underage girl. As a self-confessed sex offender, González could be barred from radio and even deported to Mexico. González, however, refused to compromise and declined to sign the confession, and he was therefore sent to San Quentin to serve his sentence.[47]

Throughout his ordeal with law-enforcement authorities, González had the support of the Mexican community. Many Mexicans understood that González's prosecution was in fact a form of political persecution for the entertainer's outspoken defense of his countrymen's interests. Thus, his support was widespread and reflected a variety of concerns. Mexican Consul General Ricardo Hill worked to gain a fair trial for him. Fans of González's radio show formed defense committees to raise money for attorney fees and to help support his family while he was in prison. During the trial itself, his supporters filled the courtroom daily. After he had been convicted and sent to prison, he continued to receive support from the Mexican community. During the first months he spent at San Quentin, he received as many as twenty supportive letters a day, many of them containing money. His supporters also continued in their efforts to have him freed. Defense committees from as far away as San Francisco organized fund-raising activities to finance appeals, entreated the Mexican government to continue its work on González's behalf, and sent petitions to the governor, asking him to free the former entertainer.[48]

Finally, in 1940, these combined efforts bore fruit. The governor of California, succumbing to pressure from the Mexican government and the Los Angeles Mexican American community, paroled the popular entertainer after he had spent more than six years in the state penitentiary. The one stipulation was that González be immediately deported to Mexico. Years later, González remembered the scene when he arrived at Union Station in Los Angeles on his way to Mexico: "My wife was there. Everybody went to see me all day long; from 7:00 in the morning. I had guards; I had my guitar; everybody stopped to say hi, crying. Since I knew that I was leaving [the country], well, they put up their children to kiss me and they would give a dollar to the child and tell the child to give it to me. . . . There were tears. There was a moment when they asked me to sing a song. I said 'Sure, why not?' And the guard says 'Uh, uh. You can't sing.' 'So what are you going to do? Throw me in jail again? I just got out of there! Throw me wherever you want, but I'm going to sing.' I didn't struggle or anything but he had to open up. So I started to sing . . . and I satisfied them." Throughout the rest of his trip into exile González enjoyed similar demonstrations of support. Hundreds of his followers came to each station at which his train stopped on its way to Mexico, to bid farewell to Pedro J. González.[49]

EL CONGRESO AND ORGANIZED PROTEST

Each of these spectacular cases demonstrated not only the community's growing awareness of the law-enforcement problem, but also a growing determination to combat official discrimination. Each of these cases also reveals the increasing political sophistication, and the concomitant political power, of the Mexican American community. For not only did

Mexican Americans continue to struggle, those struggles resulted in increasing levels of success. In the Aurelio Pompa case Mexicans organized a massive campaign, only to see their efforts frustrated when Pompa was executed. In the Juan Reyna case Mexicans again mounted an impressive campaign to save one of their compatriots, and this time their efforts initially seemed to bear fruit when Reyna received a light sentence. In the end, of course, their success turned to frustration and outrage when Reyna died under extremely mysterious circumstances and officials refused to investigate his death. Mexicans' efforts on behalf of Pedro J. González took an opposite course. At first they seemed to fail, when authorities managed to imprison the popular and politically progressive entertainer on patently false charges. Through considerable and sustained efforts, however, the Mexican community eventually persuaded California officials to grant González his freedom.

This type of agitation, however, had its limitations. Despite the success in the González case, Mexican Americans were still reacting to instances of official misconduct rather than attempting to shape policies to put an end to discriminatory law-enforcement practices in the barrio. During the 1930s, however, community organizations began to take more proactive rather than simply reactive stands regarding police practices in their community. An early example came in 1932, when the Mexican Chamber of Commerce wrote to the police commission suggesting that a special "LATIN POLICE SQUAD be created in the east side section of Los Angeles, where the Mexican population is greatest." While the police commission never so much as bothered to reply to the letter, the communication does demonstrate Mexican business leaders' concern regarding relations between the community and the LAPD.[50]

Of much more significance was the leftist El Congreso de Pueblos que Hablan Español (the Congress of Spanish-Speaking People), which was organized in 1938. El Congreso's importance stems from its role as a bridge between earlier labor and radical activists who had come into conflict with the LAPD and those Mexican Americans who would emerge to fight police misconduct during the zoot-suit hysteria. El Congreso was the brainchild of the labor organizer Luisa Moreno. Allegedly a member of the Communist Party, Moreno had previously organized chapters of the United Cannery, Agricultural, Packing, and Allied Workers of America (UCAPAWA) in Los Angeles to take up some of the slack from Mexican consul Ricardo Hill's defunct Confederación de Union Campesinos y Obreros Mexicanos (see CUCOM section in chapter 5). Because of the broad nature of the discrimination faced by Spanish-speaking people in the United States, she decided to form El Congreso, an equally broad-based organization, to fight that discrimination. Significantly, in her early efforts to form El Congreso she had worked with activists in Los Angeles who had been supporters of Ricardo Flores Magón. The magonista influence was also evident in El Congreso's other main organizer, Josefina Fierro de Bright. A native of Mexico and only eighteen years of age in 1938, Fierro de Bright was raised within a family that had supported the magonistas and, according to the historian Mario García, was "socialized . . . in the teachings of Flores Magón." The magonistas had a long history of conflict with the LAPD (see chapter 4) and predisposed El Congreso to take strong stands against police misconduct.[51]

Both in its structure and in its ideology El Congreso resembled popular-front organizations affiliated with the Communist Party. A major tenet of the popular front was to incorporate a broad representation of the political spectrum within a single organization. The ensuing inclusiveness resulted in El Congreso acting as what the historian David Gutiérrez has called "a crucial training ground for a generation of Mexican American and immigrant political and social activists." The organization included the academician George Sánchez, labor organizer Bert Corona, and, most important, liberal Edward Quevedo, who was El Congreso president at the height of its power and influence. Quevedo and Josefina Fierro de Bright would play important leadership roles in the Mexican American community during the zoot-suit crisis.[52]

Politically, El Congreso represented a dramatic advance on previous Mexican American organizations in Los Angeles. As a broadly based civil rights confederation, it sought to improve the social and economic conditions of all Spanish-speaking people in the United States. Because of the ideological orientation of its members, it focused on labor issues. An even more important goal was fighting racial discrimination against Spanish-speaking people wherever it existed. While it sought to organize Spanish-speaking people living all across the country, El Congreso was a major political force only in Los Angeles, where it was the most important Mexican American civil rights organization of its time.[53]

With its emphasis on fighting racial discrimination, El Congreso almost naturally took up the issue of police misconduct. To a certain extent it addressed the issue by reacting to specific cases of police brutality. In August 1939, for example, it protested the killing of Florentino Sánchez by Los Angeles police officer Neal Davison. Davison, in what was now becoming a pattern, claimed that Sánchez had resisted arrest and that he shot the young Mexican American in self-defense. In protest, El Congreso organized over two thousand people to attend the Sánchez funeral and burial, at which El Congreso president Edward Quevedo gave the burial oration. El Congreso also called on the governor of California to launch an investigation into the killing, but before the governor responded, a local coroner's inquest found the police officer's actions justifiable and no further investigation took place. During this period El Congreso also protested the police killing of two other Mexican American boys. Members organized a demonstration of several hundred people in front of city hall and demanded that the officer involved be tried for murder. Again the officer was exonerated, but police officials did transfer him out of the Mexican section of the city.[54]

El Congreso also believed in taking more direct action to stop specific forms of police abuse. One such occasion involved police harassment of Mexican American waitresses. Apparently, officers were in the habit of arresting these young women for prostitution and then offering to release them for sexual favors. The waitresses complained to El Congreso and the organization responded by setting up surveillance of the young women. When the officers made their demands, El Congreso members made citizens' arrests. According to Josefina Fierro de Bright, this ended the exploitative practice.[55]

El Congreso was also the first Mexican American organization in Los Angeles to make general policy statements regarding the problem of police brutality against Mexican Americans. At its December 1939 convention, El Congreso adopted several resolutions directly addressing police misconduct in the barrio. For example, in order to stop police harassment of Mexican workers, it called for the elimination of all police red squads, or other units within police departments whose function it was to break strikes and disrupt labor unions. Apparently reflecting its concerns and protests regarding the Florentino Sánchez killing, El Congreso also resolved "that this Congress protests [and] condemns the brutal action of the police upon making arrests, in using violence while conducting prisoners to jail, and every case of refusal to allow the prisoner access to legal counsel." More generally, El Congreso called for "a campaign against police brutality." Finally, making a call that would be repeated in subsequent decades, El Congreso resolved "that a movement be initiated to amend the City Charter of Los Angeles, to place the police department under the control of the people." Apparently, El Congreso hoped to end police brutality by making officers directly accountable to the people they served.[56]

In order to show their determination to end police brutality, El Congreso members also requested and held regular meetings with the chief of police. Years later Josefina Fierro de Bright recalled that the meetings were anything but friendly. "They hated us and we hated them," she remembered.[57] Friendly or not, the very fact that these meetings took place indicates a profound change in the relationship between the LAPD and the Mexican American community. Just a few years earlier, Los Angeles police officials would not have deemed representatives of a Mexican American organization important enough to meet with. The growing assertiveness of the community during the 1930s, and especially the aggressive tactics of El Congreso, changed that. More important, a few years earlier Mexican American leaders would not have considered meeting with such a high-ranking public official. This growing confidence, however, merged with an increased awareness of police misconduct to create a determination to no longer tolerate abusive police practices. That determination, along with continued police malpractice, combined to create an era of intense hostility between the LAPD and the Mexican American community—a hostility that erupted into large-scale violence only a few years later.

CHAPTER 8

Crime Fighters and Zoot Suiters

The year 1938 brought a political upheaval to Los Angeles—an upheaval that included the beginning of a genuine reform movement within the LAPD as well as profound changes in the relationship between the department and the city's Mexican American population. This political revolution resulted from the efforts of the restaurateur and county grand juror Clifford E. Clinton and his reform organization, the Citizens' Independent Vice Investigating Committee (CIVIC). A broad coalition whose members ranged from moderate reformers to radical unionists, CIVIC had as its chief goal the rooting out of protected vice in Los Angeles and the political corruption that accompanied it.

In January 1938 a car bomb almost killed CIVIC investigator and informant Harry Raymond. Raymond had information that linked Joseph Shaw, Mayor Frank Shaw's brother and executive secretary, to underworld figures. The immediate suspect in the bombing was LAPD Captain Earl E. Kynette. Throughout the rest of the year, the investigation, trial, and conviction of Earl Kynette, along with the general subject of police corruption, dominated the local news. In the midst of the uproar, CIVIC organized a recall of Mayor Shaw, with the major issue being corruption within the LAPD. The election, which took place in September, resulted in Shaw's recall and the election of superior court judge Fletcher Bowron as the new mayor.[1]

On assuming office, Bowron set out to clean up city government. Several department managers lost their jobs, and a handful, including

Joseph Shaw, faced criminal prosecution. Rather than undergo a disciplinary investigation, Chief of Police James Davis and several other high-ranking LAPD officials resigned shortly after Bowron took office. Bowron also removed close to 100 city commissioners, including the entire Board of Police Commissioners. Bowron's new appointees to the police commission quickly set about reforming the department by removing corrupt officers from the force. The commission took advantage of City Charter Section 181, which gave it the power "to retire any officer eligible for pension 'for the good of the service.' " Within three months, the new commission used this device to retire 23 high-ranking officers. Over the next two years, the commission retired over 150 corrupt or incompetent men in this manner. The first sustained and authentic reform of the LAPD had begun.[2]

The Mexican American community underwent more subtle but equally significant changes during the late 1930s and early 1940s. To a casual observer, little seemed to have changed in the Mexican neighborhoods. Mexican Americans continued to suffer various forms of racial discrimination, including police abuse. On the other hand, shifts in the demography of the Mexican-ancestry population brought about profound changes in the way in which the community related to white society. Not only did the Mexican American population grow between 1930 and 1940, it changed from being primarily an immigrant population to being one composed of the American-born daughters and sons of immigrants. This Mexican American generation brought a new, more aggressive political orientation to the Mexican American community.

The ascent of the Mexican American generation also coincided with the emergence of the zoot-suiter phenomenon. Zoot suiters and the even more hostile pachucos were Mexican American youths who, to varying degrees, had become disaffected with and alienated from American society, from which they found themselves generally excluded. Zoot suiters displayed their disaffection by wearing distinctive clothes and through general patterns of behavior designed to offend those whom they saw as their oppressors—especially figures of authority such as the police. Such conduct put the zoot suiters on a collision course with the LAPD.

These changes occurred within the context of an even more profound economic and social transformation brought about by the effects of World War II in the western United States and in particular in Los Angeles. The West's abundant natural resources, its strategic location, and the resourcefulness and aggressiveness of its civic leaders led the federal government to place much of its war production in the region. Throughout the war years the West received at least $40 billion in federal funds, with possibly half going to California. The Los Angeles metropolitan area became a center for the aircraft, shipbuilding, and related industries. Crucial to attracting these federal dollars were the efforts of western civic leaders. As early as 1941, the Los Angeles Chamber of Commerce established a lobbying office in Washington, D.C., to maximize the city's share of defense plants. Throughout the war, gaining more war-related industry was a major priority for Mayor Fletcher Bowron and Governor Earl Warren. These efforts proved spectacularly successful: California's manufacturing output jumped from $2.8 million to $10.1 million in five years, and the gains made during the war provided the basis for the future prominence of the aerospace and electronics industries in that state.[3]

These economic gains in the West had profound social consequences. The most important was a rapid increase in population. During the war years 8 million Americans moved into the region, with 3.5 million migrating to California alone. According to one estimate, between 1940 and 1943 Los Angeles saw a population growth of close to 17 percent. These figures do not take into consideration the tens of thousands of servicemen who were temporarily stationed in the area. The larger population resulted in predictable social strains. Without a doubt the most important were the severe housing shortages that affected the community as a whole, but that had the greatest effect on minority groups, who, because of segregation, had fewer housing choices. The growth in population also strained municipal services. Traffic became even a greater problem, and city agencies had an increasingly difficult time keeping track of their growing clientele. The LAPD in particular suffered from the double problem of an increased population to serve and a decreased staff resulting from men joining the armed services.[4]

POLICE PROFESSIONALISM

The 1938 recall election and the subsequent purge of corrupt officers marked the beginning of the first sustained reform movement within the LAPD. This reform took place within a very specific context in the history of American police. By the late 1930s a distinctive model had come to dominate the ideology of police reform—namely, police professionalism. This model sought to raise the status of police work by making officers' primary function fighting crime, not merely reacting to it. It posited that police work, like other professions, required special skills and training that only the police themselves could define, develop, and implement. Although the LAPD did not fully adopt police profession-alism until the 1950s, the reform movement that began in 1938 and continued through the 1940s contained many aspects of the profession-alism model. The LAPD's adoption of police professionalism helped change the nature of the relationship between the department and the Mexican American community.

To understand police professionalism and the way it affected rela-tions between the LAPD and Mexican Americans, we must first examine the historical development of the police reform movement. The origins of the national police reform movement date back to the progressive era. The middle-class reformers of the turn of the century viewed the police as brutal, corrupt, lazy, and generally inefficient. They also per-ceived the control of the police departments by the urban political ma-chines as both the major source of corruption and the major obstacle to reform. As long as the machine dictated or even influenced the actions of individual officers, the police were bound to be corrupt, and worse yet for these middle-class reformers, inefficient.

To end corruption and make the police efficient, the progressives sought to remove the police from the control of local politicians, espe-cially the ward leaders. They sought to accomplish this goal by placing authority over the police in the hands of a strong and politically secure chief of police, who would be accountable only to the mayor. The chief or an official body within the department appointed by the chief had sole authority over all personnel issues, including promotions and ques-tions of discipline. In addition, the reformers quite consciously adopted a military model for the police. They perceived the American military as politically neutral and hoped to render the police equally apolitical. The reformers also called for specific programs, such as more stringent selection methods for police recruits, extensive training of those recruits, and better pay for police officers. But they stressed again and again that these reforms would be either impossible or fruitless if the police re-mained under the control of the urban machines.[5]

During the 1920s and 1930s, the leadership of the police reform movement moved from the middle-class urban elites to members of the law-enforcement community itself. The new reformers deemphasized the military model and emphasized a professional model. Their main goal was to use police professionalism to raise the status of the policing. The police professionals argued that police officers deserved the same respect, admiration, and control over their profession as doctors, lawyers, and teachers.[6]

Like the middle-class reformers before them, the professionals stressed that policing should be carried out impartially, without regard for political considerations. They therefore reemphasized the point that police departments must be free from the control of political machines. The new reformers took the theory one step further, however, arguing for total police independence from political control. If police had the same status as other professionals, they should be allowed to establish their own criteria for entering the profession, for gaining promotions, and for deeming which actions necessitated disciplinary action. Moreover, it was only with complete independence from political influence, especially in the areas of promotions and police discipline, that police administrators could ensure that officers would fairly and equitably enforce the law for all citizens. Thus, the police professionals conceded to the politicians only the power to continue to pass laws. The police kept for themselves the power to determine how the law would be enforced, both for the public and for themselves.[7]

The professionalism movement also endeavored to improve the efficiency of the police through administrative reforms. Especially during the Depression years of the 1930s, when municipal budgets were tight and efficiency important, police administrators experimented with a variety of reforms that sought to give citizens more policing for their tax dollars. The professionals, for example, advocated the centralization of command. This not only cut back on wasteful bureaucracy at the division or precinct level, it also greatly enhanced the power of the chief of police over issues of policy and practice. During the 1930s police administrators attempted to develop scientific systems for assigning officers. By studying the times and places where police made arrests, police administrators believed they could deploy their force in ways that most effectively deterred crime. Professionals also recommended moving officers from office work to patrol assignments and the increased use of radios and automobiles in police work.[8]

In addition to the principles of police autonomy and administrative efficiency, professionalism also brought a new orientation to the police function. One of the characteristics of police in the nineteenth century and early twentieth century was that they performed many roles that had nothing to do with enforcing the law or maintaining peace. Depending on the municipality, police did everything from cleaning the streets to investigating vegetable markets. The reformers of the progressive era added to the confusion by suggesting that police also help reform society. The progressives wanted the police to play preventive and rehabilitative roles in their interactions with juveniles and adults, particularly women, who committed minor offenses. These progressive reformers thus saw the police acting very much like social workers.[9]

The police-as-social-workers concept caused much debate within law-enforcement circles through the 1920s. The public concern over the perceived crime waves of the 1920s and 1930s, however, and, more important, the publicity campaign by J. Edgar Hoover, director of the Federal Bureau of Investigation, to promote the FBI, ended the preventive and rehabilitative function of police. The crime wave of the 1930s, like the crime wave of the 1920s, existed more in newspaper headlines and in the public's imagination than it did in reality. Nevertheless, Hoover shrewdly used the exploits of his agents in shooting down gangsters like John Dillinger and Bonnie and Clyde to show the FBI's importance in stemming the crime wave that "the Director" claimed was sweeping America. Hoover stressed the danger and threat that crime posed to American society, by using provocative rhetoric that labeled criminals "vermin of the worst type" and by developing the "Public Enemy" list. Hoover warned that only the FBI and, by extension, local police forces stood between civil society and the chaos of gangsterism. Hoover and other public officials therefore declared a "war on crime," and the ambitious director dedicated his men to doing nothing else besides winning that war. Municipal police officials grasped the significance of the tremendous rise in prestige, not to mention budget, that this type of publicity gained for the FBI, and from the 1930s onward police defined themselves strictly as crime fighters.[10]

Moreover, since the FBI declared itself to be the very epitome of the professional law-enforcement agency, police professionalism became synonymous with fighting crime. Because of the emphasis on the war on crime, the law-enforcement community came to stress specific programs that made fighting crime more efficient. Although many of the programs were long-held tenets of police professionalism, the FBI led the way in institutionalizing such reforms. Hoover, for example, established high standards in education and physical fitness for men wanting to join the bureau and paid high salaries to his agents to lessen the threat of corruption. The FBI also developed a highly sophisticated training program for its agents that, among other things, stressed the fair, impartial, and, most important, constitutional enforcement of the law. In

1934 the bureau extended its training program to the National Police Academy, which police officers from throughout the country attended and where they learned the FBI's latest "scientific" techniques for fighting crime. In fact, the use of scientific methods to catch criminals became one of the cornerstones of police professionalism. The National Police Academy promoted the use of the crime lab, fingerprinting, the lie detector, and other forms of advanced technology to track down criminals and gain convictions. The bureau and the academy also promoted expertise in the use of firearms, especially the machine gun, in the war against crime.[11]

The FBI also controlled the Uniform Crime Reports (UCR), which ostensibly measured the level of crime throughout the country. While the UCR contained all the defects of other crime statistics and more, the FBI used them as a public relations tool to lobby for more funding, not only for itself but also for local law-enforcement agencies. In addition, government leaders used the UCR to evaluate the effectiveness of policing in a given community or nationwide. Since fighting crime became the only gauge of police efficiency, the UCR statistics reemphasized the war-on-crime metaphor.[12]

An unforeseen but extremely significant outcome of the new crime-fighting orientation was a changed relationship between the police and the community. A new direction arose in which police changed from a responsive force to a preventive one. Throughout the nineteenth century and during the early twentieth century police made arrests and engaged in other law-enforcement activities primarily as a response to complaints from citizens. If police were to be on the front line of the war against crime, however, they needed to take a much more active role. They needed to prevent crime—not by trying to reform would-be law violators as the social-worker model had envisioned, but by aggressively confronting the "criminal elements" in society and through a show of force that convinced potential criminals that violation of the law brought swift and severe punishment. Henceforth, officers sallied forth in their new squad cars equipped with the latest communication devices to patrol neighborhoods that the arrest statistics and the time-place studies had identified as "high-crime areas." Moreover, since most Americans violated on a regular basis some law (liquor or traffic laws, for example), the emphasis on crime fighting created an "us against them" mentality within the law-enforcement community and put the police in conflict with the general population. Every time police gave out traffic citations or made arrests for violation of the sumptuary laws, they not only angered an otherwise law-abiding citizen, they provided further evidence for themselves that the population at large disregarded the law. The police thus became alienated from the society they were supposed to serve.

The war-on-crime metaphor also increased police officers' sensitivity to all forms of criticism, but especially to attacks on their authority. After all, in a theater of war, which, for the police, took the form of the streets of urban America, there can be only two sides, and police came to believe that critics who attacked them favored lawlessness and disorder. The police therefore reacted negatively to charges of police brutality and other forms of public criticism. This attitude, which the historian Robert Fogelson has labeled "occupational paranoia," merged with the professionalism principle of police autonomy to make officers not only unsympathetic toward, but practically invulnerable to, complaints of police misconduct. The professionalism model and its war-on-crime orientation thus strained the relationship between law enforcement and society in general. Because of the increased linkage between race and criminality, however, the model had its most deleterious impact on the minority communities.[13]

REFORMING THE LAPD

While the LAPD did not fully adopt the police-professionalism model until the 1950s, the reform movement that began in 1938 incorporated many professional principles, albeit not always in their pure form. On the crucial issue of police autonomy, for example, the LAPD had a mixed record during the 1940s. The first chief of police of the reform administration, Arthur Hohmann, agreed with Mayor Fletcher Bowron that corrupt officers must be removed from the force. The chief demanded, however, that any firings take place within the letter of the law as outlined in the city charter. When the chief insisted that charter provisions precluded the firing of 170 officers whom the mayor claimed were corrupt, Bowron removed Hohmann instead. Hohmann's successor, C. B. Horrall, proved more amenable to Bowron's wishes. While Horrall deferred to the mayor on specific issues that the mayor felt might embarrass his administration, Bowron in fact found less and less reason to interfere in the day-to-day running of the department. As a consequence, Horrall enjoyed a longer single term in office than any previous twentieth-century chief, thus furthering the autonomy and therefore the professionalization of the LAPD.[14]

Even more crucial to the concept of police autonomy was internal control over personnel matters. In order to ensure that officers enforced the law fairly and impartially, the proponents of police professionalism argued that officers had to know that they would be hired or fired, promoted or demoted solely on the basis of their performance as judged by professional standards rather than on the basis of any political considerations. By 1938 the statutory requirements for internal LAPD control of personnel matters already existed. From the progressive period onward, civil-service reforms had made hiring and promotion theoretically dependent on objective civil-service examinations. While prior to 1938 these provisions were ignored more often than they were enforced, they at least laid the foundation for a rational system of hiring and promotion.

More important, by 1938 the LAPD had managed to gain statutory control of all internal disciplinary decisions. In 1934, by a margin of only 175 out of close to 190,000 votes cast, the voters passed Proposition 12A, which amended Section 202 of the Los Angeles City Charter. As amended, Section 202 gave officers a vested right to their jobs and stated that they could not be removed from the force without due process. "Due process" meant that officers accused of major violations of discipline had the right to a public trial before a board of review made up of fellow officers. Only such a trial board could dismiss an officer from the force or mete out other severe penalties. The chief could lower trial-board penalties but could not raise them. The chief and other high-ranking officers could also impose minimal penalties for minor infractions as an administrative decision. Finally, in order to protect officers from subsequent reform administrations, the 1934 amendment to Section 202 set a one-year statute of limitations on all violations.[15]

By giving total control over internal discipline to the department, Section 202 essentially removed all external control over the actions of individual officers. Henceforth, only other officers would judge the appropriateness of an officer's conduct. Individual citizens with specific complaints, as well as more general critics of the LAPD, had to rely on the police to police themselves. Given the occupational paranoia of the police, trial boards and even police administrators were loath to sustain citizens' complaints against officers charged with brutality or other excesses of authority. Since Mexican Americans and African Americans particularly resented incidents of police brutality and other misconduct, Section 202 and the question of internal control over LAPD discipline became sources of chronic tension and mutual hostility between the department and the minority communities for decades to come.

The LAPD also adopted many of the less controversial administrative reforms contained in the professionalism model. Upon taking control of the department, for example, Chief Hohmann reinstituted the training program that had lapsed during the Shaw-Davis administration. The chief also initiated a total administrative reorganization of the department, whereby power was centralized in the hands of the chief by the creation of three organizational units under which all police activity took place. Hohmann ordered the deputy chiefs who headed these units to make any additional changes they deemed necessary on the basis of three criteria: efficiency, the latest advances in the field of police science, and current or local conditions. Hohmann also abolished many of the special squads, such as the red squad, and centralized many of the functions previously dispersed throughout the department.[16] This centralization of power in the hands of the chief ensured that officers would henceforth depend on the approval of their superiors rather than on elected officials or the general public.

While Hohmann eventually lost his job while trying to assert police autonomy, his successor, C. B. Horrall, maintained his predecessor's administrative reforms and came up with a few innovations of his own. In order to attract more qualified men, Horrall succeeded in raising salaries for police officers. Between 1939 and 1945 the basic salary for an entering police officer rose by more than 26 percent. More important, during this period officers' salaries became tied to the Jacobs salary-setting formula, whereby LAPD salaries came into line with salaries paid in private industry. In time, the Jacobs formula gave LAPD officers substantial yearly pay raises—raises that made these officers among the best-paid law-enforcement personnel in the nation. The early 1940s also saw the strengthening of both the civil service system for promotion and the pension system for officers. On the other hand, World War II saw the departure of many regular officers into military service. Their replacements were less qualified and not as well trained. Moreover, there were never enough of them, which meant that throughout the war years, the LAPD was understaffed. Nevertheless, by 1945, according to the historian Gerald Woods, "the department seemed well on the way to professional status."[17]

While reform politicians and LAPD administrators were pleased with the advances toward professionalism, the general public had a greater interest in two more specific issues: how the department dealt with internal corruption and whether the LAPD would continue to be the tool of local business interests in their fight against labor unionism. The department changed significantly in respect to both issues. Whether through forced or voluntary retirements, formal dismissals, or voluntary resignations, in the 1940s most of the corrupt officers who had plagued the force during the 1930s departed. Thus, until the last months of his tenure, Horrall managed to keep the LAPD free from major scandal.

More important, at least for the purposes of this study, the department ended its subservient relationship with the business community. One of the first acts of the reform administration was the abolition of the red squad, which had served the business community by suppressing labor unions. The break with local capitalists made good sense not only to the advocates of the professionalism model but also to the businessmen who, by the 1940s and 1950s, came to accept, or at least tolerate, organized labor. Henceforth, the LAPD played, officially at any rate, only a neutral role in labor disputes.

However, the break with the Chamber of Commerce and the Merchants and Manufacturers Association had significant consequences for the LAPD. Because of the department's antilabor activities, businessmen had been major supporters of the LAPD in its budgetary and other bureaucratic battles within city government throughout most of the first four decades of the century. With the LAPD no longer acting as its private union-busting force, the business community had less incentive to support the department politically. Moreover, the LAPD's former antilabor stance had alienated it from the Los Angeles working class. The department therefore found itself with a small political base within the city.

Woods has noted, however, two factors that in the post-Depression years helped the LAPD to develop a new constituency. First, by ceasing its antilabor activities, the department "remov[ed] an old source of conflict and violence, and bridg[ed] the chasm between the police and the white working class." Second, "the reported incidence of crimes committed by minority group members provided the white community with one rationale for supporting their local police."[18] The phenomenon that most dramatically raised the specter of lawless racial groups was the hysteria regarding an alleged Mexican American juvenile crime wave that swept the city in 1942 and 1943. That hysteria combined with police professionalism's war-on-crime orientation and the LAPD's need to develop a constituency among working-class whites to permanently label Mexican Americans a criminal element within the community.

MEXICAN AMERICANS IN WARTIME LOS ANGELES

The most important factor that led to the growing popular fear of Mexican Americans was the development of a decidedly rebellious and potentially hostile Mexican American youth culture. The symbols of this youthful rebellion were the zoot suits worn by many youths, the distinctive argot they spoke, and the general attitude they displayed that demonstrated both hostility toward and scorn for white society. Only a small fraction of Mexican American youths fully adopted this attitude and the lifestyle, known as *la vida loca* (the crazy life), that went with it. These youths came to be known as pachucos, and they were the group most likely to engage in criminal and other forms of antisocial behavior. On the other hand, contemporary observers noted that as many as 67 percent of Mexican American youths adopted at least some aspect of the zoot-suit costume.[19]

Among the factors that contributed to the emergence of the zoot suit were the significant demographic changes in the Mexican American population of Los Angeles. While it is clear that the Mexican American population in the city grew substantially between 1930 and 1940, the exact size of that growth is practically impossible to determine. The problem lies with the Census Bureau, which, in 1940, did not specifically count people of Mexican descent living in the United States. Instead, the bureau attempted to identify ethnicity through the concept of the "mother tongue," which the bureau defined as "the principal language spoken in the home in [the immigrant's] earliest childhood." Not everyone who claimed Spanish as a mother tongue was of Mexican descent, and not all people of Mexican descent used Spanish in the way defined by the Census Bureau. Consequently, scholars believe that the approximations taken from the census reports seriously underestimate the size of the Mexican American population of Los Angeles.[20]

Probably the best estimates of the size of the Mexican population are based on local sources. Most of these sources place the size of that population for the city of Los Angeles during the war years at approximately 133,000, or 8.06 percent of the total population. While this figure shows an increase from the official 1930 census report of 97,000, it is still significantly lower than the 190,000 estimate for 1930 arrived at by Chicano scholars. Even considering the deportations and repatriations of the Depression era, most contemporary observers estimate that the Los Angeles Mexican American population was substantially higher in 1940 than it had been a decade earlier.[21]

The census reports are, however, reliable in illustrating another important change in the Mexican American population. By the 1940s most Mexican Americans were no longer foreign-born immigrants. Seventy-seven percent of people of Mexican descent who listed Spanish as their mother tongue were born in the United States, either to foreign- or native-born parents. As United States citizens, these Mexican Americans expected all the rights and privileges of American citizenship. Instead, they found themselves the victims of racial discrimination in many of their interactions with white society. While Mexican Americans in general found this situation reprehensible, the teenage second-generation children of the immigrants seemed to have found their status as second-class citizens unacceptable.[22]

While demographic changes created a population base that allowed a youth rebellion to flourish, the phenomenon resulted primarily from the racism, discrimination, and extreme poverty that people of Mexican descent faced in the southwestern United States. Economic and social indicators confirmed that Mexican Americans comprised the most destitute racial group in the Los Angeles area during the early 1940s. Mexican Americans still found employment only in the lowest paying, most menial jobs. Contemporary observers agreed that race was the primary cause of Mexican Americans' continued subordination. According to a confidential report by the Office of War Information, Mexican Americans suffered from employment discrimination because they were "racially different." Guy T. Nunn, the Los Angeles field representative for the Minority Group Service of the War Manpower Commission, reported that because Los Angeles Mexican Americans continued to suffer from what he called "caste discrimination" and "color discrimination," they were "confined to unskilled or semi-skilled employment, characterized by a high degree of seasonality." Other observers reported that anti-Mexican discrimination was equal to, or even exceeded, antiblack discrimination in the South. The Office of War Information, for example, equated discrimination against Mexican Americans with Jim Crowism and noted "that in some portions of the Southwest the discrimination against the Spanish-speaking people is greater than that practiced against Negroes."[23]

Captain Edward Duran Ayres of the Los Angeles County Sheriff's Department agreed in his infamous report on Mexican American criminality, noting that "Mexicans . . . are restricted in the main to only certain kinds of labor and that being the lowest paid." Ayres also maintained that discrimination prevented Mexican Americans from joining many unions, which barred them from well-paying jobs. In the early years of World War II, Mexican Americans were also effectively prevented from working in the defense industry. Part of the reason lay with federal regulations intended to decrease the risk of sabotage by reserving certain sensitive types of defense work for American citizens. Apparently, employers believed it safer not to hire anyone who looked Mexican than risk hiring a noncitizen. Equally important, however, was blatant discrimination. As one observer commented, "Americans simply will not work with Mexicans"; and a personnel manager at a southern California airplane plant commented that he would be glad to hire Mexican Americans as long as they were not "too racial—too dark."[24]

These forms of discrimination resulted in low incomes for Mexican American families. The Los Angeles County Coordinating Council reported that in 1941 Mexican Americans had a yearly median family income of only $790—more than 29 percent lower "than the minimum required for decent food and housing for the average family of five persons." As a consequence, Mexican Americans comprised more than 23 percent of the relief cases in Los Angeles County.[25]

This poverty also resulted in a variety of social conditions that made life harsh for Mexican American youths. Contemporary observers generally acknowledged that Mexicans lived in the most dilapidated housing stock in Los Angeles. The Los Angeles County Coordinating Council found that "every investigation or survey of housing in Los Angeles develops again the fact that the worse problems are among the Mexican population." Another student of the subject reported, "Generally, the Mexican is found in the blighted areas of lowest rent and lowest assessed value of properties, areas lacking in sanitary facilities, areas of high delinquency, and areas in which health conditions are relatively poor." While low income precluded most Mexican Americans from moving into better housing, racist attitudes prevented even those of greater means from living under improved conditions. In 1943, for example, white neighbors went to court to prove that Mexicans were "dirty, noisy and lawless" in order to prevent Alex Bernal and his family from moving into the Los Angeles suburb of Fullerton.[26]

In addition, while they had experienced improvements in the previous decade, Mexican Americans continued to suffer from poor health. According to the Los Angeles County Tuberculosis Association, the death rate from tuberculosis for "Latin-Americans" dropped from 326.4 per 100,000 in 1930 to 182.5 in 1940, and to 84 in 1944. In contrast, the death rate per 100,000 for whites was 73.8 in 1930, 42.7 in 1940, and 45 in 1944. The infant mortality rate for Los Angeles Mexican Americans, again despite improvement, continued to be higher than for whites. In 1923 the infant mortality for "Latin-Americans" was a staggering 250.6 per 1,000; in 1930 the rate dropped to 106.6, and in 1944 it stood at 36.2. For whites, the infant mortality rate also dropped, from 80.5 per 1,000 in 1923 to 46.3 in 1930, and to 32.3 in 1944. The major causes of death for Mexican American babies were respiratory diseases, gastroenteritis, and significantly, malnutrition.[27]

Mexican Americans, especially youths, suffered from blatant racial discrimination in a variety of other areas. Aside from bias in hiring, the most destructive form of discrimination came in the area of education. Los Angeles city school officials placed many Mexican American children in special segregated "Mexican schools." The curriculum in these schools emphasized vocational instruction and Americanization at the expense of academic course work. While not segregated by law, housing segregation and the gerrymandering of districts forced many children into these separate schools. School officials also used Mexican Americans' alleged lack of English proficiency as an excuse to segregate them. According to the historian Mario García, the prevalence of the Mexican schools resulted in children suffering from "serious cultural alienation" and "limited occupational opportunity."[28]

In addition, whether in the special Mexican schools or in mainstream schools, Mexican American children had to endure the racist attitudes and actions of southern California school officials, from superintendents to classroom teachers. These attitudes usually involved the educators' assumptions regarding Mexican American students' initiative, personal habits, and even innate intelligence. One school official, for example, stated that Mexican Americans were "lazy, have no ambition and won't take advantage of opportunities offered them." Another superintendent claimed that "social differences" existed between Mexican Americans and whites, in that he found more "undesirable behavior patterns" and "lower moral standards" among Mexican American children than among whites. In 1946 still another superintendent attempted to justify continued segregation by asserting first that Mexican Americans constituted a "distinct and therefore 'inferior' race" and later by claiming "that Mexican children were 'dirty'; that they had lice and impetigo; that their hands, face, neck, and ears were often unwashed; and that, generally speaking, they were 'inferior' to the other students in point of personal hygiene." One Los Angeles teacher returning from a workshop entitled "The Education of Mexican and Spanish-Speaking Pupils" summed it all up very neatly: "I've had a very entertaining experience," she said, "but as far as I am concerned, they are still dirty, stupid and dumb."[29]

Such attitudes translated into destructive administrative and classroom practices. The Los Angeles School District, for example, underfunded the Mexican schools, not providing such basic facilities as cafeterias, playgrounds, and auditoriums. Moreover, school administrators used assignments to the Mexican schools as punishment for unruly teachers, often sending teachers with "personality problems" to those schools. As one administrator described the situation, "There isn't a teacher in *that* school who could be kept in the Anglo school. The parents wouldn't stand for it. Mexicans don't care"[30] (emphasis in original).

Mexican American children endured the manifestations of these racist attitudes in the classroom. School officials, for example, generally prohibited Mexican American children from speaking Spanish. The penalties for violation of this rule were often severe, including corporal punishment. According to the War Manpower Commission representative Guy T. Nunn, some teachers even attempted "to impress a feeling of inferiority on Mexican students." Many teachers also had extremely low expectations of Mexican American children. "You can't force these children into the Anglo-Saxon mold or pattern of schooling," one teacher stated. "They are different—they are elemental in their conception of things. They have different temperaments."[31]

These attitudes led directly to the development of a special curriculum for Mexican American children that later placed them at a competitive disadvantage. "If you teach them attitudes and responses and how to be good citizens, how to wash and iron and scrub and bake, that's all you need to do," an elementary school principal explained. "Why teach them to read and write and spell? Why worry about it . . . they'll only pick beets anyway." Other educators developed more callous methods for dealing with overachieving Mexican American students. The head of a high school business department, for example, stated, "I have no problems with the Mexicans. I take care that the first few days' work is so difficult and involved that they become discouraged and quit." Similarly, a local high school principal revealed his rather simple technique: "We just see that none of them get to the tenth grade."[32]

These practices proved disastrous for large numbers of Mexican

American children. Many, but especially those from the poorer families, performed so poorly that school officials placed them in special contin- uation schools where, according to the sociologist Joan Moore, "they could enjoy themselves without being bothered too much by academic requirements." Many others, frustrated and angry, simply quit school.[33]

Mexican American youths also suffered from various other forms of discrimination, especially in public places. Local officials, for example, prohibited Mexican Americans from using particular parks and public pools except on certain days of the week or month. Typically, a sign at a pool read "Tuesdays reserved for Negroes and Mexicans"—Tuesday being the day before workers drained and cleaned the pool. Some the- aters seated Mexican Americans only in certain sections, and some res- taurants, dance halls, and other amusement spots refused them admit- tance at all.[34]

Even the social-service agencies designed to assist citizens and pro- mote the war effort discriminated against Mexican Americans. Accord- ing to Guy Nunn, the activities of the Civilian Defense, Red Cross, War Bonds office, Office of Price Administration Consumer Division, and Office of Defense Health and Welfare Service "have persistently been characterized by discrimination and neglect in Spanish-speaking dis- tricts." "Only the draft," Nunn concluded, "has to date shown no bias against Mexicans."[35]

In the early 1940s Los Angeles Mexican Americans were beginning to respond politically to these forms of discrimination. The most effec- tive Mexican American political organization of the period was the left- ist El Congreso de Pueblos que Hablan Español. As noted in chapter 7, this group, in collaboration with Industrial Union Council unions with large Mexican American memberships, took a leadership role in artic- ulating Mexican American concerns to city officials. During the early days of the Bowron administration, city officials had at least given El Congreso representatives a forum in which to state their grievances. As the Republican Bowron became more secure in his position, he became increasingly hostile to the more radical segments of the coalition that put him in office and chose to ignore El Congreso. Moreover, the United States' entry into World War II as an ally of the Soviet Union weakened El Congreso's resolve to raise issues such as discrimination that might weaken the unity necessary for the war effort.

Prior to the war, more conservative Mexican American groups were generally ineffective in Los Angeles. The League of United Latin Amer- ican Citizens (LULAC), the largest Mexican American organization in the nation, had focused its efforts in Texas and would not be a factor in southern California until the postwar period. More important in Los Angeles was an organization named the Mexican American Movement (MAM), which in the late 1930s attracted a grouping of upwardly mobile high school students. That grouping continued through college but disbanded after the individuals involved became professionals. Through its newspaper, the *Mexican Voice,* MAM focused on uplifting Mexican American youth by promoting education, general self-improvement, and the adoption of an American identity without abandoning their Mexican heritage. For the most part, MAM was highly critical of the zoot-suiter fad. For this reason, and because in its early years MAM eschewed politics, it had little impact on the debate regarding relations between the police and Mexican Americans during the war years.[36]

MEXICAN AMERICAN–LAPD RELATIONS

While various forms of public humiliation served to remind Mexican American youths of their inferior position in American society and to embitter many, perhaps no other form of discrimination created more anger in the Mexican American community than the mistreatment its members received from police. The police practices that most angered Mexican Americans included verbal abuse, sexual harassment, indiscriminate searches, unwarranted arrests, and, most important, excessive use of force or police brutality. It should be remembered that while these practices were pervasive within the LAPD, they were for the most part the consequence of individual officers' prejudices rather than of departmental policy.

Probably the most common type of police misconduct was verbal abuse, in particular the use of racial slurs. The future United States Congressman Edward R. Roybal, who grew up in the barrios of East Los Angeles, stated that Los Angeles police officers regularly referred to Mexican Americans as "dirty Mexicans" or "cholos." The attorney Manuel Ruiz Jr. recalled an incident that may have been typical of interactions between the police and Mexican Americans except for the way it ended. Ruiz remembered that as a young lawyer he was apprehended by a big, burly police officer for jaywalking. According to Ruiz, the officer made racial slurs and would have taken him off to jail had Ruiz not impressed upon the officer that as an attorney he knew how to defend himself legally.[37]

Sometimes officers abused their authority if they believed that Mexican Americans were stepping out of their place or putting on airs. LAPD officers, for example, regularly stopped and arrested Mexican American youths for going into white sections of the city. When a factory manager went to a police station to protest the unwarranted arrest of two of his Mexican American employees, the desk officer told him that it was departmental policy to keep Mexicans and blacks out of Hollywood. "They've got to stay in their own neighborhoods, where they belong," he was told. Other Mexican Americans reported that officers would frequently tell them, "You're way out of your district" or "you don't belong in this part of town."[38]

In a similar vein, future youth worker Henry Marín remembered an early encounter with LAPD officers in which the officers refused to believe that a Mexican could legitimately own an expensive car. Marín was driving his new 1938 Plymouth through downtown Los Angeles when an LAPD squad car pulled him over. When Marín asked the officer what the trouble was, the officer responded, "You are the trouble," and ordered him out of the car. As Marín got out of the car, the officer punched him in the stomach and demanded to know where he got the car. Marín replied that the car belonged to him, and that he had bought it with his own money. The officer then asked Marín if he had obtained the money by "pushing dope." When Marín explained that he had a full-time job, the officer let him go.[39]

The sexual harassment of Mexican American women by police officers also angered the community. In chapter 7, I noted that during the late 1930s El Congreso brought an end to the practice of officers arresting Mexican American women and demanding sexual favors. During the 1940s, Edward Roybal recalled that male officers often hand-searched women's bodies, allegedly looking for weapons or drugs. He also remembered that Mexican American families so feared the LAPD that they counseled their daughters never to accept a ride from a police officer. Roybal's parents, for example, told his sisters that if they got into trouble, they should walk home rather than ask a police officer for assistance. Thus, even the more upwardly mobile and socially integrated Mexican American families like the Roybals felt great distrust of and hostility toward the LAPD.[40]

The LAPD practice of conducting arbitrary "field interrogations" of Mexican Americans also caused anger in the community. In a typical field interrogation, officers would stop a car with Mexican American passengers, order everyone out, and then search the car and the people for some kind of contraband. Anyone of Mexican descent was subject to these searches but the police seem to have focused on the youths. Roybal remembered that in 1940, while driving home from a dance with his date, he was pulled over by an LAPD squad car. The officers ordered him to stand spread-eagled against the car in order to search him. During the search the officers stuck their hands in his pockets and made a series of racial slurs. Roybal recalled that he felt "degraded" by the experience and that he was sure he did not make a "hit" with his date. (Evidently, he was wrong on the last count: about a year later he married Lucille, the young woman he had been with that night.)[41]

Not all encounters with the LAPD ended so benignly, however. Large numbers of Mexican American youths found themselves arrested for no other reason than the fact that they were of Mexican descent. Police, for example, regularly arrested whole groups of Mexican American juveniles who congregated on street corners or on someone's front lawn and charged them with vagrancy, curfew violation, or suspicion of some other crime. The police held them for seventy-two hours and, if the suspicions were unfounded, then let them go. In this manner, Mexican American youths began compiling extensive arrest records from a very early age—in some cases as early as eleven and twelve years of age—and learned to take precautions to avoid encounters with the police. As Pete Vásquez, a young man of draft age, explained: "If the cops catch you on the street after 8 o'clock, usually they run you in—or rough you up, anyway. If you look like a Mexican you just better stay off the street, that's all."[42]

Apparently, officers viewed such actions as a form of crime control. "If a bunch of kids—say eight or ten—are standing around on the corner," explained an official of the Los Angeles County Sheriff's Department, "you are going to get trouble. If we see boys on the corner who have been in trouble, we know they are plotting more trouble, and if you want to know how I feel about it—I get mad at the officers for not picking up those kids." Police defined having "been in trouble" as having been arrested in the past, and many youths developed extensive arrest records without ever having been convicted of a crime. The author Beatrice Griffith, for example, tells of one eighteen-year-old boy who "had been arrested on suspicion seventeen times, and beaten up nine times . . . and yet had never had a conviction or even appeared in court."[43]

Officers also regularly arrested any Mexican American in the vicinity of a crime or any who vaguely resembled a suspect. This practice led to many unjust arrests, and Mexican Americans protested accordingly. Dolores Figueroa, a Mexican American woman who worked in a defense plant, wrote an angry letter to Mayor Fletcher Bowron protesting the unwarranted arrest of two of her Mexican American coworkers. According to Figueroa, LAPD officers arrested Rafael Sabala and Raymond Placencia while the two young men were in a record store, "just because they were Mexicans." Apparently, a crime had been committed in the vicinity and the two boys fit the general description in that they were both of Mexican descent. Figueroa demanded to know from Bowron if her own two young sons, ages eight and four at the time, would also have to "grow up and be thrown around like that." She told Bowron that she did not "want to even think that [her] boys will be kicked and slapped by a policeman without any cause just because they are Mexicans and make 'good suspects.' " She also noted that Raymond Placencia now even refused to go to the grocery store for fear of being arrested and missing work. Figueroa concluded that "something should be done and done quickly, otherwise the morale of these boys will be ruined."[44]

The unwarranted arrests had severely negative effects on Mexican American youths. For example, officers unjustly arrested on suspicion of robbery one young Mexican American who was sitting in a car waiting for a friend. Although police eventually set him free without filing charges, he and his family suffered serious consequences as a result of the arrest. "My mother had to mortgage the furniture to get enough money to bail me out—and I lost my job 'cause I was in jail for seventy-two hours. It's like that with the police—they arrest you, beat you up, hold you three days—and you lose your job." In addition to the personal consequences of these arrests, the wholesale overarresting of Mexican American youth inflated the arrest statistics that police used to determine crime rates in a given population, giving law enforcement more evidence that Mexican Americans were criminally inclined. The myth of Mexican American criminality became a self-fulfilling prophecy.[45]

The police practice that most angered the Mexican American community was the excessive use of force. While during the war years Mexican Americans filed relatively fewer official complaints with the police commission than they had in previous years, it seems clear that the early 1940s saw a dramatic rise in the incidence of LAPD brutality directed against Mexican Americans, especially youths. Henry Marín remembers that LAPD officers treated youths whom they suspected of being gang members "real bad." According to Marín, such youths, if arrested, could count on police beating them during interrogations.[46]

Typically, boys whom officers felt had failed to show proper respect for authority and deference to police officers could expect violent reactions. José "Chepe" Ruiz, for example, one of the defendants in the Sleepy Lagoon case, had an all-too-typical encounter with LAPD officers that ended in violence. Ruiz was playing pool when two officers walked into the establishment searching for suspects in the theft of a car. The officers began to search Ruiz, who stated he had nothing on him. The officer then pushed Ruiz; when the boy objected, the officer slugged Ruiz in the face. Ruiz swung back, and in the ensuing altercation one of the officers hit Ruiz on the head with the butt of a gun, opening a large and bloody gash. After Ruiz fell to the floor one of the officers handcuffed him, saying that he ought to kill the young man. The officers then dragged Ruiz into a squad car along with several of his friends. When the officers realized that he was bleeding onto the car, they began hitting him again. The beating inside the squad car ended only when one of Ruiz's friends put a handkerchief over the head wound and stopped the bleeding. After they arrived at the station house, officers continued to beat Ruiz in an effort either to extract a confession for the car theft or to induce Ruiz to name someone else. Eventually Ruiz went on trial for grand theft auto. His attorney, Ben Van Tress, won an acquittal and filed a formal protest before the police commission charging police brutality. The police commission, however, accepted Chief Horrall's report that officers used "no more force than was necessary" and that, anyway, "the witnesses mentioned by Attorney Van Tress all have felony records."[47]

Sometimes the police violence seemed unprovoked or a consequence of the officer's prejudice. Angel Padilla, another of the Sleepy Lagoon defendants, also had an earlier violent encounter with police officers. In this particular case, he stated that the police "beat the shit out of me. They hit me in the teeth and ribs and behind, and they kicked me below the belt. I couldn't get out of bed for a week." At the time of his arrest in the Sleepy Lagoon case, Padilla remembered an officer saying: "You Mexicans think you're smart: you guys never fight fair. . . . We ought to shoot every Mexican dog like you."[48]

Mexican American youths could expect no better treatment from Mexican American officers, who seemed to believe that they knew best how to deal with the zoot suiters. "Well, you know in Mexico we really had the answer to all this trouble we have with these kids," one high-ranking Mexican American administrator in the sheriff's department stated. "There they used a big black snake whip and really got results."

Equally important must have been the need of many Mexican American officers to distance themselves from the antisocial behavior of the pachucos and to prove to their fellow officers that they could be just as tough on their compatriots as anyone else.[49]

Whatever the reasons, Mexican American officers seemed to be particularly cruel in their treatment of Mexican American youths. One example comes from the experience of an army private home on leave. On his way to the store he was stopped by two officers, one of them Mexican American, who questioned him and demanded to see his papers. Despite protesting that only the military police had authority over him, the young serviceman complied with the officers' request. On his way back home from the store, the same two officers again stopped him and demanded to see his papers. This time the private refused, and for his insolence he received such a savage beating at the hands of the Mexican American officer that he suffered a fractured skull and had to be discharged from the army. Later he recalled that "the one cop wasn't so bad. He told him to let me alone—it was the Mexican cop that did the beating."[50]

While not every Mexican American youth who came in contact with the LAPD received this kind of beating, the practice occurred often enough to become a political issue in the community. Part of the concern arose from the growing awareness within the community that Mexican Americans in general, but particularly youths, were the victims of police abuse. Edward Roybal stated that the LAPD was "anti-Mexican" during this period. Similarly, Manuel Ruiz Jr., who probably had the closest ties to city hall of any Mexican American spokesperson, recalled that police considered Mexican Americans to be "non-American" and therefore "mistrusted" them. According to Ruiz, this mistrust and the fact that Mexican Americans lived in segregated sections of the city made it possible for the department to overpolice the community and generally keep Mexican Americans under a high level of surveillance.[51]

The intensity of the police presence in the barrios and their anti-Mexican attitudes and practices made the LAPD an important political issue in the Mexican American community. According to Roybal, the issue of the LAPD "became a subject matter of great concern" to Los Angeles Mexican Americans. People saw police abuse on a daily basis, and many came to fear and even hate LAPD officers. Consequently, according to Roybal, ending police abuse became the "uppermost" political issue in the minds of Mexican Americans during the war years.[52]

ZOOT SUITERS

The extreme poverty in which they lived, the pervasive discrimination they faced, and the police abuse and brutality they endured eventually resulted in a segment of Mexican American youth becoming alienated from and rebelling against American society. This rebellion, however, did not generally manifest itself in direct challenges to constituted authority. Rather, Mexican American youth, in varying degrees, engaged in what Joan Moore calls a "symbolic challenge to the world" through the zoot-suit style and the youth subculture that accompanied it.[53]

The zoot suit, or drapes, as the boys who wore it liked to call the outfit, can generally be described as an exercise in excess, a composition in conspicuous consumption. It consisted of very baggy pants that fit very high on the waist (in the most extreme cases, all the way to the armpits), deep "reat" pleats, and extremely narrow cuffs. The coat had wide lapels and shoulder pads that resembled epaulets and was sometimes so long it reached the knees. Accessories to the zoot suit included a wide-rimmed "pancake" hat, long watch chains, and thick-soled shoes. The female equivalent to the zoot suiters, the "cholitas," also wore distinctive, if not as outlandish, clothes. Their outfits consisted of either flared or tight short skirts, tight sweaters, and distinct styles of earrings and makeup. Zoot suiters and cholitas also wore distinguishing hair styles: the boys wore their hair long and combed it in a ducktail, and the girls stacked their hair high on their heads in a pompadour. In addition to wearing distinctive dress, some Mexican American youths, as noted earlier, spoke in an argot called Caló. The use of Caló, which was a derivative of a fifteenth-century Iberian Gypsy dialect, not only made their talk incomprehensible to both their Spanish-speaking elders and white English-speaking authority figures, it also intensified pachucos' sense of uniqueness and generational solidarity.[54] Mexican American youths who adopted the zoot suit left practically no record regarding their motives. On a conscious level for many, perhaps for most, the zoot suit was nothing more than a fad—a stylish way of dressing that appealed to them for reasons they probably did not contemplate, much less articulate. Nevertheless, even the most naive zoot suiters must have been aware of the hostility their dress and style aroused in the general public. How then do we understand the zoot-suit phenomenon?

The work of Dick Hebdige in studying the Rastafarians, punks, and other working-class British youth subcultures of the 1960s, 1970s, and 1980s has been useful for gaining an understanding of the zoot suiters.

The point that Hebdige makes that is most important here is that sub-cultures need not be overtly political—they need not have an articulated agenda for social change or a methodology for reform—to be oppositional. They can demonstrate their opposition to prevailing structures through symbols, through style as a sign of their discontent with the dominant culture. Thus, the purpose of the punks and other working-class groups was to challenge the hegemonic structure that maintained them in an exploited, subordinate position in society. The point of the subculture was to establish, at least in a superficial way, an identity that was antithetic to the values of the dominant culture. The punks, for example, donned their outlandish style (safety-pin body piercing, sa-domasochistic bondage paraphernalia, vulgar language, and so on) to realize "in a deliberate and willful fashion the direst predictions of the most scathing social critics." The punks, however, did not issue their challenge directly. Instead, their challenge was "expressed obliquely, in style. The objections [were] lodged, the contradictions displayed . . . at the profoundly superficial level, at the level of signs." Thus, Hebdige quotes social critic Umberto Eco in characterizing the punk style as a form of "semiotic guerrilla warfare" to illustrate the subversive nature of the phenomenon.[55]

Hebdige also notes that not all members of the subculture bring the same level of awareness to the significance of the style, or commitment to a total immersion in the subculture. Generally, there is a split between the hangers-on and the " 'authentic' people" who consciously make a statement through their lifestyle, between the part-timers and those whose identity is totally defined by the subculture. Despite these variations, for the subculture to gain any significant numbers of adherents "it must say the right things in the right way at the right time. It must anticipate or encapsulate a mood, a moment. It must embody a sensibility."[56]

That the zoot suiters antedated Hebdige's British subcultures by several decades does not diminish the appropriateness of the comparison. Like the lifestyle of Jamaican Rastafarians living in postwar England, the whole point of the zoot-suit style was for Mexican American youth to reciprocate the rejection they experienced from white society. That some youths wore only the pegged pants or wore the outfit only on weekends, while others were full-fledged and full-time pachucos, corresponds to Hebdige's distinction between authentic punks and part-timers. The fact that the zoot suit had previously been popular among blacks demonstrates that, at least at some level of consciousness, Mexican American youth were declaring that they understood the racial nature of their subordination. Moreover, such a declaration in the midst of a national crisis had an enhanced message. Especially during the war years when Americans prized the neat, trim look of the servicemen, when they placed high value on the conservation of basic materials such as cloth, and when they expected unity and conformity in order to defeat the common foe, Mexican American youth knew that the zoot suit offended whites. They knew, as the historian Mauricio Mazón has noted, that adult society met the zoot suiter "with anger, shock, and undoubtedly envy." The zoot suiters knew this and they reveled in the knowledge.[57]

Thus, these youths not only wore their outlandish clothes, they flaunted them. Zoot suiters, in fact, gained a measure of satisfaction and a sense of unity from the looks of ridicule and disgust that they received from "squares" when they walked down the street. Cholitas also displayed an aggressive flare. Beatrice Griffith, who wrote extensively and often stereotypically on the zoot-suit phenomenon, stated, "A bravado and swagger accentuated the dark beauty of these girls." César Chávez, future United Farm Workers Union leader, remembered that as a teenager he wore a zoot suit and that he and other zoot suiters "needed a lot of guts to wear those pants, and we had to be rebellious to do it, because the police and a few of the older people would harass us." As many as two-thirds of all Mexican American youths in Los Angeles judged wearing their zoot suits worth the harassment, for it gave them a sense of belonging to at least one group in a society from which they felt generally alienated.[58]

While a majority of Mexican American youths wore the zoot suit, the level of involvement in the subculture varied greatly from one individual to another. Many, as Chávez implied, wore only the pants. Others wore traditional fashions during the week for school or work and wore their zoot suits only on weekends. Still others wore the style on a more continuous basis but did not immerse themselves in the subculture. Only a handful of the most alienated youths, the pachucos, fully adopted *la vida loca*, the crazy life of the zoot-suit subculture with its defiant and hostile attitude and antisocial and pathological tendencies. This group comprised an infinitesimally small proportion of the Mexican American youth population (less than 3 percent, by one estimate). Nevertheless, because of their visibility within the community and the publicity they received from the press, it was the pachucos who defined what it meant to be a zoot suiter for other Mexican American youths, regardless of their level of involvement in the subculture.

According to Joan Moore, the quintessential pachucos came from the barrio of El Hoyo Maravilla, one of the most destitute Mexican American neighborhoods in southern California. As late as the 1920s, residents of El Hoyo did not even enjoy the most basic urban amenities such as running water and paved streets. During the Depression people in El Hoyo actually went hungry and had to rely on food trucks from local government agencies in order to survive. The children from this barrio performed poorly in school, and education officials sent many to special continuation schools for students with learning problems. At the continuation high school, El Hoyo Maravilla youths learned to make distinctions between themselves and Mexican American youngsters from other barrios, distinctions that often led to rivalries. While these rivalries most often worked themselves out on the basketball court or the baseball field, enough fights broke out that police began labeling as gangs the groups of boys that came together from the different barrios.[59]

Moore reports that by World War II the youths from El Hoyo Maravilla "were deeply caught up in the pachuco fad and the la vida loca (the wild life)" lifestyle that, at least for these Mexican American youngsters, went with the clothes. In addition to their drapes and ducktail haircuts, "chucos" from El Hoyo smoked marijuana and tattooed themselves with various symbols that designated their allegiance to their girlfriends, their barrio, or their race. In fact, the youths from El Hoyo Maravilla took special pride in their Mexican heritage and rejected any thought of assimilation into American culture. They spoke primarily in Caló or Spanish and ridiculed any Mexican American who spoke *gabacho* (English). Consequently, according to Moore, while the zoot suiters from El Hoyo Maravilla may have fought with other barrios, their "enmity for Anglos and their system was paramount."[60]

Because of these pachucos' open hostility toward white society, law-enforcement officials paid special attention to the inhabitants of El Hoyo during the 1940s. One former resident remembered the effects of the police presence on his community:

> Let's talk a little bit about a block in a barrio Chicano, you know, on summer nights, all the mothers and fathers would come out with the neighbors and sit on somebody's porch, someone you knew, you'd just sit half the night, just gossip, and as kids will[,] we would go out on the street, there was no sidewalks, just dirt and tar and what have you, we'd play kick the can, ring

on the view, or hide-and-go-seek, and all [the] games we'd use to play and having a hell of a lot of fun. All of a sudden a police car would appear, everybody would freeze, all the kids, mothers start yelling "get off the street, come in the yard."

They used to remind me of big sharks the way they used to cruise through the neighborhood, just looking mean, never saying a word. Soon as they passed, everything became the same way, everybody would start laughing and talking and playing around.

How far back this fear and dread or how far back this fear goes or whatever it is, I don't know, but ever since I can remember, the cops meant something evil to Mexican kids.[61]

The extreme alienation of some pachucos went beyond mere symbolic rebellion and led them into pathological and violent behavior. These alienated youths directed much of their hostility inward, within the Mexican American community. Almost all the violence reported by the press with such great alarm during the war years consisted of Mexican American youths fighting other Mexican American youths, with many of the fights resulting from real or imagined rivalries between different barrios. One older boy explained the reason for this violence: "These kids are all full of animal mad. That's why they fight each other. They can't fight the cops or the gabachos [whites], their enemies, so to get the mad from their blood they fight each other. Mad . . . mad . . . it's black and falling down that makes 'em hate the other guys. They got to fight something, you know how it is."[62]

Much of the violence, however, seemed pointless and symptomatic of anomie, as demonstrated by the following statement by one of the Sleepy Lagoon defendants: "All I want to do is stay high on tea and fight. I'm happy when I fight. I don't like to hurt people, but I like to fight. Sometimes I hit guys a lot bigger than me. They grin and knock the shit out of me. You look up my record at Jackson High. I was always fighting. I used to fight the principal."[63] This type of aimless violence became increasingly prevalent in the aftermath of the zoot-suit hysteria.

Zoot suiters, even those less committed to the subculture, also attacked the sources of racial discrimination—sometimes even consciously, albeit spontaneously. It should be noted at this point that newspaper reporters rarely bothered to interview Mexican Americans and thus discover the motivations for their actions. Nevertheless, they did print a sufficient number of stories regarding zoot suiters reacting violently to a perceived injustice to make it clear that some Mexican American youths did not fear directly confronting white society. On the same evening in late October 1942, for example, two major altercations broke out between police and zoot suiters. The first occurred at a downtown movie theater when the theater management threw three Mexican American youths out for making noises during the movie. Twenty-five to thirty other youths sitting in the balcony objected to the ejections, and the management called the police. Apparently, the officers then threw the protesters out of the theater and a fight erupted outside. According to newspaper accounts, as many as two hundred people fought with police; officers, however, made only one arrest.[64]

That same evening at a dance hall in the predominantly white west side of the city, another riot broke out between Mexican American youths and the LAPD. In previous weeks zoot suiters had crashed parties at the dance hall, causing disturbances that, in one case, resulted in an LAPD officer being injured. On the evening of the riot, the LAPD had placed a guard at the dance-hall entrance during a wedding celebration. The officer demanded to see invitations before allowing anyone to enter the dance. According to one newspaper account, those who did not possess an invitation "were ordered to disperse—or take a trip to the station house." When many of the youths refused to leave the area, officers declared it an illegal assembly and called in reinforcements. Several fights broke out between officers and zoot suiters, and at one point a crowd of youths began throwing rocks at police. Eventually the police restored order and arrested seventy-five youths. Since the newspapers took their information only from police sources, we do not know what may have provoked either incident.[65]

Zoot suiters also sometimes resisted arrest and in other ways harassed police officers. One of the more spectacular of these cases occurred in February 1943 when officers forcibly tried to remove a seventeen-year-old Mexican American boy and two Mexican American girls, ages sixteen and fourteen, from a cafe. A group of six older Mexican American boys came upon the scene and tried to restrain the two officers, causing a fight. Eventually, eight more officers arrived and arrested all but the fourteen-year-old girl, charging the six older boys with interfering with an arrest.

It also seems that zoot suiters engaged in more organized and planned actions against the police. A draft of a Sleepy Lagoon Defense Committee publication states that zoot suiters retaliated against police harassment and brutality "by '[de]pantsing' the cops and generally making life miserable for them." This kind of interaction undoubtedly worsened the already poor relationship between police and the Mexican American community.[66]

Finally, some zoot suiters went beyond reacting to police violence and harassing officers to actually displaying a political motivation for their actions. A Los Angeles schoolteacher, for example, reported that through their acts and statements Mexican American students displayed "a conscious political motivation." In September 1942 a resolution of the CIO stated that pachucos burned the American flag and tore down posters promoting the war effort. Similarly, toward the end of the war the *Belvedere Citizen* reported that police arrested three Mexican American youths for flag burning. No wonder, then, that the Los Angeles County Coordinating Council feared that the discrimination faced by Mexican American youths had led some to adopt "radical ideas." No wonder also that the vice principal at Garfield High School accused Mexican American students who formed their own organization of having "pro-Nazi designs," or that police officials became extremely alarmed when a convicted German spy waiting to be transferred to a federal penitentiary began telling his Mexican American jail mates that they were victims of racial discrimination. In fact, during the war years community leaders, both white and Mexican American, believed that the pachuco fad was somehow a scheme of an extreme right-wing and possibly pro-Axis Mexican movement known as the Sinarquistas, which allegedly hoped to disrupt the war effort by creating disunity between Mexican Americans and Anglo Americans. This belief became so prevalent that a committee of the California State Legislature conducted hearings to determine whether the zoot-suit phenomenon was part of "an axis fifth column undermining the morale of American-Mexican boys and girls."[67]

In the final analysis, however, it should be remembered that while most Mexican American youths wore zoot suits, the overwhelming majority of the youths who did wear them did not engage in illegal activities, politically motivated or otherwise. Nevertheless, Mexican American youths had plenty of reason to be rebellious, and sensitive adults at the time understood the hostile nature of the zoot-suit phenomenon. The youth worker Henry Marín remembers that these youths rebelled against the notion that whites could use Mexicans as "a bunch of clowns." These young people had grown up indoctrinated and believing in the American dream only to discover that, simply because they were Mexican, they could never fully partake of America's riches. According to Manuel Ruiz, Mexican American youths began wearing the zoot suit in order to "articulate their dissatisfaction" with the discrimination they endured daily. Ruiz, who, as a young attorney, defended many pachucos, also disbelieved the popular notions about his clients' inherent criminal nature. He found that the pachucos "were not bad at all"; instead, he found them rather "exuberant." Congressman Roybal remembered that the zoot suiters often ran afoul of the law because they demanded respect. Mexican American youths, Roybal recalls, got into trouble because they insisted on defending themselves, even if it meant getting into fights.[68]

Perhaps this last point is the most insightful, for it seems that above all, the zoot suiters wanted respect. Despite the outlandish clothes and the sometimes outlandish behavior, what the zoot suiters and even the more defiant pachucos really wanted, indeed what they demanded, was to be treated the same as the rest of society. They wanted to get the same kind of jobs, to frequent the same entertainment spots, to be treated fairly by the police, and above all, in all these interactions to be treated with respect. White society, however, was unwilling to respect Mexican Americans, especially the zoot suiters. Whites were repelled by the zoot suit precisely because of what it represented—rebelliousness against traditional forms of discrimination and subordination. Mexicans were not supposed to have jobs as good as those of whites, they were not supposed to go to the same dances or sit in the same section of theaters, and the role of the police was to keep Mexicans in their place. Moreover, Mexicans were supposed to be humble and meek and generally invisible and youths were supposed to obey figures of authority. The fact that Mexican American youths chose to attack these norms of behavior not directly through political action but symbolically through actions that showed their defiance of and hostility toward white society made it easier for whites to dismiss their protests and label all Mexicans criminal, deviant, and even pathological. That labeling, however, would have highly negative consequences for the city of Los Angeles both in the short term and in the long term.

CHAPTER 9

Facts and Origins of the Zoot-Suit Hysteria

Los Angeles white society interpreted the zoot-suit phenomenon as a sign of the inherent criminality of Mexican Americans and especially Mexican American youth. This idea of Mexican Americans' innate criminality led to a popular belief during the war years that a Mexican American crime wave was sweeping the city. Although available statistics indicate that no such crime wave existed, a variety of factors, including general wartime anxieties, pronouncements by police and other public officials, and sensational press coverage of Mexican American crime, turned that fear into full-blown anti-Mexican hysteria.

THE ZOOT-SUIT HYSTERIA: THE EVIDENCE

The first thing that must be said regarding the popular fear of a Mexican American crime wave is that it had little basis in fact. This is not to deny that juvenile delinquency was on the rise: Mexican American and white sources are in agreement about this. In addition, the more alienated and violent pachucos did indeed create a serious social problem in the community. Nevertheless, while anti-Mexican hysteria raged, Los Angeles experienced no concomitant crime wave; in fact, the most reliable police statistics indicate a decrease not an increase in crime during this period. In the mid-1940s the LAPD's *Annual Reports* began publishing trends for the total number of crimes *reported* by citizens since 1941. While crime reports still do not accurately reflect actual rates of crime—the number of crimes that are never reported cannot be determined—they nevertheless come closer to reflecting reality than arrest statistics do. It must also be remembered that these statistics do not take into account the fact that the dramatic population increase that Los Angeles experienced during the war would naturally have produced a similar increase in crime.

Table 1 shows that citizens reported significantly fewer total crimes during 1942 and 1943, the years of the alleged Mexican crime wave, than they did in the years immediately preceding and following this period. In fact, in 1942, the first full year of the war and the year in which the hysteria began, there were 25 percent fewer crimes reported than in the previous year; likewise, the number was down by almost 16 percent in 1943, the year of the Zoot Suit riots. Reported crime did not equal or surpass prewar levels until 1945, the year the war ended. Thus, during the period when police officials were issuing statements regarding the innate criminality of Mexican American youth, and when the city's press published sensational articles about a zoot-suit reign of terror, the number of reported crimes had in fact fallen.[1]

The statistics for reports of violent crimes are more ambiguous. Table 2 shows conflicting trends in reports of these types of crimes between 1941, the last year of peace, and 1942, the first year of war. Reports of murder and rape increased between these two years (by nearly 45 percent in the case of rape), but those of assault and robbery decreased (by 14 and 32 percent, respectively). Nevertheless, an analysis of the reported crime statistics throughout the period, from 1941 to 1946, shows that the total number of reports of serious crimes in fact fell in 1942 and then began a dramatic and steady rise that continued through the end of the war.

Despite the fact that the amount of reported crime was lower in 1942 and 1943 than it had been before the war, the LAPD arrested Mexican American adults at about the same rate as it had in the past. Adult Mexican Americans comprised only a slightly higher percentage of arrests on all charges during the war years than during the years immediately preceding and following the war. Similarly, except for 1942, police arrested Mexican American adults for serious violent crimes at approximately the same rate during the war as they had before and after the war. It should be noted too that 1942, the year of the highest rate of Mexican American arrests, also marks the lowest point in crime reports. Furthermore, the arrest rate for adult Mexican Americans remained relatively consistent from the mid-1930s onward.[2]

TABLE 1

NUMBER OF ALL CRIMES REPORTED, 1941–1946

	1941	1942	1943	1944	1945	1946
Crimes reported	50,951	38,115	42,879	48,053	55,696	56,552

SOURCE: LAPD, *Annual Reports.*

TABLE 2

NUMBER OF SELECTED CRIMES REPORTED, 1939–1946

	1939	1940	1941	1942	1943	1944	1945	1946
Murder	79	86	67	76	78	101	91	116
Rape	337	334	329	477	522	558	568	551
Assault	591	684	668	572	877	1,231	1,721	2,198
Robbery	1,860	2,169	2,062	1,406	2,439	2,756	3,776	3,908
Total	2,867	3,273	3,126	2,531	3,916	4,646	6,156	6,773

SOURCE: LAPD, *Annual Reports.*

The arrest statistics for juveniles show an inverse relationship to reported crime: juvenile arrests rose as reported crime fell. Table 3 also
shows that the total number of Mexican American juveniles arrested by
the LAPD rose by 73 percent between 1940 and 1942. Similarly, table
4 shows that the number of Mexican American juveniles arrested by the
LAPD for more serious violent crimes rose by 270 percent at the same
time that citizen reports for such crimes fell dramatically.[3] Interestingly,
juvenile arrests declined after the war ended although reported crime
continued to rise. As I will show shortly, however, the dramatic rise in
juvenile arrests during the war years was more indicative of changes in
the law and in LAPD practices than of a demonstrable increase in juvenile delinquency. Nevertheless, both the law-enforcement community
and the local press (and eventually the general population) came to believe that these arrest statistics reflected a wave of youth crime, and in
particular Mexican American youth crime, that was overwhelming the
city.

The statistics also show that Mexican American youths constituted
an increasingly large proportion of the juveniles arrested by the LAPD

TABLE 3

NUMBER OF ALL JUVENILE ARRESTS BY RACE, 1939–1946

Arrestees	1939	1940	1941	1942	1943	1944	1945	1946
Chicanos	1,134	1,071	1,408	1,852	2,804	3,083	3,225	2,516
Blacks	467	411	570	784	1,157	1,331	1,328	1,195
Whites	2,487	2,050	2,155	3,009	4,492	4,737	4,871	4,304
Others	38	42	41	37	29	30	33	36
Total	4,126	3,574	4,174	5,682	8,482	9,181	9,457	8,051

SOURCE: LAPD, *Annual Reports.*

TABLE 4

NUMBER OF JUVENILE ARRESTS
FOR SELECTED CHARGES BY RACE, 1939–1946

	1939	1940	1941	1942	1943	1944	1945	1946
Chicanos	58	57	111	211	285	370	350	206
Blacks	28	36	59	84	157	123	150	112
Whites	66	74	58	79	129	95	149	113
Others	1	2	7	2	2	2	0	6

NOTE: "Selected charges": homicide, rape, robbery, and felonious assault.
SOURCE: LAPD, *Annual Reports.*

during the war years. Table 5 shows that the gradual increase in the percentage of arrests of Mexican American juveniles that began in the mid-1930s continued through the early 1940s, reached a plateau during the war years, and then leveled off slightly after the war ended. Although showing significant fluctuations, overall the statistics for the war years demonstrate an even sharper increase in the percentage of Mexican American youths arrested for violent crimes. Table 6 demonstrates that in 1939 Mexican Americans accounted for close to 38 percent of juveniles arrested for violent felonies. Just three years later, that figure rose to over 56 percent, and in 1944 almost two out of every three juvenile arrests made by the LAPD for these violent crimes were of youths of Mexican descent. In fact, during the war years Mexican Americans and African Americans comprised between 77 and 83 percent of the juvenile arrests for this category of crimes in Los Angeles.

A number of factors, however, mitigate the significance of the LAPD's

TABLE 5

PERCENTAGE OF ALL JUVENILE ARRESTS BY RACE, 1939–1946

	1939	1940	1941	1942	1943	1944	1945	1946
Chicanos	27.48	29.97	33.73	32.59	33.06	33.58	34.10	31.25
Blacks	11.32	11.50	13.66	13.80	13.64	14.50	14.04	14.84
Whites	60.82	57.36	51.63	52.96	52.96	51.60	51.51	53.46
Others	0.92	1.18	0.98	0.65	0.34	0.33	0.35	0.45

SOURCE: LAPD, *Annual Reports.*

TABLE 6

PERCENTAGE OF JUVENILE ARRESTS ON SELECTED CHARGES BY
RACE, 1939–1946

	1939	1940	1941	1942	1943	1944	1945	1946
Chicanos	37.91	33.73	47.23	56.12	49.74	62.71	53.93	47.14
Blacks	18.30	21.30	25.11	22.42	27.40	20.85	23.11	25.63
Whites	43.14	43.79	24.68	21.01	22.51	16.10	22.96	25.86
Others	0.65	1.18	2.98	0.53	0.35	0.34	0.00	1.37

NOTE: "Selected charges": homicide, rape, robbery, and felonious assault.
SOURCE: LAPD, *Annual Reports.*

overall arrest statistics. To begin with, most of its arrests of Mexican
Americans, whether adult or juvenile, were for violation of sumptuary
laws and other offenses that had no victims. The statistics show, for
example, that the overwhelming majority of arrests of Mexican American adults continued to be for alcohol-related offenses. In addition,
during the war years new classes of laws came into effect that inflated
the number of Mexican American arrests. The draft laws are the most
obvious example; they did not exist prior to 1940, but they accounted
for close to 10 percent of all Mexican American arrests during the height
of the war. Toward the end of the war the LAPD began enforcing immigration laws, which also increased the arrest statistics for people of
Mexican descent. In contrast, the percentage of Mexican American
adults arrested for property crimes actually decreased during the war
years.[4]

The arrest statistics for juveniles need to be treated with even more
caution. Table 7 shows a significant rise between 1941 and 1943 in the

number of arrests in the category of "noncriminal detention." This means that much of the increase in Mexican American juvenile arrests can be attributed to arrests that were totally unrelated to any criminal activity. Also, as will be shown in the next chapter, this is exactly the category of arrest that the LAPD advocated using to curb Mexican American juvenile delinquency. The LAPD seems to have used arrest for noncriminal detention to control Mexican American youths in much the same way that it had used vagrancy laws in earlier decades to control Mexican adults.

Table 7 also shows a sharp increase in the percentage of arrests in the "Others" category and an even more dramatic rise in violent crimes. The latter will be explained later; the increase in the "Others" category resulted largely from the enactment of a new curfew ordinance in 1942. Curfew laws, even more explicitly than vagrancy laws, sought to control a segment of the population by declaring certain behavior illegal at certain times, behavior that was otherwise permitted. Authorities hoped the new curfew ordinance, by prohibiting anyone under seventeen from "loitering" in public places after 9:00 P.M., would curb the wave of juvenile delinquency they believed was sweeping the city. The LAPD, however, did not enforce the law equally. In certain sections of the city, it chose to be flexible and allow young people to congregate in public places. In other sections—namely, those in which minority youths lived—departmental policy ordered "strict enforcement" of the curfew laws. As a consequence, the number of Mexican American youths arrested for violating the curfew law increased from none prior to 1942 to close to five hundred in 1944.[5]

Another factor that mitigates the significance of the arrest statistics is the pitifully low number of actual prosecutions that resulted from LAPD arrests. From the late 1930s, the department began publishing statistics on the disposition of each arrest. While during the war years each arrest could be disposed of in one of as many as thirteen different ways, including complete exoneration or release to parents, only the filing of a petition before a court and the detaining of the suspect implied that the arresting officer actually had good cause to make the arrest. None of the other possible actions resulted in any kind of prosecution on the charges for which the police had made the original arrest. Of course, the mere fact that the district or city attorney believed that the police had developed enough evidence to file criminal charges before a judge did not imply guilt. That determination still had to be made before

TABLE 7

PERCENTAGE OF MEXICAN AMERICAN JUVENILES
ARRESTED BY CHARGE, 1939–1946

	1939	1940	1941	1942	1943	1944	1945	1946
Violent crimes[a]	5.11	5.32	8.07	11.39	10.16	12.00	10.85	8.19
Property crimes[b]	55.64	55.28	51.96	34.50	32.74	31.37	30.91	35.93
Noncriminal detention[c]	24.87	28.48	34.81	40.17	35.33	25.59	27.35	27.50
Others	14.37	10.92	5.16	13.39	21.43	31.04	30.88	28.38
Curfew[d]	—	—	—	1.35	3.53	13.56	15.01	9.82

SOURCE: LAPD, *Annual Reports*.
[a] "Violent crimes": murder, rape, manslaughter, robbery, and felonious assault.
[b] "Property crimes": burglary, fictitious checks, forgery, Dyer Act, embezzlement, grand theft, grand theft auto, obtaining money under false pretenses, petty embezzlement, petty theft, receiving stolen property, theft from a person.
[c] "Noncriminal detention": this category comprises those detained as delinquent children, dependent persons, insane persons, lost children, material witnesses, runaways, or sex delinquents.
[d] Subsection of "others" category.

a judge and/or jury. The fact, however, that so few arrests resulted in prosecutions indicates that the LAPD made a large number of unjustified and baseless arrests, especially of Mexican American youths.[6]

Table 8 shows that during the war years the LAPD became less and less efficient in actually prosecuting the people it arrested. Prosecution of adults, for example, hovered at about 90 percent before the war but plummeted to an average of 56 percent during the war years. This meant that while the LAPD generally made more arrests during the war years, the number of prosecutions that resulted in arrests was considerably lower during the war than it was during peacetime. The LAPD's prosecution rate for violent crimes was, if anything, even more dismal. Only once during the period 1939–1946 did more than 30 percent of LAPD arrests for this category of crimes result in prosecutions; indeed, in one year, 1944, only a little more than 7 percent of arrests for violent crimes actually reached the courts.

The juvenile arrest statistics show the same pattern of a large number of unjustified arrests being made by the LAPD. As table 9 shows, prior to the war close to half of all juveniles arrested in Los Angeles were prosecuted. During the war itself, that proportion dropped to as low as 27 percent. This meant that while the number of LAPD juvenile arrests more than doubled between 1939 and 1945, the number of prosecutions arising from those arrests rose by less than 33 percent. The statistics for arrests for more serious violent crimes tell much the same story. In 1939

TABLE 8

PERCENTAGE OF ADULT ARRESTS ON ALL AND SELECTED CHARGES
THAT RESULTED IN PROSECUTIONS, 1939–1946

	1939	1940	1941	1942	1943	1944	1945	1946
All charges								
Total arrests	77,407	80,962	80,971	91,711	78,451	99,587	116,754	138,627
Prosecutions	68,207	73,112	72,388	55,790	38,781	54,939	69,657	66,545
Percent prosecuted	88.11	90.30	89.40	60.81	49.43	55.17	59.66	48.00
Selected charges								
Total arrests	4,190	3,290	2,964	3,682	3,661	3,448	6,237	6,376
Prosecutions	972	948	1,218	840	1,050	248	1,105	1,314
Percent prosecuted	23.20	28.81	41.09	22.81	28.68	7.21	17.72	20.61

NOTE: "Selected charges": homicide, rape, robbery, and felonious assault.
SOURCE: LAPD, *Annual Reports.*

more than 75 percent of all juvenile arrests in this category of offense resulted in criminal prosecutions. By 1945 that proportion had dropped to below 40 percent. This meant that the number of juvenile arrests for violent crimes rose by more than 300 percent, but the number of prosecutions rose by less than 65 percent.

The discrepancies between the number of arrests and prosecutions beg for an explanation, even a speculative one. It may have been, for example, that the temporary officers hired during the wartime emergency had neither the skills nor the training to successfully bring their arrests to trial. It also may have been the case that because of their relative inexperience, these officers did indeed make a large number of unjustified arrests. The LAPD, however, may also have been responding to the general hysteria regarding Mexican American crime. In this case, the department may have used its power to arrest as a tool of social control or as a punishment—in other words, as an end in itself—rather than merely as a means of apprehending and prosecuting criminals. Whatever the explanation, the low number of prosecutions resulting from arrests made during these years clearly demonstrates the fallacy of using arrest statistics to calculate the crime rate in either the general population or a subset of it. The low number also demonstrates the validity of the Mexican American community's complaint regarding the overarresting of its youths.

These tendencies are highlighted by a unique set of statistics published

TABLE 9

PERCENTAGE OF JUVENILE ARRESTS ON ALL AND SELECTED CHARGES
THAT RESULTED IN PROSECUTIONS, 1939–1946

	1939	1940	1941	1942	1943	1944	1945	1946
All charges								
Total arrests	4,126	3,574	4,174	5,682	8,482	9,181	9,457	8,051
Prosecutions	1,940	1,205	2,002	2,033	2,388	2,486	2,575	1,953
Percent prosecuted	47.02	33.72	47.69	35.78	28.15	27.08	27.23	24.26
Selected charges								
Total arrests	153	169	235	376	573	590	649	437
Prosecutions	116	88	154	183	274	271	252	168
Percent prosecuted	75.82	52.07	65.53	48.67	47.82	45.93	38.83	38.44

NOTE: "Selected charges": homicide, rape, robbery, and felonious assault.
SOURCE: LAPD, *Annual Reports*.

by the department in the crisis years of 1942–1943. Undoubtedly because of the tremendous concern over Mexican American juvenile delinquency, the LAPD enumerated the disposition of juvenile arrests by
race in these two years. Table 10 demonstrates that in 1942, 37 percent
of all Mexican American youths arrested by the LAPD and 46 percent
of those arrested for violent crimes were prosecuted. While these statistics thus show that Mexican American juveniles were prosecuted at a
higher rate than whites for all arrests and at a lower rate for arrests for
violent crimes, they also indicate that Los Angeles police officers gained
prosecutions for only a relatively small fraction of the juvenile arrests
they made.

The 1943 statistics given in table 11 show patterns similar to those
established in 1942. Mexican American youths were still prosecuted at
about the same rate as whites for all violations and at a lower rate than
whites for violent crimes. In fact, in 1943, barely more than a quarter
of all the LAPD arrests of Mexican American juveniles resulted in prosecutions. This meant that more than 2,000 Mexican American youths
had to face the humiliation and other consequences of an arrest without
there having been good cause for the arrest. Although these statistics
cannot be compared beyond the 1942–1943 time frame, they help explain the dramatic rise in the arrests of Mexican American youths for
violent crimes shown in tables 3 and 4. In addition, a comparison of
tables 10 and 11 shows that while the total number of Mexican Amer-

TABLE 10

PERCENTAGE OF JUVENILE ARRESTS RESULTING IN
PROSECUTIONS ON ALL AND SELECTED CHARGES BY RACE, 1942

	All Charges			Selected Charges		
	Arrests	*Prosecutions*	*Percent*	*Arrests*	*Prosecutions*	*Percent*
Chicanos	1,852	679	36.66	211	98	46.45
Blacks	784	286	36.48	84	40	47.62
Whites	3,009	1,053	35.00	79	44	55.70
Others	37	15	40.54	2	1	50.00
Total	5,682	2,033	35.78	376	183	48.67

NOTE: "Selected charges": homicide, rape, robbery, and felonious assault.
SOURCE: LAPD, *Annual Reports*.

ican youths arrested by the LAPD rose by 51 percent between 1942 and 1943, the number of prosecutions rose by less than 10 percent. Another way of looking at this situation is that for the nearly 1,000 more arrests of Mexican American youths made by the LAPD in 1943, the department gained only 66 additional prosecutions.

Overall, then, the statistical evidence shows that the popular belief that Los Angeles was being overwhelmed by a Mexican American crime wave during the war years had little basis in fact. Police did arrest more Mexicans, especially more Mexican American youths, than they had in the past, but these increases in arrests resulted more from changes in the law and changes in police practices than from changes in Mexican Americans' behavior.[7] Specifically, the enactment and enforcement of new laws, such as immigration and draft laws for adults and curfew laws for juveniles, created new classes of laws that Mexican Americans violated and that therefore swelled the arrest statistics. In addition, the LAPD engaged in selective enforcement, enforcing laws such as the curfew ordinance more vigorously in the barrios than it did in white sections of the city. It also seems that the department used the curfew ordinance and noncriminal detentions as control mechanisms against Mexican American youth. Finally, the LAPD simply overarrested people during the 1940s. While the number of arrests rose to alarming numbers, only a fraction, sometimes only a small fraction, of those arrests resulted in criminal prosecutions.

A few unbiased observers understood that in fact only a handful of

TABLE 11

PERCENTAGE OF JUVENILE ARRESTS RESULTING IN
PROSECUTIONS ON ALL AND SELECTED CHARGES BY RACE, 1943

	All Charges			Selected Charges		
	Total	Prosecuted	Percent	Total	Prosecuted	Percent
Chicanos	2,804	745	26.57	285	120	42.11
Blacks	1,157	408	35.26	157	79	50.32
Whites	4,492	1,225	27.27	129	65	50.39
Others	29	10	34.48	2	2	100.00
Total	8,492	2,388	28.15	573	266	46.42

NOTE: "Selected charges": homicide, rape, robbery, and felonious assault.
SOURCE: LAPD, *Annual Reports.*

Mexican American youths actually engaged in illegal activity. Herman
G. Stark, director of the Civilian Service Corps and Coordinating Council of Los Angeles County, estimated that approximately 1.6 percent of
the boys and .6 percent of the girls ran afoul of the law. Similarly, Karl
Holton, head of the Los Angeles County Probation Department, declared that while juvenile delinquency was increasing for all groups, the
rate of increase among Mexican Americans was less than a third of that
of the general population. "In other words," he said, "there is no 'wave
of lawlessness' among Mexican children."[8]

It must nevertheless be reiterated that during the war, juvenile delinquency was indeed a problem within the Mexican American community,
and it had been a problem for a number of years. As I have previously
stated, during the 1930s, well before the wartime hysteria developed, a
relatively wide spectrum of the East Los Angeles community, from Mexican American businessmen to community newspapers to LAPD officials, all attempted to address the issue in their own ways. It is also true
that Mexican American juvenile delinquency probably got worse during
the war years. Again, as I will soon show, a wide spectrum of the community agreed on this issue, and while the LAPD's arrest statistics did
not particularly illuminate the matter, they probably do reflect, in a very
rough and indeterminable way, an increase in Mexican American juvenile crime.

SOURCES OF THE HYSTERIA

Nevertheless, as a result of a variety of interrelated factors, the general public greatly exaggerated the extent of Mexican American juvenile delinquency and came to fear Mexican American youths as a dangerous criminal element within the community. In addition to the rise of the zoot-suit phenomenon, these factors include general wartime anxieties, uncritical assessments of the arrest statistics, public announcements by police and other government officials, and the tremendous play that the press gave to the subject of Mexican American juvenile crime.

To a certain extent, the fear of juvenile delinquency was a wartime phenomenon. Public officials across the nation expected a significant rise in juvenile delinquency once the United States entered the war. The country had experienced such an increase during World War I, and Great Britain had experienced a tremendous growth in youth crime in the early years of World War II. Government officials publicly warned that the United States would have to endure a similar increase, and local authorities also voiced this concern. Karl Holton commented that "everyone seems to have expected a tremendous increase [in juvenile delinquency] after Pearl Harbor." Zoot-suited Mexican American youths were a highly visible and definitely rebellious group, making them the obvious example of a prophecy fulfilled.[9]

Wartime anxieties contributed to the anti-Mexican hysteria in other ways. The entry of the United States into World War II raised fears that often led to nonrational beliefs in the existence of internal enemy conspiracies and to demands for total conformity. Even before the United States entered the war, the Los Angeles Board of Police Commissioners recommended that the city council pass an ordinance ordering all non–U.S. citizens to register with the chief of police. After the war started, the expulsion of Japanese nationals and Japanese Americans from their homes on the West Coast and their "internment" in concentration camps was the most obvious example of this paranoia and demand for conformity. Following the removal of the Japanese, municipal officials and the public transferred much of their anxiety to the city's largest and most visible minority group, the Mexican Americans.[10]

While wartime anxieties created a general atmosphere that contributed to the zoot-suit hysteria, the tremendous fear that arose regarding Mexican American juvenile delinquency could not have developed without the sanction—and, indeed, support—of Los Angeles law-enforcement officials. The traditional interpretation of the hysteria blames Los Angeles newspapers for fomenting fears about Mexican American youths. Starting with then-contemporary articles by Carey McWilliams and other liberal commentators and continued in Mc-Williams's *North from Mexico,* this interpretation charges that the steady stream of news stories about "Zoot-Suit Gangs" and "Pachuco Gangsters" inflamed whites to the point at which they condoned vigilante action against Mexican American youths. These commentators accused the two Hearst newspapers, the *Los Angeles Examiner* and the *Los Angeles Herald and Express,* in particular, of trying to undermine the war effort by creating disunity and dissension at home. To a great extent, this interpretation has persisted to the present day.[11]

The press may indeed have incited the public to hysteria, but the newspapers generally did not fabricate the stories they printed. Rather, reporters wrote their stories with the active assistance, support, and encouragement of law-enforcement and political officials. As Nick Williams, the night news editor for the *Times* during the hysteria, noted, reporters could not have written their stories without information from police sources. Williams's recollections are supported by the many news stories that specifically acknowledged that the information they contained came from police. Thus, the press could claim, as Williams later did, that while the coverage "may have been inflammatory, ... at the time, we thought we were objectively covering the news."[12]

In fact, throughout the period of the anti-Mexican hysteria, local law-enforcement officials as well as political and community leaders fanned the flames of fear by promoting the idea that Mexican Americans, and especially Mexican American youths, presented a serious crime problem or, even worse, that they were biologically inclined toward crime and violence. A variety of factors within the LAPD contributed to this belief. Indications of a growing police animosity toward the Mexican American community were evident almost a decade before the zoot-suit hysteria. The attorney Manuel Ruiz remembered his first visit to the Los Angeles city jail in the early 1930s. He saw there a number of plaques on the wall commemorating officers killed in the line of duty. Most had no special notation, but several had a line that stated "Killed by a Mexican."[13] More important, the LAPD's arrest statistics both exemplified the department's growing interest in the linkage between race and crime and provided "scientific" evidence to support that connection. The persistent concern regarding Mexican American juvenile delinquency led to a series of studies that, without questioning the validity of the basic premise, sought to determine the cause of the delinquency and ways to combat it. Finally, the adoption of the police-professionalism model by the new reform administration in 1938 moved the LAPD further toward the war-on-crime mentality that placed it at odds with large segments of the community. During the war years rebellious Mexican American youths, with their zoot suits and general disdain for white authority, became "the criminal element," and the LAPD moved forcefully to try to control them. The press, ever alert for a sensational story, took note of the official reports and the increased police activity and began writing ever more lurid stories about the alleged pachuco crime wave. The hysteria followed.

During the war years, then, a consensus emerged among Los Angeles civic leaders that Mexican American juveniles constituted a serious crime problem. While there was general agreement on this issue, the LAPD's increased attention to the zoot-suit phenomenon laid the basis for that consensus. The department's official attitude toward zoot suiters emerged from the numerous complaints from businessmen to LAPD officials alleging increased criminal activity by Mexican American youths. The complaints included specific charges such as graffiti on walls, window breaking, and theft, but their general theme was that groups of Mexican American youths now congregated where they had not been seen in the past. The LAPD responded by acknowledging that "disturbances by Mexican gangs . . . are authentic" and by stepping up surveillance, field interrogations, and arrests in Mexican American neighborhoods. The department also called for a strengthened curfew ordinance to help officers get Mexican American youths off the streets.[14]

Another source for the growing belief that the zoot suiters constituted a crime problem consisted of the various "studies" conducted by law-enforcement and other civic agencies that reported on the extent of Mexican American crime. An early example was the 1941 annual report of the Los Angeles County Probation Department, which found that statistics on the ethnicity of youths brought before the juvenile courts indicated a higher "delinquency rate" among Mexican American youth than among the general population. The probation department did not appear to understand that the number of Mexican Americans brought before the court was a function of arrests and bore little or no relation to the actual amount of delinquency in that part of the population.[15]

A more sophisticated analysis of Mexican American crime was provided by a report produced by the Los Angeles County Coordinating Council, a volunteer organization designed to work with underprivileged youth. The coordinating council based its report on arrest statistics and intended it to address the Mexican "problem" in Los Angeles. It contended that Mexican American juveniles committed more than their share of crimes but observed that police most often arrested these youths for relatively minor crimes—crimes that usually did not lead to adult criminality. On the other hand, the council also reported the emergence of "rowdy and disorderly groups" of Mexican American youths that sometimes engaged "in serious riots involving bodily injuries [and] contests with the police." The council argued that this type of behavior emerged, at least in part, from the "social and economic discrimination" that produced "a feeling of resentment and humiliation on the part of the young Mexicans." The council also noted with alarm the "almost revolutionary attitude" that some Mexican American youths embraced.[16]

Los Angeles newspapers, noting the official concern, began running increasingly sensational headlines and news stories depicting, often in lurid detail, the latest depredations of so-called Mexican American youth gangs. The phenomenon that allowed both the press and the public to fixate on Mexican American youth was the fact that, as noted earlier, many wore zoot suits, spoke a distinctive argot, and generally displayed an attitude that was both hostile to and scornful of white society. Their distinct dress and demeanor made the zoot suiters, and especially the pachucos, highly visible targets for the fear and antagonism that resulted from the natural anxiety and frustrations of a city at war. The press capitalized on and fed these anxieties during 1942 and 1943 by publishing a seemingly endless stream of stories on so-called zoot-suit gangs and pachuco gangsters. Interestingly, the Spanish-language La Opinión published some of the most lurid stories that accepted at face value the criminality of Mexican American youth, thus also raising anxieties about zoot-suit gangsters in the Spanish-speaking community.[17]

In the spring of 1942, six months after Pearl Harbor and only weeks after the government had sent the last of the Japanese and Japanese Americans off to concentration camps, newspapers started featuring stories on Mexican American crime and juvenile delinquency. These stories continued throughout the summer, growing in intensity and reaching a crescendo after August 2, 1942, when news of the Sleepy Lagoon case broke. As a result of protests from the federal government that the news stories hurt the hemispheric unity needed for the war effort, the press cut back on its sensational coverage during December 1942 and January

1943. It resumed in February, however, and continued throughout the spring, peaking again at the time of the Zoot Suit riots.[18]

To a certain extent, the World War II–era news stories resembled earlier newspaper accounts of Mexican crime. Headlines such as "11 Mexican Youths Indicted in Gas Station Robbery" and "2 Mexicans Held as Molesters" paralleled headlines on Mexican crime from the early part of the century and from the 1920s and 1930s in that they explicitly stated that Mexicans committed the crimes. Los Angeles area newspapers thus maintained the same basic format for reporting Mexican crime that they had used throughout the century.[19]

Nevertheless, World War II–era coverage of crimes committed by Mexican Americans differed from earlier accounts in some fundamental and significant ways. Unlike the earlier periods, when newspapers reported on only the most sensational crimes committed by Mexicans, during the zoot-suit hysteria the press seemed to relate every instance of a Mexican American arrest. Alerted by the police whenever they arrested Mexican Americans, the press reported on and blew out of proportion relatively minor crimes and even trivial incidents. A story on the robbery of a gas station, not to mention the indictment of the alleged assailants, for example, would likely never have been printed during the 1920s or 1930s. Similarly, the story behind the provocative headline regarding the Mexican "molesters" was really about the arrest of two Mexican American boys on the charge of disturbing the peace for verbally harassing a white woman on the street. By printing stories about such relatively minor events, the press created the impression among the general public that Mexican Americans had become a dangerous element in the community.[20]

The local newspapers created a similar impression through headlines and articles that implied significant increases in crimes committed by Mexican American youths. Headlines such as "New Zoot Gangster Attacks Result in Arrest of 100," "Gang Attacks Spread," "Zoot Suiters Blamed in New Killing," and "6 More Mexicans Charged with Weapon Assault" gave the impression that Mexican Americans were committing crimes at an ever-increasing rate. Adding to this fear, headlines also suggested that the crime wave was well organized. One headline, for example, spoke of a ". . . Zoot Suit Revolution." Other headlines, such as "Zoot Network over L.A.," "Nab Boy Gang 'General,' " and "Zoot Arsenal," implied that zoot suiters were organized throughout the city, that they had leadership, and that they were well armed.[21]

Sometimes the newspaper assault turned positively vicious. In November 1942 a small Los Angeles weekly, the *Los Angeles Equalizer*, complained about taxing citizens so that "certain people can raise their kids by charity, go to the public schools, snatch purses, slug old folks [and] defie [*sic*] authority." Despite the additional costs to the taxpayer, the *Equalizer* proposed that "when these young Mexican hoodlums raise the hell they are raising in wartime, we should put them in a stockade and try them after the war." All the publicity and the provocative rhetoric apparently had an effect on the public. One letter writer to the *Times* called on police to treat the zoot suiters the same way they treated their victims. Pondering that this might mean that "officers might kill or seriously injure some young hoodlum," the writer concluded, "Well, why not!"[22]

As the headlines and stories quoted above indicate, the theme that dominated the Los Angeles press's treatment of Mexican American youth was that of the gang. From mid-1942 onward, local newspapers consistently assumed that any Mexican who committed a crime must belong to a gang. Consequently, headlines and news stories about Mexican, pachuco, or zoot-suit gangs became everyday items in the local press. Even when the newspapers did not use the term "gangs," the fact that the local press used the terms "Mexican," "zoot suiter," and "pachuco" interchangeably and almost always in association with some crime gave the impression that all Mexican American youths wore zoot suits and that anyone who wore a zoot suit was certainly a criminal. The effect was an increasing public apprehension about Mexican crime—an apprehension that eventually turned into hysteria.

"More Sinned Against Than Sinning"

Within this general anti-Mexican atmosphere, law-enforcement officials developed a theory of criminality that linked crime to race. In an attempt to explain the zoot-suit phenomenon, representatives from the Los Angeles Police Department and the Los Angeles County Sheriff's Department publicly embraced the notion that people of Mexican descent were biologically inclined toward criminal, indeed violent, behavior and that police needed to take harsh measures to control that population. While Mexican American civil-rights organizations and white liberals condemned this racist theory of criminality, for the most part both groups conceded that the rebelliousness of the zoot suiters was a sign of delinquency. Only a few isolated voices countered this view. This concession inevitably gave police a free hand to use whatever measures they deemed necessary to address the perceived problem. With the police unchecked and the press ready to exploit a sensational story, the popular fear of Mexican Americans reached a fever pitch in the spring of 1943.

THE COORDINATING COUNCIL FOR LATIN AMERICAN YOUTH

The ongoing concern about Mexican American juvenile delinquency and the pachuco phenomenon led local officials to take steps to try to curb it. While city and county officials relied primarily on mobilizing law-enforcement agencies to combat Mexican American juvenile delinquency, they also took the unprecedented step of organizing leaders of that community to address the perceived sources of the problem.

Local officials' main effort at using Mexican Americans to fight pachucismo came in organizing the Coordinating Council for Latin American Youth (CCLAY). The CCLAY was formed in July 1941, before the hysteria, under the auspices of Mayor Fletcher Bowron, the County Board of Supervisors, the County Probation Department, and Chief of Police C. B. Horrall. Composed primarily of middle-class Mexican American professionals and law-enforcement officials, the CCLAY's stated purpose was to fight juvenile delinquency by "raising the moral and social standards of Spanish-speaking people." Leadership of the organization stayed firmly in the hands of Mexican Americans, with former El Congreso president Edward Quevedo chairing the committee and the attorney Manuel Ruiz Jr. acting as secretary. About a year later, the Los Angeles County Board of Supervisors created a similar group called the Citizens' Committee for Latin-American Youth, with almost an identical mission and membership.[1]

The historical significance of the establishment of the CCLAY cannot be overemphasized. This was the first time since the nineteenth century that Los Angeles officials had tried to organize Mexican Americans to address a community problem. In the past, when government leaders needed to address an issue concerning the Mexican community, they usually went to the Mexican consul. The consul's office, however, often had interests different from those of the community, and any solutions reached between the city and the consul did little to empower the grass-roots leadership. In addition, groups as varied as the magonistas, the League of United Latin American Citizens, and assorted ad hoc organizations often attempted to affect public policy; but city leaders could, and usually did, ignore them with impunity. The creation of the CCLAY fundamentally altered this dynamic by giving representatives of the Mexican American community access to and influence in the highest levels of city government. Simply put, city officials could not ignore a group they themselves had organized. Moreover, access and influence became addictive; henceforth, Mexican Americans would expect a say in policy decisions that affected their community, and within a few years they would seek, and eventually gain, official representation on the city council and in other high government positions.

In the short run, however, the formation and early activities of the CCLAY helped strengthen the linkage between race and crime. As its mission statement implies, the CCLAY functioned on the dual assumptions that a major juvenile delinquency problem existed in the Mexican American community and that the causes of that problem resulted from some inherent flaw in Mexican American culture. Mayor Bowron said as much in an early meeting with CCLAY members when he told them that the trouble stemmed from their "Mexican descent" and that they, as Mexican Americans, could best deal with the issue of juvenile delinquency "because you understand the problem which exists within you." Bowron seemed to see the CCLAY as a counterforce to groups such as El Congreso de Pueblos que Hablan Español, which generally had taken the position that any problems with Mexican American youth resulted from racial discrimination, and which readily criticized the LAPD for brutality. In order to ensure the reliability of the CCLAY, the mayor chose its leadership from among a list of names provided by the Los Angeles Roman Catholic archbishop John J. Cantwell. Bowron would go on to characterize the CCLAY leadership as being "of the right sort among the Latin American people," and the CCLAY was certainly more conservative than El Congreso had been in the late 1930s.[2]

Despite the expectations of the city's political elite, the CCLAY became a focal point for Mexican American political activity. An underlying premise for the organization was that Mexican Americans should take the lead in addressing their own problems. It stressed intra-ethnic cooperation and its members saw themselves as classic ethnic brokers. Thus, the CCLAY requested monies, established youth programs, and lobbied the mayor, the police department, other governmental agencies, and the press, all in the name of the Mexican American community. As CCLAY president Edward Quevedo stated, "People of Latin-American extraction who understand their people's problems should be working in direct co-operation with any group which is interested in the problems of Latin-American youth."[3]

This position meant that the CCLAY had, on the one hand, to acknowledge that severe "problems" existed within the Mexican American community and, on the other, to concentrate its efforts within that community. Thus, the CCLAY worked with various news organizations to advise Mexican American parents on how to cope with delinquent children and publicly contemplated how to address Mexican American youth's alleged inferiority complex, which was believed to lead to delinquency.[4]

The main focus of the CCLAY's efforts was, however, to work directly with youth. In taking on this activity, the CCLAY differentiated between the bulk of Mexican American youth and the more alienated pachucos, whose activities, dress, and attitudes were rejected by whites and Mexican Americans alike. Its activities focused on boys and neglected girls, probably on the assumption that the boys were more likely to get into serious trouble. The CCLAY leadership believed that the most direct cause of these youths' delinquency was that they were "maladjusted." Unable to relate to either American culture or the Mexican culture of their parents and having had poor experiences with both "the family group and the school group," these youths joined gangs in order to gain a measure of security and satisfaction. The CCLAY also believed that a consequence of the maladjustment was a deep "inferiority complex." The CCLAY leadership thus adopted many of the concepts developed by the sociological school of criminology.[5]

Basing its work on these ideas, the CCLAY developed youth programs aimed at improving the pachucos' self-image and integrating them into the larger society. These programs included individual counseling and leadership training, but the crux of the CCLAY's efforts was its therapeutic group work. This involved group therapy in which the boys not only talked about their problems but were also given the opportunity "to do things denied them elsewhere." The CCLAY also established mentoring programs in which adults worked with boys and helped them organize group activities such as sporting events or dances—one of the few projects that included girls. Finally, the CCLAY tried to negotiate truces between and among the various neighborhood groups in order to cut down on gang violence.[6]

Sometimes CCLAY leaders, in analyzing their youth work, articulated the same sociological hypotheses regarding Mexican American youth that prevailed within the academic community. They characterized leadership training, for example, as "a not too easy task in the face of the sense of inferiority of these boys." In developing group activities, the CCLAY noted that it worked "with a group that is at a low level of social adjustment. It is necessary to start with them at their own level and stress activities which are in the upper range of their interests, gradually leading them to still more worthwhile activities." The CCLAY thus had a rather low estimation of the abilities of the youths with whom it was working. According to a document written by Manuel Ruiz assessing the CCLAY's youth activities, the pachucos' "maladjustments are too deeply rooted and too little understood by themselves to permit eradication of anti-social habits and attitudes of long standing." On the other hand, the CCLAY also understood that these habits and attitudes would not be eradicated "until there is a definite change in the attitudes of the majority group, particularly some of those in authority, and in the environmental conditions which brought about most of these maladjustments in the first place."[7]

The CCLAY understood that discrimination and police misconduct helped foster the zoot-suit phenomenon and that it also had to address those two issues. Thus it worked to end discrimination in employment, housing, and the schools. More important, at least for the purposes of this study, the CCLAY used its leverage to try to affect the policies and practices of the LAPD. It called for the department to assign more Spanish-speaking officers to Mexican American neighborhoods. It also investigated and protested cases of police misconduct. In an early case, CCLAY secretary Manuel Ruiz wrote to Chief Horrall complaining about five Mexican American boys, "of good character," who had been "kicked, cursed and beaten" by an officer from the Hollenbeck Division. Fending off the LAPD's rebuttal that it had a particularly acute juvenile delinquency problem in that area, Ruiz asserted that "a police officer should be possessed of an innate sense of proportion to enable him to distinguish between the vicious juvenile and the good juvenile." The CCLAY secretary concluded, "If an officer places them both in the same category, the inevitable result will create disrespect for the law on the part of those upon whom this Coordinating Council is depending to assist the Police Department in its program to curb juvenile delinquency."[8]

SLEEPY LAGOON

Despite the formation of the CCLAY in 1941, official concern regarding Mexican American juvenile delinquency continued to grow throughout the summer of 1942. The incident, however, that sparked a full-scale offensive by the police against Mexican American youth was the Sleepy Lagoon case. The general facts regarding Sleepy Lagoon are well known and have been recounted in numerous sources.[9] On the morning of Sunday, August 2, 1942, José Díaz was found dying by a dirt road near a gravel pit called Sleepy Lagoon. He was taken to a local hospital, where he died later that day of head injuries. The next day newspapers attributed the death to "Mexican Boy Gangs" and over the next several weeks and months the local press repeatedly charged that a "Boy Gang Terror Wave" was sweeping the city.[10]

Police officers quickly arrested more than a score of Mexican American boys who lived in the vicinity of East 38th Street and whom the press promptly dubbed "the 38th Street Gang." On the night of August 1 one of the boys, Henry Leyvas, had gone to Sleepy Lagoon with his girlfriend and gotten into a fight with a group of Mexican American boys from the Los Angeles suburb of Downey (whom the press dubbed "the Downey Boys"). Leyvas returned to his own neighborhood to round up some friends and then went back to Sleepy Lagoon to find his adversaries. By this time, however, the Downey boys had attempted to crash a party at the nearby Delgadillo home, which, after a short fight, they left but vowed to return to. When the boys from 38th Street arrived at Sleepy Lagoon, they did not find the Downey boys and instead also tried to crash the party at the Delgadillo house. After another particularly brutal fight, Leyvas and his friends left. Díaz, who had been at the party but had left sometime between the departure of the Downey boys and the arrival of the boys from 38th Street, was found unconscious later that night.[11]

The actual circumstances surrounding Díaz's death were never determined. Díaz was inebriated and no one who saw how he received his injuries ever came forward. An autopsy reported that the injuries could have been caused by repeated falls or by an automobile accident. No proof existed that anyone actually killed Díaz. Moreover, no physical evidence linked Leyvas or any of his friends to Díaz. Nevertheless, police arrested more than a score of Mexican American boys and severely beat several of them in attempts to gain confessions about the alleged killing. Within a week prosecutors obtained first-degree murder indictments against twenty-two boys from the 38th Street neighborhood. Later, police also arrested three Mexican American girls who had accompanied the boys that night, and held them as material witnesses.[12]

The Sleepy Lagoon case occurred during a period of heightened conflict and hostility between police and the Mexican American community. The previous June, four Mexican American youths had allegedly attacked, beaten, and taken the gun of an auxiliary LAPD police officer. Throughout the summer a series of party crashes, gang fights, and even a killing had prompted local officials to call a meeting to find solutions for the growing rebelliousness of Mexican American youths. Just a week before Sleepy Lagoon, a major altercation occurred when two officers attempted to stop several Mexican American boys from playing dice outside their home. According to an eyewitness, the boys complained loudly when one of the officers pocketed the five dollars that had been in the pot. After the police left, the boys, to demonstrate their defiance, resumed the dice game. The officers, however, returned and attempted to arrest the boys. Three of the boys ran into a house where a party celebrating the Confirmation of several youngsters in the Catholic religion had been in progress for several hours. When the officers tried to follow, the owner of the house turned a water hose on them. The officers called in reinforcements and a small riot broke out, with people throwing rocks at the police, resulting in a broken windshield on one patrol car. A week later, one day after Díaz's death, seven people, including a pregnant woman, involved in the altercation at the Confirmation party found themselves indicted for violation of California's lynch law. The *Times* explained that the indictments were "an example of the swift action by law enforcement agencies" to combat Mexican American crime.[13]

Law-enforcement officials used the death of José Díaz as an excuse to try to repress the growing rebelliousness of Mexican American youth. The day the story broke, spokesmen at the sheriff's department and the LAPD issued statements saying that in the two departments' efforts against Mexican American juvenile delinquency, "The kid gloves are off!" County Sheriff Eugene W. Biscailuz ordered the formation of a special squad of " 'hardened' specialists . . . to wage all-out warfare on 'chain gang' juvenile killers and clubbers." Almost immediately this "all-out war" translated into police officers harassing zoot suiters by using razor-tipped pokers to rip the youths' pegged pants as they came out of dance halls. In order to underscore their new intent, police arrested an additional thirty-four Mexican American youths in connection with José Díaz's death.[14]

The apprehension of fifty-nine people for the death of one person was just the beginning of the law-enforcement campaign against the Mexican American community. On the weekend following Díaz's death, in an effort coordinated by the LAPD, officers from various law-enforcement agencies conducted a massive three-day sweep of the Mexican American barrios, taking into custody over six hundred youths. Officers from the various jurisdictions stationed themselves at strategic intersections and stopped passing cars containing Mexican American youths. LAPD Captain Joseph Reed boasted to Chief Horrall and the press that the arrests netted "knives, guns, chains, dirks, daggers or any other implement that might have been used in assault cases."[15]

Although they could not connect the youths to a specific crime, police arrested anyone who looked like they could have committed a crime sometime in the past. Because of the flimsy pretexts for the arrests, police charged the youths only with "suspicion" of having committed some offense—usually robbery or assault with a deadly weapon. To make a connection to a specific crime, LAPD officials announced a "showup" in which the arrested youths were paraded before the public in order to make specific identifications. The weekend's activities seemed to be based on the theory articulated by an LAPD official at the time, that "a Mexican is always a good suspect." While local newspapers cheered these events, the mass arrests became a sensation in the foreign press, and those sympathetic to the Axis powers pointed to the police actions as a sign of racism and repression in the United States.[16]

In the midst of this crisis atmosphere, the Los Angeles County Grand Jury initiated hearings into the extent, nature, and causes of Mexican American juvenile delinquency. The hearings and the debate they sparked among government officials and community leaders were remarkable for a number of reasons. First, they were the clearest articulation ever of law enforcement's attitude toward the Mexican American community. The hearings also revealed the LAPD's best thinking regarding how to deal with what it saw as a serious law-enforcement problem. Finally, the hearings showed the unanimous alarm with which the various segments of Los Angeles society—conservative police officers, liberal social activists, and even the Mexican consul—viewed the growing rebelliousness of Mexican American youth as exemplified by the zoot suit; they were unanimous, too, in labeling that rebelliousness deviant, antisocial, and criminal. These various "experts" on crime and the Mexican American community might have differed about the causes and extent of, and cures for, the phenomenon, but they agreed that the zoot suiters and the pachuco lifestyle represented a grave social ill that must be repressed.

The grand jury actually held its hearings in two phases. In the first phase, which began on August 4, the jury heard primarily from law-enforcement officials. Interestingly, police differed regarding the extent and causes of Mexican American juvenile delinquency, although they agreed that strong repressive measures were needed to combat it. Captain Edward Duran Ayres of the Los Angeles County Sheriff's Department's Foreign Relations Bureau spoke of a "crime wave" and of "the great proportion of crime by a certain element of the Mexican population." Inspector E. W. Lester of the LAPD's Juvenile Division agreed that "gang activities" had greatly increased and gave as proof statistics that showed the department arresting 81 percent more Mexican American youths for robbery in 1941 than it had done in 1940, 119 percent more for assault, and 48 percent more for grand theft auto. In contrast, Captain Vernon Rasmussen of the LAPD's Homicide-Subversive Bureau maintained that "the Mexican riot activities . . . [were] not as serious a threat to law and order" as others had alleged. He concluded that he was "not unduly excited about the Mexican situation and [he believed] that it is now being, and can be properly controlled."[17]

On the issue of the causes of Mexican American crime, the police officials were in greater accord but differed in the emphasis they placed on various factors. Of the officers who testified before the grand jury, only Captain Ayres of the sheriff's department addressed the issue of discrimination as a factor in causing crime. According to Ayres, Mexican Americans were "restricted in the main to only certain kinds of labor and that being the lowest paid." Poor economic conditions, in turn, led to "a lower perspective of responsibility and citizenship." In addition, "discrimination and segregation . . . in certain restaurants, public swimming plunges, public parks, theatres and even in schools, causes resentment among the Mexican people." "All of these, and other factors," Ayres concluded, "are the cause of the Mexican youth remaining within their own racial groups, resulting in what is now practically gang warfare—not only among themselves but also between them and the Anglo-Saxons."[18]

Other police officials gave various other explanations. The LAPD's Chief Horrall took a neo–Social Darwinist approach, arguing that the parents of the troublemakers were immigrants "of the poor class of Mexicans" who could not adapt to their new environment and who could not take full advantage of the opportunities American society had to offer. This second generation "lost respect for their parents and their parents have lost the ability to properly control them." Captain Rasmussen charged that the various recreational facilities the city had established throughout the Mexican American neighborhoods, instead of alleviating juvenile delinquency as intended, had led to the organization of local gangs, each gang associated with particular recreational facilities, and developing rivalries with gangs associated with other recreational facilities. According to Rasmussen, eventually these rivalries led to the gang fights that resulted in killings like that in the Sleepy Lagoon case. Rasmussen also believed that juvenile authorities had weakened patriarchal authority within the Mexican American family. He gave as an example the story of a Mexican American father who was ordered by the juvenile court not to whip his son. Because of the court order, the father "was absolutely without means to discipline or control his boy." As a result, Rasmussen contended, the boy had become involved in gang activities and had recently been arrested.[19]

Practically all the police officials argued that the leniency of the juvenile courts contributed to Mexican American juvenile delinquency. According to this line of reasoning, when the juvenile court refused to hear a case or gave nothing more than probation to a youthful offender, that youth was considered a "big shot" by his friends and other youth, who, desiring the same notoriety and prestige, then emulated the criminal behavior. Rasmussen of the LAPD believed that this type of response was unique to "the mental reactions of the type of Mexicans who belong to these various gangs" and that it was "exactly contrary to the attitude adopted by the respectable Caucasian element."[20]

The alleged inherent differences between whites and people of Mexican descent were most fully expressed by the sheriff department's Captain Ayres. While he acknowledged that discrimination contributed to crime among Mexicans, Ayres believed that the main cause of Mexican American criminality was biological. He argued that this "biological basis" for Mexican American crime stemmed from the fact that the Mexican Americans who lived in Los Angeles were descended from Indians of Mexico. According to Ayres, these Indians were inherently lazy: even if they received high wages and improved their standard of living, "they prefer to work half a week instead of a whole week." Moreover, Ayres argued, the Indians from which Mexican Americans were descended were inherently violent. After all, the Aztecs sacrificed thirty thousand Indians in one day. "This total disregard for human life," Ayres maintained, "has always been universal throughout the Americas among the Indian population, which of course is well known to everyone."[21]

Ayres also believed that Mexicans were particularly prone to violent crime. Unlike whites, who fought as individuals and used only their fists, he maintained, Mexican Americans fought in gangs and used knives and were not content until their biological lust for letting blood was satisfied. According to Ayres, all a Mexican "knows and feels is a desire to use a knife or some lethal weapon. In other words, his desire is to kill, or at least let blood." As a way of dramatizing the difference between whites and Mexican Americans, Ayres used the analogy of the difference between a common house cat and a wild cat. A common house cat could be domesticated and treated leniently. A wild cat, Ayres argued, would always be wild and must therefore be caged.[22]

Ayres's racial theories had significant implications for law enforcement's response to Mexican American juvenile delinquency, and Ayres did not hesitate to express those implications. Since he believed in the inherent criminality of Mexican Americans, Ayres called for harsh, repressive measures against that community. He proposed that all Mexican American males over the age of eighteen be forced into the armed services. Those under eighteen should be forced to be either in school or at work, and if any in this group should break the law, "they should be incarcerated where they must work under supervision and discipline." He also thought it essential that all gang members, whether they had committed a crime or not, should be incarcerated. "The hoodlum element as a whole must be indicted as a whole." Finally, Ayres warned that if these "drastic measures are not taken to put an end to gangster-ism[,] it will increase, with resultant murders, and that which none of us want to see—race riots."[23]

The Los Angeles law-enforcement establishment fully supported the Ayres report. Sheriff Eugene Biscailuz stated that Ayres, along with the other police officers who testified before the grand jury, gave a thorough analysis of Mexican American juvenile delinquency. Chief Horrall was even more direct, stating that the Ayres report was "an intelligent statement of the psychology of the Mexican people, particularly, the youths." Ayres's racial theories of criminality thus became official policy within the southern California law-enforcement community.[24]

The other officers who testified before the grand jury echoed Ayres's harsh prescription for dealing with Mexican American youth. The LAPD's Inspector Lester gave the most detailed strategy for dealing with the problem, reiterating some of the proposals put forth by a special committee created by Judge Robert H. Scott of the juvenile court "for the investigation and control of Mexican gangs." This plan, which epitomized an aggressive, professional style of policing, centered on the "swift and sure punishment" (to use Ayres's words) of anyone involved in gang activities. Thus, police would file petitions before the juvenile court in all cases of suspected law breaking by juveniles, whether for serious or for minor offenses. Moreover, any Mexican American youths belonging to a gang, whether or not they committed a crime, would automatically fall into the category of "children who do not have proper parental supervision and control, or who are in danger of leading an idle or immoral life," and as such would be arrested and have petitions filed against them. Finally, adult members of gangs, even if unconnected with any law breaking, would have charges of contributing to the delinquency of minors filed against them "where the charges are at all tenable."[25]

Another part of Lester's plan called for all government agencies to develop as much information as possible on Mexican American youths and to share that information among themselves. The main component of this part of the strategy was intensified investigations of all arrests and a greater emphasis on "field interrogations wherein suspected youths are stopped on the street and questioned regarding their identities, activities, etc." The information thus gathered would be compiled in a central juvenile delinquency file and made available to all law-enforcement agencies. The juvenile court would also send police details of the conditions of probation for all youths involved with gangs so that police could easily identify these youths and enforce the terms of probation. In addition, Lester called for more cooperation between school and law-enforcement officials, with the schools providing police with information about troublesome youngsters.[26]

The final aspect of Inspector Lester's plan concerned "the use" of the Coordinating Council for Latin American Youth to help police suppress Mexican American juvenile delinquency. To begin with, the CCLAY would encourage Mexican American boys to enter the armed services. Lester's plan also called for the organization to admonish gang leaders about the importance of obeying the law and shouldering "their responsibilities . . . in national defense." Finally, the CCLAY would give police the names of any gang leaders "who refuse to cooperate in this program of community betterment."[27]

The overall picture that police officials gave of Mexican American youth was one of a criminal and dangerous element within the society that must be suppressed even at the cost of violating civil liberties. As Captain Rasmussen asserted, in somewhat of a contradiction to his other statements regarding the seriousness of the problem, the Sleepy Lagoon killing showed that the Mexican American juvenile delinquency problem had "reached a stage where it must be dealt with firmly and without sympathy for the individuals." Even the usually moderate and sympathetic Chief County Probation Officer Karl Holton joined in the hysterical condemnation of Mexican American youth. He charged that the "kid gangsters" were "all saboteurs" because they drained needed resources away from the war effort. Matching Captain Ayres's rhetoric, he demanded that Mexican American boys either be at work or in the military. "If these fighting boys don't enlist or go to work," he warned, "we will take them out of circulation." Within a few days, Los Angeles area police departments made good on Holton's warning with their co-ordinated mass arrests of Mexican American youths and the "showup" that followed.[28]

THE LIBERAL REACTION

While white liberals condemned both the racist explanations for Mexican American criminality and the local law-enforcement agency's repressive measures, a large segment of the liberal community agreed that the zoot suiters constituted a serious problem that needed to be addressed. Carey McWilliams, already known as a liberal activist, attorney, and journalist, expressed these concerns in a letter he wrote in the wake of the Sleepy Lagoon incident to Nelson Rockefeller, then the coordinator of Inter-American Affairs for the State Department in Washington, D.C. Characterizing the local situation as "serious," McWilliams declared that "gangs of Mexican youth" existed in the community, that these gangs were "well organized" and, quoting local newspapers, that they engaged in "juvenile gang warfare." In addition, he implied that the gangs had fascist inclinations, claiming that they wore "distinctive" black or green uniforms. McWilliams believed that the causes for gangs lay with "the generally suppressed and submerged status of the local Mexican population." Finally, he declared that he had "no reason to believe that the local authorities are competent" to deal with the problem since their only approach was "a more severe police policy—in other words, repression." McWilliams concluded, "I confidently predict that this policy will be unsuccessful."[29]

McWilliams's ideas were echoed and amplified at the second phase of grand jury hearings into Mexican American juvenile delinquency. At the urging of two liberal members, Harry Henderson and Harry Braverman, the grand jury formed a Special Committee on Problems of Mexican Youth, which held a second set of hearings on the issue of Mexican American juvenile delinquency on October 8, 1942. This time testimony came from liberal activists, government officials, and academicians such as Carey McWilliams; Guy T. Nunn, field representative for the Minority Group Service of the War Manpower Administration; the UCLA anthropology professor Harry Hoijer; Walter Laves from the Office of the Coordinator of Inter-American Affairs; and the CIO representative Oscar Fuss. In addition, the newly arrived consul general from Mexico, Manuel Aguilar, also gave testimony.[30]

Each of the speakers attacked Captain Ayres's racial explanation for

Mexican American juvenile delinquency. McWilliams stated that he knew "of no scientific warrant for the doctrine that there is any biological predisposition on the part of any race toward certain types of behavior." Harry Hoijer noted that the history of Mexico showed no evidence that the Mexican people had a biological desire to kill or let blood. "Can it be," he asked rhetorically, "that this so-called inborn desire to kill has been found only twice in the history of the Mexican people—once among the relatively pure Indians of the Aztec Empire and the second time among a certain element of the Mexican population of Los Angeles?" Guy Nunn found it "improper, misleading and dangerous" to propose that juvenile delinquency was primarily a "Mexican problem." More blandly, Consul Aguilar pleaded that since Mexicans and Mexican Americans now fought hand in hand with Americans against a common enemy, everyone should "forget entirely any notion that we are dealing with people of an inferior race."[31]

Having dismissed the Ayres report, the speakers then went on to give their own analyses of the causes of Mexican American juvenile delinquency. All these speakers based their remarks on the assumption that the rise of the zoot-suit fad demonstrated that Mexican American youth constituted a serious crime problem in Los Angeles. They also all generally agreed that discrimination and poor living conditions contributed to the rise of juvenile delinquency in the Mexican American community. Nunn and Fuss, for example, saw a direct link between job discrimination, poor housing and living conditions, and youthful criminality. Nunn made the case most succinctly when he stated, "Delinquency is not a monopoly of any racial or national group; it is a monopoly of poverty, excessive housing concentration, social and economic discrimination."[32]

McWilliams and Aguilar took more sociological or psychological approaches. McWilliams stressed " 'cultural conflict' as being at the root of our local problem" and defined cultural conflict as a "second generation problem." Consul Aguilar agreed, adding that culture conflict and the second-generation problem resulted in Mexican American children developing a "faulty character," which in turn led to crime. However, it fell to Harry Hoijer to best synthesize the economic and behavioral science approaches and to most clearly articulate the liberal position. Hoijer argued that "a scientific analysis" of the problem made evident "that our Mexican population suffers from prejudice; that they are segregated in certain portions of the city and county, many places of amusement and recreation are entirely closed to them or are open to them only

under shameful conditions, they are often restricted to poorly paid occupations and are therefore of a low economic level, and finally, because
their poverty results in their living in crowded and unsanitary quarters,
the popular mind believes them to prefer squalor and filth to comfort
and cleanliness. . . . As a consequence they are driven in on themselves
and only the rare individual succeeds in adjusting himself completely to
our language, customs and ideals."[33]

Hoijer believed that such "suppressed minority groups . . . *inevitably*
find some mode of release from the intolerable conditions under which
they must live." This release took the form of engaging in "cult activities" and/or in "sporadic acts of senselessly violent behavior." Moreover, according to Hoijer, these problems and tendencies were exacerbated in the case of Mexican American youth who, on the one hand,
were ashamed of their parents' Mexican culture but, on the other hand,
were scorned by American society precisely because of their Mexican-
ness. "Individuals misunderstood at home and regarded as inferior
abroad can express their resentments *only* by violence against those they
believe to be their enemies." Mexican American youths therefore joined
gangs, gangs that "quite *inevitably* . . . engage in hostilities with one
another and in depredations against society at large." But, Hoijer concluded, these Mexican American "gangsters" should not be regarded as
common criminals; rather, he found them to be "individuals driven to
excesses of misbehavior by circumstances beyond their control"[34] (my
italics throughout).

On the basis of this analysis, the liberals went on to condemn the
LAPD's repressive tactics for controlling Mexican American crime. Guy
Nunn, for example, complained that the police actions heightened anti-
Mexican discrimination precisely in the area that created the conditions
that fostered criminality in the first place—the area of employment. He
argued that the mass arrests and the publicity the press gave them stigmatized the Mexican American population and made it more difficult
for them to get good, well-paying jobs. Harry Hoijer charged that rather
than curbing crime, the police's heavy-handed methods only aggravated
Mexican Americans' sense of frustration and resentment. "The gangsters are already responding violently to repression, segregation, and
defeat," he argued; "to increase these pressures would increase the violence of the response." The only way for law enforcement's tactics to
work, Hoijer concluded, would be for police to put all Mexican Americans under surveillance, a practical impossibility, or, more ominously,
to place them in concentration camps.[35]

Instead of police repression, the liberals argued for social programs to address the real causes of Mexican American juvenile delinquency: discrimination, economic deprivation, and miserable living conditions. Nunn, for example, called for an end to anti-Mexican discrimination in the schools and in public accommodations. He also argued for a lifting of federal restrictions barring noncitizens from certain types of defense work and for vocational training for adults and youths in order to prepare them for work in southern California's burgeoning military industry. Carey McWilliams focused on improving housing for Mexican Americans and Consul Aguilar called for more recreational facilities and activities for idle youth. Hoijer went one step further, urging that Mexican American youth be organized around an educational program that instructed them about "their rights and privileges as American citizens."[36] Clearly, Hoijer did not realize that Mexican Americans understood only too well their rights and privileges, and that it was exactly the discrepancy between that understanding and the reality of their lives that drove many into the symbolic rebellion of the zoot suit and a few into the nihilism of pachucismo.

Despite this liberal group's critique of police tactics and their recommendations of alternative ways to end Mexican American juvenile delinquency, their basic assumptions about the seriousness of the Mexican crime problem and, more important, their explanation for its causes in fact supported the harsh tactics of the police. Their fundamental error was that they failed to distinguish between the most alienated and pathological pachucos (comprising 1 to 3 percent of the youth population) and the Mexican American youths who wore zoot suits but who were generally law abiding. Instead, these liberals accepted the notion that the zoot suit was synonymous with delinquency and as such constituted a grave social problem, and that the root cause of this problem was discrimination. The irony of this analysis is, of course, that it was every bit as deterministic as Captain Ayres's racial explanation for Mexican American juvenile delinquency. Ayres may have believed that Mexicans were biologically inclined toward crime and violence, but the belief that discrimination and economic deprivation caused crime led every bit as "inevitably" to the same conclusion: that Mexican Americans were inherently criminal.

Given the pervasiveness of that discrimination, most Mexican American youths could be expected to become alienated from American society. Moreover, as long as Mexican American youths suffered from racial discrimination, they would continue to engage in delinquent behavior. Consequently, although these liberals railed against the repressive tactics of the police, their deterministic analysis in fact supported law enforcement's repressive measures. Since the function of the police was to fight crime, and since Mexican Americans were either biologically or environmentally inclined toward criminality, the police had to do everything within their power to try to suppress the evident danger that Mexican American youths posed to society. To do anything else would be contrary to the major tenets of the police professionalism model.

All this is not to say that no one dissented from the prevailing view. In a long article, County Chief Probation Officer Carl Holton presented evidence from probation department records showing that, compared with a similar period in 1941, fewer Mexican American youths faced prosecution during the first half of 1942. From these statistics he concluded that "there is no 'wave of lawlessness' among Mexican children" in Los Angeles. Edward Quevedo, chairman of the Coordinating Council for Latin American Youth, made the same point even more emphatically. Newspapers reported that in response to the liberals' testimony before the grand jury on October 8, Quevedo angrily declared that "there was no Mexican gang problem, no organized gangs, 'only a lot of disorganized, idle, unhappy boys, against whom discrimination has been practiced since babyhood.' "[37]

In addition, "The Report of [the] Special Committee on [the] Problems of Mexican Youth of the 1942 Grand Jury" gave an eloquent defense of the Mexican American community. This report, written by liberals Harry Henderson and Harry Braverman, ignored the Ayres report and the general law-enforcement explanation for Mexican crime and instead adopted the view that pervasive racial discrimination and its economic and social consequences created delinquency among Mexican American youth. Nevertheless, it accepted the argument that the overwhelming majority of Mexican American juveniles did not commit crimes and that "for every delinquent there are a host of splendid youth, good citizens, loyal to the highest American ideals." The report concluded "that young people of Mexican ancestry have been more sinned against than sinning, in the discrimination and limitations that had been placed on them and their families."[38]

The recommendations made by this committee emerged directly from its analysis of the causes of Mexican American juvenile delinquency. These recommendations included the classic liberal agenda of ending employment discrimination and discrimination in public accommodations, improving housing conditions, increasing educational opportu-

nities (but only in the area of "technical training"), providing more recreational facilities, and putting an end to police brutality against
prisoners. The committee also recommended that "the Board of Education, so far as possible, employ only teachers who speak the Spanish
language" in schools with high numbers of Mexican American children
and that the various law-enforcement agencies "assign to districts inhabited by Mexican people only officers with special qualifications for
this duty." Finally, in a seeming contradiction of the generally sympathetic tone of its analysis, the committee endorsed and attached to its
own recommendations the report of the Special Committee on Older
Youth Gang Activity in Los Angeles appointed by Judge Robert H.
Scott.[39]

The inclusion of the Scott committee's report demonstrated the Los
Angeles liberal community's confusion on the issue of Mexican American crime. The Scott report uncritically presented law enforcement's
agenda for dealing with Mexican American juveniles and through its
rhetoric and recommendations reinforced the idea that a Mexican American crime wave was sweeping the city. For example, the report stated
that in order to provide for the "immediate protection of [the] community . . . all organizations and citizens" must give police "every assistance and encouragement in taking into custody anyone suspected of
implication in assaults and gang activity." The overwhelming majority
of the report's recommendations addressed law-enforcement issues, such
as laying down conditions for probation and parole and suggesting
where to jail convicted juveniles. It also reiterated the proposals made
the previous August before the grand jury by the LAPD's Inspector Lester. In some cases it went even further. While Lester had recommended
that school officials give police the records of only troublesome children,
the Scott committee proposed that records of all students be made ac-
cessible to police during summer vacation.[40]

Only at the end of its report did the Scott committee address social
concerns, calling for increased "technical training" and recreational activities for Mexican American youths. The committee also noted that
social and economic conditions helped incite "these acts of crime and
violence" and stated that "the community at large, labor and management, church and school, adult as well as youth" needed to undergo
"an improvement of mind and attitude" if these social factors were to
be addressed. It is noteworthy that the Scott committee did not list law
enforcement among the segments of the community that required an
improvement in attitude for juvenile delinquency to be prevented.[41]

THE MEXICAN AMERICAN RESPONSE

White liberals' confusion regarding the causes, extent, and nature of Mexican American criminality and the measures that public officials should take to combat the phenomenon was echoed within the Mexican American community. Most believed, like Harry Hoijer, that juvenile delinquency was the result of discrimination. For educator George I. Sánchez, one of only a handful of Mexican Americans in the country holding a Ph.D., "the seed for the pachuco was sown . . . by unintelligent educational measures, by discriminatory social and economic practices, by provincial smugness and self-assigned 'racial' superiority." Sánchez placed the blame on school segregation and employment discrimination, which made Mexican American youth "a caste apart, fair prey to the cancer of gangsterism." Criminal gang members should be punished, he asserted "but what of the society which is an accessory before and after the fact?"[42]

Nevertheless, despite Edward Quevedo's angry remarks at the time of the second grand jury hearings, Mexican American leaders and their organizations took essentially defensive positions regarding police actions against their community in the wake of the Sleepy Lagoon incident. Throughout the pachuco hysteria, for example, *La Opinión,* the city's leading Spanish-language newspaper, faithfully reported police officials' various pronouncements regarding juvenile delinquency and even exceeded the most virulent rhetoric of English-language newspapers. Similarly, before Sleepy Lagoon, Fred Rubio, who was affiliated with both the Mexican American Movement and the Coordinating Council for Latin American Youth, had defended Mexican American youth, claiming that some groups, such as the East First Street Gang, were not violent gangs but functioned just like "other social and athletic groups." As the zoot-suit hysteria gained momentum, however, Rubio became more critical, and by the time of Sleepy Lagoon he was equating "extreme dress" with juvenile delinquency and calling on merchants, including public dance managers, to refuse service to "extra-drape" zoot suiters.[43]

More surprising was the changed attitude of El Congreso de Pueblos que Hablan Español. As noted in chapter 7, El Congreso was a leftist Mexican American civil-rights organization that during the late 1930s had taken a leading role in protesting LAPD misconduct. With the United States' entry into World War II on the same side as the Soviet Union, however, El Congreso attenuated its emphasis on discrimination and focused instead on the struggle to defeat fascism. It thus responded to the anti-Mexican hysteria by taking a position similar to that of white liberals, but with the added twist of emphasizing the alleged link between pachucismo and the Mexican pro-Axis group, the Sinarquistas.[44]

In a press release apparently issued shortly after Sleepy Lagoon and the mass arrests, El Congreso ignored the issue of police misconduct and declared that its prime concern was maintaining home front "harmony and unity" and fighting the Sinarquistas. El Congreso blamed Mexican American "gang activities" on "fascist-minded elements among the Mexican people [who] were spreading hatred against the American government and people." Discrimination and lack of opportunity were indeed problems for Mexican Americans, the press release stated, but primarily because they created "a constantly worsening problem of juvenile delinquency, which . . . could result in unsuspecting youths being utilized for fifth column work by fascist agents or sympathizers." Demanding a cessation of these alleged Sinarquista activities, El Congreso even called for an FBI investigation of the Mexican American community to determine the extent of fascist influence. Other El Congreso members took even harsher positions, arguing that juvenile delinquents between the ages of sixteen and eighteen should be summarily drafted into military service. Later, however, individual members of El Congreso, such as Josephina Fierro de Bright and Bert Corona, would take the lead in establishing a defense committee for the youths accused in the Sleepy Lagoon case.[45]

The Coordinating Council for Latin American Youth took a somewhat more aggressive, if not less confused, stance regarding events surrounding Sleepy Lagoon. To begin with, law-enforcement officials "indirectly" consulted the CCLAY leadership regarding the "crackdown" that resulted in the mass arrests of August 1942. While it is not clear how the CCLAY leaders responded to these inquiries, there is no record that they ever publicly protested the mass arrests, or that they officially denounced Captain Ayres's racist theories of criminality. Instead they sought to assist the youths caught up in the police roundups. CCLAY secretary Manuel Ruiz, for example, as a member of another committee, went before the California State Bar Association to request legal aid for the youths apprehended in the mass arrests. The CCLAY also officially appointed two investigators to seek information regarding the mass arrests and to assist attorneys in defending the youths. CCLAY president Edward Quevedo's angry statement that "there was no Mexican gang problem" at the time of the grand jury hearings was the closest that organization's leadership ever came to deviating from the prevailing wisdom on the criminality of Mexican American youth.[46]

To a certain extent, the CCLAY leadership's reticence to speak out on the issues of Mexican American criminality and police tactics was understandable. The organization was brought into being to combat juvenile delinquency. Participation in this activity gave young professionals like Quevedo and Ruiz status and access to people with power. This not only meant their appointment to various committees and leadership within the Mexican American community, it also meant they could affect the policies of the LAPD and other agencies of city and county government. If, on the other hand, they minimized the importance of Mexican American juvenile delinquency, they also minimized the importance of their work. Similarly, a public denunciation of the activities of the police would alienate them from the department hierarchy and preclude any chance they might otherwise have had to affect LAPD policies and practices.[47]

Consequently, those who spoke against the idea that Mexican American youth were inherently criminal or who denounced the activities of the LAPD were few and isolated. A group called the Youth Committee for the Defense of Mexican American Youth wrote to Vice President Henry Wallace in September 1942 protesting the Sleepy Lagoon mass arrests and complaining that the police "treat us like criminals [for] just being Mexican." Similarly, an anonymous letter was sent to the Los Angeles County Grand Jury the following month, calling the mass arrests "provocative, persecutory, and uncalled for by the actual extent of delinquency among such youth" and requesting an investigation of the roundups. More to the point, a petition circulated in the Mexican American community accused local law-enforcement agencies of harboring "adherents to the social doctrine of 'suppression and segregation' [who] have implanted in the public mind the lie that delinquency among juveniles of Mexican extraction has increased." Referring to the Ayres report, the petition went on to demand that the sheriff's department "cease to sanction . . . unproved sensational and fantastic charges concerning Mexican youth" and called for cessation of the mass arrests and equal enforcement of the law. The existing copies of both the letter to the grand jury and the petition are unsigned and there is no evidence that local public officials responded in any way to the charges or demands contained in either document.[48]

THE OFFICIAL RESPONSE

The confusion and ambivalence among both white liberals and Mexican American leaders not only allowed public officials to ignore the few isolated voices of protest, they left no significant political force to counter those who advocated the repression of the zoot suiters. Thus, politicians and police officials had a free hand to shape the debate regarding the nature of and the appropriate response to Mexican American crime. The combination of provocative language from public officials, severe law-enforcement measures, and sensational press coverage generated an irrational public fear that Mexican American youths were engaged in a crime wave that threatened the entire community.

One of the points that city officials almost immediately contested was the critics' charge that the police discriminated against Mexican Americans. As early as November 1942, police commission president Van Griffith told a delegation from El Congreso and other groups that the LAPD had not engaged in discrimination during the mass arrests of the previous August. Mayor Fletcher Bowron supported Griffith's contention and for good measure tried to intimidate critics of the LAPD by insinuating that people who charged the department with discrimination were in fact "enemy agents." "We believe," Bowron stated in an address to the city, "that someone behind the scenes is trying to suggest that we are persecuting Mexicans in Los Angeles for the purpose of stirring up misunderstanding and discord." He added that the LAPD was working with the FBI to find out who was "stirring up the people to foment trouble." Bowron would continue to deny throughout the period of the hysteria that any anti-Mexican bigotry existed in Los Angeles.[49]

Instead of condemning the mass arrests or the LAPD's other repressive tactics, Mayor Bowron supported the department's stern measures. In response to a petition calling for the initiation of programs to better integrate Mexican Americans into the community, Bowron stated that he would cooperate with county government in attacking the causes of Mexican American juvenile delinquency, but promised that the city was "not going to mollycoddle a lot of tough kids[,] and we are going to enforce the law." The district attorney took a similar position, promising "an all out war . . . against 'zoot suit' hoodlums." Hearing this type of language from city officials only served to heighten whites' fears of Mexican American youths.[50]

What government officials meant by waging an "all out war" on the zoot suiters soon became apparent during the trial of the young men accused of killing José Díaz. The trial of the Sleepy Lagoon defendants took place in a circus atmosphere. Throughout the trial, newspapers ran banner headlines broadcasting the latest depredation by "Zoot Suit Boy Gangsters" and "Pachuco Killers." Los Angeles newspapers referred to the trial itself with headlines such as "Zoot Suit Trial" and "Gang Trial," and one newspaper even called it a "Mass Murder" trial, although only one person had died. The worst offender was the *Los Angeles Herald and Express,* which referred to the trial as the "Goon" or "Gooner Trial" and which described the defendants as "the goons of Sleepy Lagoon."[51]

The press could not, however, compete with police officials when it came to inciting popular sentiment against the Sleepy Lagoon defendants. In December 1942, in the middle of the thirteen-week trial, Clem Peoples, chief criminal investigator for the sheriff's department and the person in charge of preparing the prosecution testimony, published a highly provocative article in *Sensation* magazine, in which he gave his version of the events at the Delgadillo house the previous August. Peoples named each of the defendants in the case and identified Henry Leyvas as the "ring leader of the blood thirsty mob" that killed José Díaz. Although no one ever saw how Díaz received the fatal injury, Peoples described a scene in which the "ruffians" chased Díaz from the house and began beating him brutally. While Díaz lay on the ground begging for mercy, according to Peoples, "one of the demons lifted his bludgeon above his shoulder and brought it down with all his strength on the head of the moaning man." Peoples charged that the only reaction from the assailants came when one of them inspected the body and "spat from the edge of his mouth: 'Guess we croaked 'im all right.' " The Peoples article received wide publicity in Los Angeles during the final month of the trial.[52]

The trial itself was a travesty. The heart of the prosecution's case was the assertion that, in retaliation for the beating Henry Leyvas had received earlier, the defendants had entered into a conspiracy to commit murder. In words reminiscent of the Ayres report, the prosecution charged that the defendants entered this conspiracy "as the result of their malignant hearts . . . [and] in satisfaction of their lust for revenge." To underscore their collective guilt, the district attorney's office did not allow the defendants to get their hair cut or wear a change of clothes. The prosecuting attorney, Clyde C. Shoemaker, gave this directive in an effort to maintain the defendants' "distinctive" appearance, which, according to Shoemaker, was in itself important evidence. George Shibley, one of the defendants' attorneys, stated that through this practice "Mr. Shoemaker is purposely trying to have these boys look like mobsters, like disreputable persons, and is trying to exploit the fact that they are foreign in appearance." Shoemaker also repeatedly alluded to the boys' Mexican ethnicity and referred to them in front of the jury as "gangsters" and members of the 38th Street Gang. The prosecution's prejudicial tactics continued until a delegation, which included representatives from the Mexican Chamber of Commerce and El Congreso, met with the district attorney, who subsequently agreed to allow the defendants to have a change of clothes and haircuts. Nevertheless, in another calculated allusion to the Ayres report, Shoemaker, in his summation to the jury, stated that "there was 'a smidgeon of truth' to the proposition that all Mexicans are cowards and do not fight fair."[53]

One of the reasons the prosecution could violate the defendants' rights with impunity was that the presiding judge in the case, Charles W. Fricke, was biased. Coming into the case, Fricke already had a reputation for being avidly pro-prosecution and for having an anti-Mexican attitude. He denied the defendants the right to sit with their attorneys during the trial, and consequently the boys conferred with their lawyers only during breaks from the proceedings. Throughout the proceedings, Fricke rebuked and ridiculed the defense attorney, thus prejudicing the jury. He accused one defense attorney of being a ventriloquist's dummy and told another to look up a point of law during the lunch hour. He also characterized a defense attorney's statement as "absolutely unworthy of any respectable member of the Bar" and accused another of "serious misconduct" for objecting to a prosecution witness using notes during testimony. Fricke also effectively prevented Henry Leyvas's attorney, Anna Zacsek, from testifying about the beating her client took at the hands of police by ruling that if she testified, she could not continue as Leyvas's counsel. As an appellate court would later rule, Fricke admitted into evidence information that was prejudicial to the defense and erroneously denied defense attorneys' motions to admit evidence that helped their clients. He also made contradictory rulings on the same points of law, depending on whether the ruling helped or hindered the prosecution. Fricke once even referred to the defendants as members of a "gang" similar to the organized crime gangs of Chicago.[54]

Given the atmosphere in the community and the antics in the courtroom, the jury's verdict was virtually a foregone conclusion. Although the prosecution presented no evidence in court that any of the defendants so much as assaulted José Díaz, on January 13, 1943, the jury found three of them, including Henry Leyvas, guilty of first-degree murder, nine others of second-degree murder, and five of assault. Fricke sentenced those convicted of first-degree murder to life imprisonment, those convicted of second-degree murder from five years to life, and the five boys found guilty of assault to six months in the county jail.[55]

THE SLEEPY LAGOON DEFENSE COMMITTEE

The trial, conviction, and sentencing of the Sleepy Lagoon defendants aroused Los Angeles liberals and leftists, both white and Mexican American, as no case involving Mexican Americans had in the past. On October 21, 1942, in the early stages of the trial, a small group came together to discuss the Sleepy Lagoon prosecutions. On November 1, Josephina Fierro de Bright, who had previously helped organize El Congreso, chaired a second meeting, this time open to the public, and attended by about sixty people, most of them Mexican American. Under the leadership of Fierro de Bright and LaRue McCormick, of the International Labor Defense, these two meetings produced the Citizens' Committee for the Defense of Mexican-American Youth, which eventually became known as the Sleepy Lagoon Defense Committee (SLDC).[56]

Like other liberal and leftist groups during the war, the SLDC had as its initial central concern maintaining unity and strength for the fight against fascism. Working on the assumption that the trial, statements from the police and the press, and generalized discrimination were demoralizing the Mexican American community, the committee at first attempted to address all these issues. It soon became apparent, however, that such a broad scope was logistically impossible, and the committee narrowed its focus solely to assisting in the Sleepy Lagoon defense. During the trial this meant raising money for the attorney fees and sending delegations to the district attorney to protest prosecutor Shoemaker's prejudicial tactics. After the convictions, the committee continued to focus on fund-raising, but now for the appeal and this time on a massive national scale.[57]

The SLDC differed from other organizations of the time in that it had to focus on a case of official discrimination against Mexican American youths instead of on juvenile delinquency. Unlike El Congreso it could not equate pachucismo with juvenile delinquency and blame it all on the Sinarquistas. As an early document noted, "It will be difficult to prove, both to the courts and the public, that Mexican youth under arrest have been incited to illegal outbreaks by Sinarquistas and are at the same time innocent, in the main, of criminal activities." Similarly, the SLDC could not work to uplift Mexican American youths in the way the CCLAY could, because to do so would distract it from its focus of mounting an appeal of the Sleepy Lagoon convictions.[58]

Because the heart of the SLDC's argument was that the Sleepy Lagoon defendants were the victims of a biased criminal justice system, it publicized the idea that Mexican Americans as a group were victims of systemic racial prejudice. Thus, immediately after the trial ended, the SLDC issued a broadside entitled "We Have Just Begun to Fight!" This pamphlet claimed that the convictions were gained by "calloused" and "ambitious" prosecutors and through " 'confessions' and 'admissions' plainly gotten through beatings and terror by the notorious Los Angeles police and sheriff's offices." Characterizing the trial as "grimy with prejudice," it placed the proceedings within the context of "an ancient campaign of bigotry and persecution of an entire people, the Mexican-Americans of California, a half million decent citizens long leashed in 'second-class' status by profiteers of labor and an indifferent public." While this type of rhetoric may have already been familiar within segments of the Mexican American community, the fact that it became part of a nationwide fund-raising effort meant that now thousands of whites throughout the United States became aware for the first time of anti–Mexican American discrimination in the Southwest.[59]

The SLDC's campaign, however, could only have a limited effect on the growing zoot-suit hysteria in Los Angeles. This was so because instead of discussing generalized discrimination against Mexican Americans, the SLDC focused its efforts on the immediate issue of publicizing the injustice of the Sleepy Lagoon trial in order to raise funds for the appeal. Its main effort in the spring of 1943 was aimed at writing and publishing *The Sleepy Lagoon Case,* a pamphlet that stressed the need for national unity and touched on the atmosphere of discrimination against Mexican Americans, but that centered on raising sympathy for the seventeen "boys" convicted in the case. This necessary but limited focus proved successful in raising funds but had little impact in the spring of 1943 on the rising hysteria in Los Angeles regarding Mexican American criminality.[60]

HYSTERIA ON THE RISE

The conviction and sentencing of the Sleepy Lagoon defendants also allowed the press to resume its campaign against Mexican American youths—a campaign that continued throughout the spring. In the aftermath of the verdict, newspapers fed a growing hysteria by printing provocative stories that highlighted alleged pachuco attacks on innocent whites. In early February 1943, for example, several newspapers ran stories about a fourteen-year-old white girl who was dragged off the street and into a car by four zoot suiters; she was gagged and was about to be raped when she hit one of her assailants with a pop bottle and managed to escape. Another story told how two Mexican American youths jumped into a white woman's car as she stopped at an intersection and forced her to drive to a hotel, where they allegedly raped her. During the same period one particularly pathetic headline read, " 'Zoot Suiters' Rob Lad of His Movie Money." Another story, headlined " 'Zooters' Threaten Teacher at Dance," told how "A gang of Mexican 'zoot suiters' . . . threatened to 'cut down' a school teacher." Still another story told how " 'twin zoot suiters' . . . bound and gagged a 65-year-old woman and her 2-year-old granddaughter" in order to rob them of a total of fifteen dollars. Although this particular piece did not identify the assailants as Mexicans, it did make it a point to mention that the suspects were "dark-skinned."[61]

As the public's reaction to these stories turned from concern to fear to hysteria, the press became even more provocative in the stories it published, and began using traditional stereotypes of Mexicans. A piece in early March 1943 referred to alleged suspects in a kidnapping case as "a knife-wielding 'zoot-suit' gang." This same story told of another group of Mexicans who assaulted a man by throwing him to the ground and "beat[ing] him in the face with a large rock." Some newspapers also made thinly veiled references to the Indian ancestry of Mexican Americans in their reports. In a story on an alleged zoot-suit "rampage," the *Wilmington Press* stated that "zoot-suited Mexican gangsters staged a foray here tonight, according to the police, when seven of their tribe assaulted S. Rodriguez."[62]

Again, however, the rhetoric of the local press paled in comparison with the actions of the police. On May 7 and 8, 1942, newspapers reported that LAPD officer O. W. Andrews shot and killed twenty-two-year-old Patrick Nuñez. According to the *Herald and Express,* the episode started when officers tried to stop a car containing "three pachuco-suited youths" in downtown Los Angeles. The young men tried to outrun the police but crashed their car into a curb. Two of the occupants of the car immediately surrendered, but Nuñez tried to run and Andrews gave chase and eventually caught him. The *Times* reported that Andrews shot Nuñez three times in the stomach after Nuñez hit the officer on the mouth with a rock or piece of concrete. None of the newspaper accounts explained why the officers decided to stop the car in the first place.[63]

At around the same time as the Nuñez killing, another incident took place that raised tensions between Mexican Americans and whites even higher. On Saturday, May 8, a group of Mexican American youths, several of whom wore zoot suits, went dancing at the Aragon Ballroom on Lick Pier in Venice Beach, west of downtown Los Angeles. Local white high school students, resenting the fact that Mexicans had invaded their territory, began spreading rumors that zoot suiters had "taken over the beachfront" and promised to "straighten things out." Soon a large group of sailors joined the crowd and someone yelled, "A sailor's been stabbed . . . let's get the zooters." An LAPD officer on duty tried to calm the crowd, assuring everyone that no one had been stabbed and that the Mexican American boys and girls inside the ballroom were not troublemakers.[64]

Despite the officer's efforts, the rumors spread, and when the Mexican American dancers tried to leave the ballroom the crowd attacked them, yelling, "Let's get them[,] . . . let's get the chili-eating bastards." The rioters indiscriminately beat the Mexican Americans they encountered. According to one eyewitness, "They didn't care whether the Mexican kids wore zootsuits or not, . . . they just wanted Mexicans." Another source later claimed that zoot suiters fought back, even attacking police officers. The fighting continued until 2:00 A.M., when a combined force of Los Angeles and Santa Monica police officers and the shore patrol dispersed the mob. Interestingly, despite the fact that white high school students and servicemen were clearly the aggressors, police arrested only Mexican Americans. One officer explained this disparate enforcement of the law by claiming, "Our actions are limited by what the public thinks. The sailors and high-school kids got hold of rumors, everybody was upset with jittery emotions wanting to let off steam. So you had a riot, and the zootsuiters were the safety valve. You'll have to admit the only thing we could do to break it up was arrest the Mexican kids."[65]

The aftermath of the riot caused almost as much furor as the battle itself. Two days later a major fire gutted the Merchants Building located a block from the pier, causing a hundred thousand dollars' worth of damage and injuring four firefighters. Newspapers reported that police and fire officials suspected that zoot suiters set the blaze in reprisal for the previous riot and arrests. The only evidence that officials gave to support this version of events was that someone saw two youths wearing zoot suits "loitering" near the building shortly before the fire. The newspapers never reported whether anyone was ever arrested for the blaze.[66]

The trial of the eleven Mexican American boys arrested at the Venice riot also caused controversy and demonstrated the hostile attitude that criminal justice officials had toward Mexican Americans and the resentment that Mexican American youths felt toward the justice system. At the trial, Anna Zacsek, the attorney for several of the boys, argued that her clients were not near the scene of the riot, but "were arrested by police in amusement places and on the streets." When Officer M. W. Pugh hesitated in identifying the defendants, Zacsek moved for a dismissal for lack of evidence.[67]

Before Judge Arthur Guerin ruled on Zacsek's motion, however, he gave the boys a stern twenty-minute lecture from the bench on Americanism, on their patriotic role as Mexican Americans, and on the zoot-suit crime wave he believed was sweeping the city. Obviously feeling compelled to grant the dismissal, Guerin echoed the recommendation made by other law and order advocates for solving the juvenile delinquency problem: "If any of you actually were involved in this fracas or have any such belligerent ideals, then I suggest that you go to a recruiting office where you can find the proper outlet for it." Only then did Guerin grant Zacsek's motion.[68]

Guerin's admonitions, however, did not go unchallenged. Alfred Barela, one of the boys on trial that day, wrote Guerin a letter that, in its straightforward eloquence, articulated the indignation that many Mexican American youths must have felt at the anti-Mexican campaign being waged against them in the newspapers and by the police and the courts:

> You gave us quite a severe lecture, said we were a disgrace to our people and you said that Mexican boys are a grave problem and you don't understand yourself what's wrong. . . . I was sore at your lecture because instead of bawling out the cops, you bawled us out and took it for granted that we really had been doing something we shouldn't. . . . We had nothing to do with any riot or any fighting. The cops picked us up, pushed us around, made fun of our clothes, grabbed some of us by the hair and said they're going to give us a haircut. . . .
> Ever since I can remember I've been pushed around and called names

because I'm a Mexican. I was born in this country. Like you said I have the same rights and privileges of other Americans. Pretty soon I guess I'll be in the army and I'll be glad to go. But I want to be treated like everybody else. We're tired of being pushed around. We're tired of being told we can't go to this show or that dance hall because we're Mexican or that we better not be seen on the beach front, or that we can't wear draped pants or have our hair cut the way we want to.

Why didn't you bawl those cops out? How come he [Officer Pugh] dais [sic] there were twenty-five hundred people in that mob and only a few Mexican kids, but all the arrests were of the Mexican kids and none of the others arrested? Why do cops hate the Mexican kids and push them around? You should see the way the cops searched us for knives and guns as though we were gangsters. They didn't let us call up our folks and my ma was plenty worried about what happened to me. You say we've got rights like everybody else. Then how can they do this to us?

Other Mexican kids are like me and my friends. Their [sic] may be a few tough ones like their [sic] are in every neighborhood, but it's not because they're Mexican. Maybe it's because they're poor.

I don't want any more trouble and I don't want anyone saying my people are in disgrace. My people work hard, fight hard in the army and navy of the United States. They're good Americans and they should have justice.[69]

Barela's voice, however, like so many others that protested the mistreatment of Mexican Americans, went unheard and unheeded. Instead, throughout the spring the anti-Mexican hysteria continued and eventually engulfed Los Angeles. Back in March, the *Herald and Express* reported that it had learned from police that "a cowardly horde of 'pachucos' " had committed still another assault. April and May saw a steady stream of stories, also originating with police, in which the press accused Mexican American youths of everything from assault and robbery to arson, rioting, murder, and even sabotage. The SLDC complained and called a meeting to discuss the matter, but to no avail. By the end of May, the campaign reached fever pitch. On May 25 the *Los Angeles Times* began a story on four alleged assaults that took place the night before with the following sentence: "In a veritable reign of terror four separate gangs of zoot-suiters yesterday launched attacks on peaceful citizens at widely scattered points." Anyone who read this story must have believed that the war had come home to Los Angeles; that "Zoot Suit gangsters" roamed the streets at will, attacking "peaceful citizens"; that police, by and large, could provide little defense; and that citizens therefore had to take the law into their own hands to end the "Pachuco menace." In a little more than a week, Los Angeles citizens did just that.[70]

CHAPTER 11

The Riots and
Their Aftermath

The Zoot Suit riots that raged in Los Angeles between June 3 and June 10, 1943, were the direct result of the anti-Mexican hysteria of the preceding year. For months, government and police officials, the press, and a variety of civic leaders had all trumpeted the idea that anyone who wore a zoot suit was a criminal. Now, through their ritual beating and stripping of the zoot suiters, the servicemen were meting out what most agreed was well-deserved justice. The fact that the police condoned and even assisted the servicemen indicated the broad local support for the servicemen's actions. When the rioting ended, however, as a result of a War Department order declaring Los Angeles off-limits to military personnel, many people began reassessing not only the wisdom of the mayhem but also the more general treatment of Mexican Americans in southern California.[1]

The Zoot Suit riots in fact shook Los Angeles as no other single event had at least since the bombing of the Times Building in 1911. As the rioting subsided, a debate emerged over who was responsible for the violence and how to prevent its recurrence. At the national level, a broad political spectrum, from *Time* magazine on the right to the *People's World* on the left, put into print what became the prevailing interpretation: that the riots resulted from racial discrimination. In contrast, Los Angeles's civic leaders steadfastly denied any racial motives for the violence and instead looked toward the alleged Mexican American crime wave as the cause of the riots. The debate that developed shows how

234 The Riots and Their Aftermath

various ideological groups viewed the riots. More important, the synthesis that evolved from this debate had a profound impact on the future of race relations in the city, shaping the relationship between the LAPD and the Mexican American community for decades to come. Mexican Americans became Los Angeles's principal "oppressed minority" group, and Mexican American youth were stigmatized as a criminal element within the community.

THE RIOTS

The Zoot Suit riots resulted from the public hysteria over the alleged Mexican American crime wave and from the anti-Mexican campaign conducted by public officials and the press. That campaign apparently had a particularly profound effect on the thousands of servicemen stationed in and around Los Angeles. The servicemen, many of them away from their families for the first time and facing the imminent danger of combat, read the newspaper accounts of "pachuco crime" and feared for their safety. Every actual incident created greatly exaggerated rumors of pachuco depredations, and the servicemen decided to deal with the zoot suiters themselves.[2]

The actual basis for the servicemen's fears is difficult to determine and may have been misdirected. Captain Martin Dickinson, commander of the naval base at Chávez Ravine, publicly stated that zoot suiters "insulted or attacked" ten of his men in April 1943 and twenty in May. A report issued by the navy as the rioting was ending recounted several altercations between sailors and zoot suiters that allegedly had taken place in the previous months. While it is impossible to determine the veracity of these reports, to the extent that these incidents actually occurred they undoubtedly led to anger and fear among servicemen. Other sources indicate, however, that those emotions, instead of being focused on zoot suiters, should more accurately have been directed elsewhere. The historian Mauricio Mazón surveyed local sources and found that in the weeks before the riots, servicemen did indeed face danger when they went into the city, but that that danger came more from other servicemen and from white civilians than from Mexican Americans. According to Mazón, eighteen major violent incidents involving servicemen in southern California were reported in the *Los Angeles Times,* seven of which ended in death. None of the seven incidents ending in death involved a zoot suiter, and only one of the other eighteen incidents, the Venice riot of May 8, included any Mexican American participants. As noted earlier, in the Venice riot the servicemen were the aggressors, and the judge dismissed the charges against the Mexican American youths arrested by the police.[3]

Whatever the factual basis for their fear, servicemen concluded that they and their loved ones were unsafe in Los Angeles. A typical attitude was shown by a serviceman who wrote to the Mexican American attorney Manuel Ruiz during the rioting, signing only his first name, Johnny. Johnny believed that "god-damn mexican punks" were "raping women and knifing lone soldiers" in Los Angeles. "I'll be damned," Johnny declared, "if my buddies and I want to fight and defend the rights of our countries while over seas [sic], when just as great, if not greater an enemy[,] is right at our door step, commiting [sic] rape, murder, and endangering the lives of our loved ones." He said he was disgusted that the police could not handle the situation and threatened that if he and his buddies had to go into Los Angeles, "there will be a lot of sorry mexicans." "I for one," Johnny stated, "would kill any of them that hurt any body [sic] I know, soldiers or any of the women I know in L.A." Other servicemen echoed Johnny's attitude. "We do not intend," said a marauding serviceman, "to be beaten and seriously injured while on leave here. If the police can't handle these little gangsters, then we will."[4]

The trouble began on Sunday, May 30, when a group of zoot suiters fought with eleven sailors as they walked through the heart of the Mexican American barrio of Alpine. According to the youth worker Henry Marín, the attack may have been in retaliation for two of the sailors dating the girlfriends of two Mexican American boys. Whatever the cause, elements within the LAPD decided to act. In what amounted to a vigilante action, a group of fourteen off-duty LAPD officers led by a detective lieutenant descended on the Alpine barrio to summarily punish the zoot suiters. In addition, in the days following the May 30 fight, groups of sailors in taxicabs reconnoitered the Mexican American neighborhoods, looking for places where zoot suiters congregated. By Thursday, June 3, the sailors were prepared to strike.[5]

That evening, several dozen sailors from the Chávez Ravine naval base rampaged through the Alpine district, beating every zoot suiter they found. At one point they entered the Carmen theater, pulled Mexican American boys as young as twelve years old from their seats, and beat them viciously. Ironically, a group of zoot-suited boys who had attended a meeting at LAPD headquarters to discuss ways of reducing juvenile delinquency happened on the scene and were attacked by the marauding sailors. The sailors next roamed down side streets, entering restaurants and beer parlors and attacking any Mexican American wearing a zoot suit. Although the shore patrol issued a riot call, neither the shore patrol nor the LAPD managed to arrive at the scene of any incident until after the sailors had left. The evening's violence did not end until the shore patrol arrested several sailors near downtown and sent the rest back to their base. Later that night authorities released all the prisoners without filing any charges.[6]

Thursday's events set the stage for the next several days of rioting. On Friday, June 4, in what the *Los Angeles Daily News* called "open warfare," two hundred sailors hired a fleet of taxicabs and drove through downtown Los Angeles and later through East Los Angeles, beating a score or so of zoot suiters and sending five to the hospital. The shore patrol and the LAPD never managed to intercept the rioting sailors until they returned to their bases, where several were arrested. Again, no charges were filed and the combination of few arrests and no prosecutions gave implicit sanction to the sailors continuing their attacks. The manner in which the press reported the rioting demonstrated that the wider community also condoned the lawlessness. The *Los Angeles Herald and Express,* for example, described the evening's events with the headline "Sailor Taskforce Hits L.A. Zooters," and the story in the *Los Angeles Times* had the headline "Zoot Suiters Learn Lesson in Fight with Servicemen."[7]

With the apparent approval of law enforcement and the press, the sailors, now joined by army personnel and marines on leave for the weekend, set out to rid the city of the hated pachucos. On the evening of Saturday, June 5, scores of servicemen swarmed through downtown Los Angeles, accosting Mexican American youths and giving them twenty-four hours to shed their zoot suits or face severe consequences. Other servicemen went into East Los Angeles, where they again attacked individuals wearing drapes. On Sunday evening, despite the presence of an additional three hundred LAPD and sheriff's department officers on the streets, the servicemen made good on the previous night's threat, invading East Los Angeles and attacking any zoot suiters they found. One group of sailors, for example, chased zoot suiters into a dance hall on First and State Streets. According to the *Daily News,* the sailors left the Mexican American youths "crawling about with battered heads and smashed noses." Throughout the night, the servicemen continued their attacks, always managing to leave the scene of a beating "just ahead of the shore patrol and the police," as the *Daily News* coyly reported.[8]

The LAPD seemed to have adopted an informal policy of allowing the violence to continue as long as the servicemen had the upper hand. According to *Time* magazine, "The police practice was to accompany the [servicemen's] caravans in police cars, watch the beatings and jail the victims." Although LAPD officials denied any partiality during the violence, local Mexican American observers and the press confirmed that officers often stood by while servicemen assaulted Mexican American boys. If zoot suiters tried to fight back, however, police leapt into action. At the same time that the officers were refusing to arrest servicemen for rioting, the LAPD and the sheriff's department arrested as many as six hundred Mexican American youths.[9]

Moreover, police and other government officials encouraged the servicemen to expand their attacks on Mexican American youth. One anonymous police officer, during the height of the violence, stated that "the only way to handle these gangster kids is to whale the daylights out of them." Los Angeles County Supervisor Roger Jessup publicly echoed this attitude, stating, "All that is needed to end lawlessness is more of the kind of action as is being exercised by the servicemen—if this continues[,] zooters will soon be as scarce as hen's teeth." Police also incited even more rioting by issuing highly provocative statements. After they arrested a group of sixteen zoot suiters who had somehow arranged to "have it out" with a gang of sailors on California and Temple Streets, police told reporters that "those arrested were armed with broken bottle necks, steel bars, truck wrenches, tire irons and hammers." The *Daily News* reported that, according to police officials, "the zooters admitted they planned to attack more sailors and would jab the broken bottle necks in the faces of their victims. . . . Beating sailors' brains out with hammers and irons was also on the program."[10]

Newspaper stories such as these had a profound impact on the servicemen who read them. One group of eight men traveling through Los Angeles read such a story at the train station and, instead of catching their train, recruited a larger band and went out looking for zoot suiters to beat up. Eventually the shore patrol caught them and locked them up. According to military officials, incidents such as these showed "how excited they [servicemen] get . . . from just reading the papers."[11]

The Mexican American community reacted to the rioting with anger and alarm. Manuel Ruiz reported that Mexican American boys were "bitter . . . since they feel they are being attacked without cause and they are not receiving the protection which is their due." Rudy Sánchez, a boy from the Alpine barrio who attended the community meeting at

LAPD headquarters the first night of rioting, wrote an angry letter to Edward Quevedo, chairman of the CCLAY, conveying the bitterness of many. According to Sánchez, "Pityless [sic] sailors" beat and sent to the hospital boys as young as twelve years old, "just because their [sic] Mexican." Dan G. Acosta, another Mexican American youth, asked why the police ignored or "even hurrahed" the rioting sailors. He wanted to know why police arrested only " 'pachucos' " whom the servicemen had yanked out of theaters and restaurants "in Hitlerite fashion, [and] pounded with bottles, clubs, belt buckles, etc. [Not] until these questions are answered," Acosta asserted, "will we the Mexican people feel at ease from the fear of a possible internment at a concentration camp for feeling free to wear what we wish." Rudy Sánchez asked the question that must have gone through the minds of many Mexican Americans: "On who's [sic] side is the Navy on anyway, Uncle Sam or Hitler?"[12]

The Mexican American middle-class leadership responded more cautiously than these young men did to the crisis. The Coordinating Council for Latin American Youth waited until its regular meeting on June 7 to discuss the rioting. The group that met that day, and which included several white guests, heard Rudy Sánchez's letter and reports both on meetings with city and police officials and on the inflammatory stories in the local newspapers. After some discussion, which included deliberation on the possibility of fascist or "fifth column" influence as a cause for the zoot-suit phenomenon, the only action the CCLAY took was to send a telegram to the Office of War Information requesting that the OWI persuade local newspapers to tone down their inflammatory coverage of the riots.[13]

A more heated discussion took place at the meeting of the Citizens' Committee for Latin-American Youth. The debate there revolved around the issues of police conduct and whether the War Department should declare Los Angeles off-limits to military personnel in order to stop the rioting. Attending the meeting were representatives of the Mexican American community, of law enforcement, of the Mexican consul, of the Sleepy Lagoon Defense Committee, and of the federal government, as well as Los Angeles County Supervisor John Anson Ford, one of the few high-level elected officials in southern California who had championed Mexican American causes. Chairman Manuel Ruiz Jr., Edward Quevedo, and other community representatives gave reports describing servicemen's attacks on Mexican American youths while police stood by and did nothing. The community representatives also stated that, contrary to reports in the newspapers, Mexican American youths had not yet retaliated, but if they did not receive police protection, they warned, "there will be serious trouble." Captain Brewster of the sheriff's department characterized reports of police inactivity as "erroneous" and noted that police officers could make arrests only if they witnessed an actual violation of the law. Brewster also revealed, however, that the sheriff's deputies regularly ordered "all Mexican groups" found congregating on the streets to disperse or face arrests. No mention was made of similar orders being given to servicemen.[14]

In the hope of stopping the rioting, Josephina Fierro de Bright, who represented the Sleepy Lagoon Defense Committee, recommended that the Citizens' Committee ask the army and navy to declare the Mexican American neighborhoods of Los Angeles out-of-bounds for military personnel. Law-enforcement representatives reacted with hostility to this recommendation. The LAPD's Captain Reid replied "that if Navy men were forbidden to go into certain sections, the Pachucos should be forbidden to go where they pleased." Lt. Edward Duran Ayres of the sheriff's department agreed, adding that local merchants would lose business if federal authorities declared Los Angeles off-limits. Law-enforcement representatives also insisted that their respective departments could handle the situation and that the out-of-bounds order was unnecessary. Because of so much controversy, the Citizens' Committee only managed to reach two innocuous decisions—one that called for "an impartial community agency to study the situation and present an unbiased statement of fact," and a second that requested "increased facilities for social guidance among Mexican youth."[15]

Contemporary liberal chroniclers of the riots echoed the assertions made by Ruiz and Quevedo at the Citizens' Committee meeting that the zoot suiters did not retaliate against the servicemen. Carey McWilliams, for example, contended that in the first few days of the riots Mexican Americans made no counterattacks against the servicemen; instead, he portrayed servicemen and police as the aggressors and Mexican Americans as powerless victims. Most modern scholars have generally agreed with this interpretation. It stretches credulity, however, that the proud and rebellious pachucos, who readily fought each other over minor affronts, would sit passively while strangers invaded their neighborhoods and even their homes.[16]

The events of Monday, June 7, the climactic day of the riots, show that the zoot suiters in fact fought back vigorously. The violence began with the press and servicemen going on the offensive. That afternoon, newspapers ran special editions with headlines announcing that zoot suiters planned "TO KILL EVERY COP WE SEE" and gave details of when and where the attacks were to occur. On schedule, thousands of servicemen and civilians converged on the appointed location in the heart of downtown Los Angeles and started hunting down, beating, and stripping every Mexican American boy they found. The crowd surged through the downtown, bursting into restaurants, bars, penny arcades, pool halls, and theaters, dragging out unsuspecting Mexican American boys, beating them, and leaving them lying naked in the gutters. The scene at the Orpheum theater exemplified what happened throughout the downtown area that night. Servicemen grabbed Mexican American boys wearing zoot suits, took them onto the stage, and stripped them of their clothes, thus humiliating them in front of the audience. At least half the victims, however, did not wear zoot suits and were attacked simply because they were Mexican. According to Carey McWilliams, Mexican American boys were so fearful of the mayhem that they pleaded with police to arrest them. "Charge me with vagrancy or anything," McWilliams quoted one boy as saying, "but don't send me out there!"[17]

The dynamics of the violence changed, however, after the servicemen left the immediate downtown area. After three days of being victimized, Mexican American youths apparently decided to defend themselves and took the fight to the servicemen. According to the *Daily News,* zoot suiters had decided "to stop fighting among themselves and concentrate on the United States navy." The *Los Angeles Herald and Express* reported that on that Monday night, "police estimated more than 700 of the grotesquely-clad hoodlums . . . roamed Los Angeles bent on the common purpose of . . . engaging in battle with service men." While the press and the police undoubtedly exaggerated the numbers to make the zoot suiters look more menacing, it is clear that Mexican Americans fought back.[18]

The best-documented battle of June 7 took place on the corner of Central Avenue and 12th Street. Rudy Leyvas, the brother of the Sleepy Lagoon defendant Henry Leyvas, gave an account of what happened that night—an account that emphasized the determination of Mexican American youths to defend themselves and even strike back at their enemies:

> The sailors had been beating up zoot suiters for about a week. The radio was even broadcasting when and where they were coming. This time we were going to be ready for them. All day we were just transferring guys from the

neighborhoods into the city. The black people loaned us their cars to use. . . . We rounded up at least 500 guys.

Toward evening, we started hiding in alleys. . . . Then we sent about 20 guys right out into the middle of the street as decoys. Then they came up in U.S. Navy trucks. There were many civilians, too. There were at least as many of them as us. They started coming after the decoys, then we came out. They were surprised. It was the first time anybody was organized to fight back. Lots of people were hurt on both sides. I was about 15 then, and I had a baseball bat. I came out OK, but I know I hurt a lot of people.[19]

The fighting became even fiercer when the mob crossed the bridges over the Los Angeles River and invaded the barrios of East Los Angeles. There, the servicemen not only hunted down Mexican American youths on the streets and in public places, they even entered people's homes. Jews who lived in the area wondered if they were witnessing a pogrom. But again, the Mexican American youths fought back. According to Beatrice Griffith, it was in the homes of Mexican American families that the most violent battles were fought.[20]

Mexican American women also defended their barrios and retaliated against attacks on their communities. Police arrested one woman for cursing them as they interrogated a group of Mexican American boys near her home. Although her husband was away in the navy himself, she clearly did not identify with the rampaging sailors and told reporters at the county jail that she believed that police should stop harassing zoot suiters. Another young woman stated that she paid seventy-five dollars for her zoot suit and added: "Nobody is going to take it off me, either." Like their male counterparts, Mexican American women also developed organized resistance against their antagonists. The *Daily News* reported that a group of young Mexican American women "vowed to enter the fighting in force, in revenge for attacks on boy friends by servicemen."[21]

Shortly after midnight on the morning of June 8, military officials declared downtown Los Angeles out-of-bounds for military personnel. Commander Clarence Fogg, the officer in charge of the shore patrol, called for the restriction because "hundreds of service men [were] prowling downtown Los Angeles mostly on foot—disorderly—apparently on the prowl for Mexicans." Despite the continued assertions by the press that the servicemen were only defending themselves, the naval commandant for southern California characterized his men's activities as "mob violence" and declared that "the [military] men now engaging in these demonstrations are actuated mainly by a desire for excitement." Indicating that he believed that the LAPD had allowed the rioting to go on unabated, Rear Admiral David W. Bagley also promised to maintain the restrictions "until I am assured that Los Angeles can . . . provide, with their police, the safety of both civilians and Navy people[,] and I shall not follow the recommendation to take off [the] restriction and put on heavier [shore] patrol because I want them to do it themselves."[22]

Despite these official efforts to restore order, local newspapers continued to inflame public opinion against Mexican American youth. In a signed editorial on June 9, Manchester Boddy, the powerful publisher of the *Daily News,* excoriated Mayor Bowron, the LAPD, and even other Los Angeles newspapers for not taking a tougher stance against the zoot suiters. "The time has come," Boddy declared, "to serve notice that the city of Los Angeles will no longer be terrorized by a relatively small handful of morons parading as zoot suit hoodlums." He charged that past "temporizing" on "the hoodlum problem" had led to the rioting that rocked the city and claimed, mistakenly, that military officials had declared Los Angeles out-of-bounds because "organized hoodlums began assaulting servicemen." He demanded that the LAPD guarantee that "every street . . . will be made safe for any man, woman or child 24 hours of every day." According to Boddy, failure to acquire the resources to make good that guarantee "borders mighty close on criminal negligence." The Los Angeles City Council, apparently taking its cue from Boddy, passed an ordinance outlawing the wearing of the zoot suit.[23]

While the out-of-bounds order effectively ended the zoot-suit riots downtown, the disturbances spread to outlying districts such as Watts and Pasadena for the next two days. In Watts, for example, groups of servicemen disembarked from Pacific Electric railway cars at 103rd Street, barged into stores and theaters, and cut the cuffs of any Mexican American boys wearing pegged pants. Initially no one challenged the servicemen, and no police appeared until a shouting match developed between several Mexican Americans and the servicemen. As they had done downtown, police took into custody only the Mexican Americans, allowing the servicemen to leave. When Henry Marín asked the officer in charge why the LAPD arrested only the Mexican American boys, the officer said that he considered anyone wearing any part of the zoot-suit costume to be a hoodlum. In apparent retaliation for the servicemen's attacks and the LAPD's hostility, zoot suiters stoned Pacific Electric trains as they went through Watts for the next several days. According to the *Daily News,* "nearly every window of an outbound Long Beach tow-car train was smashed when it was caught in crossfire of pachuco stoning." Sporadic violence of this kind continued throughout southern California until the end of the week.[24]

THE DEBATE

As the rioting wound down, residents and officials began to debate the causes of and remedies for the violence. The most widely accepted opinion regarding its main causes pointed to long-standing anti-Mexican racism, the resultant poverty and alienation among Mexican Americans (especially among the youth), police misconduct, and journalistic irresponsibility. Proposed cures for these problems included ending discrimination against Mexican Americans, integrating Mexican Americans into the American mainstream, improving the relationship between the police and the minority communities, and curbing the excesses of the press. Variations existed within this interpretation depending on political ideology, but at the state and national levels a general consensus emerged that Mexican Americans were the victims, not the aggressors, in the riots.

Los Angeles civic leaders, however, in particular the mayor and the local press, refused to accept any responsibility for the disorders and angrily rejected the notion that any anti-Mexican sentiments existed in their city. Instead, they publicly declared the riots to be a minor flare-up between an unruly element within the community and rambunctious servicemen looking for excitement. This view called for increased law-enforcement actions against the zoot suiters and for military authorities to control the servicemen.

The prevailing interpretation began to take shape even as the violence wound down. On June 11 an ad hoc group called the Los Angeles Committee for American Unity, consisting of Mexican American, African American, and white liberals and leftists, issued a report that not only asserted the racial motivations for the riots but also placed primary responsibility for the atmosphere of racial hysteria that led to the outbreaks directly on the police and the press. According to this unity committee, official statements, police tactics (such as the mass arrests), and irresponsible press coverage all converged to convince the public and the servicemen stationed at nearby bases that all Mexican American youths were zoot suiters and that all zoot suiters were criminals who needed punishment. As proof that the riots were racially motivated, the committee noted that servicemen attacked Mexican Americans and African Americans whether they wore zoot suits or not, but left alone zoot suiters of other racial groups.[25]

The committee stated it had "clear and convincing evidence" that the LAPD aided and abetted the rioting. It cited as an example the servicemen's attack on Mexican Americans at the Meralta theater on the evening of Monday, June 7. Although the theater was only three hundred feet from the LAPD's Hollenbeck Division headquarters and although "many carloads of policemen" were available at the time, the officer in charge refused to send help to stop the rioting. The committee also claimed that it had evidence that officers "actually assisted the rioters by clearing the streets of women and very young children in anticipation of the rioters" and verbally encouraged the servicemen to continue in the rioting. Even more alarming was the committee's charge that officers actively participated in the rioting and beatings of Mexican American youth. Finally, the committee called for a grand jury investigation into the rioting and the apparent bias of the police in handling the violence.[26]

The views of the Committee for American Unity were echoed by the report of the official inquiry into the riots. Even as the violence peaked, Governor Earl Warren appointed a "Citizens Committee" to investigate the causes of and remedies for the civil strife. Chaired by Catholic Auxiliary Bishop T. McGucken and including only one Mexican American, actor Leo Carillo, the committee issued its report on June 12. While couching the report in diplomatic language, the McGucken committee's findings and recommendations were still stunning rebukes to Mayor Bowron, local newspapers, and especially law-enforcement agencies. Noting that most of the victims were either Mexican American or African American, the committee linked the rioting to "race prejudice" and called for an educational program "to combat race prejudice in all its forms." The committee had particularly harsh criticism for the mass arrests of the previous year, saying that such "group accusations foster race prejudice" and lead the public "to believe that every person in the accused groups is guilty of crime." Within this context, the report reiterated that only a handful of Mexican Americans committed crimes, that Mexican American juvenile delinquency was growing at a slower rate than that among the general population, and that simply wearing a zoot suit or belonging to a neighborhood "gang" did not necessarily make a person a criminal. The committee stated the novel premise that "it was a mistake in fact and an aggravating practice to link the phrase 'zoot suit' with the report of a crime."[27]

The McGucken committee's recommendations emerged directly from this analysis. The main recommendation under the heading of "Delinquency," for example, called for police to make arrests "without undue emphasis on members of minority groups." Other recommendations under this category directed law-enforcement agencies to hire more Mexican American police officers and to provide training to officers already on the force for "dealing with minority groups." While the committee called for more detention facilities for juvenile offenders, it also requested that local lawyers' groups work "to protect the rights of youth arrested for participation in gang activity." In addressing what actions should be taken against those guilty of rioting, the committee dealt the LAPD what was perhaps its cruelest blow. Putting the LAPD and zoot suiters on the same plane, the report called for punishing all law breakers "regardless of the clothes they wear—whether they be Zoot suits, police, army or navy uniforms." It was one thing for liberals to accuse the LAPD of wrongdoing; it was quite another for a committee appointed by a Republican governor to equate a police uniform with a hated zoot suit.[28]

A broad range of publications across the national political spectrum agreed with this interpretation, from the staunchly Republican *Time* magazine and *Chicago Tribune* to the liberal *PM* and the Communist Party's *People's World*. *Time*, for example, blamed the *Los Angeles Times* and the two Hearst papers, the *Examiner* and the *Herald and Express*, for inciting the worst of the rioting on Monday, June 7. *Time* also specifically criticized the LAPD for contributing to the violence by allowing the servicemen to go free and continue rioting while arresting only their Mexican American victims. *PM* also blamed the press for the rioting and additionally gave several examples of police brutality toward Mexican Americans. The Los Angeles CIO Council issued a statement condemning the press, in particular the Hearst newspapers, for inciting the mobs, and censuring the LAPD and the Los Angeles County Sheriff's Department for their biased handling of the riots.[29]

Eleanor Roosevelt, wife of President Franklin D. Roosevelt, succinctly summed up the prevailing attitude when she characterized the turmoil in Los Angeles as a race riot. At a press conference on June 16 she traced the origins of the riots to "long-standing discrimination against Mexicans in that part of the country." Placing the riots within the context of growing racial problems in the United States, she added that she had long "worried about the attitude toward Mexicans in California and the States along the border."[30]

Finally, Mexican American leaders and their organizations also criticized the police and the press for their roles in the riots and helped shape the debate by obtaining firsthand accounts from the Mexican American youths. Most prominent among these leaders was Edward Quevedo, who not only sat on the executive committee of the Committee for American Unity but was also chairman of the Coordinating Council for Latin American Youth (CCLAY) and an outspoken member of the Citizens' Committee for Latin-American Youth. Undoubtedly, much of the Unity Committee's "clear and convincing evidence" of LAPD misconduct came from Quevedo's contacts in the community. Within the CCLAY and the Citizens' Committee, Quevedo took the lead in denouncing the LAPD for its "negligence and passiveness" and the press for continuing to incite violence. Moreover, while the CCLAY never issued a public statement on the riots, it wrote a letter to Eleanor Roosevelt "commending . . . her bold and unequivocal stand, to the effect that race prejudice was the controlling fundamental factor inciting the recent riots." Thus, even the group that Mayor Bowron characterized as being "of the right sort among the Latin American people" now condemned his police department and agreed with those who said the riots resulted from a racist strain within Los Angeles society.[31]

Los Angeles civic leaders vehemently disagreed, arguing that no anti-Mexican sentiments existed in their city. As the violence wound down, city officials, newspaper editors, and other civic leaders attempted to limit the damage done to the city's reputation by the riots. Of most immediate concern was the off-limits order that prohibited servicemen from entering the downtown area, thus hurting the profits of local merchants. Even more important, however, was the possibility that negative publicity from the riots would impair southern California's ability to continue procuring the lucrative military contracts that were enriching the region.[32] To put the best light on a bad situation, community leaders—politicians, newspaper editors, and other business people—developed a strategy that placed primary responsibility for the riots on Mexican American youths and on the military, and that denied that either anti-Mexican racism or police misconduct had anything to do with the violence.

The official reaction to the riots initially took the form of statements issued by Mayor Bowron on June 9 that set out the basic themes of the city's explanation for the civil strife. Bowron categorically stated that the violence was "not in any manner directed at Mexican citizens or even against persons of Mexican descent." "Nothing that has occurred can be construed as due to prejudice against Mexicans or discrimination against young men of any race," he said. In addition, the mayor declared the accusations that police had discriminated against Mexican Americans during the riots as having no basis in fact. He characterized those who in any way linked the rioting to racism as "sentimentalists" who cared only about protecting "the disturbing element in the community."[33]

Rather than attribute the riots to racism, Bowron placed the blame on "the formation and activities of youthful gangs" and servicemen who "pile into Los Angeles for the purpose of excitement and adventure and what they might consider a little fun by beating up young men whose appearance they do not like." While the mayor expected that the army and navy would control their men, he promised that LAPD officers would discard their "powder puffs" and resort to "two-fisted action" to control the Mexican American gangs. "If young men of Mexican parentage or if colored boys are involved it is regrettable," Bowron declared, "but no one has immunity and whoever are the disturbers are going to be sternly dealt with."[34]

The Los Angeles newspaper establishment supported Bowron's position. The *Los Angeles Times,* which just a few weeks earlier had declared that zoot suiters were engaged in a "veritable reign of terror" over the city, now called for "sanity." For the *Times,* sanity meant rejecting the notion that the riots had anything to do with racial prejudice or official discrimination. In a rare, if not unprecedented, front-page editorial, the *Times* declared that such charges were not only "unthinking" and "unsupported," they were also a threat to the unity needed to prosecute the war. The *Times,* the city's most important newspaper, said it understood the seriousness of the situation but dismissed the riots as only a "flare-up of retributive violence" for zoot-suit "gangsterism." It thus saw "no reason . . . to permit unfounded charges of racial strife to bring about an overemphasized reaction."[35]

One of the local newspapers' major themes in the days following the violence was the negative impact that the military's off-limits order was having on local merchants and the need for the federal government to lift the ban. The press's primary strategy was therefore to minimize the significance of the riots. Manchester Boddy, editor of the *Daily News,* thus changed his position of just a few days earlier, now declaring that "only a ridiculously small percentage of the local Mexican population is involved in the *so-called 'gang' demonstrations*" (my italics). In what was perhaps the biggest reversal of editorial policy at the time, the *Los Angeles Herald and Express* wrote that because of "erroneous reports," many people saw East Los Angeles, the section of the city with the largest Mexican American population, as unsafe. Nothing, it now reported, was further from the truth. Responding to area merchants' complaints of reduced sales, the newspaper concluded that East Los Angeles was in fact "populated by high-class, energetic and cultured people who are both proud of their district and jealous of its good name."[36]

The biggest long-term difficulty that civic leaders had to combat, however, was the widespread belief that the riots were racially motivated. The *Times,* for example, attacked "the attempt of certain political and pressure groups to pervert the flare-up into 'racial persecution' or 'race riots.' " It also cautioned the governor's Citizens Committee to focus on eradicating "juvenile gangsterism" and "not be diverted from its purpose by those who seek to inject race hatred into a situation that is difficult enough as it is."[37]

When the theme of racial motivation came directly from the White House, in the form of Eleanor Roosevelt's statement characterizing the violence as a race riot, Los Angeles civic leaders reacted almost hysterically. Preston Hotchkis, the president of the California State Chamber of Commerce, declared that the "so-called 'zoot-suit' riots have never been and are not now in the nature of race riots." Moreover, he continued, "the statement that the citizens of California have discriminated against persons of Mexican origin is untrue, unjust and provocative of disunion among people who lived for years in harmony." The *Los Angeles Times* denounced Mrs. Roosevelt in even angrier terms. Denying that any anti-Mexican discrimination existed in Los Angeles, the *Times* charged that Mrs. Roosevelt's statement "shows an amazing similarity to the Communist party line propaganda, which has been desperately devoted to making a racial issue of the juvenile gang trouble here."[38]

In addition to this public campaign, local leaders, in particular Mayor Bowron, worked behind the scenes to save the city's reputation. In a series of letters written in the summer of 1943, some of them quite remarkable, Bowron attempted to reconstruct the history of the zoot-suit hysteria in order to castigate his critics and exonerate his administration. These letters, however, said very little new. For the most part they restated the position that the mayor had articulated since the earliest days of the hysteria: in them he claimed that no anti-Mexican discrimination existed in his city, that the source of the problems was the zoot-suit gangs that just happened to be made up of Mexican American youths, and that the LAPD acted properly and without any prejudice in trying to suppress the gangs. It was not their restatement of the mayor's position that made these letters extraordinary; rather, it was the transparent manner in which Bowron attempted to manipulate and perhaps even misrepresent facts in order to manipulate federal officials' perceptions of the riots.

Bowron began with a bitter letter to Elmer Davis of the Office of War Information (OWI), complaining of the activities of OWI representative Alan Cranston. Responding to international criticism, the OWI had sent Cranston to Los Angeles at the time of the Sleepy Lagoon incident and the subsequent mass arrests to try to gain information and develop remedies for the situation. Cranston had achieved temporary success in persuading local newspapers to tone down their coverage of Mexican American crime. He had also worked with some of the more liberal Mexican American leaders and had given his moral support to the formation of the Sleepy Lagoon Defense Committee. In the wake of the riots, Cranston returned and began working with those who sought to end anti-Mexican discrimination. It was these activities that raised the mayor's ire.[39]

What enraged Bowron was that during Cranston's visit to Los Angeles, he had allied himself with those who claimed that anti-Mexican racism was at the heart of the hysteria and the riots. The mayor characterized these people as "busybodies," "radicals," and "disturbers and agitators" who, "by rushing to the defense of the young hoodlums . . . and raising a hue and cry about racial discrimination and minority groups," had caused "irreparable damage to the City of Los Angeles." Cranston, in Bowron's eyes, had thus "busied himself with many things that are not appreciated either by myself or others who feel that their responsibility for local conditions is our own." Bowron thus "respectfully suggest[ed]" that local officials be allowed to deal with the local situation "without federal interference."[40]

In an even more remarkable letter, Bowron wrote to Chief of Police C. B. Horrall, directing him to rewrite his official report on the riots and giving him explicit and detailed instructions on what the report should contain. Bowron clearly intended that Horrall issue a report that countered the various charges that his administration, and in particular the LAPD, had mishandled the situation. For example, to forestall the effects of an official Mexican government protest over the riots, Bowron instructed Horrall to state that an LAPD investigation of the riots "shows that no Mexican citizen was arrested by the Police Department" and that, to the department's knowledge, no Mexican citizen was attacked by servicemen. Only parenthetically did Bowron note that if Horrall had knowledge to the contrary, he should state the facts.[41]

Most important, Bowron wanted the chief's report to state that the LAPD's actions had been necessary to combat the criminal "Mexican gangs" and that these actions were not the products of anti-Mexican discrimination. To accomplish this, the zoot suiters had to be vilified. Consequently, the mayor directed his chief of police to state that at the small riot at the Venice Beach pier the previous May, zoot suiters had attacked police officers with brass knuckles and saps and had later burned down a city block in retaliation for being arrested. Bowron also instructed Horrall to state that in response to increasing violence, "some of the substantial local Mexican residents appealed to the Police Department for protection, urging vigorous action against the members of the gangs." This proved, Bowron asserted, "that it was the Mexicans themselves and not the members of the Police Department that brought about numerous arrests of youths of Mexican parentage." There appears to be no evidence to substantiate Bowron's claim.[42]

Bowron also wanted the police report to show that in all their activities regarding Mexican American youths, police officers had been instructed "that racial discrimination would not be tolerated and that any action of the police officer in any arrest should be without reference to race, color or creed." Police officers might sometimes need to take "vigorous action," but only because of the criminal activities of "the young hoodlums involved" and not because of their ethnic background. "It is unfortunate that many local young men of Mexican blood have been arrested," the mayor stated, "but it is at the same time regrettable that young men of Mexican blood have violated the law."[43]

Finally, in order to explain why the LAPD only arrested Mexican American youths during the riot and not the marauding servicemen, Bowron believed that "an inferential criticism of the Navy Shore Patrol might be conveyed in the report." Bowron thus instructed Horrall to state that the LAPD had always deferred to the shore patrol when it came to arresting sailors and that the shore patrol should have had more men on patrol during the violence. "While we cannot disclaim all responsibility for acts of violence in which there were sailors involved," the mayor declared in logic and prose more convoluted than normal, "necessarily police officers could not be on the scene wherever a fight occurred, and it was very difficult, if not impossible, to identify sailors, and therefore few, if any, arrests of sailors were made by police officers."[44]

Two weeks later, Bowron used Horrall's revised report, along with other documents, to support the contention that no anti-Mexican discrimination existed in Los Angeles. In a confidently written letter to Philip W. Bonsal, the state department chief of the Division of American Republics, Bowron stated as accepted fact many of the points he had been making for several weeks: that the riots "were not prompted by prejudicial or even unfriendly feelings toward the Mexican people"; that police had to take "vigorous" actions to curb the zoot-suit gangs; and that those who attempted to make a racial incident out of the hysteria and the riots "are doing irreparable damage, interfering with proper understanding and friendly relations between ourselves and the Mexican people, and at the same time hurting the war effort."[45]

Bowron's confidence resulted from the fact that as well as the LAPD report, he could also transmit to the state department the findings and recommendations of the 1943 Los Angeles County Grand Jury regarding the juvenile delinquency. This document displayed the extent to which civic leaders rallied around Mayor Bowron and the LAPD in an attempt to salvage the city's reputation. The grand jury virtually ignored the issue of racial discrimination and concentrated instead almost completely on the extent and nature of Mexican American juvenile delinquency. By doing so it turned attention away from the depredations of the rioting servicemen and the malfeasance of the LAPD and toward the alleged delinquency of Mexican American youths. The whole point of the grand jury report thus seems to have been to support the claims of the mayor and the press that the zoot suiters caused the riots. In addition, the report further stigmatized Mexican American youths as a criminal element within the community.[46]

The grand jury's findings for the most part reiterated and supported law enforcement's views on Mexican American juvenile delinquency. Using LAPD arrest statistics, the report found an alarming rise in youth crime, among Mexican Americans in particular but also among African American youths. Dismissing the racial theories contained in the Ayres report, the grand jury focused instead on the social causes of delinquency. The major factor on which the report concentrated was the "present lower economic and educational status" of minority youths. Other factors that the grand jury identified as leading to delinquency among Mexican American youths included the conflict between their parents' Mexican culture and American culture; the resultant decline in parental authority (which the report also attributed to women working in war industries); the rise of gangs; and the use of alcohol and drugs. Finally, the grand jury report paid special attention to the alleged leniency of juvenile authorities, complaining that it led to a small number of court filings against juvenile offenders and a disrespect for the law.[47]

The grand jury went to considerable lengths to attack the liberals' contention that racial discrimination caused Mexican American juvenile delinquency. The report specifically refuted any connection between "the outrages committed by these zoot suit gangs . . . [and] the dislike or hatred created in the minds of Mexican youth by repressive and discriminatory treatment inflicted upon them by the Anglo-Americans." It found "no evidence that these activities were in any sense due to or incited by race prejudice or anti-Mexican feelings." The report also disputed any connection between Mexican American juvenile delinquency and Sinarquismo. Having found no connection between youth crime and discrimination, the grand jury went even further in condemning "ill-informed and reckless persons" for making "unfounded charges of racial discrimination against the Mexican people."[48]

The grand jury also stretched truth and logic in its attempt to blame the zoot suiters for the June riots. Citing LAPD statistics for the period between January 1 and June 16, 1943, it found twenty-three felonious assaults, six misdemeanor assaults, and fourteen fights in which zoot suiters allegedly attacked servicemen. It also found a total of 316 zoot suiters involved in felonies. The period utilized by the grand jury, however, included the eight days of the rioting when the LAPD arrested hundreds of Mexican American youths, thus inflating the number of arrests. Nevertheless, the grand jury concluded from these statistics that it was "little to be wondered that a zoot suit has become, in the eyes of many, an emblem of gangsterism and crime."[49]

The grand jury's recommendations emphasized a repressive, law-enforcement solution. It called on juvenile authorities to adopt "a realistic approach" and incarcerate more youngsters, especially repeat offenders. It recommended increasing penal capacity for juveniles, involving superior court judges in juvenile cases, improving enforcement of narcotic and alcohol laws, and increasing police personnel, especially Mexican American and African American officers. It also made a series of recommendations regarding the social problems that it believed caused juvenile delinquency. These included improving housing conditions in minority communities, hiring teachers in those communities "who are genuinely interested in the social welfare of their pupils," and employing only women who can find supervision for their children left at home. Only in its last recommendation did the grand jury advocate that "Negro and Mexican citizens be given impartial opportunity for employment and advancement in industry, and that members of all races and nationalities be permitted to use the public facilities without discrimination."[50]

The 1943 grand jury report represented the most the Los Angeles civic leaders could salvage from a very bad situation. With the city's reputation sullied and its potential for continuing to attract military contracts into the area threatened, area leaders tried to shift the blame for the violence away from structural problems within southern California society. Instead, they blamed their troubles on the temporary problem of the criminal zoot suiter that, while serious, could be addressed by determined leadership and vigorous law enforcement. In so doing, the grand jury, along with the mayor and the press, stigmatized Mexican American youths as constituting a criminal element within the community. In the final analysis, however, they had to at least partially acknowledge the existence of anti-Mexican racial discrimination in their city. That concession would have profound implications for future relations between Mexican Americans and the white power structure, especially the LAPD.

CHAPTER 12

A Statue to the
Unknown Zooter

Despite the grand jury's protestations to the contrary, Los Angeles civic leaders understood that they needed to develop a new relationship with the Mexican American community. The growing but as-yet-undirected rebellion of Mexican American youths, the hysteria and riots that such rebellion caused, the widespread criticism of the city that resulted, and the growing political consciousness and sophistication of the Mexican American minority all meant that that community could no longer be ignored, much less abused and exploited with impunity.

Civic leaders responded by taking a number of initiatives intended to placate the city's critics. For the first time in the twentieth century, the city's elite focused on the issue of race relations, providing forums in which Mexican Americans and other minority groups could air their grievances. The LAPD in particular developed strategies and programs to improve its relationship with Mexican Americans. Specifically, the department developed a multifaceted police-community relations program that included creating formal lines of communication between the department and the Mexican American community; it instituted training programs that emphasized the need to protect the civil rights of all individuals and to show sensitivity toward the special needs of racial and cultural minority groups; it created the Deputy Auxiliary Police, through which officers worked directly with minority youth; and it introduced procedures to guarantee that the department did not give out information that the press could use to write defamatory stories about Mexican

Americans. The significance of these developments was not that they had a particularly long-lasting effect on police-Chicano relations—they did not; rather, they demonstrated the growing political maturity, sophistication, and power of Mexican Americans and an understanding by local political leaders that they needed to respond to that community.

One of the reasons that Mexican Americans became such a political force was that wartime experiences changed the way the community saw itself. The riots and the whole zoot-suit hysteria that preceded them politicized Mexican Americans as no issue had done before, and led to the rise of organizations such as the Coordinating Council for Latin American Youth and the Sleepy Lagoon Defense Committee. These organizations, whether by attempting to improve communications between the community and the police or through their fund-raising efforts, brought to the forefront of Los Angeles Mexican Americans' consciousness the notion that they must become politically active to end police misconduct and other forms of discrimination. That notion had an immediate effect during the war years on how city and police officials interacted with the Mexican American community, and it had an even greater impact after the war as returning veterans formed new political organizations that turned Mexican Americans into a potent political force. The zoot-suit hysteria and the riots launched Los Angeles into an era of racial group politics from which it has yet to emerge.

THE RISE OF GANGS

One of the legacies of the zoot-suit era was the rise of a truly pathological youth gang culture that would plague the Chicano community for the rest of the century. According to the sociologist Joan Moore, who did a longitudinal study of three representative youth gangs, the war years were "the turning point" toward criminal behavior for the East Los Angeles Hoyo Maravilla and White Fence gangs and the rural and suburban San Fernando gang. Prior to the war, these gangs were at most loosely organized. The boys from White Fence had first come together as a result of youth activities sponsored by the local Catholic church, and the San Fernando gang had not yet been established. Only El Hoyo Maravilla had accepted the pachuco fad; but while boys from this barrio developed an openly hostile attitude toward white society, they were nevertheless more "interested in most of the same activities that interested other adolescents—sports, dances, and parties." Aside from occasional fights with boys from other barrios, there was scant criminal activity and police paid them little attention. Drug abuse, aside from alcohol and to a lesser extent marijuana, was practically unheard of.[1]

Evidence suggests that the hysteria and the riots transformed the relatively innocuous prewar youth groups into the predatory, ultraviolent gangs that today plague the Mexican American community. According to Moore, the rise of a new generation of American-born Mexican Americans, the "overt racism" of the Zoot Suit riots, and the hostile attitude of the police gave "the barrio gangs a degree of self-consciousness quite different from earlier years." This consciousness manifested itself in ways that suggest a deepening alienation within the pachuco and zoot-suit subcultures. According to historian Maurico Mazón, "During and after the Zoot Suit Riots[,] Mexican-American youth were known to have shaven their heads—a kind of scarification that indicated their victimization by servicemen." Mazón suggests that the "youths sported their smooth pates as a badge, meaning they had survived contact with the enemy." Sociologist Moore states that the impact of the riots was most prominent in El Hoyo Maravilla, where the subsequent generation of gang members saw the boys who fought the white servicemen "as heroes in a race war." One young man consciously modeled himself after "the pachucos, the first men to openly meet the enemies and defy the law." He said that he was proud of his "brother for fighting the sailors, for wearing a zoot suit[;] he was one of the soldiers."[2]

The aftermath of the rioting saw the rise of gang-related criminal activity, in particular the institutionalization of violence and the use of hard drugs. White Fence's reputation as a particularly fierce fighting gang, for example, stems from the zoot-suit era. It was also in this period that El Hoyo Maravilla gang members began experimenting with heroin; as early as 1947 police conducted raids against the barrio, arresting large numbers of men whose skin showed needle marks. The semirural San Fernando gang became organized during the war years in response to the pachuco fad and quickly adopted the violence and drug use that was becoming an integral part of the culture of the more urban East Los Angeles gangs. By the 1950s and 1960s most Chicano youths associated with these gangs had become addicted to heroin and had been incarcerated for drug-related and violent crimes.[3]

REFORMS

The rise of these violent gangs and the closer scrutiny that the city received in the wake of the riots led Los Angeles civic leaders to institute a series of reforms designed to improve the relationship between Mexican Americans and white city officials—in particular the police. For the most part, the reforms followed the recommendations made by the Citizens Committee appointed by Governor Earl Warren to investigate the June riots. These recommendations included measures to combat youth crime by addressing the social problems that the committee members believed led to delinquency and by developing rehabilitative experiences for youths caught up in the criminal justice system. The recommendations also included more sensitivity and responsiveness on the part of police to the needs of the Mexican American community; an end to discrimination by law enforcement and in public accommodations; and an education program to create better understanding of minority groups.[4]

State and local officials and civic leaders, working in an almost crisis atmosphere, set out immediately to implement the committee's recommendations. Believing that the Mexican American youths were responsible for the riots, officials strengthened or created a plethora of public, private, and semipublic groups to address the social problems they believed led to juvenile delinquency. Parks, playgrounds, and school facilities expanded their hours of operation so that Mexican American youths would have greater opportunity for wholesome recreational activities. Radio programs, movie short features, and literature were developed so that the majority community could gain a "better understanding of the Latin-Americans" and also "to give Latin-Americans a pride of place in the community, and thus overcome their inferiority complex." Government agencies gave additional support to the CCLAY and provided more resources to groups as varied as the juvenile court system, the YMCA, and the probation department to develop their preventive and rehabilitative programs. This support often resulted in demonstrable successes. A program led by the probation department in the Hazard area of East Los Angeles resulted in not a single youth from that neighborhood being prosecuted during July, August, and September 1943.[5]

The rush of activity created a desperate need for coordination. The state government established a special committee, Youth in Wartime, to coordinate delinquency-prevention efforts throughout California. In the

Los Angeles area, the YMCA, the YWCA, the Girl and Boy Scouts, the
International Institute, the Camp Fire Girls, the Catholic Welfare Bureau, and the Church Welfare Bureau all reported that they had mobilized "every present available resource" to address the problems leading
to juvenile delinquency. These organizations called for additional resources to coordinate their efforts with those of government agencies.
One document drafted at the end of 1943 listed twenty-two different
groups "working on [the] Latin-American situation" and added thirty-
two others that might be approached to also get involved. So many
groups formed in the wake of the riots that the Citizens' Committee for
Latin-American Youth held a special meeting to discuss its own role "in
view of the numerous organizations and committees which have recently
been set up to interest themselves in minority problems." No wonder,
then, that Mexican American youths were awed by all the attention they
were suddenly receiving. As one young zoot suiter from Watts stated,
"They ought to erect a statue in the Plaza to the unknown zooter. Cause
it wasn't until then[,] . . . until the riots, when a lot of kids got beat up[,]
. . . that they gave us our clubs."[6]

Of the agencies that emerged from the zoot-suit crisis, one of the most
important was the Los Angeles Youth Project (LAYP). The LAYP
evolved from a proposal by ten social service agencies in the wake of
the riots to establish "a special cooperative project for an enlarged group
program for youth of the major racial minorities of Los Angeles, particularly of Mexican and Negro origin." The proposal succeeded in acquiring for the organization more than $234,000 to conduct its activi-
ties. The LAYP worked closely with the California Youth Authority,
and the programs it created became the national model for delinquency
prevention.[7]

The LAYP was not, however, always sensitive to the interests of the
Mexican American community. As first constituted, its governing board
had no Mexican American representatives. When Mexican American
leaders active in the CCLAY inquired about the omission, the LAYP
promised to include them on the organization's advisory board. Perhaps
because of the lack of input from the community, the LAYP and its
affiliates sometimes took actions that offended Mexican Americans and
that even undermined the organization's specified goal. In December
1943, for example, the Southern California Council of Inter-American
Affairs (SCCIAA), a local group of businessmen and politicians working
with the State Department to improve relations between the United

States and Latin America, sent a letter protesting publicity material used by the War Chest (LAYP's funding agency) that depicted Mexican American youths wearing zoot suits behind bars. The SCCIAA, which had just added a Mexican American to its governing board, pointed out that a community agency distributing pictures of jailed zoot suiters undermined the council's own efforts to dissuade newspaper publishers from printing similar depictions, libeled innocent youngsters, and, according to the current psychological theory, might even encourage delinquents who enjoyed the publicity they received from such pictures.[8]

The LAYP's mission and the specific projects it undertook were similar to the efforts of the CCLAY in combating juvenile delinquency. Like the CCLAY's goal of "uplifting" Mexican American youth, the LAYP sought to "aid youth in their progress into mature American citizenship." Also like the CCLAY, the LAYP aimed at developing a coordinated effort of youth workers interacting with potential delinquents, their parents, the schools, clergy, and police "to direct the energies of the young people into useful channels." These "useful channels" included the youths participating in establishing community youth centers, holding dances and sporting events, going on camping trips, and organizing pageants and other festivals. Undoubtedly because it received ample funding, the LAYP provided services for many more youngsters than the CCLAY could ever reach. In its first full year of operation, the LAYP reported that it had served 13,659 youths. Ironically, however, only 27 percent of those served were Mexican American; the majority were white.[9]

Of longer-lasting importance in addressing racial conflict in the city was the Los Angeles County Commission on Human Relations (LACCHR), created by the Los Angeles Board of Supervisors. The oldest of its kind in the nation, the commission was established in direct response to the crisis created by the Sleepy Lagoon case and the Zoot Suit riots. The LACCHR's initial objectives included identifying and eliminating the causes of racial tension and preventing racial conflict. In regard to law enforcement, the commission has attempted to achieve these objectives by tackling issues as broad as racism within the LAPD and the sheriff's department and as narrow as officer training and citizen-complaint procedures. It has functioned most prominently, however, in times of crisis, providing forums for community groups to state their grievances and perhaps vent their anger against police officials. The LACCHR's impact on the Mexican American community, however, has been limited by the lack of Chicano representation on the commission; in its fifty-year history, only a handful of its more than two hundred commissioners have been Mexican American.[10]

The flurry of activity by public and private social service agencies was understandable given the national and international scrutiny the city received in the wake of the riots. More interesting, however, are the efforts that the LAPD made to improve relations with the Mexican American minority. The reforms that the LAPD undertook flowed from the recommendations made by Governor Warren's Citizens Committee to investigate the Zoot Suit riots. Those recommendations included diminishing—though not eliminating—race as a factor in making arrests; increasing the number of Spanish-speaking officers and officers "who understand the psychology of the Spanish speaking groups in Los Angeles"; and providing "special training for officers dealing with minority groups." The department attempted to implement each of these recommendations; in addition, it tried to improve its communications with both Mexican American leaders and Mexican American youths. Finally, the LAPD addressed the issue of its actions during the riots by developing a training manual for dealing with civil disturbances.[11]

Prior to the riots, the LAPD had never seen fit to issue a statement regarding the impropriety of racial discrimination in police work. The combination of criticism that the department received for its handling of the riots and the growing assertiveness of the Mexican American community, however, forced the LAPD to address racism within its ranks. It did so by making broad declarations of policy that directed officers to refrain from acting on any prejudicial attitudes they might hold and by instituting special training sessions on minority issues.[12]

The LAPD's clearest declaration of its new attitude toward racism within its ranks came in its training manual on civil disturbances. While the document addressed potential riots and riotous situations, the department clearly intended officers to apply its dictums to more generalized police work. The introduction, for example, stated that a "trained officer will prevent serious disturbances by alert and intelligent police action." It defined intelligent police action as promoting "good public relations," "treat[ing] all police problems in a fair and impartial manner and avoid[ing] the show of bias or prejudice, especially on controversial issues." The LAPD's Chief Horrall echoed these sentiments in his foreword to the manual, stating that one of an officer's primary responsibilities was to protect every citizen, "without regard to his race, color, creed or political views." The law, the chief continued, "must be enforced equally against all transgressors" and officers must be "nonpartisan."[13]

As the above statement indicated, properly trained police officers were necessary in preventing riots. During the corrupt Shaw-Davis administrations, training of police recruits had all but lapsed. By the time the riots broke out, the police academy had been reinvigorated, although many of the temporary officers pressed into service during the war emergency remained undertrained. In the wake of the riots, demands came from a variety of sources that LAPD training include special instruction in how officers should interact with members of racial minority groups, especially Mexican Americans. In addition to the governor's Citizens Committee, organizations as varied as the federally sanctioned Southern California Council of Inter-American Affairs and the ad hoc 13th (Councilmanic) District Citizens' Committee called for minority-relations training for officers.[14]

The requests for officer training differed in emphasis, depending on the orientation of the organization making the request. The SCCIAA, dominated by conservative businessmen, called for the police academy curriculum to include training in "the *special problem* of contact with minority groups" (my italics). The resolution passed by the 13th District Citizens' Committee and forwarded directly to the police commission focused on the need for unbiased police work. The committee prefaced its resolution by remarking that it understood "the manifold problems involved in making the benefits of democratic government applicable to all persons, regardless of race, religious belief or national origin." It then called upon the department to incorporate in its training program "material or courses, that inculcate sound American attitudes toward minority groups, and that teach the special responsibilities of police officers in situations in which incitement or discrimination against minority groups may be a factor." Chief Horrall and the police commission responded that officer training addressed these concepts "to some degree," in the section on courtesy and conduct, and stated that they were "treated at length in a special theme on 'Tolerance in Police Work.'" Nevertheless, the LAPD institutionalized special classes in minority relations in its training curriculum.[15]

In addition to the general classes on race relations, the LAPD made classes on various aspects of Mexican American culture available for officers. The University of Southern California, for example, created a course especially for police officers to develop "among them an understanding and sympathy for the culture and background of our Latin-

American population." The University of California at Los Angeles offered a special class for officers who worked with juveniles, on how to
speak to parents about their "responsibility . . . for the welfare of their
children." Spanish-language instruction became an integral part of the
training curriculum. Another group of thirty juvenile officers took a
course in conversational Spanish that included a special section on "Pachuco slang."[16]

The emphasis on Spanish-language instruction indicated the perceived need among many reformers for more Mexican American police
officers. Mexican Americans had been on the LAPD since the turn of
the century; in the early years, when government officials and civic leaders saw Mexican immigrants and the possible spillover of radical ideology from the Mexican Revolution as a threat to local order, they employed a fairly significant number of Mexican American officers. The
role of these officers was to control the Mexican immigrant community.
After the Mexican Revolution, local leaders perceived the immigrant as
less threatening and Mexican American officers' role in controlling their
community diminished in importance. Mexican Americans did not,
however, disappear from the force—the historian Gerald Woods
counted approximately twelve officers with Spanish surnames on the
department roster in 1924. Throughout the 1920s and 1930s, the Mexican American officers who remained on the force continued to be either
commended for outstanding performance or condemned for misconduct. Among the officers purged at the beginning of the Bowron administration, a number of allegedly corrupt Mexican American officers either retired or were removed from the force.[17]

The advent of the zoot-suit hysteria brought about calls for more
Mexican American law-enforcement officers. The 1942 grand jury report, for example, recommended that Mexican American districts be
policed "only [by] officers with special qualifications for this duty."
Chief Horrall responded that the department could hire only people who
had passed the civil service examination for police officers, and claimed
that not enough Mexican Americans took the test. In addition, many of
the Mexican American officers already on the force had been promoted
into the detective bureau and were not available for patrol duty.[18]

In the wake of the riots, constituent groups redoubled their calls for
the LAPD to hire more Mexican American officers. As noted earlier, the
governor's Citizens Committee to investigate the riots called for an increase in the number of Spanish-speaking officers—"Spanish-speaking"

often being a euphemism for Mexican Americans. Responding to those recommendations, Governor Warren reportedly expressed "chagrin" that although Los Angeles had a Mexican American population of approximately 240,000, it had only a few police officers of Mexican descent. Other groups, from the SCCIAA to the CCLAY, and Sleepy Lagoon defense attorney Ben Margolis, writing on behalf of the National Lawyers Guild, all called on the LAPD to make provisions to hire more Mexican American officers.[19]

The LAPD responded in an almost typical fashion: the department stood on bureaucratic principle while still managing to accommodate the requests for more Mexican American officers. Chief Horrall replied to Ben Margolis's insistent requests by stating that the department had long sought to assign officers who understood "the Mexican language to areas in which this nationality dwell." These efforts had not been more successful, the chief explained, because of "the inability of Mexican-Americans to successfully pass Civil Service examinations which are written in English." Nevertheless, the wartime need to use temporary police officers (who did not have to meet the same civil service requirements) offered the opportunity to increase the number of Mexican Americans on the force. Horrall estimated that this strategy would result in as many as a dozen new Mexican Americans being added to the force. Moreover, after the war, the LAPD succeeded in attracting a significant number of returning Mexican American veterans into permanent positions on the force. Thereafter, maintaining a Mexican American presence in the department became a priority for LAPD administrators.[20]

While race relations courses in the police academy and the recruitment of more minority officers were seen by many as positive steps for the LAPD, no effort better demonstrated the department's determination to improve its relationship with the Mexican American community than the creation in September 1943 of the Deputy Auxiliary Police (DAPS). DAPS focused on working with Mexican American "predelinquent" youth, and it was the LAPD's primary effort at juvenile crime prevention in the 1940s and 1950s. Its objectives were similar to those of many other social service agencies. According to Mayor Bowron, who claimed the idea was his, DAPS's goals included promoting "among the youth of the community good citizenship, a sense of responsibility to the community, cooperation with law enforcement agencies, development of leadership and the encouragement of wholesome leisure-time activities." Remarkably, these goals were to be accomplished by a police department that, in molding itself to the professionalism model, was in the midst of moving away from a social service role into one strictly of crime prevention.[21]

All of this was achieved through activities organized and led by LAPD personnel. Many of these activities were rather traditional in nature, and included individual and group counseling, handicraft training, sporting events, camping, the event that would become the annual DAPS picnic, and the citywide celebration known as DAPS Week. Youth involved in DAPS, however, also gained special instruction on "the organization, and function and purpose" of the LAPD. They visited crime labs, heard lectures from FBI agents, and received instruction from the National Rifle Association on the proper use of firearms. They took examinations on this material to determine what rank they would achieve, the ranking system being similar to that within the department. Those who achieved high enough rank even assisted police in crowd control at parades and other large gatherings. In its first year of operation four thousand youngsters joined DAPS; by the end of the decade, it had close to twelve thousand members. The unit continued until 1954, when Chief of Police William Parker disbanded it as an inappropriate police function.[22]

CCLAY YOUTH WORK AND PROTEST

The Coordinating Council for Latin American Youth (CCLAY) emerged from the Zoot Suit riots as the most influential Mexican American group in the city. By the summer of 1943, it had developed close ties to city hall and a good working relationship with the LAPD. The riots infused the CCLAY with an assertiveness and a determination to prevent a recurrence of the hysteria that had led to the violence. As noted earlier, the CCLAY explicitly criticized the LAPD for its handling of the riots and publicly agreed with Eleanor Roosevelt that the fundamental cause of the rioting was racism. The organization combined these fundamental assumptions with its ongoing youth work to develop its agenda for the next several years. In particular, it identified three major factors that fed the anti-Mexican sentiments that led to the violence: Mexican American juvenile delinquency, irresponsible journalism, and police misconduct. In the aftermath of the riots, the CCLAY set out to combat all three.[23]

Despite their new assertiveness, the middle-class leaders of the CCLAY were also saddled with assumptions and strategies that limited their impact. They understood that Mexican Americans suffered from discrimination, but they argued that anti-Mexican discrimination had nothing to do with race; rather, they believed that it resulted from "Anglo" Americans not realizing that Mexicans were also "white." Their solution was to do away with this misconception by fighting the worst examples of discrimination and helping Mexicans to integrate into American society; in this way, they argued, Anglos would come to their senses and stop discriminating. Because of this basic accommodationist and assimilationist philosophy and the CCLAY leaders' roles as ethnic brokers, the group accepted the generally held belief that the symbolic rebellion of zoot suiters constituted a severe social problem. The CCLAY therefore concentrated its efforts on uplifting the Mexican American community, demanding responsible journalism, and calling for modest reforms in police practices.[24]

In the immediate aftermath of the riots, the CCLAY took the lead in addressing the issue of juvenile delinquency through their reform work with Mexican American youths. The CCLAY made its general outlook evident in a July 1943 General Assembly it sponsored. The purpose of the meeting was to discuss "the problem of the 'pachucos' " and to determine how Mexican American groups could "best aid in the rehabilitation of our youth." Along the same vein, the CCLAY redoubled its efforts in youth work and in particular its work with boys from the Alpine Street neighborhood. This program took place in a clubhouse, where recreational activities and individual and group counseling were available for the boys. CCLAY leaders touted their Alpine Street project as the model for reforming "maladjusted" youths.[25]

The CCLAY's approach to juvenile delinquency sometimes created friction with other groups or drew criticism even from its own members. Several CCLAY members, for example, objected to the formation of a youth group called "Club Los Pachucos" organized by a well-meaning Englishwoman named Christine Sterling. The CCLAY members complained that the use of the term *pachuco* was "impolitic" and said it tended to give publicity to and glamorize a segment of the Mexican American population that the group sought to diminish. In a slightly different vein, the county probation officer Stephen Keating reported that "many" boys had come to believe that the CCLAY was setting them up to be arrested by having them congregate in one place. Keating reported that he responded vehemently to the boys' concern, telling them that the CCLAY "was not a stool pigeon agency." A few months later, youth worker Tom García reported that police had in fact raided a CCLAY-sponsored clubhouse in the Happy Valley area. Complaining that the CCLAY executive committee should have taken some "affirmative action" in the matter, Dr. Camilo Servín, who had helped develop the Alpine Street project and was thus an influential member of the council, moved to censure the committee. The motion, however, failed.[26]

Despite these controversies, the CCLAY took a determined stand against what it saw as anti-Mexican discrimination during the two years after the riots. Along with its allies inside and outside the Mexican American community, the CCLAY used a series of sensational cases to redefine the relationship between itself and the LAPD and, more broadly, the city's white power structure. The ways in which Mexican American political leaders acted in these cases showed a new determination not to allow police misconduct to go unchallenged; they also showed a new political sophistication, and, perhaps as significant, civic leaders and police officials showed a new appreciation for the growing political strength and acumen of the Mexican American community.

The first case, which took place less than three months after the riots, demonstrated not so much the politicization of the Mexican American community as the extent to which liberal groups and the Mexican government had come to see people of Mexican descent as an oppressed group in need of protection. Early on the morning of August 30, 1943, two LAPD officers shot Perfecto López Rojas, a young Mexican national, in the leg. The next day, Vicente Peralta C., the Mexican consul general in Los Angeles, sent a telegram to Chief Horrall characterizing the shooting as "hasty[,] unwarranted and unjustified" and calling for Horrall to take measures to "prevent repetition of incidents of this nature that naturally create unrest among the Mexican colony." A week later, the Los Angeles chapter of the National Lawyers Guild sent a formal protest to the police commission. The guild wanted not only an investigation into the shooting but also a broader "inquiry into the repeated charges of police brutalities insofar as Mexicans and Negroes are concerned."[27]

The significance of the LAPD's investigation resulted not so much from its conclusion—the officers involved in the shooting of López were exonerated of any wrongdoing—as from the almost solicitous manner in which the department responded to the protesters. The gist of the department's explanation was that the shooting had been a tragic misunderstanding. On the evening in question, police dispatchers had received a call that a man had shot a gun from a taxicab in a warehouse district just northeast of downtown Los Angeles. The department issued an "all units" call, and officers from a patrol car reported they had seen "a Mexican" walking from the vicinity of the shooting. Officers R. W. Wise and C. E. Larson drove to the area where the suspect had been seen, and stopped López. The twenty-two-year-old López, however, did not speak English. In an interview with police from his hospital bed, López stated that when the police stopped him they spoke to him, but since he did not understand, he reached into his pocket to give them his passport. Officer Wise said in his report that he thought López was reaching for a pistol and therefore shot the young Mexican in the thigh. In his interview López stated that he understood that the shooting resulted from a misunderstanding and indicated that the officers treated him kindly and with respect.[28]

The LAPD went to unusual lengths to mollify both Consul Peralta C. and the National Lawyers Guild. To begin with, it responded to the Mexican consul's August 31 telegram almost without delay. Acting Chief of Police Henry S. Eaton replied two days later with a thorough account of the shooting. Eaton's letter also expressed both the department's "regret" that a Mexican citizen had become "involved in this unfortunate incident" and its sympathy for the injured man. Finally, Eaton attempted to assure Peralta C. that the LAPD would continue to cooperate with the consul in preventing "the unnecessary repetition of similar incidents." While the department did not respond as promptly to the National Lawyers Guild protest, it did take the unprecedented step of sending the guild the entire López file, including normally confidential internal documents such as the original incident report. On the other hand, the department refused to conduct the broader inquiry that the guild had requested, arguing that such an investigation would be "futile" without "specific information" of instances of police brutality.[29]

One of Mexican Americans' main concerns was that of addressing the public's perception of them as a criminally inclined racial group. Not only did the crescendo of the riots fail to end official or public preoccupation with Mexican American crime, the hysteria and violence permanently fixed in the popular imagination the image of the pachuco and the Mexican American youth gang. One of the reasons for the persistence of this image was the continued coverage of Mexican American youth crime by the press. Albeit at a greatly reduced rate and with lowered rhetoric, area newspapers continued to print stories, sometimes with sensationalized headlines, about "Zoot Suit" crime. Within a few weeks of the riots, for example, one newspaper ran the headline "Zooters in Attack on Park Cripple," while other papers printed stories about zoot suiters stabbing soldiers and raping women. Similar stories continued throughout the war years, and after the war, media representations regarding violent youth gangs produced periodic public scares and chronic popular and official anxiety regarding Mexican American crime.[30]

In response, Mexican American groups addressed what they saw as journalistic irresponsibility that contributed to anti-Mexican attitudes among the general public. The CCLAY, for example, along with other groups, took a direct role in protesting an article in the *Los Angeles Times* that it believed had the potential to reignite the zoot-suit hysteria. On Sunday, July 16, 1944, thirteen months after the riots, the *Times* ran a news story on the front page of its city section under the headline "Youthful Gang Secrets Exposed." The article charged that "gang members . . . perform sadistic mutilations upon unwilling neophytes, . . . smoke marihuana costing $5 per reefer . . . [and] gather on the streets to fight, to steal and to rob." The *Times* also claimed that girl gang members wore pompadour hairstyles in order to hide weapons in their hair and, suggesting sexual impropriety, that they had to "obey and yield" to boy gang members "in all things." In what was, to the CCLAY, the most alarming passage, the *Times* story charged that "gang members are taught to hate servicemen" and that they walked the streets armed and ready for an altercation. Characteristically, the *Times* blamed the situation on "the influence of subversive elements[,] . . . [the] mollycoddling of racial groups and . . . war-depleted police forces."[31]

The CCLAY's response to the *Times* story demonstrated the organization's determination not to allow the pachuco hysteria to resume. At its regular meeting the day after the article's publication, the CCLAY passed a resolution "taking exception" to the *Times* piece. It charged that the story was "inimical to good Latin-American relations" and "an incitement to open riot." The CCLAY instructed its secretary, Manuel Ruiz, to write a letter to the *Times* expressing the organization's concern and appointed a subcommittee to meet with the *Times* publisher, Norman Chandler. In his letter to the *Times*, Ruiz noted that while the writer made no reference to zoot suits, he nevertheless wove his story "around current taboos in directing attention to particular racial groups." Ruiz characterized the story as "vicious" and as the type of news story condemned by various government agencies, including the United States Department of War Information and the special committee established by Governor Warren to investigate the Zoot Suit riots. Ruiz also took particular exception to the story's assertion that gang members hated servicemen, noting that most "gang members" had family members in the service. He ominously added that such stories had preceded the Zoot Suit riots.[32]

Other groups also protested the *Times*'s story. The Sleepy Lagoon Defense Committee issued a statement decrying the article as a "journalistic provocation against Mexican-American juveniles" and a "vicious slander unsubstantiated by statistics or source or authority." Echoing the CCLAY's fears, the SLDC charged that "this is exactly the kind of newspaper incitement which preceded the Sleepy Lagoon case— which continued throughout the trial and which continued after it to culminate in the shameful anti-Mexican riots of June 1943." The SLDC concluded by asking people to write letters to the *Times* protesting the story. In an even more alarmed fashion, the Council for Civic Unity, one of several groups that came together after the riots to promote home front stability, issued a broadside condemning the *Times* and calling for a meeting of interested parties "to help combat racism on every front." Finally, the business-oriented Southern California Council of Inter-American Affairs also protested the *Times* article and sent a delegation to talk with Norman Chandler. The broad nature of the protest was unprecedented and demonstrated the extent to which a wide range of community groups were unwilling to allow resumption of the zoot-suit hysteria.[33]

The *Times* responded by attacking its critics. In an August 8 editorial, it characterized the protests as coming "from certain groups and individuals—some of them no doubt sincere, some noted for their efforts to stir up trouble on any pretext and others who should know better." Rather than promoting racial strife, the city's newspaper of record stated that it had "the highest regard for racial minorities who are law-abiding, self-respecting citizens." The *Times* claimed that it was only trying to shed light on the increasing gang problem and that the story in question had nothing to do with race. Those who attempt to inject racial issues into such a discussion, the editorial asserted, undermine efforts at "youth regeneration." Finally, any linkage between law-enforcement efforts to suppress juvenile delinquency and race prejudice, the *Times* concluded, contributes "to the very 'disunity' which some of the groups criticizing publication of the article in question profess to deplore."[34]

With the *Times*'s refusal to curb its provocative coverage, the CCLAY sought to use its enhanced influence in city government to change the type of information the LAPD gave the press on juvenile cases. The best example of the organization's new assertiveness and influence is seen in its response to the sensational newspaper coverage of a minor riot involving Mexican American youths that erupted in December 1944. On the evening of December 22 the County Probation Department sponsored a dance for youths from three Mexican American boys' clubs. Not only were club members invited, the sponsors told the youths that they could also invite friends and relatives. Witnesses gave essentially two explanations for the outbreak of violence. Some said that fights broke out when servicemen attending the dance insulted young men who had not entered the military. Others believed that an element from the Alpine Street gang that had not been invited decided to crash and started a fight. In either case, a brawl erupted in which numerous people were slashed with a razor or a very sharp knife. Police arrested several people at the scene and more later that night at hospitals.[35]

The next day Los Angeles area newspapers ran sensational headlines such as "Goof Ball Gang Battles Servicemen." The stories that accompanied the headlines claimed that the Alpine Street gang had crashed a holiday dance for servicemen and that the gang members attacked the soldiers with knives, bicycle chains, and metal pipes. The stories also indicated that the attacking gang members were high on marijuana and, as the headline indicated, amphetamine pills called "goof balls."

CCLAY members and other community leaders worried that such news articles would incite another wave of rioting between servicemen and Mexican American youths. What concerned community activists as much as the inflammatory news stories was the fact that articles stated that reporters got their information from the LAPD. In two similarly worded letters, Manuel Ruiz, writing for the CCLAY, and Maurice Hazen, from the office of the Coordinator of Inter-American Affairs, complained that the news stories were "grossly inaccurate" and "highly inflammatory" and that "the writers quote[d] the Police Department as the source of the information." Ruiz and Hazen called on the department to "take steps toward having more accurate presentation of its news releases."[36]

In response, the department launched a full-scale investigation into how the reporters received their information. In their internal report, Inspector E. C. Biffle and Sergeant John T. Shields found practically no basis for the allegations contained in the newspaper articles. The most that they could speculate was that newspaper reporters may have picked up a broadcast teletype calling for the arrest of one of the participants in the fight that made reference to "a service mens party." None of the officers that Biffle and Shields interviewed admitted any knowledge as to how the press received information about the use of tire chains or metal pipes during the fight. In his official report to the police commission, Chief Horrall noted the special importance of the CCLAY's complaint, but supported his investigators' conclusion that the department bore no responsibility for the information in the inflammatory news stories. At the same time, however, he asserted what was the emerging department policy—that all officers were responsible "for judicious and impartial treatment of all police problems, racial or otherwise." The chief also warned that "any officer who willfully releases detrimental information will be subject to disciplinary action." Horrall thus acquiesced to the request that the department take more care in what it said to newspaper reporters.[37]

Horrall's statement regarding the impartial enforcement of the law resulted from the general empowerment of the Mexican American community and more directly from the aggressive efforts of the CCLAY. The CCLAY was even more aggressive in responding to what it perceived to be instances of LAPD misconduct—in particular, assertions of police brutality. While it protested a number of incidents, the case that best illustrates how the CCLAY worked began with the beating of seventeen-year-old Raymond Morales by LAPD officer Wilfred Wilson. On the evening of April 1, 1945, Easter Sunday, Morales and his eighteen-year-old cousin Juan Cruz Morales had gone to a movie and stopped afterward to get a bite to eat along Olvera Street, a historic section of Los Angeles with many Mexican shops and restaurants. After eating, the boys had begun to walk home when they were stopped by Wilson and his partner, Officer Joe Castro. The officers demanded to see identification, and although they had no reason to suspect the boys of any wrongdoing (the two boys were not even wearing zoot suits), the officers searched them. Because Raymond Morales was under eighteen and thus technically in violation of the curfew ordinance, Officer Wilson ordered him to go home.[38]

As the two boys started to leave, Morales turned and looked at Wilson in a way that obviously offended the officer. According to eye witnesses, Wilson responded by calling Morales a "son of a bitch" and beating the boy with a nightstick about the head, shoulders, back, legs, and kidneys and eventually arresting him. While the beating was severe enough to necessitate several stitches in Morales's head, neither boy was charged with any crime. At this point the incident would have gone unnoticed and unpunished had it not been for the fact that a white merchant by the name of Arthur Whipple witnessed the disturbance and tried to intervene. Whipple protested that Wilson continued to beat an already bloodied Morales even after the officer had handcuffed the boy. For his trouble, Whipple found himself arrested and charged with resisting an officer in the performance of his duty. It was Whipple's trial, in which he was represented by the Sleepy Lagoon Defense Committee's chairman, Carey McWilliams, that brought the case to public attention.[39]

Even before Whipple's trial, however, the CCLAY had written a strong letter to the police commission characterizing the incident as "an unprovoked assault" and asking for an "immediate investigation" and hearing into the case. The CCLAY's position was strengthened by the outcome of the trial. In pronouncing Whipple innocent of all charges, Judge James H. Pope found that the police officers had provoked the incident through "vulgar" language and the use of excessive force, and that the defendant had acted properly with the intent of protecting the boy from serious injury. Pope also aided the CCLAY by sending the organization his extensive notes on the trial.[40]

Officially, the LAPD responded to the CCLAY's accusations in a defensive manner. The department claimed in a letter written a month after the trial that the officers properly detained Morales for being in violation of the curfew ordinance and that the boy became "very belligerent" when questioned. According to Captain Richard Simon, the commander of the Personnel Division, young Morales "went so far as to charge one of the officers," forcing him to retreat twenty or thirty feet. Only after this had occurred, did the officer resort to using his nightstick to subdue Morales. Wilson attempted to "strike at his shoulder," Simon claimed, "but, due to his [Morales's] movement at that time, the blow accidentally struck his head." Simon also maintained that this information was not presented at the Whipple trial because of the officers' inexperience. Had the two officers given the proper testimony, Simon implied in his letter, the trial would not have ended with an acquittal. Despite this spirited defense, just three months later the LAPD found cause to fire Officer Wilson from the force. Consequently, while the department officially refused to admit misconduct, it nevertheless found a way to accommodate the CCLAY.[41]

THE SLEEPY LAGOON DEFENSE COMMITTEE

While the CCLAY may have had considerable influence with government officials, the Sleepy Lagoon Defense Committee (SLDC) did more to publicize the issue of police misconduct and official discrimination against Mexican Americans than any other organization in Los Angeles. What began in the fall of 1942 as a modest effort to gain a fair trial for the Sleepy Lagoon defendants turned, after their convictions, into a nationwide campaign to raise the funds for an appeal. This campaign was significant for at least two reasons. First, it was the most extensive effort ever to gain justice for people of Mexican descent who were victims of wrongful prosecution and conviction. Second, the SLDC strategy and argument catapulted Mexican Americans to the forefront of the civil-rights debate in California and helped define them at the national level as an oppressed minority group.

The SLDC's primary strategy involved trying to gain sympathy for "the boys" by demonstrating the blatantly unjust nature of the arrests and prosecutions. It also placed the whole case within the context of anti-Mexican discrimination and charged that the case and the general discrimination hurt the national and international unity necessary to win the war. In pursuance of these basic themes, the committee held rallies, published pamphlets and newsletters, conducted mass mailings, circulated petitions, hired lawyers, and at the same time, tried to maintain the morale of the defendants in prison.[42]

While the SLDC came into existence in October 1942 to aid the defendants in the initial Sleepy Lagoon trial, its main organizing efforts did not begin until after the trial ended in January 1943 with convictions of seventeen of the youths. On March 15 the committee held an organizing conference that developed the strategy for the fund-raising effort but also gave an indication of the kind of resistance from governmental officials that the committee would have to overcome. Carey McWilliams gave the keynote speech, in which he placed the Sleepy Lagoon case within the context of historic anti-Mexican discrimination, explained the international implications of the case, and told of the urgency of gaining justice for the defendants. George Shibley, the conference's main speaker and the lead defense attorney during the trial, gave a rousing speech in which he also placed the case within the context of anti-Mexican racism and vividly illustrated the prejudicial actions of the judge and prosecutor during the trial.[43]

The minutes from this conference demonstrate the broad support that existed for gaining justice for the Sleepy Lagoon defendants. Mexican American representatives took a strong leadership role. El Congreso leader Josephina Fierro de Bright and the labor activist Frank López led subcommittees that reported back to the larger group with suggestions on how to raise public awareness. These suggestions included developing a publicity subcommittee and a speakers' bureau, holding mass meetings, and enlarging the committee to include members from all interested organizations. In addition, organized labor, in particular some of the more progressive CIO unions, pledged support for the committee. Assistance from the Mexican American community, labor unions, and leftist and liberal organizations would prove crucial over time to the success of the SLDC.[44]

The minutes of the conference alsò, however, demonstrated the law-enforcement community's deep antagonism toward the SLDC's work. Because of the committee's connection with the Communist Party, Deputy District Attorney Clyde Shoemaker, the lead prosecution lawyer at the Sleepy Lagoon trial, threatened to remove the tax-exempt status of a local Unitarian church if it hosted the meeting. This action forced the SLDC to find a different conference site at the last minute. The conference attendees passed a resolution condemning Shoemaker's interference with free speech and charged a delegation to meet with Mayor Bowron and District Attorney Houser, as well as with local newspapers, to denounce the action. Despite these efforts, the SLDC would be red-baited by public officials throughout its existence.[45]

In the subsequent months the SLDC concentrated on putting together a publicity campaign to raise the twenty thousand dollars the committee estimated it needed for the appeal. The primary effort in this regard was the writing, production, publication, and distribution of the pamphlet *The Sleepy Lagoon Case,* which was issued in June 1943. Before the pamphlet could be written, however, the committee needed funds for its production and distribution, and it was at this point that support from organized labor proved crucial. The CIO state convention passed a resolution condemning the continued imprisonment of "the Sleepy Lagoon victims," petitioning Governor Warren for a pardon, and going "on record as supporting the Sleepy Lagoon Defense Committee both morally and financially." In mid-April the SLDC, citing the adopted resolution, sent out an appeal to CIO unions throughout the state to raise the twenty thousand dollars needed. State and local CIO unions, especially those with a large Mexican American membership, responded enthusiastically to the call for support. For example, the Southern California District of the International Workers Order pledged two thousand dollars to the campaign and individual locals contributed smaller but significant amounts. By late spring the SLDC managed to publish the pamphlet and retain the San Francisco labor attorney Ben Margolis to take charge of the appeal.[46]

The main theme of the SLDC pamphlet was the fact that the baseless conviction of the Sleepy Lagoon defendants hurt the unity needed to defeat fascism. It opened with a discussion of the optimism created by the hemispheric solidarity against the Axis powers and contrasted that with the injustice of the trial, the earlier mass arrests, and the more generalized anti-Mexican hysteria. According to the SLDC, it was not only the Sleepy Lagoon defendants who were convicted at the trial, it was "the whole Mexican people, their children, and their grandchildren. It was the whole of Latin America with its 130,000,000 people. It was the Good Neighbor Policy. It was the United Nations and all for which we fight." The SLDC took particular aim at the Ayres report, which had asserted that Mexican Americans had a biological inclination toward crime and violence. It quoted extensively from the report and likened it to Nazi theories of racial superiority that resulted in the oppression of the Jews. The SLDC also hinted at a conspiracy among Ayres, the Hearst newspapers, other right-wing "appeasers," and Axis propagandists who used the case to undermine Latin American enthusiasm for an alliance with the United States. Finally, the pamphlet gave a short summary of the case and biographies of the convicted youths, and made a request for support to fund the appeal. Because of the importance of reaching the Mexican American community, the SLDC also printed a Spanish-language version of the pamphlet.[47]

With the publication of *The Sleepy Lagoon Case*, the SLDC launched a mass national mailing campaign to raise money for the appeal. Typically, a request included a copy of the pamphlet and a cover letter explicitly requesting contributions. The letter noted that any donations would not only help overturn a miscarriage of justice based on race prejudice, they would also help maintain home front unity for the prosecution of the war. While the mailing effort concentrated on labor unions, the SLDC made use of mailing lists obtained from radical groups, such as the International Labor Defense based in New York, to make appeals to individuals. The broad nature of the campaign contributed to a growing national recognition of Mexican Americans as an oppressed racial minority group.[48]

The SLDC, however, understood that its efforts would bear most fruit in California, where the problems faced by Mexican Americans were better understood, and where the citizenry could put pressure on elected officials. The committee thus launched two petition drives to try to compel state government officials to intervene in the case. They directed one to Governor Warren, asking him to free the Sleepy Lagoon defendants.

The SLDC directed the second petition to Attorney General Robert W. Kenny. Because of his firm stand condemning racial discrimination, the petition requested that Kenny go before the appeals court and officially acknowledge that the trial court had made errors. Such a stipulation would have led the appeals court to immediately overturn the convictions. The SLDC obtained over ten thousand signatures on this petition, and while Attorney General Kenny did not intervene in the case in the way the committee wanted, he did feel compelled to respond to various petitioners, promising them that the state's response before the appeals court would be fair and "without prejudice."[49]

As the success of the petition drive indicates, the SLDC gathered strong support for its efforts to free the Sleepy Lagoon defendants. That support was also broad based. The New York office of the Communist Party's International Labor Defense (ILD), for example, provided logistical help in the form of mailing lists and other organizational assistance. Local ILD representatives such as LaRue McCormick provided early leadership and ongoing logistical assistance. Labor unions made substantial financial contributions to the defense fund, helped with staffing, and passed resolutions at the local, state, and national levels demanding the release of the defendants. Celebrities from the entertainment industry as varied as actor-director Orson Welles, jazz singer Nat King Cole, and classical violinist Yehudi Menuhin allowed use of their names as sponsors, entertained at fund-raising events, wrote essays, and contributed money.[50]

Assistance also came from other American racial and ethnic groups. Carlotta Bass, publisher of the *California Eagle,* southern California's largest African American newspaper, was an early member of the SLDC and consistently promoted its objectives both within the African American community and to white city officials. Support also came from a variety of Jewish organizations and other Latino groups. For example, the New York–based Spanish-language newspaper *Pueblos Hispanos* serialized *The Sleepy Lagoon Case* in order to publicize the SLDC's efforts to Spanish-speaking groups outside the Southwest, and the Latin American delegates to the International Labor Organization conference expressed their support. Finally, in April 1944, the SLDC issued a press release announcing that a group of Japanese and Japanese Americans interned at the concentration camp at Manzanar had signed the petition to Attorney General Kenny. The press release noted that the petition linked the Sleepy Lagoon case to racial prejudice.[51]

The SLDC made a special effort to gain support from the Mexican American community. At the beginning of the campaign, most Mexican American involvement came from leftists such as Josephina Fierro de Bright and from Mexican Americans in progressive labor unions. Unions with large numbers of Mexican American members placed the resolution pledging support for the SLDC before the California state CIO convention. In contrast, the more conservative elements within the Mexican American community were initially hostile or ambivalent to the efforts to free the Sleepy Lagoon defendants. The Spanish-language newspaper *La Opinión* was at first antagonistic to the SLDC's efforts to publicize the case, and Manuel Ruiz of the CCLAY took a curiously philosophical approach to the verdicts. While Ruiz found the convictions unjust, he also believed that, given the nature of the charges, the jury could just as easily have found all the defendants guilty of first-degree murder. The fact that the jury reached a variety of verdicts ranging from not guilty to first-degree murder demonstrated to Ruiz that the members of the jury had tried to reach a just verdict.[52]

In order to overcome these attitudes, the SLDC endeavored to maintain a strong link with the broader Mexican American community. Much of this responsibility fell to Alice McGrath, secretary to the SLDC and the committee's only paid employee. She maintained communications with other Mexican American groups and worked to sustain the morale of the defendants and their families by involving them in the fund-raising efforts. Mexican American CIO members distributed the Spanish-language edition of *The Sleepy Lagoon Case* pamphlet along with other Spanish-language literature publicizing the case at patriotic festivities such as Mexican Independence Day. The SLDC also worked closely with officials of the Mexican government, in part to deflect even a hint of impropriety (the Mexican consul helped audit SLDC financial records), and also to allay fears that Communists and radicals may have been using the case to advance their own agenda.[53]

These efforts apparently proved successful, and as the fund-raising campaign gained momentum, Mexican Americans came more and more to see the Sleepy Lagoon case as just one additional example of anti-Mexican discrimination. Raymond G. McKelvey, executive secretary of the Southern California Council of Inter-American Affairs, stated that Mexican Americans believed that "the convictions and severe sentencing of so many boys indicates hostility on the part of the Anglo-American community toward its Mexican members. They are convinced that if the boys had been Anglos their treatment by the court would have been different."[54]

This attitude was more concretely manifested in the efforts of Mexican American grassroots organizations to aid in fund-raising. For example, the Pico Gardens Residents Council, the tenants' organization for the inhabitants of the Pico Gardens public housing project, sponsored a fund-raising dance, with proceeds going to the defense fund. Similarly, three hundred residents from the Palo Verde barrio met at a local church and sent a telegram to Attorney General Kenny worded in a way similar to the SLDC petition. The SLDC's fragmentary records also indicate that the overwhelming majority of the individual contributions from California came from Mexican Americans, demonstrating that the SLDC's campaign seems to have had a significant impact on ordinary Mexican Americans.[55]

Important institutions within the Mexican American community also provided needed endorsements. After initial hostility, La Opinión came to support the campaign and in January 1944 the editor of the smaller El Pueblo officially joined the defense committee. The efforts to garner support from the Mexican government also proved successful. The Mexican consul general, Vicente Peralta C., publicly congratulated the SLDC, describing its efforts as "magnificent work" and "a valuable service to the community." More important, former Mexican President Lázaro Cárdenas, probably the most popular chief executive of Mexico in the twentieth century, also praised the SLDC for its "spirit of justice" and its efforts "to end racial discrimination which is incompatible with the democratic ideals of the people of North America."[56]

Racial discrimination was the main issue taken up in the second SLDC pamphlet, The Sleepy Lagoon Mystery, written by the novelist and screenwriter Guy Endor and published in June 1944. In his introduction, SLDC chairman Carey McWilliams directly tied the Sleepy Lagoon case to the issue of racism. According to McWilliams, the case symbolized "the struggle of the Mexican minority to free itself from a pattern of racial ostracism and discrimination which has too long prevailed in Southern California." McWilliams characterized the defense effort as "the first well-organized and widely-supported effort in Southern California to bring the case of the Mexican, or the citizen of Mexican descent, to the attention of all the peoples of the area." McWilliams described the work of the SLDC as important not only in overcoming the injustice done to the Sleepy Lagoon defendants, but also in correcting "those stereotyped attitudes which have long resulted in more than one type of discrimination against the Mexican."[57]

Guy Endor's text consisted of a sensationalized account of the case. It attempted to lay the blame for the zoot-suit hysteria and the prosecution and conviction of the Sleepy Lagoon defendants on a conspiracy initiated by William Randolph Hearst in collaboration with conservative, even reactionary, elements within the Los Angeles law-enforcement community. Endor quoted liberally from the trial transcripts to demonstrate prosecutor Shoemaker's use of racial themes during the trial. He also charged that police beat the Sleepy Lagoon defendants in order to get confessions and that the LAPD initiated the Zoot Suit riots to distract the public from highly publicized cases of police brutality. The overall picture painted by Endor was of an unholy but shadowy alliance that aggravated racial divisions so as to disrupt the war effort.[58]

Such charges of racial discrimination, prosecutorial misconduct, police brutality, and disloyalty did not go unchallenged. East and West Coast distributors refused to handle *The Sleepy Lagoon Mystery* because they feared that William Randolph Hearst, the "villain of the book," would retaliate against them. As a result, the SLDC had to market the book itself. Opponents also used the Communist Party affiliation of LaRue McCormick, who had helped start the SLDC, as proof of its subversive intent. Right-wing politicians employed the Communist connection not only to try to discredit the committee but also to stop it from functioning. As already noted, Deputy District Attorney Clyde Shoemaker intimidated a Unitarian church into not hosting an SLDC convention in March 1943. Later, Shoemaker testified before the California legislature's Joint Fact-Finding Committee on Un-American Activities in California (also known as the Tenney Committee after its chairman, Senator Jack Tenney), regarding the SLDC's Communist affiliation. Shoemaker stated that he knew that the SLDC was a Communist organization because from the very day that SLDC attorney George Shibley took over the defense at the Sleepy Lagoon trial, he started making charges of prosecutorial and judicial misconduct, police brutality, and societal racism. The Tenney Committee concluded that the SLDC was a Communist front organization and charged that SLDC chairman Carey McWilliams had Communist inclinations. It cited as proof his opposition to racial segregation and the fact that his "views on racial intermarriage are identical with *Communist Party* ideology"[59] (emphasis in original).

280   A Statue to the Unknown Zooter

More moderate elements in Los Angeles were also alarmed at the SLDC's success in publicizing the injustices in the Sleepy Lagoon case and worried that the committee might radicalize the Mexican American community. As mentioned in chapter 11, the *Los Angeles Times* attacked the committee for charging that the Zoot Suit riots were racially motivated, and Mayor Fletcher Bowron complained bitterly of the contacts the Office of War Information representative Alan Cranston had with the SLDC. They, however, were not alone. More explicit was the Southern California Council of Inter-American Affairs, which worried that only the "radical leadership" had championed the cause of the Sleepy Lagoon defendants. Referring to the SLDC, the business-oriented SCCIAA believed that the radicals stood "to win the reputation among Mexicans of being the only element in our community ready to go to bat to see that the legal rights of these convicted boys have been adequately protected." The SCCIAA thus noted that "the radicals have a splendid chance to dramatize themselves and build their prestige and potential opportunities for leadership among our Mexican-Americans. We can only guess the consequences of this for the community in the years ahead."[60]

Raymond McKelvey, the executive director of the SCCIAA, proposed a solution to this problem. He recommended that the Los Angeles County Bar Association form a committee "composed of distinguished men" to investigate the Sleepy Lagoon case and file an amicus brief with the appeals court. This committee's work would be given wide publicity. Such a course of action would have two benefits, according to McKelvey. First, "much local racial tension would be alleviated" if the bar committee's inquiry found that "the case was in fact handled in a way prejudicial to the defendants, and . . . it can honestly be said that racial bias showed itself in the prosecution of the case, and in the severity of the sentence." Second, and perhaps more important, through its work, the bar committee would help "correct the impression now being fostered among the Mexican colony that only left-wingers are concerned with their problems, and that when they need assistance, advice, and counsel they should look to the various radical groups who thrive on discontent." While McKelvey and the SCCIAA may have exaggerated the SLDC's actual influence in the Mexican American community, these conservative civic leaders' eagerness to enter the case on the side of the defendants, their willingness to attribute the misconduct of the prosecution and the judge to racial prejudice, and their concerns regarding the radicals' stature among Mexican Americans give an indication of the effectiveness of the SLDC's work.[61]

Despite the red-baiting, the obstacles put before the organization, and the maneuvering of civic leaders to limit its effectiveness, the SLDC and its attorney, Ben Margolis, succeeded, on March 1, 1944, in filing a brief appealing the convictions of the Sleepy Lagoon defendants. The principal point made in the original brief, the subsequent supplements, and the oral arguments was that the prosecution presented no evidence linking the defendants with the death of José Díaz and that the defendants did not receive a fair trial because of the "atmosphere of anti-Mexican prejudice which could not have helped but influence the jury." Margolis submitted as evidence of that atmosphere copies of newspaper stories, the Clem Peoples article in *Sensation* magazine, and the Ayres report. The brief also gave as examples of misconduct by prosecutor Shoemaker and Judge Fricke their refusal to allow the defendants to get haircuts and a change of clothes or to sit or consult with their attorneys during the trial proceedings.[62]

On October 4, 1944, the Sleepy Lagoon Defense Committee's two-year struggle finally bore fruit. In a unanimous decision, the Second District Court of Appeals of the State of California overturned the convictions of the seventeen young Mexican American men convicted in the death of José Díaz and all related charges. In a 121-page opinion, the court stated that it had painstakingly reviewed the 6,000-page transcript of the trial as well as the 1,400 pages of appeal briefs and had as a result concluded that the prosecution had presented no evidence that the defendants had entered into a conspiracy to commit murder. "Our examination of the record in this case," the court stated, "convinces us that there is a complete lack of evidence from which the Jury could properly find or infer that the appellants formed a conspiracy of the kind and type or for the purposes claimed by the prosecution." Having dismissed the conspiracy charges, the heart of the prosecution's case, the appeals court proceeded to find no evidence, either material evidence or testimony, that any of the individual defendants had assaulted, much less murdered, José Díaz or, with one exception in terms of assault, anyone else at the Delgadillo home on the night of August 1, 1942.[63]

How then had the jury reached the guilty verdicts? The appeals court found that much hearsay and other inadmissible evidence was presented to the jury. Despite the lower court's admonition that these points of evidence must not be considered in reaching verdicts, the appeals court declared that "to hope that they might be forgotten by the jury in their deliberations is to belie human nature and challenge human experience." The appeals court also found that the trial judge, Charles W. Fricke, had committed a number of procedural errors and was guilty of serious judicial misconduct, as the SLDC had charged all along. The court ruled, for example, that the mass trial of multiple defendants and Fricke's ruling that they could not sit with their attorneys deprived them of their constitutional "right to the effective and substantial aid of counsel at all stages of the proceedings." Citing the United States Supreme Court's decision in the Scottsboro case, the California court stated, "To do that 'is not to proceed promptly in the calm spirit of regulated justice, but to go forward with the haste of the mob.' "[64]

The appeals court was particularly harsh in criticizing Fricke's attempts to ridicule the defense attorneys before the jury. The court declared "that the trial judge injured materially the defense of appellants by the character of rebukes administered in the presence of the jury, when, in most instances, not even a mild rebuke was deserved." It cited as an example Fricke's charge of "severe misconduct" against a defense attorney who objected to a prosecution witness using prepared notes on the stand. The defense's objection was not only appropriate, the court ruled, Fricke's "severe castigation . . . was as undeserved as it was unwarranted." It also censured Fricke for allowing the prosecution attorney to coach witnesses by reading to them their previous grand-jury testimony, a practice the appeals court found "neither proper nor legal." Finally, the court reprimanded Fricke for not allowing testimony that showed the defendants had been beaten and intimidated by the police into making self-incriminating statements to them.[65]

However, despite the appellate court's finding that no evidence existed to support the conviction, despite its harsh criticism of the hostile atmosphere set by the trial judge, and even despite its allusion to mob rule and the Scottsboro case, the court rejected the SLDC's contention that the prosecution and conviction were motivated by racial prejudice against Mexican Americans. In its published opinion, the court stated that no evidence was "revealed by the record upon which it can be said that this prosecution was conceived in, born, or nurtured by the seeds of racial prejudice." The court gave as proof for this contention the fact that the victim of the crime, José Díaz, was Mexican American and thus the prosecution "was instigated to protect Mexican people in the enjoyment of rights and privileges which were inherent in everyone." As the SLDC and other observers noted, such a narrow view ignored "the total context of anti-Mexican racial hysteria in which the trial took place, the same context which soon erupted like a volcano in the 'pachuco,' or 'zoot-suit,' riots." Guy Endor, writing for the SLDC, said much the same thing, adding that, other than racial prejudice, there were few other explanations for Judge Fricke's obvious bias against the defendants.[66]

On October 23, 1944, Los Angeles Superior Court Judge Clement D. Nye, on the recommendation of Deputy District Attorney John Barnes, dismissed all charges against the Sleepy Lagoon defendants. Two hours later authorities released the eight defendants who remained in jail to a throng of approximately 250 family, friends, and well-wishers. That evening, the three young men who had been convicted of first-degree murder, Henry Leyvas, Robert Telles, and Chepe Ruiz, appeared on a CIO radio program to express their thanks to everyone who had worked on their defense and contributed to the defense fund. Chepe Ruiz told Vernon Partlow, the show's host, that all the defendants understood the important role organized labor had played in their defense and that it was "only right" that they spend their first day of freedom thanking the unions. Partlow ended the interview by noting that "winning the Sleepy Lagoon Case was just a step in the fight to end discrimination not only in our courts but in every aspect of American Life."[67]

Two months later, on December 29, 1944, Carey McWilliams, national chairman of the Sleepy Lagoon Defense Committee, announced the dissolution of the committee effective January 1, 1945. Claiming complete vindication for the positions the committee had taken, McWilliams stated that the committee's work had also improved relations between the United States and its Latin American neighbors, thus contributing to the war effort. For McWilliams, however, the SLDC's accomplishments were only a beginning. "The larger task, which must be undertaken in California and throughout the Southwest," McWilliams proclaimed, "is to organize the Mexican minority along democratic lines for the achievement of a larger measure of social, economic and political democracy throughout the area and to remove all vestiges of discrimination." McWilliams concluded by charging those who had supported the SLDC to continue the struggle to bring justice to the Mexican American community.[68]

McWilliams underestimated the significance of the SLDC's work. Not only did the committee correct, as McWilliams observed, "an obvious miscarriage of justice," it also publicized across the nation the fact that Mexican Americans were the victims of racial discrimination. Despite the appellate court's refusal to acknowledge that racism had played a role in the case, the court's reversal of the convictions did indeed vindicate the SLDC's argument, and gave Mexican Americans roughly the same status as African Americans as an oppressed racial minority group. More important, the SLDC's two-year campaign helped politicize the Mexican American community. If the fears of SCCIAA spokesman Raymond McKelvey and the support the SLDC received from the Mexican American community are any indication, Mexican Americans learned important lessons from the Sleepy Lagoon case. Not only did they begin to define themselves as an oppressed minority group, they also learned that through organized political activity and collective ethnic politics they could begin to overcome at least the worst aspects of their oppression. The net result was a more assertive attitude on the part of the Mexican American community toward the LAPD, the press, and the white city establishment.

Conclusion

On May 31, 1949, Edward R. Roybal, who had lived through the zoot-suit hysteria and had been a victim of LAPD misconduct, became the first person of Mexican descent to be elected to the Los Angeles City Council in the twentieth century. Roybal had campaigned in 1947 and lost. In the intervening two years a grassroots civil-rights group, the Community Service Organization, composed primarily of World War II veterans, registered more than fifteen thousand additional Mexican American voters. The additional voters seemingly responded to one of Roybal's main campaign themes, reforming the LAPD in order to end police brutality, thus providing the margin of victory in the city's ninth district. During his years on the city council and later as a United States congressman, Roybal consistently addressed issues of police misconduct and called for reform of the LAPD.[1]

Roybal's campaign, victory, and subsequent career illustrate the multiple legacies of the previous half century of interactions between Mexican Americans and the LAPD. One of the most important of those legacies was the institutionalization within the police department of the linkage between race and criminality. This linkage changed the way the LAPD policed the Mexican American community, and it led to a deterioration of the relationship between the department and the Mexican American community.

While in the immediate aftermath of the Zoot Suit riots the LAPD attempted to accommodate the Mexican American community through programs such as the Deputy Auxiliary Police and by working closely with the Coordinating Council for Latin American Youth, these efforts were effectively undermined by the belief that Chicanos were criminally inclined. By the end of the war, the department had institutionalized in its operations the idea that Mexican Americans constituted a criminal population, and it began training officers, both formally and informally, to expect more crime from Mexican Americans than from the white population. Since theories of scientific management and other aspects of police professionalism directed that police personnel be aggressively deployed in high-crime areas, the concentration of police officers became much greater in Mexican American neighborhoods than in other areas of the city. The combination of these two factors and the department's more aggressive posture in fighting crime resulted in chronic over-arresting of Mexicans. Since the police used arrest statistics in their calculations to determine the crime rate within a given population, officers' belief that Mexican Americans were criminally inclined became a self-fulfilling prophecy. Officers arrested more Mexican Americans because they believed them to be criminally inclined. Similarly, officers who were trained to expect violent behavior from Mexican Americans were more likely to resort to violence themselves in response to a perceived threat. Thus, the years after World War II saw a dramatic rise in the number of police-brutality complaints made by Mexican Americans.[2]

The LAPD's preoccupation with minority crime meant that the department's subsequent history became inextricably intertwined with that of the minority communities. To begin with, the issue of minority group crime helped develop a constituency for the department's bureaucratic agenda. Beginning with the Zoot Suit riots, the LAPD cultivated the mystique of being the defender of the white middle and working classes against the depredations of inherently criminal racial groups. In the 1950s and 1960s Chief of Police William H. Parker described the LAPD as "the thin blue line" that stood between civilization and chaos. No one who heard his words doubted that to Parker, "civilization" meant whites and "chaos" meant the Chicano and black communities of Los Angeles. The department brokered this view into increased appropriations and also into political support when Chicanos and blacks protested police misconduct. Department managers used protests from minority groups as proof of their inherent criminality and of the need for whites to support their local police. Because it succeeded in gaining this support, the LAPD became virtually insulated from criticism emanating from the citizenry and even from public officials. Thus, to a great extent, the LAPD attained its increased budgets and its much-desired autonomy from political control precisely because whites feared black and Chicano crime.[3]

But the hostile relationship with the minority communities was not an unmixed blessing for the LAPD. While this strategy succeeded in the short run in creating a constituency supporting the department's agenda, it also resulted in an immutable hostility on the part of many minority citizens. During the second half of the twentieth century, the constant barrage of criticism from Chicanos and blacks eventually permeated and corrupted the very core of the department. Officers who had already been taught that minorities represented the criminal element in society found in criticism from that quarter further proof of Chicanos' and blacks' hostility toward law enforcement, and all too often they engaged in what the Kerner Commission would later call "abrasive" police practices. Police administrators developed policies regarding citizens' complaints, officer training, and deployment of officers that adversely affected the minority groups and increased tensions. When Chicanos and blacks protested police misconduct, the LAPD attempted, often through illegal means, to suppress that protest. The resultant hostilities erupted into the Watts uprising of 1965 and the violence associated with the Chicano Moratorium demonstrations of 1970 and 1971. During the relatively quieter 1980s, the idea that minority males were criminally inclined governed, to an even greater extent, the work habits of police officers. One needed only to see the video tape of the 1991 beating of Rodney King by Los Angeles police officers, recall the nationwide debate that it generated, and remember the massive violence that erupted when a jury acquitted the accused officers to understand the long-term consequences of the hostility between minority groups and the LAPD.[4]

If the linkage between race and criminality helped define the postwar LAPD, it also changed the racial identity of Mexican Americans. One of the ironies of the World War II experience is that while European ethnic groups lost their separate racial identity—they laid "a secure claim to whiteness," in the words of the historian Gary Gerstle—the racial identity of Mexican Americans became even more clearly defined and firmly entrenched. One of the main characteristics of this new identity was the alleged criminal nature of Mexican American youth. It is not an exaggeration to say that the youth gang became the prism through which much of white society came to view the Chicano community. One need only see the depictions of Chicanos in the local news-papers or on television or in Hollywood films to comprehend the prom-inence of the gang stereotype.[5]

Unfortunately, such depictions had a basis in fact. The antisocial and self-destructive youth gangs that today prey on the Chicano community originated in the zoot-suit era. As some scholars have suggested, the limited opportunities afforded Mexican American youth and the official rhetoric regarding their inherent criminality may have combined to pro-duce the gang culture that has been passed along to succeeding gener-ations. But while the gangs are now a reality—a reality with which the community must contend—they are not the totality of the late-twentieth-century Chicano experience. Violent gang members still rep-resent only a small minority of Chicano youth. Nevertheless, they define the Chicano community in the eyes of much of white America.[6]

Mexican Americans' racial identity changed in another important way as a result of the zoot-suit hysteria and the broader interaction with the LAPD: white society came to see Mexican Americans as an op-pressed racial minority group. Primarily as a result of the efforts of the Sleepy Lagoon Defense Committee, the plight of Mexican Americans in Los Angeles received national prominence. At the local level, civic lead-ers' fear that the SLDC might radicalize the Mexican Americans led to the development of a broad range of social-welfare programs to benefit the community, especially the youth. That same fear raised the status of the more conservative Coordinating Council for Latin American Youth. The CCLAY used its elevated standing to push for even more social services for Mexican Americans and to enhance the influence both of itself as an organization and of its individual members.

Edward Roybal came out of the tradition established by the CCLAY. During his tenure on the city council Roybal attempted to improve the relationship between the Chicano community and the LAPD. On the one hand, this meant supporting at least part of the department's pro-gram for professionalization. Roybal generally endorsed the depart-ment's requests for additional funding, and he also attempted to act as a conduit between the LAPD and the community on issues of mutual concern, such as growing problems with drugs and gangs in East Los Angeles. At the same time, however, he vigorously protested LAPD ac-tions when he felt it necessary to do so. He advocated improved officer training on minority issues, called for the creation of a civilian review board, and once even demanded the resignation of the LAPD's Chief William H. Parker for declaring that Mexican Americans were genetically inclined toward criminality. Although the department almost never publicly acceded to his demands for reform, Roybal became a force to be reckoned with on the issue of police treatment of Mexican Americans.[7]

The historical significance of Roybal's career, however, goes well beyond the issues he addressed; equally important was the fact that he was in a position to address these issues at all. In 1949 Mexican Americans voted in record numbers to elect him to office. They voted for him precisely because he was Mexican American and because he promised to try to make city government—especially the LAPD—more accountable to the Mexican American community. Although Roybal publicly stated that he would represent all his constituents, regardless of race, both he and the Mexican American community understood the significance of his election. As *La Opinión* editorialized, Roybal represented "not only the Ninth District that elected him, but also the hundreds of thousands of Mexicans and Mexican Americans who reside in the city." While the returning veterans brought home an increased confidence, the ethnic solidarity and sense of political identity necessary to elect Roybal would not have been possible without Mexican Americans' passage through the crucible of the pachuco hysteria. Edward Roybal's political career, and the new power of the Mexican American community it symbolized, was another legacy of the zoot-suit era.[8]

In the final analysis it would seem, then, that the zoot suiters achieved some successes—albeit unwittingly. In response to the symbolic protest of the zoot suiters, postwar Mexican Americans found themselves with a level of political prominence no one would have imagined just a few years earlier. This new prominence cut both ways. Police, the press, and society at large continued to view Chicano youth as inherently delinquent, a view that would to a large extent define the Mexican American minority for the rest of the century. On the other hand, Mexican Americans' status as an oppressed racial minority group gave them the political clout to end their explicit exclusion from public accommodations and other forms of public discrimination and to demand that public officials create a broad spectrum of public and social services devoted to meeting the needs of the community. Mexican Americans' new political strength also meant that civic leaders, politicians, and even the police had to consider the potential response of the community when making public policy decisions. While during the 1950s and 1960s officials generally chose to disregard the Chicanos' wishes, they nevertheless knew they would have to pay some political price for ignoring the community. Mexican Americans both helped create their new status and were transformed by it. The election of Edward Roybal was but one manifestation of the changed way in which they saw themselves and the way they related to white society. As a champion and defender of the Mexican American community, Roybal would articulate the community's needs and protest its grievances. Mexican Americans emerged from the wartime experience with a confidence and sophistication that exemplified a new political identity and a new political style. Simply put, they would no longer be ignored.

Notes

CHAPTER 1

1. The Zoot Suit riots are fully described in Jones, *Government Riots of Los Angeles;* McWilliams, *North from Mexico;* Mazón, *Zoot-Suit Riots;* Acuña, *Occupied America.*

2. *Time* magazine, June 21, 1943, quoted in Jones, *Government Riots of Los Angeles,* 29; Citizens' Committee for Latin-American Youth, Minutes, June 7, 1943; Manuel Ruiz Jr. Papers (hereafter Ruiz Papers), Box 3; *Los Angeles Times* (hereafter *Times*), June 7, 1943; *Los Angeles Daily News* (hereafter *Daily News*), June 7, 1943.

3. For a discussion of youth subcultures, see Hebdige, *Subculture.*

4. In this study, I will use the following terminology to designate people of Mexican descent living in the United States: *Mexican* will identify first-generation immigrants from Mexico; the term *Mexican American* will denote the second-generation children of the immigrants; the term *Chicano* will primarily refer to people of Mexican descent in the postwar period. In addition, the terms *white* and *Anglo* will designate Americans of European descent. In general, I will use Mexican to describe actors during the period from 1900 to 1930 and Mexican American for people from 1930 to 1945.

5. For two typical examples of the social science literature, see Bayley and Mendolson, *Minorities and the Police;* and Mann, *Unequal Justice.* Examples of historical studies that follow this pattern are Fogelson, *Big City Police;* Woods, "Progressives and the Police." For a critique of law-enforcement institutional history that is still valid, see Robinson, "Criminal Justice History Research in Progress in the United States."

6. National Advisory Committee on Civil Disorders, *Report of the National Advisory Committee on Civil Disorders* (henceforth, Kerner Commission), 301.

7. United States Commission on Civil Rights, *Mexican Americans and the Administration of Justice in the Southwest,* 88.

8. The Kerner Commission, for example, stated, " 'Harassment' or discourtesy may not be the result of malicious or discriminatory intent of police officers. ... Calling a Negro teenager by his first name may arouse resentment because many whites still refuse to extend to adult Negroes the courtesy of the title 'Mister.' A patrolman may take the arm of a person he is leading to the police car. Negroes are more likely to resent this than whites because the action implies that they are on the verge of flight and may degrade them in the eyes of friends or onlookers." Kerner Commission, 300–304; Skolnick, "Police in the Urban Ghetto," 224–225; also see Westley, *Violence and the Police;* Mann, *Unequal Justice,* 116–165; Skolnick, *Justice without Trial,* 80–83.

9. Fogelson, *Big City Police,* 112–116, 146, and 236–242; Woods, "Progressives and the Police," 2–6, 410–411, and 497–499; also see Morales, "Study of Mexican American Perceptions of Law Enforcement Policies and Practices in East Los Angeles," 260; Skolnick, *Justice without Trial,* 42–70; and Westley, *Violence and the Police,* 48–152.

10. U.S. Civil Rights Commission, *Mexican Americans and the Administration of Justice in the Southwest,* 88.

11. For a more recent articulation of these basic themes, see Independent Commission of the Los Angeles Police Department, *Report of the Independent Commission of the Los Angeles Police Department.*

12. Haney López, "Social Construction of Race"; also see Gould, "Geometer of Race."

13. This discussion draws heavily from Omi and Winant, *Racial Formation in the United States;* and Haney López, "Social Construction of Race." Race of course does not apply only to minority groups; people of European descent also have race and they usually fall into the category of white. For a discussion of whiteness, see Haney López, *White by Law;* Lipsitz, "Possessive Investment in Whiteness"; George J. Sánchez, "Reading Reginald Denny"; Taylor, "Hidden Face of Racism," 395–408; Williams, "Tragic Vision of Black Problems"; Lipsitz, "Toxic Racism"; and Fishkin, "Interrogating 'Whiteness,' Complicating 'Blackness.' " For the view that scholars ought not even use race as a category of analysis, see Miles and Torres, "Does 'Race Matter'?" and Fields, "Slavery, Race and Ideology in the United States of America."

14. Horsman, *Race and Manifest Destiny.*

15. DeLeón, *They Called Them Greasers,* 104; Gutiérrez, *Walls and Mirrors,* 29.

16. Reisler, *By the Sweat of Their Brow,* 151–176; Gutiérrez, *Walls and Mirrors,* 54 and 55.

17. Reisler, *By the Sweat of Their Brow,* 178–183. Reisler quotes S. Parker Fisselle saying that "like a pigeon, he [the Mexican] goes back to roost."

18. Omi and Winant, *Racial Formation,* 14–20; Haney López, "Social Construction of Race," 20–24.

19. Analyses of the origins of American urban police departments can be found in Lane, *Policing the City;* Richardson, *New York Police;* and the Center for Research on Criminal Justice, *Iron Fist and the Velvet Glove,* 19–23. The

role of police protecting the interests of the capitalist class during the period in question is most thoroughly explored in Haring, *Policing a Class Society;* Friedman, *Crime and Punishment in American History,* 104.

20. Friedman, *Crime and Punishment,* 104; quoted in Skolnick, *Justice without Trial,* 45–46; *New York Times,* May 10, 1998.

21. In a democratic society the police theoretically perform their order maintenance function under the rule of law. This means that police officers are not only subject to the same laws as the rest of society, they must also perform their official duties in accordance with a whole set of rules and regulations explicitly intended to curtail their power. As the sociologist Jerome Skolnick has observed, the twin goals of "law and order" are sometimes inconsistent and often in conflict with one another. Skolnick, *Justice without Trial,* 17–22 and 230–245; also see Wilson, *Varieties of Police Behavior.*

22. For discussions on the role of the state, see Barrera, *Race and Class in the Southwest,* 157–173; Davis, *City of Quartz,* 250–253; Independent Commission, *Report.* Sometimes, however, police become too aggressive in their actions against minority groups and create disorder rather than order. In such instances elites step in and reestablish control. Such was the case in the wake of the 1991 beating of motorist Rodney King by Los Angeles police officers when the intransigence of Police Chief Daryl Gates not only became an embarrassment but threatened to provoke a wholesale restructuring of the LAPD. The consummate corporate lawyer and power broker Warren Christopher stepped in to head a commission that called for the removal of Gates and for reforms, which came nowhere close to dealing with the mutual hostility between the minority communities and the LAPD.

23. This does not mean that Mexicans had not been racialized earlier nor that this was the first time Mexicans had been seen as a criminally inclined race. Part of the nineteenth-century stereotype that whites had of Mexicans was that they were a violent, criminal group. That view softened, however, during the early twentieth century, when American industries attracted hundreds of thousands of Mexicans to work in the factories, fields, and mines of the Southwest. In fact, while the stereotype of the violent and brutal Mexican never totally disappeared, by the 1920s it was to a great extent replaced by that of the "docile" Mexican. See Horsman, *Race and Manifest Destiny;* DeLeón, *They Called Them Greasers,* 63–74; and McWilliams, *North from Mexico,* 189–190.

24. I use the concept of politics here and throughout the study broadly to encompass all activity that seeks to change power relationships. My thinking is strongly influenced by the work of the feminist social scientists Ann Bookman and Sandra Morgen, who define "politics as activities that are carried on in the daily lives of ordinary people who are enmeshed in the social institutions and political-economic processes of their society. When there is an attempt to change the social and economic institutions that embody the basic power relations in our society—that is politics." See Morgen and Bookman, "Rethinking Women and Politics," 4.

25. For social banditry see Castillo and Camarillo, *Furia y Muerte.*

26. The generational analysis of Chicano history was first articulated in Al-

varez, "Psycho-Historical and Socioeconomic Development of the Chicano in the United States." The most thorough analysis of the Mexican American generation comes in García, *Mexican Americans;* also see George J. Sánchez, *Becoming Mexican American.*

27. Gutiérrez, *Walls and Mirrors;* George J. Sánchez, *Becoming Mexican American.*

CHAPTER 2

1. Griswold del Castillo, *Treaty of Guadalupe Hidalgo.*

2. Quoted in Weinberg, *Manifest Destiny,* 167.

3. Quoted in Horsman, *Race and Manifest Destiny,* 236.

4. Escobar, "Chicano Protest and the Law," 46–107; Bell, *Reminiscences of a Ranger,* 13–18; *El Clamor Público,* July 26, 1856.

5. Gutiérrez, *Walls and Mirrors,* 29; for an overview of Mexicans' violent response to white domination, see Castillo and Camarillo, *Furia y Muerte.*

6. Fogelson, *Fragmented Metropolis,* 56 and 78–79. Also see Carey McWilliams's impressionistic but highly insightful *Southern California;* and Nelson and Clark, *Los Angeles Metropolitan Experience,* passim.

7. Fogelson, *Fragmented Metropolis,* 76–83.

8. Ibid., 81. Singleton, *Religion in the City of Angels,* 100–107.

9. Fogelson, *Fragmented Metropolis,* 76–83.

10. Ibid., 76; Castillo, "Making of a Mexican Barrio," 19–20; Camarillo, *Chicanos in a Changing Society,* 200.

11. Quoted in Stimson, *Rise of the Labor Movement in Los Angeles,* 104.

12. McWilliams, *Southern California.*

13. For example, Otis once described unionism in the *Times* as an "insufferable despotism . . . odious to free men and injurious . . . to public safety." He characterized the union boycott as a "cowardly, mean, un-American, assassin-like method of establishing a petty despotism." Even the union label did not escape Otis's ire. In 1900 he stated that the union label was "a form of blackmail, levied by organized ruffianism upon invertebrate employers, weak-kneed politicians and poltroons who [do] not assert . . . their manhood or stand for their inalienable rights." Quoted in Stimson, *Rise of the Labor Movement in Los Angeles,* 37, 119, and 248.

14. In 1903 the *Times* ran the following editorial: "Employers of labor should be ready to meet and vanquish those who make unreasonable and arrogant demands upon them. To be forewarned is to be forearmed. Employers of labor in Los Angeles, have been thus forewarned, should prepare for possible disturbances by quietly arranging with skilled workingmen in various parts of the country, who they may, if necessary, summon at a moment's notice by telegraph, to take the place of their present employees, in case the latter should be persuaded to walk out and leave their work. The latter might then be notified to go about their business and never to darken the doors of the establishment again. At the same time a watch should be kept over the weak and faithless, and all interlopers. Those who are found to be acting the part of the traitor and fomenting disturbance, should be weeded out, and replaced by men who believe

in respecting the interests of their employer, as well as their own." Quoted in ibid., 259.

15. Good treatments of the Southern Pacific's control over California politics can be found in Mowry, *California Progressives*, 1–22; and Bean, *California*, 252–263. For a detailed discussion of the railroad's power in Los Angeles, see Fogelson, *Fragmented Metropolis*, 206–209.

16. Fogelson, *Fragmented Metropolis*, 212–213.

17. For a discussion of the sumptuary laws and their effects on ethnic minority groups, see Fogelson, *Big City Police*, 29–39, 137, and 192.

18. Mowry, *California Progressives*, 55–56, 92–94, and 97. For a thorough treatment of the labor movement in Los Angeles, see Stimson, *Rise of the Labor Movement in Los Angeles;* and Perry and Perry, *History of the Los Angeles Labor Movement, 1911–1941.*

19. Mowry, *California Progressives.*

20. Woods, "Progressives and the Police," 15–23 and 25.

21. Fogelson, *Big City Police*, 13–39.

22. Ibid., 21.

23. Fogelson, *Fragmented Metropolis*, 213. A good national treatment of the progressives' agenda for the police can be found in Fogelson, *Big City Police*, 40–66 passim. For a detailed discussion of the progressive program for the police in Los Angeles, see Woods, "Progressives and the Police," 15–83.

24. Lane, *Policing the City;* Richardson, *New York Police;* Center for Research on Criminal Justice, *Iron Fist and the Velvet Glove;* Haring, *Policing a Class Society.*

25. Cardoso, *Mexican Emigration to the United States, 1897–1931;* Reisler, *By the Sweat of Their Brow.*

26. Castillo, "Making of a Mexican Barrio," 19–20 and 132–190; also see George J. Sánchez, *Becoming Mexican American*, 188–206.

27. For the role that Mexican labor played in the economic development of Los Angeles and the Southwest, see Barrera, *Race and Class in the Southwest;* Camarillo, *Chicanos in a Changing Society;* Romo, *East Los Angeles;* and García, *Desert Immigrants.*

28. Quoted in Ríos-Bustamante and Castillo, *Illustrated History of Mexican Los Angeles, 1781–1985*, 113.

29. Quoted in Camarillo, *Chicanos in a Changing Society*, 203.

30. Romo, *East Los Angeles*, 67–80; the housing conditions of Los Angeles Mexicans are also thoroughly described in Castillo, "Making of a Barrio," 91–97; Camarillo, *Chicanos in a Changing Society*, 126–141; George J. Sánchez, *Becoming Mexican American*, 6–83.

31. The LAPD did not even begin to compile arrest statistics by race until 1923. For a discussion of the nineteenth-century stereotype of Mexicans as criminals, see DeLeón, *They Called Them Greasers.*

32. *Times*, April 13–14, 1903, and October 21, 1907.

33. Examples of Mexican burglaries and robberies can be found in the *Los Angeles Record* (hereafter *Record*) throughout the period from 1912 to 1920; *Los Angeles Herald* (hereafter *Herald*), September 28 and 29, 1908; *Record*, May 19, 1914; November 3, 1913.

34. *Record,* June 3–7 and 10, 1913.

35. *Los Angeles Express* (hereafter *Express*), August 23, 1907.

36. *Times,* February 1, 1903. The only connections between Gonzales and the murder were that the morning after the killing, he was found sleeping in a stairway several blocks from the murder, and one of Underwood's companions stated that the two men had had an altercation earlier that night. Although several people witnessed the murder, no one could identify Gonzales as the killer.

37. *Times,* March 3 and 15, 1903.

38. Ibid.

39. Ibid., January 4, 6, 7, and 14, 1903. *Record,* January 3, 13, and 14, 1903.

40. *Times,* January 6, 7, 13, 21, and 22, 1903. *Record,* January 5, 6, 12–17, 19–21, 24, and February 5, 1903. During the grand jury hearings, the dead man's brother, Ralph Sepúlveda, produced a note allegedly written by the victim that read, "Ralph, they have killed me here with a bunch of keys. The one who takes care of the jail." LAPD spokesmen claimed the note was a forgery.

41. *Record,* February 24, 1912, October 30, 1916, and January 15, 1917. Because the *Record* was the city's only daily newspaper with pro-labor sentiments, it was also the only paper that consistently published stories critical of the LAPD. In the Parra case, for example, the *Record* stated that the boy worked full-time to support his widowed mother and attended night school in order to improve himself.

42. Los Angeles Board of Police Commissioners, Minutes (hereafter P.C., Minutes), January 1900 to December 1919. Charges were brought by or on behalf of Mexicans in the following categories: five for excessive force, four for conduct unbecoming an officer, two for undue use of authority, two for extortion, two for neglect of duty, one for illegal entry, and one not specified. During a short period, from May 1911 to November 1913, as a result of controversy over the killing of several civilians by police officers, the police commission also heard reports regarding police shootings. During this period the minutes show that officers shot six Mexicans. The police commission ruled all the shootings justified.

CHAPTER 3

1. Stimson, *Rise of the Labor Movement,* 266–267; Wallenberg, "Working on El Traque," 96; *Times,* February 12, 1903, and April 25, 1903; *Record,* April 24, 1903.

2. *Times,* March 15 and May 3, 1903.

3. Ibid., April 28, 1903.

4. Ibid., April 25, 1903; *Record,* April 25, 1903.

5. *Times,* April 26, 1903; *Record,* April 28, 1903. On the fame of Teresa Urrea, see McWilliams, *North from Mexico,* 199–200.

6. *Record,* April 28, 1903; *Times,* April 26, 1903.

7. *Times,* April 26 and 27, 1903.

8. *Record,* April 25, 1903; *Times,* April 27, 1903.

9. *Times*, April 26, 1903; *Record*, April 25, 1903.

10. *Times*, April 28–29, 1903.

11. Ibid.

12. Ibid.

13. Ibid., May 1, 1903. Mexican railway workers went out on strike again in 1904, 1910, and 1917, but without much controversy. The only notable interference came during the 1917 strike, when police officers distributed circulars from the Mexican consul asking that Mexican workers stay neutral in the dispute. Los Angeles Police Department, *Daily Bulletin* (hereafter *Daily Bulletin*), March 17, 1917.

14. *Record*, December 22–24, 1913. It is also interesting to note that in early December the police commission, perhaps because of the unemployment situation, had authorized the appointment of an additional twenty-five patrolmen. P.C., Minutes, December 1, 1913.

15. *Times*, December 27, 1913. Also see *Record*, December 26, 1913.

16. *Record*, December 26, 1913.

17. Ibid.; *Times*, December 26, 1913. It was rumored that several other people were killed by the police. However, only one body was ever found.

18. *Record*, December 27, 1913.

19. *Times*, December 26, 1913.

20. Ibid.

21. Ibid. The hostility of Los Angeles officials toward the Wobblies resulted in part from recent IWW activities in other parts of southern California. In 1912 the Wobblies had organized a free-speech movement in San Diego to protest that city's public-speaking ordinance. Hundreds of IWW members had converged on what was then only a small seaside resort, made public speeches in defiance of the ordinance, and practically demanded to be arrested. As the population of the local jail swelled beyond its limits, vigilantes rounded up all the Wobblies and led them out into the countryside. The vigilantes then forced the Wobblies to kneel and kiss the American flag and run a gauntlet in which all received beatings. One man later died as a result of the injuries he received that day. These incidents created a firestorm of protest throughout the state, and Los Angeles officials may have feared that the Christmas Day rally was only the opening of a series of Wobbly activities in that city. McWilliams, *Southern California*, 287–289.

22. *Times*, December 27, 1913.

23. *Record*, December 26, 27, 29, 30, 1913, and January 3, 1914. Also see *Times*, December 27 and 30, 1913, and January 3, 1914. The committee report was technically correct. The Plaza itself was a free-speech zone and not subject to the public-speaking ordinance. The speaker, however, had placed his makeshift platform on the firmer cement sidewalk that surrounded the Plaza but that was outside the free-speech zone.

24. *Record*, December 30, 1913.

25. Ibid., December 27 and 29, 1913. The *Times*, in reporting Wheeler's assertion, responded that the problem could be solved by sending "the horde of Spanish-Indian half breeds" to the border area and eventually back to Mexico. *Times*, December 29, 1913.

26. *Record,* December 27 and 30, 1913; *Times,* December 28 and 30, 1913.

27. *Record,* January 21–23, 1914.

28. Ibid., January 30, 1914. A good example of the tactics used by the defense came during the cross-examination of the last prosecution witness, Patrolman E. E. Brown. According to the *Record,* Brown had been saved until the end of the trial because he was the prosecution's "trump card," the kind of man who "knew exactly what he had seen and was not the character of a man to be bulldozed from his testimony." During direct testimony Brown pointed out twelve men whom he stated had been throwing rocks during the riot. Under questioning by Harriman, however, Brown was unable to give the order in which he saw the men committing the alleged crime, or other important details of the incident.

29. Ibid., February 2, 6, and 9, 1914.

30. Ibid., February 7, 1914.

31. Ibid. An incident that occurred three weeks after the sentencing is of some interest. On February 25 the *Record* revealed that the convicted men had been taken to a work camp run by the County Sheriff's Department and tortured when they refused to work. According to the *Record*'s story, which was not denied by the sheriff's office, the men's ankles were tied by wire to a sycamore tree and their handcuffed wrists were draped back around the tree and secured by a rope. The longer the men refused to work, the higher their arms were slung over the branch. The length of time the men stayed in this position ranged from six hours to three and half days, depending on when they agreed to join the work gang. According to Judge White, who had presided over the trial and now ordered the torture stopped, the men "were standing squarely on their legal rights when they refused to work," because their case was then on appeal.

32. Ibid., August 18, 1917.

33. Ibid.

34. Ibid. and August 20, 1917.

35. Whitten, "Criminal Syndicalism and the Law in California"; Bernstein, *Lean Years,* 83–143; Perry and Perry, *History of the Los Angeles Labor Movement,* chapters 4–6. The *Daily Bulletin* published the Red Flag ordinance on February 11, 1919.

36. *Record,* September 16, 1917; *Express,* August 15 and October 7, 1919.

CHAPTER 4

1. Gómez-Quiñones, *Sembradores,* 17–29; also see Raat, *Revoltosos* and MacLachlan, *Anarchism and the Mexican Revolution.*

2. Raat, *Revoltosos,* 107–199. Easily the most influential American investor in Mexico was David E. Thompson, American ambassador to Mexico from 1906 to 1909. Thompson held large investments in Mexico (including part ownership in the Pan American Railway) and did not hesitate to use his office to enhance his personal finances. He strongly advised his superiors at the State Department to aid in the suppression of the PLM. Ibid., 109–111.

3. Ibid.

4. Myers, "Mexican Liberal Party," 229. The *Los Angeles Citizen* (hereafter

Citizen), the official newspaper of the Los Angeles Labor Council, claimed in the October 4, 1907, issue that in the months immediately preceding the arrests, Harrison Gray Otis of the *Times* had "received great gifts of land from the president of Mexico."

5. *Express*, August 30, 1907. Also see *Herald*, August 30, 1907.

6. Raat, *Revoltosos*, 109–111. Also see Gómez-Quiñones, *Sembradores*, passim.

7. PLM organized labor unions had been particularly active in New Mexico and Arizona; Gómez-Quiñones, *Sembradores*, 27–31 and 118.

8. *Herald*, August 24, 1907; *Times*, August 24, 1907; *Express*, August 24, 1907; *Citizen*, August 30, 1907; Gómez-Quiñones, *Sembradores*, 36–37.

9. *Herald*, August 24, 1907; *Times*, August 24, 1907. According to the *Times*, when Modesto Díaz was arrested, he gave up without a fight, saying only, "*Carramba*. I was to have been ze [sic] Consul-General at San Francisco."

10. Raat, *Revoltosos*, 92–93. The most celebrated kidnapping case came on the morning of June 30, 1907, when Sam J. Hayhurst, an Arizona Ranger, kidnapped PLM member Manuel Sarabia, "spirited" him across the border, and handed him over to Mexican officials; ibid., 142–146.

11. *Herald*, August 24, 1907. Also see *Times*, August 24, 1907.

12. *Times*, August 24, 1907.

13. Ibid.; *Express*, August 27, 1907.

14. *Herald*, August 25, 1907; *Times*, August 27, 1907.

15. *Times*, August 27–29 and November 13, 1907. The *Times* also reported that at the same rally, in reaction to one of the speeches, "Mexicans snarled and growled like wolves." For a more balanced account of the same rally, see *Herald*, November 13, 1907, and *Citizen*, November 15, 1907.

16. *Times*, November 13, 1907. For discussions of American radical support for the PLM, see Gómez-Quiñones, *Sembradores*, 37 and Raat, *Revoltosos*, 48.

17. *Herald*, August 27, 1907. On the day that Talamantes and the Ricos pressed their charges of resisting arrest, the court showed its partiality by holding a special noon session so that the new charges could be filed before the defense could file its writ of habeas corpus in the afternoon; *Express*, August 26, 1907. Three days later, Judge Wilbur ruled that "under the circumstances" the PLM leaders were justified in resisting arrest; *Express*, August 30, 1907.

18. *Express*, August 26 and 30, 1907; *Herald*, November 13, 1907; *Citizen*, November 15, 1907; and *Times*, August 24, 1907.

19. *Times*, October 11, 1909, and *Herald*, October 11, 1909. Presumably, the police did not arrest the Mexican woman orator (and thus did not give us her name) for fear of arousing sympathy for the protesters.

20. *Herald*, October 19, 1909; *Times*, November 27, 1907, and October 21, 1909; Gómez-Quiñones, *Sembradores*, 34 and 55; Raat, *Revoltosos*, 54.

21. Raat, *Revoltosos*, 54.

22. *Herald*, October 11, 20, 24, and 25, 1909.

23. Ibid., October 23 and 24, 1909. The *Herald* was careful to point out that the rally was "deliberative, rather than inflammatory" and that "the rabid element was lacking [with] nearly every walk of professional and business life

. . . represented." The *Times* did not comment on the rally. Also see the *Express,* October 23 and 25, 1909.

24. *Express,* October 13, 1909. Progressive support for Gutiérrez de Lara, however, was not monolithic. At the time of Gutiérrez de Lara's first incarceration in the fall of 1907, progressive journalist Charles Lummis wrote to Caroline Severance chastising her for her support of the Mexican lawyer. "Go slow on Gutiérrez de Lara," Lummis warned. He argued that because "there is no country to which we owe more . . . kindness and helpfulness," the United States should seek to "aid Mexico," not harm it. "Díaz governs Mexico well," Lummis maintained, and "there is no more persecution for politics in Mexico than there is in Los Angeles." Consequently, "any attempt to overthrow the present government of Mexico is as far from patriotic as any attempt to overthrow the government of the United States." Charles F. Lummis to Caroline Severance, January 17, 1908, Caroline Severance Papers. My thanks to Gayle Gullett for this citation.

25. *Herald,* October 22 and 24, 1909. Gutiérrez de Lara also ingratiated himself with Los Angeles whites by reinforcing negative stereotypes of Mexican immigrants. For example, in denying that he had threatened the lives of Presidents Díaz and Roosevelt, Gutiérrez de Lara declared that he would be "crazy . . . to make such a statement to poor ignorant peons." He also stated that if released he would devote himself to the "uplift" of the Mexican people because he believed "that when they learn the ways of this country and become better educated they will be among the best citizens of Los Angeles"; *Express,* October 29, 1909. Many examples of whites' attitudes toward Mexicans can be given. In its report on the original arrest, the *Express,* the city's most prominent progressive newspaper, referred to Gutiérrez de Lara's Mexican audience as "the rabble"; *Express,* October 11, 1909. For progressives' views about immigrants in general, see Higham, *Strangers in the Land.* For progressives' views regarding American racial and ethnic minorities, see Allen, *Reluctant Reformers.* The best treatment of white attitudes toward Mexicans can be found in DeLeón, *They Called Them Greasers.*

26. The evidence against Limón was, in fact, so weak and the police were so eager to convict him and to discredit Gutiérrez de Lara that the judge publicly censured them for giving prejudiced testimony. As a consequence, the jury took only three minutes to acquit Limón; *Herald,* October 27, 1909.

27. Ibid.

28. Ibid.

29. Ibid., November 16, 1909.

30. Other instances of wrongdoing against Talamantes and the Ricos were reported in a November 4, 1909, *Herald* story stating that Talamantes "probably will be confronted . . . in criminal court with a charge of contempt" for failing to respond to a subpoena. The story also stated that Talamantes may have taken money from a Mexican prisoner, J. José Gonzales, who was subsequently acquitted of any wrongdoing. The following month the *Herald* charged Talamantes and the Ricos with "one of the most brazen attempts to 'railroad' a man into the penitentiary." The man in question was the same J. José Gonzales, and, as in the previous case, all charges were dropped against him. Gon-

zales's attorney, S. S. Sanders, charged that the whole matter was the result of the police department attempting to gain revenge for the embarrassment Gonzales had caused them in the earlier case; ibid., November 4 and December 25, 1909.

31. *Record,* August 1, 1910; *Times,* August 2, 1910; *Herald,* October 11, 1910.

32. *Herald,* October 11, 1910; P.C., Minutes, November 7, 1910; *Times,* November 8, 1910.

33. P.C., Minutes, October 10, 17, 24, and 31, November 7, 10, and 14, 1910; *Herald,* November 11, 15, and 17, 1910; *Times,* November 8, 1910.

34. P.C., Minutes, November 23 and 28, December 5 and 27, 1910. *Herald,* November 22 and 28, and December 6, 1910; *Times,* November 22 and December 6, 1910. The main testimony given on behalf of Talamantes and the Ricos pertained to their good character.

35. Gómez-Quiñones, *Sembradores,* 52–54; *Record,* April 1, 1912.

36. Gómez-Quiñones, *Sembradores,* 53–54; *Record,* June 22, 1912; June 25, 1912.

37. *Record,* April 1, 1912; June 25–July 1, 1912.

38. Ibid.; July 11 and 17–18, 1912. The police commission passed the following resolution regarding the June 25 riot: "Resolved, that the Police Commission recognizes the splendid service performed by the Los Angeles Police Department on June 5th, 1912, in quickly subduing a riotous demonstration in the vicinity of the Federal Building which, but for the prompt and effective work done, might have been accompanied by loss of life and property"; P.C., Minutes, June 26, 1912.

39. For example, Harry Chandler, who became the owner of the *Los Angeles Times* after Harrison Gray Otis's death, was indicted for violation of the neutrality laws for buying and transporting military supplies to conservative forces in Baja California, Mexico, where Chandler owned large parcels of land; *Record,* February 19, 1915.

40. Romo, *East Los Angeles,* 90.

41. *Record,* July 29–31 and August 2, 1913. Other examples of the revolution spilling over into Los Angeles can be found in the *Record,* August 9, and September 16, 1913.

42. Romo, *East Los Angeles,* 89–111. Romo reports that even prior to the periods of diplomatic tension, the LAPD violated the rights of Los Angeles Mexicans in response to revolutionary activity. In November 1913, for example, the *Times* published an alarmist editorial claiming that Mexican revolutionaries were ready to raid American cities along the border, including Los Angeles. The next day the LAPD began making arbitrary arrests of Mexicans and stepped up surveillance in the barrio; ibid., 96–97.

43. Cline, *United States and Mexico,* 157–160. Womack, *Zapata and the Mexican Revolution,* 185–186. Only Pancho Villa, among leading revolutionary figures, did not protest the American action.

44. *Record,* April 20, 1914.

45. Ibid., April 22, 23, and 28 and May 15, 1914.

46. Ibid., May 27, 1915; May 8, 1915; July 7, 1915; August 12, 1915.

Among other things, the *Plan de San Diego* called for the massive uprising of Mexicans living in the southwestern states of Texas, New Mexico, Colorado, Arizona, and California, the independence of those states, and the expulsion or execution of all white males in the newly freed territories.

47. Cline, *United States and Mexico,* 174–183.

48. Ibid.

49. *Record,* March 14 and 16 and April 8, 19, and 21, 1916.

50. Ibid., May 11, 1916.

51. Ibid., June 26–27 and 30 and July 24, 1916.

52. Romo, *East Los Angeles,* 101–102.

53. Romo, "Mexican Workers," 115. *Record,* March 16, 1916; March 18, 1916; March 19, 1916.

54. *Record,* March 20, 1916; Los Angeles Police Department, *Daily Bulletin,* March 25, 1916.

55. *Record,* June 21, 27, 29, and 30, 1916. P.C., Minutes, June 27, 1916.

56. Romo, *East Los Angeles,* 105–110.

57. Ibid.; *Record,* May 14, 1917.

58. *Times,* May 15, 1917.

59. *Record,* May 28, 1917. The *Record* also stated that Carrillo told his audience "that if the United States wanted Mexicans to aid them in Europe, Americans should give them an interest in the country by marrying 500,000 Mexicans to American girls." Carrillo evidently practiced what he preached, for he was himself convicted of refusing to register for the draft and sentenced to one year in the county jail. After his release, he was deported to Mexico.

CHAPTER 5

1. Kasun, *Some Social Aspects of Business Cycles in the Los Angeles Area,* 9. Findley, "Economic Boom of the 'Twenties in Los Angeles," 29.

2. Findley, "Economic Boom," 33 and 20; Fogelson, *Fragmented Metropolis,* 76; Castillo, "Making of a Mexican Barrio," 19–20; Camarillo, *Chicanos in a Changing Society,* 200.

3. Romo, *East Los Angeles,* 67–80. In 1929 the Los Angeles Chamber of Commerce, using information from the Los Angeles Board of Education, placed the Mexican population of the city at 189,850, thus supporting the higher estimate of the Chicano scholars; Clements Papers.

4. Romo, *East Los Angeles,* 120 and 122; Kasun, *Some Social Aspects of Business Cycles,* 32.

5. Kasun, *Some Social Aspects of Business Cycles,* 9 and 23; Leader, "Los Angeles and the Great Depression," 1–18; Balderrama, *In Defense of La Raza,* 1.

6. Kasun, *Some Social Aspects of Business Cycles,* 32; George J. Sánchez, "Barrio in Crisis," 41–45; Balderrama, *In Defense of La Raza,* 1–3 and 15–25. For Mexican workers as a buffer group, see Barrera, *Race and Class in the Southwest.*

7. The corruption within the LAPD and city government as a whole is richly detailed by Woods in "Progressives and the Police," chapters 3–9.

8. LAPD, *Daily Bulletin*, November 22, 1919; *Express*, November 22, 1919.

9. United States Senate, Committee on Education and Labor, *Violations of Free Speech and Rights of Labor*, Hearings before a subcommittee of the Senate Committee on Education and Labor, 76th Congress, Third Session, Senate Resolution 266 (1940; hereafter *Violations of Free Speech*), pt. 64, 23509–23510; Hopkins, *Our Lawless Police*, 53–54.

10. *Violations of Free Speech*, pt. 64, 23514–23516. For an example of a red-squad attack on a group of citizens addressing the Los Angeles City Council, see Taft, *Fifteen Years on Freedom's Front*, 41–42.

11. *Violations of Free Speech*, pt. 64, 23518–23519 and 23528. The La-Follette Committee published seventy-five volumes of testimony and documents it had collected. The document cited here (and most other LAPD documents) was obtained by the subcommittee under subpoena.

12. Ibid., pt. 64, 23640–23641; pt. 54, 20049; pt. 64, 23645; pt. 71, 26160; Taft, *Fifteen Years on Freedom's Front*, 38–41.

13. *Violations of Free Speech*, pt. 53, 19481–19483; Woods, "Progressives and the Police," 345.

14. Taft, *Fifteen Years on Freedom's Front*, 35–36.

15. P.C., Minutes, January 1930 through December 1938; Perry and Perry, *History of Los Angeles Labor Movement*, 237. The one case where the police commission resolved the conflict in favor of a labor complainant came from the protest of the Millinery Branch Needle Trades Workers Industrial Union. The chief of police advised the commission that the red squad had been removed from the strike area. P.C., Minutes, September 25, 1933.

16. Hoffman, *Unwanted Mexican Americans in the Great Depression*, 26–30; Acuña, *Occupied America*, 185–188.

17. Hoffman, *Unwanted Mexican Americans*, 39–41.

18. George J. Sánchez, "Barrio in Crisis," 42–43 and 45; quoted in Balderrama, *In Defense of La Raza*, 2.

19. George J. Sánchez, "Barrio in Crisis," 45; quoted in Balderrama, *In Defense of La Raza*, 2; Hoffman, *Unwanted Mexican Americans*, 35–37.

20. Visel to Arthur M. Woods, January 6, 1931, George P. Clements Papers, Bundle 15, Box 80 (hereafter Clements Papers); quoted in Hoffman, *Unwanted Mexican Americans*, 42–44.

21. Quoted in Hoffman, *Unwanted Mexican Americans*, 170–171 and 48; quoted in Balderrama, *In Defense of La Raza*, 17.

22. Hoffman, *Unwanted Mexican Americans*, 53.

23. *La Opinión*, February 27, 1931.

24. Ibid.; also see Hoffman, *Unwanted Mexican Americans*, 59–63.

25. Balderrama, *In Defense of La Raza*, 16–20; Clements to Arthur G. Arnoll, January 31, 1931, Clements Papers; Hoffman, *Unwanted Mexican Americans*, 57 and quoted on 65.

26. Hoffman, *Unwanted Mexican Americans*, 52.

27. Ibid., 53–54.

28. Kerr to Ortiz Rubio, June 6, 1931; Arnold to Visel, January 8, 1931; Clements to Arnoll, January 31, 1931, Clements Papers; for the Chamber of Commerce's position on the need for Mexican workers, also see Clements to

Arnoll, June 11, 1931, Clements Papers; and Hoffman, *Unwanted Mexican Americans,* 53–54.

29. George J. Sánchez, *Becoming Mexican American,* 209–252.

30. Pesotta, *Bread upon the Waters,* 19–20 and 23; Perry and Perry, *History of Los Angeles Labor,* 252 and 254.

31. Pesotta, *Bread upon the Waters,* 24–25.

32. Ibid., 24–25, 29–30, and 34; Perry and Perry, *History of Los Angeles Labor Movement,* 252–253.

33. *Times,* October 13, 1933; Pesotta, *Bread upon the Waters,* 38–43; Perry and Perry, *History of Los Angeles Labor Movement,* 252–253.

34. *Times,* October 16, 20, and 26, 1933; *Violations of Free Speech,* pt. 64, 23588.

35. Perry and Perry, *History of Los Angeles Labor Movement,* 254; Pesotta, *Bread upon the Waters,* 44 and 52; *Times,* October 12 to November 4, 1933. See the *Times,* October 19, 1933, for a discussion of the Protestant ministers' protest over "police violence." These same ministers filed a complaint before the police commission regarding "police brutality" during the strike; P.C., Minutes, November 3 and 13, 1933. On the other hand, the police commission received several commendations of the red squad from dressmaking companies; ibid., October 20 and November 10, 1933; and the Merchants and Manufacturers Association sent a letter to Mayor Shaw commending the red squad for its "work in protecting employees remaining at work"; *Times,* October 22, 1933.

36. *Times,* October 17, 1933; Pesotta, *Bread upon the Waters,* 44.

37. *Times,* October 18, 1933, and October 19, 1933; Pesotta, *Bread upon the Waters,* 45–46.

38. *Times,* October 21, 31, and November 1, 1933.

39. Ibid., October 27, 1933.

40. Ibid., October 24, 1933.

41. Cletus E. Daniel, *Bitter Harvest,* 15–39.

42. Ibid., 40–70.

43. Ibid.

44. Ibid., 71–104.

45. Balderrama, *In Defense of La Raza,* 95–97; quoted in Weber, "Organizing of Mexicano Agricultural Workers," 331; *Violations of Free Speech,* pt. 64, 23637.

46. *Violations of Free Speech,* pt. 70, 23855; *Times,* April 18, 1936.

47. Balderrama, *In Defense of La Raza,* 101–102; *Open Forum,* May 16, 1936; *Violations of Free Speech,* pt. 70, 25855–25873.

48. *Violations of Free Speech,* pt. 64, 23693.

49. *Times,* April 25, 1936.

50. Ibid., April 26, 1936.

51. *Open Forum,* May 2, 1936; *Times,* April 27, 1936.

52. *Open Forum,* May 2, 1936.

53. Ibid.; *Violations of Free Speech,* pt. 64, 23595.

54. *Open Forum,* May 2 and 9, 1936; *Violations of Free Speech,* pt. 64, 23693; Balderrama, *In Defense of La Raza,* 101–102.

55. *Open Forum,* May 9 and 16, 1936.

56. P.C., Minutes, May 6, June 9 and 23, and July 14, 1936.

57. *Violations of Free Speech,* pt. 70, 25855–25873; pt. 65, 23949.

58. Balderrama, *In Defense of La Raza,* 99; *Violations of Free Speech,* pt. 70, 25855–25873.

59. *Violations of Free Speech,* pt. 64, 23637.

60. Balderrama, *In Defense of La Raza,* 106.

61. Ibid., 106–107.

62. *Times,* August 10–11, 1936; Balderrama, *In Defense of La Raza,* 106–107.

63. *Violations of Free Speech,* pt. 64, 23637–23638 and pt. 63, 23001.

64. Balderrama, *In Defense of La Raza,* 106–107.

65. Clements to Arnoll, November 27, 1936, Clements Papers.

CHAPTER 6

1. *Times,* June 19 and 20, 1921.

2. Ibid., June 19 and 23, 1921. The *Times* also gave a heartrending description of how Fitzgerald's wife, carrying their five-year-old child, "swooned" into the arms of other officers when she learned of her husband's death; ibid., June 19, 1921.

3. LAPD, *Daily Bulletin,* December 22, 1921; *Times,* June 20, 1921.

4. *Times,* June 19–26, 1921.

5. Ibid., June 21, 1921.

6. Ibid.; LAPD, *Daily Bulletin,* June 19–25, 1921.

7. *Times,* June 21 and 25, 1921; LAPD, *Daily Bulletin,* July 1, 1921, August 4, 1921, and December 22, 1921.

8. *New York Times,* October 4 and 7, 1925, and April 4, 1926. Contemporary observers had heated debates over whether the nation was indeed suffering a crime wave. In contrast to the popular press, for example, the President's Research Committee on Social Trends concluded that the country had experienced an increase in crime between 1900 and 1925, "but hardly a crime wave, if by that is meant an extraordinary rise in the number of criminal acts committed." Whether extraordinary or not, the committee's statistics indicate that crime did increase by 175 percent in the United States during the period in question. President's Research Committee on Social Trends, *Recent Social Trends in America,* vii.

9. Woods, "Progressives and the Police," 138 and 164. In chapters 3 to 8, Woods details the importance of the crime and vice issues in Los Angeles during the 1920s and 1930s.

10. Walker, *Critical History of Police Reform,* 151–153.

11. Woods, "Progressives and the Police," 270–364.

12. For the different schools of criminology, see Sutherland and Cressey, *Principles of Criminology,* 53–60. Also see Quinney, *Criminology,* 4–12.

13. Sutherland and Cressey, *Criminology.*

14. Ibid.

15. Ibid.

16. I made a thorough study of the *Journal of Criminal Law and Criminology* from 1920 through 1929. The one article that advocated the sociological school was John Koren's "What We Do Not Know about Crime," 447–448.

17. Hewes, "Study of Delinquent Girls at Sleighton Farm," 600–602; H. H. Goddard, as quoted in Parmelee, *Criminology,* 159. For a sampling of the debate on the effects of intelligence, see Doll, "Comparative Intelligence of Prisoners," 33–46; Erickson, "Study of the Relationship between Intelligence and Crime," 592–635; and Murchison, "American White Criminal Intelligence," 239–316 and 435–494.

18. Doll, "Study of Multiple Criminal Factors," 42; Doll, "Comparative Intelligence," 194; Willis, "Success Record of Delinquent Boys in Relation to Intelligence," 177; Erickson, "Intelligence and Crime," 624.

19. Doll, "Study of Multiple Criminal Factors," 40–41. Another author, Calvin P. Stone, discovered that differences did exist between African Americans and whites in terms of the numbers and types of crimes for which each group was incarcerated. He reached a far different conclusion, however, regarding the causes of this phenomenon. Also working with a prison population, Stone found that African Americans were incarcerated more than whites for crimes against persons but less so for crimes against property and public order. This occurred, he observed, because "the courts are a trifle more severe with the negro than with the white in order that he may be kept in the approved degree of subordination"; Stone, "Comparative Study of 399 Inmates of the Indiana Reformatory and 653 Men of the United States Army," 254.

20. Bingham, "Determinants of Sex Delinquency Based on Intensive Studies of 500 Cases," 505–506.

21. Brasol, "Foundations of Criminology," 33–35.

22. Ibid., 35–36.

23. May, "Our Anti-Social Mexican Class," typed manuscript, Box 62, Ernesto Galarza Papers. A note on the manuscript states that the article was published in the *Los Angeles County Employee* magazine in March 1929. It is also interesting to note that May supports his contention that Mexicans were intellectually inferior with the fact that no Mexicans were enrolled at the Stanford University Medical School.

24. Bogardus, *Mexican in the United States,* 52–58, 61, and 68–75.

25. Taylor, "Crime and the Foreign Born: The Problem of the Mexican," 237–243.

26. Warnshuis, "Crime and Criminal Justice among the Mexicans of Illinois," 271 and 328–329. Later, Bogardus expressed the same ideas regarding Mexicans' alleged tendency to steal; see Bogardus, *Mexican in the United States,* 52.

27. Handman, "Preliminary Report on Nationality and Delinquency," 253 and 256–258.

28. Warnshuis, "Crime and Criminal Justice among the Mexicans of Illinois," 267–268.

29. Taylor, "The Problem of the Mexican," 216, 241, 234–235, and 229.

30. Ibid., 220; Warnshuis, "Crime and Criminal Justice," 268.

31. Taylor, "The Problem of the Mexican," 218.

32. Warnshuis, "Crime and Criminal Justice," 281–284; Taylor, "The Problem of the Mexican," 240 and 229–230.

33. Taylor, "The Problem of the Mexican," 241, 219, 234–235, and 243.

34. Ibid., 219 and 229–230.

35. Ibid., 231–232.

36. California Governor C. C. Young's Mexican Fact-Finding Committee, *Mexicans in California,* 197–207. This report was in general agreement with the mental testers school of criminology when it noted that the Mexican inmates at the Preston School for Boys had "a decidedly lower level of intelligence" than the white inmates.

37. Ibid.

38. Sutherland and Cressey, *Criminology,* 25; quoted in Quinney, *Criminology,* 56.

39. Quinney, *Criminology,* 56 and 63–64. Quinney goes on to argue that "crime rates finally have to be understood for their political construction and the political uses they serve." For example, police departments often manipulate crime statistics by raising them, in order to increase their budgets, or by lowering them, in order to show that they are doing their jobs. Similarly, Quinney asserts that politicians and law-enforcement officials use crime statistics to reify theories of the inherent criminality of racial groups and to justify suppressing the political activism of minority groups and women.

40. For the difficulty in measuring the Mexican population of Los Angeles, see the "note" in Camarillo, *Chicanos in a Changing Society,* 200.

41. S. H. Bowman, "Brief Study of Arrests of Mexicans in Los Angeles for a Twelve Month Period," in August Vollmer, "Survey of the Los Angeles Police Department, 1923–1924," unpublished manuscript, in Los Angeles Police Department Archives, 3–4.

42. Ibid., 7–8.

43. Ibid., 10.

44. Ibid., 27.

45. Ibid., 3–4.

46. Camarillo, *Chicanos in a Changing Society,* 199.

47. Unless otherwise noted, the following discussion will be based on LAPD, *Annual Report,* multiple volumes, 1925–1939.

48. Los Angeles Board of Playground and Recreation Commissioners, "Resolution," August 30, 1934, Chief of Police General Files, City Records Center (hereafter COP, General Files, CRC), Box 35288; Captain W. M. Littell to Chief of Police James Davis, September 9, 1934, COP, General Files, CRC, Box 35288; P.C., Minutes, January 4, 1938. For other indications of early LAPD concern, see *Daily Bulletin,* "Commendation," September 6, 1935; P.C., Minutes, January 28, 1936.

49. Acuña, *Community under Siege,* 16; Acuña also lists all headlines from the *Citizen* and the *Eastside Sun* dealing with Chicanos in the "Community Bulletin Board" section of his book; P.C., Minutes, December 26, 1939.

50. Quinney, *Criminology,* 270–273 and 279–289. For a full discussion of the use of discretion among police officers and the effect of discretion on the police function, see Skolnick, *Justice without Trial.*

51. Taylor, "The Problem of the Mexican," 229.

52. Quinney, *Criminology,* 286; Bowman, "Brief Study of Arrests of Mexicans," 7.

53. Woods, "Progressives and the Police," 288–289. The disposition of the department on this issue is best demonstrated by Chief of Police Roy Steckel's response to criticism of the dragnets: "Suppose it is against the law," he replied; "is that any good reason why it shouldn't be done? It's practical. It gets results[;] . . . we have no intention of stopping"; ibid.

CHAPTER 7

1. Romo, *East Los Angeles,* 148–155.

2. Quoted in ibid., 149; Balderrama, *In Defense of La Raza,* 38; for discussions of Los Angeles area Spanish-language newspapers of the era, see Ríos-Bustamante and Castillo, *Illustrated History of Mexican Los Angeles,* 118–122; and Medeiros, *"La Opinión,* A Mexican Exile Newspaper," 65–87.

3. Acuña, *Occupied America,* 183.

4. For a thorough discussion of the role of the Mexican consulate in Los Angeles, see Balderrama, *In Defense of La Raza;* also see Sánchez, *Becoming Mexican American,* 108–125.

5. García, *Mexican Americans,* 13–22.

6. LAPD, *Annual Reports,* 1926–1939; P.C., Minutes, January 1920–December 1939.

7. P.C. Minutes, January 1920–December 1939.

8. Ibid., June 18, 1929.

9. Ibid., June 25, 1929.

10. Ibid., July 2 and 12 and August 13, 1929.

11. Ibid., January 1920–December 1939.

12. Ibid., August 9 and December 20, 1927, and January 24, 1928.

13. Ibid., January 31, 1928. In addition to making complaints to the police commission, Mexicans sometimes also used the courts to redress their grievances against the LAPD. In 1930, for example, J. P. Román sued Officer Clyde Plummer for assault and battery, claiming damages of one hundred thousand dollars. According to the complaint, a handcuffed Román was standing in Plummer's office asking to see his wife when Plummer struck him "full in the face and knocked him to the floor and jumped upon his postrate [*sic*] form." With Román on the floor, Plummer "placed both knees upon plaintiff's stomach, grabbed him by the throat with both hands and bounced his head upon the cement floor at least eight times, with all his might, causing blood to spurt from plaintiff's mouth and to flow upon the floor and upon the wall." At the time of the arrest, Plummer bragged to newspaper reporters that he had roughed up Román. When the suit was filed, however, Plummer claimed that he had not touched Román and that the young Mexican had been under the influence of marijuana at the time of the arrest. *Record,* November 11, 1930. The *Record* does not indicate the outcome of Román's suit.

14. LAPD, *Annual Reports,* 1926–1939.

15. *Times,* October 20, 1922.

16. *El Tucsonense,* April 5, 1924; Ricardo Romo, *East Los Angeles,* 158–159; J. L Schleimer to Alvaro Obregón, n.d.; Obregón to Mexican consulate in Los Angeles, March 21, 1923; Obregón to Richardson, February 25, 1924; *Hispano America,* n.d. My special thanks to F. Arturo Rosales for sharing his file on the Pompa case with me.

17. Gamio, *Mexican Immigration to the United States,* 103–107.

18. *La Opinión,* May 9, 1931; *Times,* May 12, 1930.

19. *Times,* May 12 and 14 and October 30, 1930; *Record,* May 12–13, 1930.

20. *La Opinión,* May 10, 1931; *Times,* October 30 and September 2, 1930.

21. *La Opinión,* May 8, 1931.

22. Ibid., May 8, 1931; *Times,* August 29, September 6 and 11, 1930.

23. *Times,* October 29, 30, November 2, 4, and 6, 1930; *La Opinión,* May 7, 1931.

24. *La Opinión,* May 8, 1931; quoted in Armando Morales, "Study of Mexican American Perceptions of Law Enforcement Policies and Practices in East Los Angeles," 71–72.

25. *La Opinión,* May 5 and 10, 1931.

26. Ibid., May 5–14, 1931.

27. Ibid., May 10 and 5, 1931; *Times,* May 4, 1931.

28. *La Opinión,* May 5–6, 1931. *La Opinión* published twenty-three of his letters to his family and friends on May 10, 1931.

29. Ibid., May 8 and 9, 1931.

30. Ibid., May 6–10, 1931.

31. Ibid., May 10, 1931. Although a handwriting analysis is no longer possible, a comparison of texts of the alleged suicide letter and Reyna's twenty-three letters published in *La Opinión* do give some indications, not totally conclusive, regarding its authenticity. On the one hand, the suicide letter was much more somber, rambling, and, as *La Opinión* noted, philosophical than Reyna's regular letters to his family; in addition, Reyna made reference in the suicide letter to going to Mass, which, since he was a practicing Methodist, was not a mistake he was likely to make. On the other hand, the suicide letter contained a long soliloquy on the importance of life's experiences as opposed to religious teachings as a means to gaining an understanding on how to get along in the world. This argument was similar to one he made in a section of one of his letters to his mother. In the final analysis, it is impossible to tell whether Reyna wrote the letter himself or, for that matter, whether he committed suicide or was murdered.

32. Ibid., May 6, 1931; the PLM and other Mexican organizations also helped raise money to support the Reyna family. Ibid., May 14, 1931.

33. Ibid., May 6–7, 1931.

34. Ibid., May 8, 1931.

35. Ibid., May 9, 1931. Because the LAPD refused to provide police officers to direct traffic, the large crowd created quite a bit of confusion in the area around the church and en route to the cemetery.

36. Ibid.

37. Ibid. Most of the other speakers echoed Flores's call for an official in-

vestigation. Mrs. Jesús Vda. de Robles, for example, dramatically produced a
torn and tattered cross and stated that it symbolized how justice as exemplified
by the Reyna case had been destroyed in the United States. Another speaker,
Mrs. Elena de la Llata, the president of La Cruz Azul Mexicana, ended her
speech by saying that Juan Reyna, was "a good Mexican [and] a martyr"; ibid.

38. Ibid.

39. Ibid.

40. Ibid., May 10–12 and 23, 1931.

41. Transcript of interview with Pedro J. González, n.d., Audio Visual Services, University Research Library, University of California, Los Angeles, 118–
119.

42. Ibid., 184–185.

43. Ibid., 113. *San Diego Tribune,* October 6, 1983.

44. *San Diego Tribune,* October 6, 1983.

45. González transcript, 120–126.

46. Ibid., 126–133.

47. Ibid., 195–196.

48. Ibid., 173–178 and 180–181.

49. Ibid., 178–180.

50. P.C., Minutes, November 7, 1932.

51. García, *Mexican Americans,* 145–159.

52. Ibid.; Gutiérrez, *Walls and Mirrors,* 111.

53. García, *Mexican Americans,* 145–159; Camarillo, *Chicanos in California,* 58–64; also see Sánchez, *Becoming Mexican American,* 245–249, and Gutiérrez, *Walls and Mirrors,* 110–116.

54. García, *Mexican Americans,* 161; also see Acuña, *Community under
Siege,* 17.

55. García, *Mexican Americans.*

56. Spanish Speaking People's Congress of California, "Resolutions
Adopted by the Second Convention of the Spanish Speaking People's Congress
of California," December 9 and 10, 1939, Ernesto Galarza Papers.

57. García, *Mexican Americans,* 161.

CHAPTER 8

1. Woods, "Progressives and the Police," 350–364.

2. Ibid., 364–373.

3. Nash, *American West Transformed,* 17–36. I have chosen the lowest of
three separate figures that Nash gives (in one chapter) for federal expenditures
in the West. This kind of confusion is unfortunately symptomatic of this book.
On page 11, for example, he states that over 600,000 Mexican Americans lived
in East Los Angeles; on pages 107–108, he states that the Mexican American
population for all California was 354,432 and 219,000 for Los Angeles.

4. Ibid., 38–39, 42–43, 58, and 62–66.

5. Fogelson, *Big City Police,* 51, 57, 58–60, 97, 111–112, 136–138, and
158–160.

6. Ibid., 142–143, 145.

7. Ibid., 59, 99–100, 104–105, 144–145, 158–160, 175–176, 184, 223–224, 225, and 282–287.

8. Walker, *Critical History of Police Reform,* 139–146. See the LAPD's *Annual Reports* throughout the 1930s for examples of these time-and-place studies.

9. Fogelson, *Big City Police,* 16–17; Walker, *Critical History of Police Reform,* 79–106 and 146–151.

10. Walker, *Police Reform,* 151–152.

11. Ibid., 143 and 156–166. Hoover was so enthusiastic about the potential application of fingerprinting to law enforcement that he advocated universal fingerprinting for residents of the United States; ibid., 157–159.

12. Ibid. In addition to having all the faults that have already been noted regarding crime statistics, the UCR relied on local police departments collecting and reporting crime rates in their areas. Since the municipalities used different methods for collecting statistics, and since local departments often had reason to manipulate the figures (either up or down), the UCR was an extremely unreliable measure of crime; ibid.

13. Fogelson, *Big City Police,* 99–100, 104–105, 112–116, 158–160, and 236–242.

14. Woods, "Progressives and the Police," 372–373 and 381–385.

15. Los Angeles City Charter; Woods, "Progressives and the Police," 337–338.

16. LAPD, *1939 Annual Report;* Woods, "Progressives and the Police," 373–374.

17. LAPD, *Annual Reports,* 1939–1945; Woods, "Progressives and the Police," 394–397.

18. Woods, "Progressives and the Police," 436.

19. Griffith, *American Me,* 45.

20. Quoted in Gutiérrez, "Ethnicity, Ideology, and Political Development," 186.

21. Anon., "Mexican Population as of June, 1942," typed table, Sleepy Lagoon Defense Committee Papers (now titled the Alice McGrath Papers), Special Collections Room, University Research Library, University of California, Los Angeles (hereafter SLDC Papers), Reel 2; Los Angeles County Coordinating Council, "Notes on the Mexican Population in Los Angeles County," typed manuscript, December, 1941, SLDC Papers, Reel 2, also available in the John Anson Ford Papers; also see McWilliams, "Testimony of Carey McWilliams [before the Los Angeles County Grand Jury]," October 8, Carey McWilliams Papers (hereafter McWilliams Papers).

22. Gutiérrez, "Mexican Immigration as a Political Issue," 187.

23. Quoted in Clete Daniel, *Chicano Workers and the Politics of Fairness,* 20; Nunn, Testimony before the Los Angeles County Grand Jury, October 8, 1942, McWilliams Papers; Special Services Division, Bureau of Intelligence, United States Office of War Information, "Spanish-Americans in the Southwest and the War Effort," Report No. 24, August 18, 1942, Research Group 228, Division of Review and Analysis of the Fair Employment Practices Committee, National Archives, Washington, D.C.; my special thanks to Ruth Needleman for this source.

24. Edward Duran Ayres, "Statistics" (henceforth "Ayres Report"), in Jones, *Government Riots of Los Angeles,* 85; quoted in Scott, "Mexican-American in the Los Angeles Area, 1920–1950," 205; quoted in Special Services Division, "Spanish-Americans in the Southwest and the War Effort."

25. Los Angeles County Coordinating Council, "Notes on the Mexican Population in Los Angeles County," December 1941, McWilliams Papers.

26. Ibid.; Harvey, "Delinquent Mexican Boy in an Urban Area, 1945," 53; also see Griffith, *American Me,* 137 and 142. For a detailed report on the status of housing in a Mexican *colonia,* see "A Tabulation of Facts on Conditions Existent at Hicks Camp," October 8, 1942, SLDC Papers, Reel 2; and Scott, "Mexican-American in the Los Angeles Area," 197.

27. Griffith, *American Me,* 131–133. In 1945 the community newspaper the *Belvedere Citizen* corroborated the lack of progress when it reported that Mexican Americans still had the city's highest death rate from tuberculosis. *Belvedere Citizen,* August 17, 1945, quoted in Acuña, *Community under Siege,* 417.

28. García, "Americans All," in de la Garza et al., *Mexican American Experience,* 204–205.

29. Quoted in Ruiz, "Latin-American Juvenile Delinquency in Los Angeles," 492–494; quoted in McWilliams, *North from Mexico,* 281–282; quoted in Griffith, *American Me,* 156. Griffith reported that one school screened Mexican American girls for lice or nits in their hair before allowing them to walk across the auditorium stage and receive their graduation diplomas.

30. Jones, "Government Riots," 53.

31. Nunn, Testimony; quoted in Griffith, *American Me,* 158.

32. Quoted in Griffith, *American Me,* 167.

33. Moore, *Homeboys,* 56–57; Los Angeles County Coordinating Council, "Notes on the Mexican Population."

34. "Ayres Report."

35. Nunn, Testimony.

36. Sánchez, *Becoming Mexican American,* 255–269; also see Muñoz, *Youth, Identity, Power,* 28–42; and García, *Memories of Chicano History,* 80–83.

37. Congressman Edward R. Roybal interviewed by Escobar, January 5, 1988; Manuel Ruiz Jr. interviewed by Escobar, January 14, 1988.

38. Griffith, *American Me,* 205–206.

39. Henry Marín interviewed by Escobar, January 18, 1988.

40. Roybal interview.

41. Ibid.

42. Griffith, *American Me,* 203–204; Stephen J. Keating to Karl Holton, June 29, 1942, Ford Collection, Box 65; Citizens' Committee for the Defense of Mexican-American Youth (hereafter CCDMAY), *Sleepy Lagoon Case,* 1.

43. Griffith, *American Me,* 203–204.

44. Jones, "Government Riots," 10; Figueroa to Bowron, reprinted in untitled newspaper clipping, n.d., McWilliams Papers.

45. Quoted in Griffith, *American Me,* 204.

46. Marín interview.

47. Anon., typed manuscript, n.d., SLDC Papers, Reel 2; P.C., Minutes, May 30, 1942.

48. Anon., typed manuscript, n.d., SLDC Papers, Reel 2; quoted in Jones, "Government Riots," 13.

49. Quoted in Griffith, *American Me*, 208. For the attitudes of minority police officers, see Cooper, *Police and the Ghetto*, 114–115.

50. Quoted in Griffith, *American Me*, 209.

51. Roybal interview; Ruiz interview.

52. Roybal interview.

53. Moore, *Homeboys*, 36–37; Mazón, *Zoot-Suit Riots* discusses the symbolic nature of the zoot suit and pachucismo in great detail.

54. For a picture of a ducktail haircut, see "Hair Style Used in Identification of Hoodlums," *Examiner*, October 27, 1942; Daniels, "Depression Children," 3 and 15; Mazón, *Zoot-Suit Riots*, 2–3. It should be noted that the overwhelming majority of the historical sources deal exclusively with the male zoot suiters. Cholitas received relatively little attention, both at the time of the hysteria and in subsequent historical analyses.

55. Hebdige, *Subculture*, 79, 17; Eco, "Toward a Semiotic Enquiry into the Television Message," quoted in ibid., 105.

56. Hebdige, *Subculture*, 122.

57. The historian Mauricio Mazón states, "The narcissistic self-absorption of the zoot-suiter in a world of illusory omnipotentiality was in opposition to the modesty of individual selflessness attributed to the defense worker and the soldier. Zoot-suiters transgressed the patriotic ideals of commitment, integrity and loyalty with non-commitment, incoherence, and defiance." See Mazón, *Zoot-Suit Riots*, 7–9.

58. Chávez, quoted in Daniels, "Depression Children," 21; Griffith, *American Me*, 45 and 47; Chávez, quoted in Daniels, "Depression Children," 31.

59. Moore, *Homeboys*, 56–57.

60. Ibid., 57–59.

61. Ibid., 59–60.

62. Quoted in Griffith, *American Me*, 49.

63. Anon., typed manuscript, n.d., SLDC Papers, Reel 2.

64. *Daily News*, October 26, 1942. Most of the other Los Angeles daily newspapers also carried the story. With the exception of references to *La Opinión*, the newspaper citations for chapters 8–12 are available in the form of newspaper clippings in either the Carey McWilliams Papers or the Sleepy Lagoon Defense Committee Papers. I've given normal newspaper citations in the notes to assist scholars who may not have easy access to either of these collections.

65. Ibid.; *West Adams Tribune*, October 30, 1942.

66. *Times*, August 5 and October 7, 1942; *Daily News*, February 27, 1943; *Examiner*, February 28, 1943; anon., untitled typed manuscript, n.d., SLDC Papers, Reel 2. In addition, zoot suiters in the city of Oxnard, about sixty miles to the north, were in the habit of stoning police cars that cruised the barrio; *Oxnard Press Courier*, March 22, 1942.

67. Anon. (but probably Carey McWilliams), typed manuscript, n.d., McWilliams Papers; Mexicans of the Industrial Union Council (CIO), Resolution, September 18, 1942, SLDC Papers, Reel 2; *Belvedere Citizen,* March 23, 1945, quoted in Acuña, *Community under Siege,* 417; Los Angeles County Coordinating Council, "Notes on the Mexican Population"; Coordinating Council for Latin American Youth, Minutes, June 7, 1943; *Examiner,* September, 1942; *Bell Industrial Post,* December 17, 1942. I found no direct evidence linking the Sinarquistas with the zoot-suit phenomenon; for contemporary analyses of Sinarquismo, see Prado, "Sinarquism in the United States," 97–102, and Eulau, "Sinarquismo in the United States"; *Inter-American* 3 (March, 1944), 25–27 and 48; for the Mexican American interpretation of Sinarquista activities in southern California, see Spanish Speaking People's Congress, "Statement on Youth Activities," n.d., and Spanish Speaking People's Congress, typed manuscript, October 14, 1942, SLDC Papers, Reel 2; for a historical analysis of the pachuco-Sinarquista connection, see Mazón, *Zoot-Suit Riots.*

68. Marín interview; Ruiz interview; Roybal interview.

CHAPTER 9

1. The LAPD's *Annual Reports* did not publish crime report statistics for all crimes before 1941. Whenever possible, and for the sake of illustrating longer-term trends, I have used the years 1939–1946 for all appropriate tables and graphs.

2. LAPD, *Annual Report,* 1939–1946.

3. It should be remembered that the total number of reported crimes is not available before 1941 and therefore a strict comparison is not possible.

4. LAPD, *Annual Reports,* 1939–1946.

5. Horrall to all officers, October 29, 1942; Horrall to police commission, October 9, 1944, COP, General Files, CRC Box 35288.

6. It should be noted, however, that police have always had broad discretion not only on whether to make an arrest but also on whether to recommend filing charges even when they believe a crime has been committed. In addition, in Los Angeles County it is either the district attorney, the city attorney, or juvenile authorities who make the final decision on filing charges before the court, and each also may use discretion in making that judgment. As will be shown in chapter 11, the LAPD was very critical of each of these offices but especially of the juvenile authorities for their unwillingness to file charges against juvenile offenders.

7. Changes in the law and in police practices also affected the arrest rate for women; see Steffensmeier, Rosenthal, and Shehan, "World War II and Its Effect on the Sex Differential in Arrests," 403–416.

8. Herman G. Stark, quoted in Malaret, "Press and the Zoot-Suit Riots," 38.

9. For the fear of juvenile delinquency during the war, see Gilbert, *Cycle of Outrage,* 24–41; Holton, "Delinquency in Wartime," n.d., SLDC Papers, Reel 2.

10. P.C., Minutes, June 4, 1940; for civilian hysteria during the war, see Ma-

zón, *Zoot-Suit Riots,* 15–19 and 31; for the transference of anxiety from Japanese Americans to Mexican Americans, see McWilliams, *North from Mexico,* 227.

11. McWilliams, "Hearst Press Incited Campaign against Mexicans," *PM,* June 12, 1943; McWilliams, "Zoot-Suit Riots," 818–820; McWilliams, *North from Mexico,* 226–258; *San Francisco People's World,* July 28, 1943; CCDMAY, *Sleepy Lagoon Case;* Tuck, "Behind the Zoot Suit Riots," 313–316. A more recent example of the persistence of this interpretation can be seen in the stage setting for the first act of the play *Zoot Suit* by Luis Valdez, which displays a collage of lurid headlines regarding pachuco crime.

12. *Times,* May 9, 1978.

13. Ruiz interview; Ruiz also stated that the jail was segregated at the time, with Mexicans separated from whites.

14. See P.C., Minutes, January 21 and August 12, 1941; February 24, April 21, April 24, June 30, July 28, August 26, and October 20, 1942; February 2, November 2, November 30, and December 14, 1943; and November 28, 1944; for information on the curfew ordinance, also see *Times,* August 9, 1942.

15. Los Angeles County Probation Department, "Annual Report," 1941, Ford Papers, Box 29.

16. William Burk to Herman Stark, December 1, 1941, SLDC Papers, Reel 2; Los Angeles County Coordinating Council, "Notes on the Mexican Population in Los Angeles County." Burk, who wrote the report, noted that a report that dealt with Mexican Americans only as a problem gave only a partial picture of that community.

17. For the English-language newspaper coverage of the zoot-suit phenomenon, see the McWilliams Papers and the SLDC Papers, both of which contain a large number of clippings; also see *La Opinión,* June 1942–July, 1943, passim; for an analysis of three newspapers' coverage of the zoot-suit phenomenon prior to the riots, see Malaret, "Press and the Zoot Suit Riots."

18. McWilliams, *North from Mexico,* 227.

19. *Daily News,* August 9, 1942; *San Pedro News-Pilot,* October 26, 1942.

20. *Daily News,* August 9, 1942; *San Pedro News-Pilot,* October 26, 1942.

21. *Times,* October 27, 1942; *Wilshire Press,* October 29, 1942; *Examiner,* February 23, 1943; *Daily News,* November 11, 1942; *Times,* April 20, 1943; *Los Angeles Herald and Express* (hereafter *Herald and Express*), October 7, 1942; *Examiner,* April 30, 1943; also see *Hollywood Citizen-News* (hereafter *Citizen-News*), April 30, 1943.

22. *Los Angeles Equalizer,* November 1942; *Times,* October 8, 1942.

CHAPTER 10

1. LAPD Chief of Police C. B. Horrall to Friend, August 6, 1941, Edward Quevedo Papers (hereafter Quevedo Papers), Box 7; Ruiz to Los Angeles County Board of Education, August 26, 1941, Ruiz Papers, Box 2; press release, n.d., Ruiz Papers, Box 3; Coordinating Council for Latin American Youth (hereafter CCLAY), Minutes, August 8, 1941, Ruiz Papers, Box 3.

2. Untitled and undated newspaper clipping, Ruiz Papers, Box 3; Bowron to State Department, August 3, 1943; Bowron to Elmer Davis, June 28, 1943, Fletcher Bowron Collection (henceforth Bowron Collection), Box 1.

3. Quevedo quoted in CCLAY, Minutes, January 18, 1943, Ruiz Papers, Box 3; also see García, "Americans All," 202–210.

4. Manuel Ruiz Jr. to Dick Conner, August 12, 1942, Ruiz Papers, Box 2; Manuel Ruiz Jr. to José Garduño, October 21, 1943, Ruiz Papers, Box 2.

5. CCLAY, "Leadership Training Program," typed manuscript, Ruiz Papers, Box 3.

6. Manuel Ruiz Jr., "Narrative Report and Evaluation of the Conditioning Program Undertaken by the Co-ordinating Council of Latin-American [sic] Youth with the So-called 'Pachuco' Gangs in Los Angeles, California," typed manuscript, n.d. (but probably late 1943), Ruiz Papers, Box 3.

7. Ibid.

8. García, "Americans All," 202–210; CCLAY, Minutes, January 4, 1943; CCLAY, Minutes, January 18, 1943, Ruiz Papers, Box 3; Ruiz to Horrall, November 14, 1941; Ruiz to Lt. E. M. Quibell, November 27, 1941, Ruiz Papers, Box 2.

9. See, for example, Acuña, Occupied America, 253–256; and McWilliams, North from Mexico, 228–233; Jones, "Government Riots," 13–19. For a psycho-historical interpretation, see Mazón, Zoot-Suit Riots, 15–30. For a contemporary account, see CCDMAY, Sleepy Lagoon Case; and Rita Michaels, untitled typed manuscript, April 30, 1943, SLDC Papers, Reel 1. The most recent and most detailed account of Sleepy Lagoon can be found in Eduardo Pagán's dissertation "Sleepy Lagoon: The Politics of Youth and Race in Wartime Los Angeles." Unfortunately, this source became available too late to be more fully incorporated into this study.

10. Jones, "Government Riots," 13; Times, October 6, 1942.

11. McWilliams, North from Mexico, 228–229; Michaels, manuscript, April 30, 1943, SLDC Papers, Reel 1; Pagán, "Sleepy Lagoon," 120–137.

12. McWilliams, North from Mexico, 228–229; Michaels, manuscript, April 30, 1943, SLDC Papers, Reel 1; Pagán, "Sleepy Lagoon," 120–137, 187–196; Times, August 5, 1942.

13. Stephen Keating to Karl Holton, June 29, 1942, Ford Collection, Box 65; anon., untitled typed manuscript, October 15, 1942, SLDC Papers, Reel 2; La Opinión, June 12, 19, 21, 26, and 30, July 3, 10, 17, 19, 21, 22, and 24, 1942; Times, August 4, 1942; Daily News, August 4, 1942. The Sleepy Lagoon Defense Committee document states that six boys received sentences of eighty-five days hard labor and the pregnant woman received sixty days in the county jail from Los Angeles Superior Court judge A. A. Scott. In contrast, the husband of the pregnant woman, who was on leave from the army and who was also arrested by the LAPD but turned over to the military police, received only thirteen days of K.P. duty from the army.

14. Times, August 4, 1942; La Opinión, August 4, 6, 7, and 10, 1942; CCDMAY, Sleepy Lagoon Case, 10; Daily News, August 4, 1942.

15. Reed to Horrall, August 12, 1942, McWilliams Papers; Times, August 10, 1942; La Opinión, August 11–12, 1942; also Daily News, August 11, 1942.

16. Of the ninety-seven arrests of Mexican American youths made by the Reserve Division of the LAPD on August 8, all but twelve were for suspicion of robbery or suspicion of assault with a deadly weapon; LAPD Reserve Division Report, August 10, 1942, SLDC Papers, Reel 2; *Times,* August 10, 1942; also *Daily News,* August 11, 1942; quoted in Sleepy Lagoon Defense Committee, "The Ayres Law," handwritten press release draft, n.d., SLDC Papers, Reel 1; quoted in Ruiz, "Latin-American Juvenile Delinquency in Los Angeles: Bomb or Bubble!" 492–494; McWilliams, *North from Mexico,* 228–229.

17. "Ayres Report" in Jones, *Government Riots;* E. W. Lester, "Information for the 1942 Los Angeles County Grand Jury," August 11, 1942, McWilliams Papers; Rasmussen to Ernest W. Oliver, August 12, 1942, McWilliams Papers.

18. "Ayres Report," in Jones, *Government Riots.*

19. Horrall to Ernest W. Oliver, August 13, 1942, McWilliams Papers; Rasmussen to Oliver, August 12, 1942, McWilliams Papers; also see "Ayres Report," in Jones, *Government Riots.*

20. Rasmussen to Oliver, August 12, 1942, McWilliams Papers; also see "Ayres Report," in Jones, *Government Riots.*

21. "Ayres Report," in Jones, *Government Riots.*

22. Ibid.

23. Ibid. Ayres also proposed that everyone stopped by the police be fingerprinted, whether arrested or not.

24. Biscailuz to Oliver, August 20, 1942, SLDC Papers, Reel 2; Horrall to Oliver, August 13, 1942, McWilliams Papers.

25. "Ayres Report," in Jones, *Government Riots;* Lester, "Information," August 11, 1942, McWilliams Papers.

26. Lester, "Information," August 11, 1942, McWilliams Papers.

27. Ibid.

28. Rasmussen to Oliver, August 12, 1942, McWilliams Papers; *Times,* August 5, 1942.

29. McWilliams to Rockefeller, August 6, 1942, McWilliams Papers.

30. *Daily News,* October 9, 1942; McWilliams, *North from Mexico,* 237. Only those specifically invited by Harry Henderson, the chairman of the Special Mexican Relations Committee of the grand jury, could give testimony; Henderson to "Those Interested in Youth," October 2, 1942, McWilliams Papers.

31. Carey McWilliams, "Testimony of Carey McWilliams . . . before the Los Angeles County Grand Jury," October 8, 1942; Harry Hoijer, "The Problem of Crime among the Mexican Youth of Los Angeles," October 8, 1942; Manuel Aguilar, "Paper Presented by Consul Aguilar," October 8, 1942: all of the preceding are in the McWilliams Papers.

32. Guy T. Nunn, "Testimony of Guy T. Nunn," October 8, 1942, McWilliams Papers; Oscar Fuss, transcript of testimony before the Los Angeles County Grand Jury, October 8, 1942, SLDC Papers, Reel 2.

33. McWilliams, "Testimony," October 8, 1942; Aguilar, "Paper," October 8, 1942; Hoijer, "Problem," October 8, 1942: all of the preceding are in the McWilliams Papers. For a similar line of analysis, see the comments of Dr. Willsie Martin, pastor of the Wilshire Methodist Church, in the *Herald and Express,* November 24, 1942.

34. Hoijer, "Problem," October 8, 1942, McWilliams Papers.

35. Nunn, "Testimony," October 8, 1942; Hoijer, "Problem," October 8, 1942: both of the preceding are in the McWilliams Papers.

36. Nunn, "Testimony," October 8, 1942; McWilliams, "Testimony," October 8, 1942; Aguilar, "Paper," October 8, 1942; Hoijer, "Problem," October 8, 1942: all of the preceding are in the McWilliams Papers.

37. Holton, "Delinquency in Wartime," McWilliams Papers; *Daily News,* October 9, 1942.

38. H. F. Henderson and Harry Braverman, "Report of Special Committee on Problems of Mexican Youth of the 1942 Grand Jury of Los Angeles," December 22, 1942, McWilliams Papers.

39. Ibid.

40. McKibben et al., "Summary and Recommendations & Progress to Date of the Special Committee on Older Youth Gang Activity in Los Angeles and Vicinity," December 10, 1942, McWilliams Papers. The only Mexican American on the committee was Manuel Ruiz of the CCLAY.

41. Ibid.

42. George I. Sánchez, "Pachucos in the Making," 12–20.

43. See, for example, *La Opinión,* October 7 and 9, 1942; Malaret, "Press and the Zoot Suit Riots," 86–129; Rubio, "Our Life," August 13, 1941, and September 9, 1941, newspaper clippings, Ruiz Papers, Box 3; CCLAY, Minutes, August 3, 1942.

44. García, *Mexican Americans,* 165–174; George J. Sánchez, *Becoming Mexican American,* 248–249; also see Camarillo, *Chicanos in California,* 58–64; and García, *Memories of Chicano History,* 108–126.

45. Spanish Speaking People's Congress, "Statement on Youth Gang Activities," typed manuscript, n.d., SLDC Papers, Reel 2; a separate anonymously written document that was probably authored by an El Congreso member stated this position most precisely by claiming that Sinarquismo was "the perfect ideological and philosophical ground for the pachuco gangs of Los Angeles"; anon., typed manuscript, n.d., SLDC Papers, Reel 2; CCLAY, Minutes, August 3, 1942. El Congreso founder Josephina Fierro de Bright spoke on the same theme on a number of occasions. See Josephina Fierro de Bright and John Bright, "Prospectus for the Office of Inter-American Affairs on the Mexican-Americans of [the] Southwestern United States," typed manuscript, November 10, 1942, SLDC Papers, Reel 2, and Fierro de Bright, typed manuscript, n.d., SLDC Papers, Reel 1. Other Mexican Americans took similar positions. See Local 26, ILWU, "Resolution," n.d., SLDC Papers, Reel 1.

46. Ruiz, "Latin-American Juvenile Delinquency in Los Angeles," 492–494; *Daily News,* August 12 and October 9, 1942. It should be noted that the CCLAY leadership, but especially Manuel Ruiz, belonged to many organizations that addressed the issue of Mexican American juvenile delinquency. Ruiz, for example, went before the state bar as part of a subcommittee of the All Nations Foundation. Subsequently he would become chairman of the Citizens' Committee for Latin-American Youth, which should not be confused with either the Coordinating Council for Latin American Youth or the Citizens' Committee for the Defense of Mexican-American Youth, the latter of which would later be

less confusingly renamed (to at least this historian's relief) the Sleepy Lagoon Defense Committee.

47. Although there is no evidence that the CCLAY leaders sought to gain personally from their activities on behalf of the Mexican American community, there may also have been some financial rewards for the individuals involved. Both Quevedo, as an "international consultant," and Ruiz, as a lawyer, must have gained important contacts and perhaps client referrals as a result of their activities. See the biographical sketches in the Quevedo Papers and the Ruiz Papers for information about other aspects of the two men's lives.

48. Reginald García to Henry Wallace, quoted in Jones, *Government Riots,* 17; anon., to Los Angeles County Grand Jury, October 10, 1942; SLDC Papers, Reel 2; anon., petition, n.d., Ruiz Papers, Box 3. John M. Clark, the director of the Emergency Rehabilitation Division of the Office of the Coordinator of Inter-American Affairs, responded to García's letter, stating that Coordinator Nelson Rockefeller himself was "personally very concerned with the problem" and that their office was "working on a program for cooperation with the resident Spanish speaking people"; Clark to García, November 24, 1942, SLDC Papers, Reel 2.

49. *Daily News,* November 3 and 7, 1942; *Times,* November 7, 1942; *Herald and Express,* November 7, 1942; *Examiner,* November 7, 1942.

50. *Herald and Express,* November 24, 1942; *Daily News,* March 17, 1943.

51. *Herald and Express,* October 5, 1942; *Examiner,* October 30, 1942; *Times,* November 5, 1942; untitled newspaper clipping, January 1943, SLDC Papers, Reel 2; *Herald and Express,* October 27 and 30, November 4–5, 1942 and January 9, 11, and 18, 1943; also see CCDMAY, *Sleepy Lagoon Case;* Pagán, "Sleepy Lagoon," 143–187.

52. Peoples, "Smashing California's Baby Gangsters." Throughout the article, Peoples used exceedingly provocative language, referring to Mexican American youths as "gangsters," "hoodlums," "terrorists," and "Mexican mobsters." He also blamed the alleged "unreasoning brutality and senseless vandalism . . . [on] the gangsters' addiction to marijuana." He explained that "after smoking this 'loco weed,' people are known to go berserk, committing incredible crimes of violence for no cause whatsoever."

53. SLDC, "Excerpts from the Decision of the Second District Court of the State of California in the Sleepy Lagoon Case," typed manuscript, October 4, 1944, SLDC Papers, Reel 2; McWilliams, *North from Mexico,* 230–231; CCDMAY, *Sleepy Lagoon Case,* 21; Shibley, quoted in Michaels, manuscript, April 30, 1943; *Herald and Express,* clipping, n.d., McWilliams Papers; *Daily News,* October 27, 1942; anon., "A Statement on the Sleepy Lagoon Case," n.d., Corona Papers, Box 20.

54. Fricke had previously sentenced five Mexican American boys to 250 years in prison each in a rape case, SLDC, typed statement, n.d., SLDC Papers, Reel 2; Michaels' manuscript, April 30, 1943; anon., "A Statement on the Sleepy Lagoon Case," n.d., Corona Papers; SLDC, "Excerpts." Fricke also made it impossible for former District Court of Appeal Judge Lester Roth to enter the case for the defense by refusing to postpone the trial for a week in order for Roth to familiarize himself with the evidence.

55. *La Opinión,* January 13, 1943; anon., "A Statement on the Sleepy Lagoon Case," n.d., Corona Papers; McWilliams, *North from Mexico,* 231.

56. LaRue McCormick to anon., October 16, 1942; anon., "Proposed Objectives of a Mexican Defense Committee," October 21, 1942; Valida Dávila to Mrs. Cullen, November 1, 1942; SLDC Papers, Reel 2.

57. Anon., "Proposed Objectives of a Mexican Defense Committee," October 21, 1942; Valida Dávila to Mrs. Cullen, November 1, 1942; SLDC Papers, Reel 2.

58. Anon., "Proposed Objectives of a Mexican Defense Committee," October 21, 1942;

59. CCDMAY, "We Have Just Begun to Fight!" n.d., Ruiz Papers, Box 15.

60. CCDMAY, *Sleepy Lagoon Case.*

61. *Citizen-News,* February 9, 1943; *Pasadena Star News,* February 9, 1943; *Examiner,* February 10, 1943; *Examiner,* March 9, 1943; *Citizen-News,* March 24, 1943; *Pasadena Independent,* April 4, 1943; *Examiner,* March 29, 1943.

62. *Alhambra Post-Advocate,* March 3, 1943; *Wilmington Press,* March 16, 1943.

63. *Herald and Express,* May 7, 1943; *Pasadena Star News,* May 7, 1943; *Huntington Park Signal,* May 7, 1943; *Times,* May 8, 1943.

64. Griffith, *American Me,* 18–19.

65. Ibid.; in his recent dissertation, Eduardo Pagán reports that zoot suiters severely beat at least one police officer. Pagán, "Sleepy Lagoon," 340.

66. The newspapers gave various estimates regarding how long before the fire it was that the zoot suiters were seen in the building. The *Culver City Star News* stated that "several hours prior to the fire two zoot suit youths were assertedly seen near the Merchants Building," while the *Herald and Express* claimed they were seen a half hour before the blaze. *Culver City Star News,* May 12, 1943; *Herald and Express,* May 11 and 12, 1943; also see *South Bay Daily Breeze,* May 12, 1943; *Citizen-News,* May 12, 1943; *Times,* May 12, 1943.

67. Quoted in Jones, *Government Riots,* 21; *Culver City Star News,* May 18, 1943.

68. Quoted in Jones, *Government Riots,* 21.

69. Barela to Guerin, May 21, 1943, Ruiz Papers, Box 15.

70. *Herald and Express,* March 24 and May 15 and 28, 1943; *Citizen-News,* March 29 and 31, May 15 and 17, 1943; *Examiner,* March 29, 1943; *Daily News,* April 6, 1942; *Huntington Park Bulletin,* April 8 and 22, 1942; *Wilmington Press,* March 31 and April 19, 1943; Joe L. Marty to "Friend," May 22, 1943, Ruiz Papers, Box 15; *Times,* April 7 and May 25, 1943.

CHAPTER 11

1. The Zoot Suit riots are fully described in Jones, *Government Riots;* McWilliams, *North from Mexico;* Mazón, *Zoot-Suit Riots;* and Acuña, *Occupied America.*

2. For details about the psychological strains on the servicemen, see Mazón,

Zoot-Suit Riots, 54–55; for the impact of rumors on the servicemen, see Griffith, *American Me,* 19.

3. Griffith, *American Me,* 19; Nash, *American West Transformed,* 115–117; Mazón, *Zoot-Suit Riots,* 68–69. Eduardo Pagán's recent dissertation would seem to refute Mazón's findings. Pagán argues that the riots emanated from a year of violent turmoil between sailors and zoot suiters. The evidentiary basis for his argument is, however, sailors' reports taken at the height of the rioting, and we do not know the context within which the reports were given. For example, had the sailors giving the reports been rioting themselves? Were they under arrest at the time they made their allegations of previous attacks by zoot suiters? We do not know the answers to these questions, but under any circumstances the sailors had plenty of motivation to lie or at least exaggerate. Pagán, "Sleepy Lagoon," 211–230.

4. Johnny to Manuel Ruiz, n.d. (but probably June 11, 1943), Ruiz Papers, Box 1; *Daily News,* June 7, 1943.

5. The *Hollywood Citizen-News,* however, lamented that the "first swoop of the vengeance squad—formed by police to clean up the gangs of Zoot-Suiters terrorizing Los Angeles citizens, soldiers and sailors—came to naught today." Quoted in Jones, *Government Riots,* 23–24; Marín interview; Griffith, *American Me,* 19.

6. Citizens' Committee for Latin-American Youth, Minutes, June 7, 1943, Ruiz Papers, Box 4; CCLAY, Minutes, June 7, 1943, Ruiz Papers Box 3; Rudy Sánchez to Sir [Edward Quevedo], June 6, 1943, Quevedo Papers, Box 6; Jones, *Government Riots,* 23; McWilliams, *North from Mexico,* 244–245; Griffith, *American Me,* 19.

7. *Daily News,* June 7, 1943; McWilliams, *North from Mexico,* 245–246; Griffith, *American Me,* 19; quoted in Jones, *Government Riots,* 25–26.

8. McWilliams, *North from Mexico,* 246–247; Jones, *Government Riots,* 26–29; *Daily News,* June 7, 1943.

9. *Time* magazine, June 21, 1943, quoted in Jones, *Government Riots,* 29; Citizens' Committee for Latin-American Youth, Minutes, June 7, 1943, Ruiz Papers, Box 4; *Times,* June 7, 1943; *Daily News,* June 7, 1943.

10. *Time* magazine, June 21, 1943, quoted in Jones, *Government Riots,* 29; *Times,* June 7, 1943; *Daily News,* June 7, 1943. For other accounts of police acting passively toward servicemen but aggressively toward zoot suiters, see *Daily News,* June 8, 1943; *PM,* June 10, 1943.

11. Transcript of telephone conversation between Captain Heim and Admiral Bagley, June 11, 1943, reprinted in Mazón, *Zoot-Suit Riots,* 132–134.

12. Citizens' Committee for Latin-American Youth, Minutes, June 7, 1943, Ruiz Papers, Box 4; Sánchez to Sir [Edward Quevedo], June 6, 1943, Quevedo Papers, Box 6; Dan G. Acosta, "We 'Pachucos' Fight for a Free World," June 9, 1943, McWilliams Papers. Some Mexican Americans, however, approved of the servicemen's attacks on the zoot suiters; see Mr. Flores's comments in Citizens' Committee for Latin-American Youth, Minutes, June 7, 1943, Ruiz Papers, Box 4. Also see *PM,* June 10, 1943. A twelve-year-old boy who had had his jaw broken by marauding sailors echoed Sánchez's feelings: "So our guys

wear tight bottoms on their pants and those bums wear wide bottoms. Who the hell they fighting, Japs or us?" *Time* magazine, June 21, 1943.

13. CCLAY, Minutes, June 7, 1943, Ruiz Papers, Box 3.

14. Citizens' Committee for Latin-American Youth, Minutes, June 7, 1943, Ruiz Papers, Box 4.

15. Ibid. Also see *Examiner,* June 6, 1943.

16. McWilliams, *North from Mexico,* 246–253; also see Griffith, *American Me,* 3–28; for historians' interpretations, see Mazón, *Zoot-Suit Riots;* Jones, *Government Riots;* and Acuña, *Occupied America,* 256–259.

17. Jones, *Government Riots,* 29–30; *People's World,* June 9, 1943; McWilliams also describes how the mob pulled an African American man from a streetcar and gouged out an eye with a knife. McWilliams, *North from Mexico,* 248–251; Scott, "Mexican-American in the Los Angeles Area," 240.

18. *Daily News,* June 8, 1943; *Herald and Express,* June 8, 1943.

19. Leyvas said that the unprovoked attacks on Mexican American boys were what motivated him to fight. "I knew one guy personally who got yanked off a streetcar. They ripped his clothes off and beat the hell out of him right in front of his mother. That really got me steamed, that they would do something like that in front of his mother." *Times,* May 9, 1978.

20. *People's World,* June 10, 1943; Griffith, in *American Me,* 11–12, gives a vivid description of a fight in a home; also see McWilliams, *North from Mexico,* 248–251.

21. *Times,* n.d.; *Daily News,* June 10, 1943; *Times,* n.d.

22. Memo from Clarence Fogg to District Patrol Officer, June 8, 1943, reprinted in Mazón, *Zoot-Suit Riots,* 123; memo from DCGO 11nd Long Beach to All Units Under My Command, June 10, 1943, reprinted in Mazón, *Zoot-Suit Riots,* 127–128; transcript of telephone conversation between Captain Heim and Admiral Bagley, June 11, 1943, reprinted in Mazón, *Zoot-Suit Riots,* 132–134. The word "entirely" on the June 9 memo was crossed out in subsequent versions of the memo and replaced with the word "mainly"; see memo from Comeleven to "Activities Los Angeles and San Diego area, Santa Barbara Advance Depot Hueneme," June 9, 1943, reprinted in Mazón, *Zoot-Suit Riots,* 125.

23. *Daily News,* June 9, 1943; *Citizen-News,* June 9, 1943.

24. Marín interview; *Daily News,* June 9, 1943; *Examiner,* June 9, 1943; *Daily News,* June 9, 1943.

25. Braverman to Robert W. Kenny and Joseph T. McGucken, June 11, 1943, in Jones, *Government Riots,* 101–105. The committee was chaired by former grand jury member Harry Braverman and included representatives of both the African American and Mexican American communities, including the CCLAY president, Edward Quevedo.

26. Ibid.

27. Joseph T. McGucken et al., "Report and Recommendations of Citizens Committee," typed manuscript, June 12, 1943, Ruiz Papers, Box 4.

28. Ibid. The committee called for an end to racial discrimination in public accommodations. For the academic version of this argument, see Bogardus, "Gangs of Mexican-American Youth," 55–66.

29. *Time* magazine, June 21, 1943; *PM,* June 11, 1943. Also see *San Francisco People's World,* June 14, 1943; *New York Times,* June 14, 1943; and Carey McWilliams writing in the *New Republic,* June 21, 1943. For reference to the *Chicago Tribune*'s interpretation of the rioting, see *Times,* June 18, 1943; Los Angeles CIO Council, "Statement on Recent Race Riots Here," June 22, 1943, SLDC Papers, Reel 1.

30. Untitled newspaper clipping, June 17, 1943, McWilliams Papers; *Times,* June 18, 1943.

31. CCLAY, Minutes, June 14 and 21, 1943, Ruiz Papers, Box 3; Citizens' Committee for Latin-American Youth, Minutes, June 14 and 21, 1943, Ruiz Papers, Box 4; Bowron to Elmer Davis, June 28, 1943, Bowron Collection, Box 1.

32. The Bowron Collection contains extensive evidence that the mayor placed a high priority on maintaining a positive image of Los Angeles in order to attract more war-related industry. For the importance of military industries for Los Angeles and the West in general, see Nash, *American West Transformed,* 17–36.

33. "Statement of Mayor Fletcher Bowron," June 9, 1943, Bowron Collection, Box 34; untitled newspaper clipping, June 9, 1943, McWilliams Papers; *Examiner,* June 10, 1943; *Daily News,* June 10, 1943.

34. "Statement of Mayor Fletcher Bowron," June 9, 1943, Bowron Collection, Box 34; untitled newspaper clipping, June 9, 1943, McWilliams Papers; *Examiner,* June 10, 1943; *Daily News,* June 10, 1943.

35. *Times,* May 25 and June 11, 1943. In what I can only describe as a perverse distortion of fact and logic, the *Times*'s June 11 editorial also stated that the previous summer's mass arrests had nothing to do with race, and, referring to the Ayres report, that "no responsible person at any time condemned Latin Americans, as such, because some irresponsibles were causing trouble."

36. *Daily News,* June 10, 11, and 15, 1943; *New York Times,* June 11, 1943.

37. *Times,* June 15, 1943.

38. *Times,* June 18, 1943. In order to demonstrate the error of Mrs. Roosevelt's remarks, the *Times* pointed to local pride in the missions, participation in Mexican fiestas, the Hispanic heritage of Los Angeles County sheriff Eugene Biscailuz, and Olvera Street—"a bit of old Mexico"—as signs of friendly relations between whites and Mexican Americans.

39. Bowron to Davis, June 28, 1943, Bowron Collection, Box 1. In the same letter Bowron also asserted that "several of those of Mexican blood who were named on the committee are not representative of the local Mexican population."

40. Bowron to Davis, June 28, 1943, Bowron Collection, Box 1.

41. Bowron to Horrall, July 19, 1943, Bowron Collection, Box 1. The very fact that the mayor considered it appropriate to dictate to a chief of police the contents of an official police report demonstrates how far the LAPD was from becoming a truly professional police department. At the very heart of the police professionalism model is the lack of political interference in internal police procedures. No mayor after Fletcher Bowron would have even considered writing a letter such as this.

42. Ibid.

43. Ibid. A glimpse into Bowron's racial attitudes can be found in two letters regarding the migration of Southern blacks into Los Angeles. Orville R. Caldwell, the executive deputy to the mayor, called for the federal government to halt the migration of blacks into the city. Bowron disavowed his deputy's proposal but disagreed with those who "insist upon treating every Negro as a member of a minority group who should receive special treatment" and stated that in general there should be "less emphasis on minority groups." Caldwell to Ed V. Izac and Bowron to Lou Rossner, November 10, 1943, Bowron Collection, Box 1.

44. Bowron to Horrall, July 19, 1943, Bowron Collection, Box 1.

45. Bowron to Bonsal, August 3, 1943, Bowron Collection, Box 1.

46. Los Angeles County Grand Jury, "Findings and Recommendations of the Grand Jury of Los Angeles County for 1943, Based upon Its Inquiry into Juvenile Crime and Delinquency in That County," July 21, 1943, McWilliams Papers.

47. Ibid. The report cited two pieces of evidence to support its claim of excessive leniency among juvenile authorities: the discrepancy between rising arrests and declining court filings; and assurances of police that they had the evidence to prosecute youthful offenders.

48. Ibid.

49. Ibid. The report did not make clear whether these statistics were based on arrests, crime reports, or some other source.

50. Ibid.

CHAPTER 12

1. Moore, *Homeboys,* 55–74.

2. Mazón, *Zoot-Suit Riots,* 17; Moore, *Homeboys,* 55–74.

3. Moore, *Homeboys,* 55–74.

4. McGucken et al., "Report and Recommendations of Citizens Committee," McWilliams Papers.

5. Joseph T. McGucken, "List of Projects Undertaken in the Los Angeles Area in Accordance with the Recommendation of the Governor's Committee," October 13, 1943, McWilliams Papers; anon. (but probably Ben Margolis), typed manuscript, n.d., McWilliams Papers.

6. McGucken, "List of Projects," McWilliams Papers; Young Men's Christian Association of Los Angeles et al., to James R. Page, August 7, 1943, Ruiz Papers, Box 4; George Gleason, "List of Groups Working on Latin-American Situation," Ford Papers, Box 65; Citizens' Committee for Latin-American Youth, Minutes, October 11, 1943, Ruiz Papers, Box 4; quoted in Griffith, *American Me,* 73.

7. YMCA et al., to James R. Page, August 7, 1943, Ruiz Papers, Box 4; McGucken, "List of Projects," McWilliams Papers; Los Angeles Youth Project (LAYP), typed report, November 22, 1943, Ruiz Papers, Box 4; for the long-term impact of the LAYP and the California Youth Authority, see Mazón, *Zoot-Suit Riots,* 99–102, and Walker, *Popular Justice,* 213.

8. Citizens' Committee for Latin-American Youth, Minutes, October 11,

1943, Ruiz Papers, Box 4; Southern California Council of Inter-American Affairs (SCCIAA), Minutes, December 1, 1943, Ford Papers, Box 65.

9. McGucken, "List of Projects," McWilliams Papers; LAYP, "Report of Summer Activities," typed manuscript, September 21, 1944; Program Analysis and Evaluation Committee, LAYP, "Objectives of the Los Angeles Youth Project and the Youth It Served in 1944," August, 1945, Ruiz Papers, Box 4.

10. Los Angeles County Commission on Human Relations (LACCHR), *50th Anniversary Celebration;* LACCHR, "Procedural Rules and Administrative Practices," Ruiz Papers, Box 4; also see LACCHR, "We Strive for Improved Intergroup Relations," typed outline, COP General Files, CRC Box 35306; LACCHR, "Ordinance Relating to the Establishment of the Commission of Human Relations of the County of Los Angeles," Quevedo Papers, Box 4.

11. McGucken et al., "Report and Recommendations of Citizens Committee," McWilliams Papers; the committee specifically stated that arrests "should be made without *undue* emphasis on members of minority groups" (my italics); LAPD, *Civil Disturbance Control.*

12. The department had addressed racial issues in the past, but usually to enforce traditional racial restrictions, see P.C., Minutes, April 23 and May 3, 1929, for examples. In addition, the racial beliefs of police officers sometimes caused the department embarrassment. A minor scandal erupted in 1922 because LAPD officers, including the chief of police, admitted they were members of the Ku Klux Klan. The issue at the time, however, was not that the KKK was a racist organization, it was that police officers should not be members of secret organizations; Woods, "Progressives and the Police," 144–146. By the 1940s the racial climate had changed sufficiently to force the department to address societal racism. In response to the hanging of an effigy of an African American child at a public school, the police commission instructed officers "to use every effort . . . to prevent any acts of racial, religious or political intolerance or prejudice in the public schools of the City, or elsewhere." The commission added that such acts had the potential to become "a serious menace" to the city. It was not until after the riots, however, that the department issued policy directives demanding that officers enforce the law impartially, without regard to race. LAPD, *Daily Bulletin,* April 25, 1941; also see P.C., Minutes, March 26, April 7, May 15 and 22, 1941.

13. LAPD, *Civil Disturbance Control.*

14. Woods, "Progressives and the Police," 396–397; SCCIAA, "Recommendations of the SCCIAA," typed manuscript, June 22, 1943, Ford Papers, Box 65; 13th District Citizens' Committee, Resolution, typed manuscript, September 27, 1943, P.C., Supplementary Files.

15. SCCIAA, "Recommendations," Ford Papers; the police commission did not respond to this recommendation because the SCCIAA did not directly petition the police department; 13th District Committee, Resolution; Horrall to P.C., October 15, 1943; Arthur G. Baraw to Agnes Cordy, October 19, 1943. P.C. Supplementary Files.

16. McGucken, "List of Projects," McWilliams Papers; CCLAY, Minutes, January 3, 1944, Ruiz Papers, Box 3; Citizens' Committee for Latin American Youth, Minutes, January 17, 1944, Ruiz Papers, Box 4.

17. Woods, "Progressives and the Police," 197; for commendations, see LAPD, *Daily Bulletin,* March 8, 1928, February 3, 1931, and January 11, 1934; for examples of alleged misconduct, see *Record,* February 19, 1919, September 16, 1920, and September 21, 1920; P.C., Minutes, July 5, 1939.

18. Los Angeles County Grand Jury, "Report of the Special Committee"; Citizens' Committee for Latin American Youth, Minutes, December 2, 1942, Ruiz Papers, Box 4.

19. McGucken et al., "Report and Recommendations of Citizens Committee"; untitled newspaper, n.d., McWilliams Papers; SCCIAA, "Recommendations," Ford Papers; CCLAY, resolution, n.d., Ruiz Papers, Box 3; P.C., Minutes, November 2, 1943.

20. Horrall to P.C., November 18, 1943, P.C., Supplementary Files; Roybal interview.

21. Bowron, "Statement Re Anniversary Celebration of DAPS," n.d., Bowron Papers, Box 34.

22. Ibid.; LAPD, Volunteer Services Section, typed report, ca. 1949; William H. Parker and Robert W. Bowling to Jesse W. Callahan, October 26, 1950, COP General Files, CRC Box 35296.

23. The CCLAY seemed to take to heart the advice it received at its June 21, 1943, meeting from the Office of War Information representative Alan Cranston. Cranston told the CCLAY that the community had a guilty conscience as a result of the riots and that the time was propitious to initiate community programs. CCLAY, Minutes, June 21, 1943, Ruiz Papers, Box 3.

24. García, "Americans All," 208–210; Manuel Ruiz to Judge Robert H. Scott, September 3, 1942, Ruiz Papers, Box 2; CCLAY, Resolution, n.d.; Manuel Ruiz, untitled newspaper article, n.d., Ruiz Papers, Box 3.

25. CCLAY, press release, n.d., Ruiz Papers, Box 3; for the CCLAY's work in the Alpine Street district, see CCLAY, Minutes, June 8, August 23, and November 15, 1943, Ruiz Papers Box 3; and Manuel Ruiz Jr., "Narrative Report and Evaluation of the Conditioning Program Undertaken by the Co-Ordinating Council of Latin-American [sic] Youth with the So-called 'Pachuco' Gangs of Los Angeles, California: The Alpine Street Project," typed manuscript, n.d., Ruiz Papers, Box 3. Consistent with this attitude, the CCLAY objected to the creation of a social club called "Club los Pachucos"; see CCLAY, Minutes, November 8 and 15, 1943, Ruiz Papers, Box 3.

26. CCLAY, Minutes, August 2 and November 8 and 15, 1943, Ruiz Papers, Box 3.

27. Peralta C. to Horrall, August 31, 1943; Laurence M. Weinberg to Board of Police Commissioners, September 7, 1943, P.C. Supplementary Files.

28. R. W. Wise and C. E. Larson, "LAPD Arrest Report," August 30, 1943; Perfecto López Rojas, "Statement of Perfecto López Rojas," typed manuscript, September 1, 1943; Detective Lieutenant C. E Ream and Sergeant A. A. Ruiz to Captain J. A. Donahoe, September 1, 1943; Lieutenant B. M. Johnson to Captain Paul E. Harrison, September 2, 1943; Acting Chief Henry S. Eaton to Vicente Peralta C., September 2, 1943, P.C. Supplementary Files. Interestingly, in their interview with López, police asked him whether his statement had been

"free and voluntary" and whether anyone had used "threats or force upon you to induce you to answer these questions."

29. Eaton to Peralta C., September 2, 1943; Alfred A. Cohn to P.C., September 21, 1943; Arthur G. Baraw to Laurence M. Weinberg, September 21, 1943, P.C., Supplementary Files.

30. *Huntington Park Bulletin,* July 22, 1943; *Alhambra Post,* July 10, 1943; *Herald and Express,* July 17, 1943.

31. *Times,* July 16, 1944.

32. CCLAY, Minutes, July 18, 1944 (the original is misdated 1943), Ruiz Papers, Box 3; Ruiz to *Los Angeles Times,* July 18, 1943, Ruiz Papers, Box 2; Ruiz forwarded his letter to the Office of War Information. Ruiz to Office of War Information, July 19, 1944.

33. SLDC to anon., n.d., SLDC Papers, Reel 2; anon., broadside, n.d., McWilliams Papers; SCCIAA, Minutes, July 17, 1944, Ford Papers, Box 65. The *Times,* however, was unrepentant, even defiant. In an editorial published three weeks later, Los Angeles's leading newspaper attacked the protesters and claimed that it had published the piece so that "properly constituted authorities and those honestly interested in juvenile matters would take steps to see that corrective measures were immediately instituted to prevent any outbreak of gang warfare." *Times,* August 8, 1944.

34. *Times,* August 8, 1944.

35. Lt. C. P. Wallace, typed memorandum, December 22, 1944; Sgt. Robert L. Parker and Sgt. Earl A. Langdon, typed memorandum, January 9, 1945; Sgt. E. M. Nelson and Officer Hugh D. Ward, typed memorandum, January 10, 1945, Ruiz Papers, Box 3.

36. Hazen to Van M. Griffith, December 26, 1944, Ruiz Papers, Box 3.

37. Inspector E. C. Biffle and Sgt. John T. Shields to Captain Paul E. Harrison, January 11, 1945; LAPD, "Broadcast 1," transcribed teletype broadcast, December 23, 1944, Horrall to P.C., January 29, 1945; also see Arthur G. Baraw to Ruiz, January 30, 1945, Ruiz Papers, Box 3. Interestingly, in an apparent attempt to diminish the legitimacy of the complaints, Biffle and Shields charged that the probation department had in fact solicited the Ruiz and Hazen letters in order to embarrass the LAPD. Horrall ignored this assertion in his official reply, but since the department forwarded the entire file to the complainants, the CCLAY saw the allegations and, in a strongly worded response, vigorously denied that it had been "used as an instrument of the Probation Department." Ruiz to Van M. Griffith, February 21, 1945, Ruiz Papers, Box 3.

38. CCLAY to police commission, May 11, 1945; Richard Simon to Manuel Ruiz Jr., June 18, 1945; testimony of Joe Castro (Officer Castro's testimony, and the testimonies of all other witnesses involved in the case, was transcribed informally by James H. Pope, the presiding judge in the case), June 11, 1945; testimony of Wilfred William Wilson, June 18, 1945; testimony of Arthur W. Whipple, June 18, 1945; testimony of Raymond Morales, June 18, 1945; testimony of Juan Cruz Morales, June 18, 1945; testimony of Mary Ratcliffe, June 18, 1945; testimony of Faye Whipple, June 18, 1945; affidavit of Arthur W. Whipple, April 1945, Ruiz Papers, Box 3. All of the sources agree with these

essential facts about the case. The CCLAY letter claims that the officers frisked the boys "brusquely." The nonpolice witnesses testified that the officers cursed at the boys while interrogating them and ordering them home.

39. Raymond Morales testimony; Juan Cruz Morales testimony; Arthur Whipple testimony; Mary Ratcliffe testimony; Faye Whipple testimony; Arthur Whipple affidavit; Carey McWilliams (Whipple's attorney in the case) to Manuel Ruiz; during the trial, Officer Wilson claimed that he did not hit Morales after he had cuffed him; both officers asserted that Whipple tried to strike them; Wilson testimony; Castro testimony, Ruiz Papers, Box 3.

40. CCLAY to Police Commission, May 11, 1945; Carey McWilliams to Manuel Ruiz, June 12, 1945; James H. Pope to Ernest R. Orfila, June 25, 1945; statement of James H. Pope, June 11, 1945, Ruiz Papers, Box 3.

41. Simon to Ruiz, June 18, 1945; anon., handwritten note on letter from James H. Pope to Manuel Ruiz Jr., September 7, 1945, Ruiz Papers, Box 3.

42. The SLDC almost always referred to the Sleepy Lagoon defendants publicly as "boys." Although somewhat paternalistic and inaccurate (the defendants' ages ranged from seventeen to twenty-four), the committee's intent was undoubtedly to gain sympathy for the defendants. See, for example, various issues of the *Appeal News,* SLDC Papers, Reel 2; for biographies of the defendants, including their ages, see CCDMAY, *Sleepy Lagoon Case,* 27–29.

43. Ella Kube, "Report on Conference Held under the Auspices of the Citizens' Committee for the Defense of American-Mexican [*sic*] Youth," typed manuscript, n.d., McWilliams Papers; "Minutes Conference Citizens' Committee for the Defense of Mexican-American Youth Held March 14, 1943, Belmont Studios," typed manuscript, n.d., SLDC Papers, Reel 2.

44. Kube, "Report on Conference," McWilliams Papers; "Minutes Conference Citizens' Committee for the Defense of Mexican-American Youth," SLDC Papers, Reel 2.

45. Kube, "Report on Conference," McWilliams Papers; "Minutes Conference Citizens' Committee for the Defense of Mexican-American Youth," SLDC Papers, Reel 2; "Resolution of Interference of D A's Office with Meeting Place of Conference," typed manuscript, n.d., SLDC Papers, Reel 2.

46. United Electrical Radio and Machine Workers of America et al., "Resolution on Sleepy Lagoon Case," n.d., SLDC Papers, Reel 2; anon., to All State CIO Unions, April 17, 1943, SLDC Papers, Reel 2; García, *Memories of Chicano History,* 103–107 and 114–115; *San Francisco People's World,* May 29, 1943; SLDC, press release, n.d., SLDC Papers, Reel 1.

47. CCDMAY, *Sleepy Lagoon Case.*

48. See copies of various such fund-raising letters in SLDC Papers, Reel 2.

49. Anon., to Friend, n.d.; anon. to Governor Warren, n.d.; Alice Greenfield to Kenny, May 15, 1944; Kenny to Santiago Campbell, March 9, 1944, SLDC Papers, Reel 2. The term "without prejudice," of course, has a precise legal meaning. Kenny, however, must have known that the use of such language had special symbolism for the petitioners.

50. For the relationship between the SLDC and the International Labor Defense, see Chairman to International Labor Defense, July 15, 1943, and Dorothea Stein to Bertha Marshall, August 20, 1943, SLDC Papers, Reel 3; for sup-

port from organized labor and the entertainment industry, see *Appeal News,* April 7, 1943, to March 4, 1944, SLDC Papers, Reel 2; and *Labor Herald,* July 1, 1944. Orson Welles wrote the introduction to *The Sleepy Lagoon Case.*

51. *Appeal News,* November 19 and August 3, 1943; SLDC, press release, April, 1943, SLDC Papers, Reel 2; SLDC, press release, May 15, 1944, SLDC Papers, Reel 1.

52. United Electrical Radio and Machine Workers of America et al., "Resolution on Sleepy Lagoon Case," n.d.; *Appeal News,* November 19, 1943, SLDC Papers, Reel 2; Ruiz to Alan Cranston, February 11, 1943, Ruiz Papers, Box 2.

53. For the importance the SLDC placed on relations with the Mexican American community and Alice McGrath's role in maintaining those relations, see Joan to Alice, October 21, 1943, SLDC Papers, Reel 3; for a typical letter from McGrath to the defendants, see Alice to Guys, August 31, 1943, SLDC Papers, Reel 2; *Appeal News,* September 23, 1943; Ben Margolis to Vicente Peralta C., November 24, 1943, SLDC Papers, Reel 2.

54. McKelvey to Wm. C. Mathes, October 28, 1943, Ford Papers, Box 65.

55. SLDC, "A la Colonia Mexicana . . . ," flyer, n.d.; *Appeal News,* September 23, 1943; *Pico Garden News,* January 14, 1944; for individual support, see the order forms for the *Sleepy Lagoon Mystery,* SLDC Papers, Reel 2.

56. *Appeal News,* January 17, 1944, SLDC Papers, Reel 2; Peralta C. to SLDC, reprinted in SLDC press release, July 27, 1943; Cárdenas to Carey McWilliams, reprinted in SLDC press release, August 21, 1944, SLDC Papers, Reel 1.

57. Endor, *Sleepy Lagoon Mystery.* This pamphlet was also translated into Spanish.

58. Ibid.

59. Lev Gleason to Harry Braverman, August 1, 1943, SLDC Papers, Reel 2; Mark Day, "The Pertinence of the 'Sleepy Lagoon' Case," *Journal of Mexican American History* 4 (1974): 92; McWilliams, *North from Mexico,* 232–233.

60. Raymond G. McKelvey to Wm. C. Mathes, October 28, 1943, Ford Papers, Box 65.

61. Ibid.

62. SLDC, press releases, March 1, May 9, and May 16, 1944, SLDC Papers, Reel 1.

63. SLDC, "Excerpts from the Decision of the Second District Court of Appeal of the State of California in the Sleepy Lagoon Case," typed manuscript, October 4, 1944, SLDC Papers, Reel 2. Testimony was given at the trial stating that one of the defendants, Ismael Parra, had stabbed someone at the party. That evidence was so contradictory that the appeal court found it "unsatisfactory and as well unconvincing." As the SLDC noted, "This is the only charge of the 36 against the 12 defendants on which the Court found that the evidence was merely insufficient. In the other cases the evidence was totally lacking." Ibid.

64. Ibid.

65. Ibid.

66. Ibid.; Eulau, "Sleepy Lagoon Case"; Guy Endor, "Victory for Democracy," Los Angeles: Sleepy Lagoon Defense Committee, n.d., SLDC Papers, Reel 2.

67. SLDC, press release, October 28, 1944; transcript, October 23, 1944, SLDC Papers, Reel 1.

68. SLDC, press release, December 29, 1944, SLDC Papers, Reel 1.

CONCLUSION

1. *La Opinión,* May 29 and June 1–3 and 5, 1949; Gutiérrez, *Walls and Mirrors,* 168–169; Acuña, *Community under Siege,* 29–30, 278, and 423; Roybal interview.

2. On the development of police professionalism, see Fogelson, *Big City Police;* for the police professionalism movement in Los Angeles, see Woods, "Progressives and the Police." On police practices in the Los Angeles Mexican American community during the 1950s and 1960s, see Morales, *Ando Sangrando (I Am Bleeding)* and Escobar, "Dialectics of Repression," 1483–1514.

3. Fogelson, *Big City Police;* Woods, "Progressives and the Police"; Morales, *Ando Sangrando (I Am Bleeding);* Escobar, "Dialectics of Repression," 1483–1514.

4. Fogelson, *Big City Police;* Woods, "Progressives and the Police"; Morales, *Ando Sangrando (I Am Bleeding);* Escobar, "Dialectics of Repression," 1483–1514; Independent Commission, *Report.*

5. Gerstle, "Liberty, Coercion, and the Making of Americans," 553; also see Erenberg and Hirsch, *War in American Culture;* and Slotkin, *Gunfighter Nation,* 313–326; for depictions of Chicanos in the cinema, see Keller, *Hispanics and United States Film,* 150–178.

6. Moore, *Homeboys;* Vigil, *Barrio Gangs;* also see Horowitz, *Honor and the American Dream.*

7. Roybal interview; Morales, *Ando Sangrando (I Am Bleeding);* Woods, "Progressives and the Police," 462–464.

8. *La Opinión,* May 29 and June 1–3 and 5, 1949.

Select Bibliography

ARCHIVAL AND MANUSCRIPT COLLECTIONS

American Civil Liberties Union Collection. Department of Special Collections, University of California, Los Angeles.

Fletcher C. Bowron Collection. Huntington Library and Art Collection, San Marino, California.

George P. Clements Collection. Department of Special Collections, University of California, Los Angeles.

Bert Corona Collection. Department of Special Collections, Stanford University, Stanford, California.

John Anson Ford Collection. Huntington Library and Art Collection, San Marino, California.

Ernesto Galarza Papers. Department of Special Collections, Stanford University, Stanford, California.

Los Angeles Board of Police Commissioners. Minutes. Los Angeles City Records Center, Los Angeles, California.

Los Angeles Board of Police Commissioners. Supplementary Files. Los Angeles City Records Center, Los Angeles, California.

Los Angeles City Council Files. Los Angeles City Records Center, Los Angeles, California.

Los Angeles Police Department. Chief of Police General Files. Los Angeles City Records Center, Los Angeles, California.

Los Angeles Police Department Archives. Los Angeles City Records Center, Los Angeles, California.

Alice McGrath Papers (previously known as the Sleepy Lagoon Defense Committee Papers). Department of Special Collections, University of California, Los Angeles.

Carey McWilliams Collection. Department of Special Collections, University of
    California, Los Angeles.
Manuel Ruiz Jr. Collection. Department of Special Collections, Stanford Uni-
    versity, Stanford, California.
Urban Police Research Institute Papers. Southern California Social Science Li-
    brary, Los Angeles.

GOVERNMENT PUBLICATIONS

California Governor C. C. Young's Mexican Fact-Finding Committee. *Mexi-
    cans in California*. San Francisco: California State Printing Office, 1930.
California State Assembly Interim Committee on Juvenile Delinquency. "Prelim-
    inary Report." Sacramento: California State Printing Office, 1944.
Independent Commission of the Los Angeles Police Department. *Report of the
    Independent Commission of the Los Angeles Police Department*. Los An-
    geles, 1991.
Lewin, Molly, ed. *The City of Los Angeles: The First 100 Years*. Los Angeles:
    Police Printing Bureau, 1950.
Los Angeles County Commission on Human Relations. *50th Anniversary Cel-
    ebration: Serving Los Angeles County* (program). Los Angeles: Los Angeles
    County Commission on Human Relations, 1994.
Los Angeles Police Department. *Annual Reports, 1915–1945*. Los Angeles: Los
    Angeles Police Department.
———. *Civil Disturbance Control* (training manual). Los Angeles: Los Angeles
    Police Department, July 1944.
National Advisory Committee on Civil Disorders. *Report of the National Ad-
    visory Committee on Civil Disorders*. New York: Bantam Books, 1968.
President's Research Committee on Social Trends. *Recent Social Trends in
    America*. New York: McGraw Hill, 1933.
United States Commission on Civil Rights. *Mexican Americans and the Admin-
    istration of Justice in the Southwest*. Washington, D.C.: U.S. Government
    Printing Office, 1970.
United States Senate, Committee on Education and Labor. *Violations of Free
    Speech and Rights of Labor,* hearings before a subcommittee of the Senate
    Committee on Education and Labor, 76th Cong., 1st sess., Senate Resolution
    266 (1940).

NEWSPAPERS

Hollywood Citizen-News
Los Angeles Citizen
Los Angeles Daily News
Los Angeles El Clamor Público
Los Angeles Examiner
Los Angeles Express
Los Angeles Herald

Los Angeles Herald and Express
Los Angeles La Opinión
Los Angeles Open Forum
Los Angeles Record
Los Angeles Times
New York PM
New York Times
San Diego Tribune
San Francisco People's World

THESES, DISSERTATIONS, AND OTHER UNPUBLISHED
SECONDARY SOURCES

Anti-Defamation League of B'nai B'rith. "A Study of Police Training Programs in Minority Relations." Prepared for the Police Relations Committee of the Los Angeles County Conference on Community Relations, Los Angeles, 1950.

Arroyo, Luis Leobardo. "Industrial Unionism and the Los Angeles Furniture Workers Industry." Ph.D. diss., University of California, Los Angeles, 1979.

Bond, Max J. "The Negro in Los Angeles." Ph.D. diss., University of Southern California, Los Angeles, 1936.

Case, Fred E., and James H. Kirk. "The Housing Status of Minority Families: Los Angeles, 1956." Ms., Los Angeles Urban League, Los Angeles, 1958.

Castillo, Pedro G. "The Making of a Mexican Barrio: Los Angeles, 1890–1920." Ph.D. diss., University of California, Santa Barbara, 1979.

Daniels, Douglas Henry. "Depression Children: The Zoot Suiter, the Pachuco, and the Hipster." Paper presented at the Seventy-second Meeting of the Pacific Coast Branch of the American Historical Association, Honolulu, Hawaii, August 9–12, 1979.

Duus, Louise. "There Ought to Be a Law: A Study of Popular Attitudes toward 'the Law' in the 1920's." Ph.D. diss., University of Minnesota, Minneapolis, 1967.

Erie, Steven P. "The Cognitive Structure of Los Angeles Patrolmen." Institute on Law and Urban Studies, Los Angeles, 1972. Mimeographed.

———. "Trends in the Provision of Public Services: Los Angeles Police Expenditures and Manpower Allocations, 1930–70." Institute on Law and Urban Studies, Los Angeles, 1972. Mimeographed.

Findley, James Clifford. "The Economic Boom of the 'Twenties in Los Angeles." Ph.D. diss., Claremont Graduate School, Claremont, Calif., 1958.

Gutiérrez, David G. "Ethnicity, Ideology and Political Development: Mexican Immigration as a Political Issue in the Chicano Community, 1910–1977." Ph.D. diss., Stanford University, 1987.

Harvey, Louise. "The Delinquent Mexican Boy in an Urban Area, 1945." Master's thesis, University of California, Los Angeles, 1947.

Johnson, Wendell F. "Citizens in Action: The Forty Year History of the Coordinating Council Movement in Los Angeles County." Federation of Coordinating Councils, Los Angeles, n.d.

Leader, Leonard J. "Los Angeles and the Great Depression." Ph.D. diss., University of California, Los Angeles, 1972.

Malaret, Jesús Francisco. "The Press and the Zoot-Suit Riots." Master's thesis, California State University, Sacramento, 1995.

Monroy, Douglas. "Mexicanos in Los Angeles 1930–1941: An Ethnic Group in Relation to Class Forces." Ph.D. diss., University of California, Los Angeles, 1978.

Morales, Armando. "A Study of Mexican American Perceptions of Law Enforcement Policies and Practices in East Los Angeles." Ph.D. diss., University of California, Los Angeles, 1972.

Myers, Ellen Howell. "The Mexican Liberal Party, 1903–1910." Ph.D. diss., University of Virginia, Charlottesville, 1971.

Pagán, Eduardo Obregón. "Sleepy Lagoon: The Politics of Youth and Race in Wartime Los Angeles, 1940–1945." Ph.D. diss., Princeton University, Princeton, N.J., 1996.

Reese, Charles D. "Police Academy Training and Its Effects on Prejudice." Master's thesis. Pepperdine University, Los Angeles, 1972.

Sánchez, George Joseph. "Barrio in Crisis: The Making of the Chicano Community in Los Angeles during the Great Depression." Senior thesis, Harvard University, Cambridge, Mass., 1981.

Scott, Robin Fitzgerald. "The Mexican-American in the Los Angeles Area, 1920–1950: From Acquiescence to Activity." Ph.D. diss., University of Southern California, Los Angeles, 1971.

Urban Policy Research Institute. "The Los Angeles Fire and Police Protective League: History of a Triumphant Police Lobby, 1960–1973." Urban Policy Research Institute, Los Angeles, 1973. Mimeographed.

Ward, James Randolph. "The Texas Ranger, 1919–1935: A Study in Law Enforcement." Ph.D. diss., Texas Christian University, Fort Worth, 1972.

Woods, James Gerald. "The Progressives and the Police: Urban Reform and the Professionalization of the Los Angeles Police." Ph.D. diss., University of California, Los Angeles, 1973.

PUBLISHED SOURCES

Acuña, Rodolfo. A Community under Siege: A Chronicle of Chicanos East of the Los Angeles River, 1945–1975. Los Angeles: Chicano Studies Research Center Publications, University of California at Los Angeles, 1984.

———. Occupied America: A History of Chicanos. 3ᵈ ed. San Francisco: Harper and Row, 1988.

Alamguer, Tomás. Racial Fault Lines: The Historical Origins of White Supremacy in California. Berkeley and Los Angeles: University of California Press, 1994.

"Aliso Village, Los Angeles." Architect and Engineer 152 (January 1943): 13–21.

Allen, Robert. Reluctant Reformers: Racism and Social Reform Movements in the United States. Garden City, N.Y.: Anchor Press, 1975.

Alvarez, Rodolfo. "The Psycho-Historical and Socioeconomic Development of the Chicano in the United States." *Social Science Quarterly* 5 (1973): 920–942.

Balderrama, Francisco E. *In Defense of La Raza: The Los Angeles Mexican Consulate and the Mexican Community, 1929 to 1936.* Tucson: University of Arizona Press, 1982.

Barrera, Mario. *Race and Class in the Southwest: A Theory of Racial Inequality.* Notre Dame, Ind.: University of Notre Dame Press, 1979.

Bayley, David H., ed. *Police and Society.* Beverly Hills: Sage Publications, 1977.

Bayley, David H., and Harold Mendolson. *Minorities and the Police: Confrontation in America.* New York: Free Press, 1968.

Bean, Walton. *California: An Interpretive History.* 3ᵈ ed. San Francisco: McGraw-Hill, 1978.

Bell, Horace. *Reminiscences of a Ranger, or Early Times in Southern California.* Santa Barbara, Calif.: Wallace Hebberd, 1927.

Bernstein, Irving. *The Lean Years: A History of the American Worker, 1920–1933.* Boston: Houghton Mifflin, 1963.

Bingham, Anne T. "Determinants of Sex Delinquency Based on Intensive Studies of 500 Cases." *Journal of Criminal Law and Criminology* 13 (February 1923): 519–536.

Bogardus, Emory S. "Gangs of Mexican-American Youth." *Sociology and Social Research* 28 (September 1943): 55–66.

———. *The Mexican in the United States.* University of Southern California Social Science Series, no. 8. Los Angeles: University of Southern California, 1934.

Bottles, Scott. *Los Angeles and the Automobile: The Making of the Modern City.* Berkeley and Los Angeles: University of California Press, 1987.

Brasol, Boris. "Foundations of Criminology." *Journal of Criminal Law and Criminology* 17 (May 1926): 13–39.

Camarillo, Albert. *Chicanos in a Changing Society: From Mexican Pueblos to American Barrios in Santa Barbara and Southern California, 1848–1930.* Cambridge: Harvard University Press, 1979.

———. *Chicanos in California: A History of Mexican Americans in California.* San Francisco: Boyd and Fraser, 1984.

Cardoso, Lawrence A. *Mexican Emigration to the United States, 1897–1931.* Tucson: University of Arizona Press, 1980.

Carte, Gene E., and Elaine H. Carte. *Police Reform in the United States: The Era of August Vollmer.* Berkeley and Los Angeles: University of California Press, 1975.

Carter, David L., and Thomas Barker, eds. *Police Deviance.* Cincinnati: Pilgrimage, 1986.

Castillo, Pedro, and Albert Camarillo, eds. *Furia y Muerte: Los Bandidos Chicanos,* Monograph no. 4. Los Angeles: Aztlán Publications, Chicano Studies Center, University of California at Los Angeles.

Center for Research on Criminal Justice. *The Iron Fist and the Velvet Glove: An Analysis of the U.S. Police.* 3ᵈ ed. Berkeley: Center for Research on Criminal Justice, 1977.

Citizens' Committee for the Defense of Mexican-American Youth. *The Sleepy*

Lagoon Case. Los Angeles: Citizens' Committee for the Defense of Mexican-American Youth, 1943.

Cline, Howard F. *The United States and Mexico*. Rev. ed. New York: Atheneum, 1969.

Cohen, Norman S., ed. *Civil Strife in America: A Historical Approach to the Study of Riots in America*. Hinsdale, Ill.: Dryden Press, 1972.

Collier, Peter, ed. *Crisis: A Contemporary Reader*. San Francisco: Harcourt, Brace and World, 1969.

Conot, Robert. *Rivers of Blood, Years of Darkness. Rebellion in the Streets: The First Full Story of America's Long Hot Summer of Hate*. New York: Bantam Books, 1967.

Daniel, Clete. *Chicano Workers and the Politics of Fairness: The FEPC in the Southwest, 1941–1945*. Austin: University of Texas Press, 1991.

Daniel, Cletus E. *Bitter Harvest: A History of California Farmworkers, 1870–1941*. Berkeley and Los Angeles: University of California Press, 1981.

Davis, Mike. *City of Quartz: Excavating the Future in Los Angeles*. New York: Vintage Books, 1990.

de la Garza, Rodolfo O., et al. *The Mexican American Experience: An Interdisciplinary Anthology*. Austin: University of Texas Press, 1985.

DeLeón, Arnaldo. *They Called Them Greasers: Anglo Attitudes toward Mexicans in Texas, 1821–1900*. Austin: University of Texas Press, 1983.

Doll, Edgar A. "The Comparative Intelligence of Prisoners." *Journal of Criminal Law and Criminology* 11 (May 1920): 191–197.

———. "A Study of Multiple Criminal Factors." *Journal of Criminal Law and Criminology* 11 (May 1920): 33–46.

Douthit, Nathan. "Police Professionalism and the War against Crime in the United States, 1920s–1930s." In *Police Forces in History*, edited by George Mosse, 317–333. Beverly Hills: Sage Publications, 1975.

Endor, Guy. *The Sleepy Lagoon Mystery*. Los Angeles: Sleepy Lagoon Defense Committee, 1944.

Erenberg, Lewis A., and Susan E. Hirsch, eds. *The War in American Culture: Society and Consciousness during World War II*. Chicago: University of Chicago Press, 1996.

Erickson, Milton Hyland. "A Study of the Relationship between Intelligence and Crime." *Journal of Criminal Law and Criminology* 19 (February 1929): 592–635.

Escobar, Edward J. "Dialectics of Repression: The Los Angeles Police Department and the Chicano Movement, 1968–1971." *Journal of American History* 79 (March 1993): 1483–1514.

Eulau, Heinz. "Sinarquismo in the United States." *Inter-American* 3 (March 1944): 25–27.

———. "The Sleepy Lagoon Case." *New Republic* (December 11, 1944): 795–796.

Farrell, Barry. "The Power Political behind the Badge: A Cop Who Would Be King." *New West* (December 19, 1977): 28–36.

Fields, Barbara Jeanne. "Slavery, Race, and Ideology in the United States of America." *New Left Review* 181 (May-June 1990): 95–98.

Fishkin, Shelley Fisher. "Interrogating 'Whiteness,' Complicating 'Blackness': Complicating American Culture." *American Quarterly* 47 (September 1995): 428–466.

Fogelson, Robert M. *Big City Police*. Cambridge: Harvard University Press, 1977.

———. *The Fragmented Metropolis: Los Angeles, 1850–1930*. Cambridge: Harvard University Press, 1967.

Friedman, Lawrence M. *Crime and Punishment in American History*. New York: Basic Books, 1993.

Gamio, Manuel. *Mexican Immigration to the United States: A Study of Human Migration and Adjustment*. New York: Dover Press, 1971.

García, Mario T. "Americans All: The Mexican American Generation and the Politics of Wartime Los Angeles, 1941–1945." In *The Mexican American Experience: An Interdisciplinary Anthology*, edited by Rodolfo O. de la Garza et al. Austin: University of Texas Press, 1985.

———. *Desert Immigrants: The Mexicans of El Paso, 1880–1930*. New Haven, Conn.: Yale University Press, 1981.

———. *Memories of Chicano History: The Life and Narrative of Bert Corona*. Berkeley and Los Angeles: University of California Press, 1994.

———. *Mexican Americans: Leadership, Ideology, and Identity, 1930–1960*. New Haven, Conn.: Yale University Press, 1989.

Gerstle, Gary. "Liberty, Coercion, and the Making of Americans." *Journal of American History* 84 (September 1997): 524–558.

Gilbert, James. *A Cycle of Outrage: America's Reaction to the Juvenile Delinquent in the 1950s*. New York: Oxford University Press, 1986.

Gómez, David F. "Chicanos Besieged: The Bloody Fiesta." *The Nation* (1971): 326–328.

Gómez-Quiñones, Juan. *Chicano Politics: Reality and Promise, 1940–1990*. Albuquerque: University of New Mexico Press, 1990.

———. *Sembradores; Ricardo Flores Magón y el Partido Liberal Mexicano: A Eulogy and Critique*. Los Angeles: Chicano Studies Center Publications, University of California at Los Angeles, 1973.

Gould, Stephen Jay. "The Geometer of Race." *Discover* 15 (November 1, 1994): 65–69.

Gourley, G. Douglas. *Public Relations and the Police*. Springfield, Ill.: Charles C. Thomas, 1953.

Grebler, Leo, Joan W. Moore, and Ralph Guzman, *The Mexican-American People: The Nation's Second Largest Minority*. New York: Free Press, 1970.

Griffith, Beatrice. *American Me*. Westport, Conn.: Greenwood Press, 1973.

Griswold del Castillo, Richard. *The Los Angeles Barrio, 1850–1890: A Social History*. Berkeley and Los Angeles: University of California Press, 1979.

———. *The Treaty of Guadalupe Hidalgo: A Legacy of Conflict*. Norman: University of Oklahoma Press, 1990.

Grove, Gene. "Sorry about That, Jack Webb." *Scanlan's Monthly* 1 (May 1970): 27–34.

Guerin-Gonzales, Camille. *Mexican Workers and American Dreams: Immigra-*

tion, *Repatriation and California Farm Labor, 1900–1939.* New Brunswick, N.J.: Rutgers University Press, 1994.

Gutiérrez, David G. *Walls and Mirrors: Mexican Americans, Mexican Immigrants, and the Politics of Ethnicity.* Berkeley and Los Angeles: University of California Press, 1995.

Hammarley, John. "Inside the Mexican Mafia." *New West* (December 19, 1977): 67–71.

Handman, Max Sylvus. "Preliminary Report on Nationality and Delinquency: The Mexican in Texas." In *The Mexican American and the Law,* edited by Carlos E. Cortés, 245–264. New York: Arno Press, 1974.

Haney López, Ian F. "The Social Construction of Race: Some Observations on Illusion, Fabrication, and Choice." *Harvard Civil Rights–Civil Liberties Law Review* 2 (winter 1994): 1–62.

———. *White by Law: The Legal Construction of Race.* New York: New York University Press, 1996.

Haring, Sidney L. *Policing a Class Society: The Experiences of American Cities, 1865–1915.* New Brunswick, N.J.: Rutgers University Press, 1983.

Hebdige, Dick. *Subculture: The Meaning of Style.* London: Methuen, 1979.

Hewes, Amy. "A Study of Delinquent Girls at Sleighton Farm." *Journal of Criminal Law and Criminology* 15 (February 1925): 599–610.

Higham, John. *Strangers in the Land: Patterns of American Nativism, 1860–1925.* New York: Atheneum, 1963.

Hoffman, Abraham. *Unwanted Mexican Americans in the Great Depression: Repatriation Pressures, 1929–1939.* Tucson: University of Arizona Press, 1979.

Hopkins, Ernest J. *Our Lawless Police: A Study of the Unlawful Enforcement of the Law.* New York: Viking Press, 1931.

Horowitz, Ruth. *Honor and the American Dream: Culture and Identity in a Chicano Community.* New Brunswick, N.J.: Rutgers University Press, 1983.

Horsman, Reginald. *Race and Manifest Destiny: The Origins of American Racial Anglo-Saxonism.* Cambridge: Harvard University Press, 1981.

James, Thomas H. *Chief Steckel Unmasked.* Los Angeles: Thomas H. James, 1931.

Jones, Solomon James. *The Government Riots of Los Angeles, June, 1943.* San Francisco: R and E Publications, 1973.

Kairys, David. *The Politics of Law: A Progressive Critique.* New York: Pantheon, 1982.

Kasun, Jacqueline Rorabeck. *Some Social Aspects of Business Cycles in the Los Angeles Area: 1920–1950.* Los Angeles: Haynes Foundation, 1954.

Kazin, Michael. "The Great Exception Revisited: Organized Labor and Politics in San Francisco and Los Angeles, 1870–1940." *Pacific Historical Review* 40 (August 1986): 371–402.

Keller, Gary D. *Hispanics and United States Film: An Overview and Handbook.* Tempe, Ariz.: Bilingual Review/Press, 1994.

Kennedy, Randall. *Race, Crime, and Law.* New York: Pantheon, 1997.

Koren, John. "What We Do Not Know about Crime." *Journal of Criminal Law and Criminology* 12 (November 1922): 447–448.

Lane, Roger. *Policing the City: Boston, 1822–1885.* New York: Atheneum, 1975.

Lipsitz, George. "The Possessive Investment in Whiteness: Racialized Social Democracy and the 'White' Problem in American Studies." *American Quarterly* 47 (September 1995): 369–387

———. "Toxic Racism." *American Quarterly* 47 (September 1995): 416–427.

Loza, Steven. *Barrio Rhythm: Mexican American Music in Los Angeles.* Chicago: University of Illinois Press, 1993.

MacLachlan, Colin M. *Anarchism and the Mexican Revolution: The Political Trials of Ricardo Flores Magón in the United States.* Berkeley and Los Angeles: University of California Press, 1991.

Manes, Hugh R. "A Report on Law Enforcement and the Negro Citizen in Los Angeles." Los Angeles: Hugh R. Manes, 1963.

Mann, Coramae Richey. *Unequal Justice: A Question of Color.* Bloomington: Indiana University Press, 1993.

Margolis, Ben. "The Sleepy Lagoon Case." *Los Angeles Guild Lawyer* 1 (December 1944).

Marx, Gary T. "Thoughts on a Neglected Category of Social Movement Participant: The Agent Provocateur and Informant." *American Journal of Sociology* 80 (1974): 402–442.

Masotti, Louis H., and Don R. Bowen, eds. *Riots and Rebellion: Civil Violence in the Urban Community.* Beverly Hills: Sage Publications, 1968.

May, Carl L. "Our Anti-Social Mexican Class." *Los Angeles County Employee* (March 1929): 12.

Mazón, Mauricio. *The Zoot-Suit Riots: The Psychology of Symbolic Annihilation.* Austin: University of Texas Press, 1984.

McWilliams, Carey. *North from Mexico: The Spanish-Speaking People of the United States.* New York: Greenwood Press, 1968.

———. *Southern California: An Island on the Land.* Santa Barbara: Peregrine Smith, 1973.

———. "The Zoot-Suit Riots." *New Republic* 108 (June 21, 1943): 818–819.

Medeiros, Francine. "*La Opinión,* a Mexican Exile Newspaper: A Content Analysis of Its First Years." *Aztlán, International Journal of Chicano Studies Research* 11 (spring 1980): 65–87.

Miles, Robert, and Rudy Torres. "Does 'Race Matter'? Transatlantic Perspectives on Racism after 'Race Relations.' " In *Re-situating Identities: The Politics of Race, Ethnicity and Culture,* edited by Vared Amit-Talai and Caroline Knowles, 24–46. Orchard Park, N.Y.: Broadview Press, 1995.

Monroy, Douglas. *Thrown among Strangers: The Making of Mexican Culture in Frontier California.* Berkeley and Los Angeles: University of California Press, 1990.

Montejano, David. *Anglos and Mexicans in the Making of Texas, 1836–1986.* Austin: University of Texas Press, 1987.

Moore, Joan W. *Going Down to the Barrio: Homeboys and Homegirls in Change.* Philadelphia: Temple University Press, 1991.

———. *Homeboys: Gangs, Drugs and Prison in the Barrios of Los Angeles.* Philadelphia: Temple University Press, 1978.

Morales, Armando. *Ando Sangrando (I Am Bleeding): A Study of Mexican American–Police Conflict*. La Puente, Calif.: Perspectiva Publications, 1972.

Morgen, Sandra, and Ann Bookman, eds. *Women and the Politics of Empowerment*. Philadelphia: Temple University Press, 1988.

Morín, Raúl. *Among the Valiant: Mexican-Americans in World War II and Korea*. Alhambra, Calif.: Borden Publishing, 1966.

Mosse, George L., ed. *Police Forces in History*. Beverly Hills: Sage Publications, 1975.

Mowry, George E. *The California Progressives*. Chicago: Quadrangle Books, 1963.

Muñoz, Carlos, Jr. *Youth, Identity, Power: The Chicano Movement*. New York: Verso, 1989.

Murchison, Carl. "American White Criminal Intelligence." *Journal of Criminal Law and Criminology* 15 (August and November 1924): 239–316 and 435–494.

Nash, Gerald D. *The American West Transformed: The Impact of the Second World War*. Bloomington: Indiana University Press, 1985.

National Committee to Free Los Tres. *The Case of Los Tres and the U.S. Involvement in Drug Traffic*. Los Angeles: National Committee to Free Los Tres, 1973.

Nelson, Howard J., and William A. V. Clark. *The Los Angeles Metropolitan Experience: Uniqueness, Generality, and the Goal of the Good Life*. Cambridge, Mass.: Ballinger Publishing, 1970.

Niederhoffer, Arthur, and Abraham S. Blumberg, eds. *The Ambivalent Force: Perspectives on the Police*. San Francisco: Rinehart Press, 1973.

Omi, Michael, and Howard Winant. *Racial Formation in the United States: From the 1960s to the 1990s*. 2d ed. New York: Routledge, 1994.

Parmelee, Maurice. *Criminology*. New York: Macmillan, 1921.

Paz, Octavio. *The Labyrinth of Solitude: Life and Thought in Mexico*. New York: Grove Press, 1961.

Peoples, Clem. "Smashing California's Baby Gangsters." *Sensation*, December 1942.

Perry, Louis B., and Richard B. Perry. *A History of the Los Angeles Labor Movement, 1911–1941*. Berkeley and Los Angeles: University of California Press, 1963.

Pesotta, Rose. *Bread upon the Waters*. New York: Dodd, Mead, and Company, 1945.

Pitt, Leonard. *The Decline of the Californios: A Social History of the Spanish-Speaking Californians, 1846–1890*. Berkeley and Los Angeles: University of California Press, 1971.

Prado, Enrique. "Sinarquism in the United States." *New Republic* 109 (July 26, 1943): 97–102.

Quinney, Richard. *Criminology*. 2d ed. Boston: Little, Brown, and Company, 1979.

Raat, W. Dirk. *Revoltosos: Mexico's Rebels in the United States, 1903–1923*. College Station: Texas A and M University Press, 1981.

Reisler, Mark. *By the Sweat of Their Brow: Mexican Immigrant Labor in the United States, 1900–1940.* Westport, Conn.: Greenwood Press, 1976.

Richardson, James. *The New York Police: Colonial Times to 1901.* New York: Oxford University Press, 1971.

Ríos-Bustamante, Antonio, and Pedro Castillo. *An Illustrated History of Mexican Los Angeles, 1781–1985.* Los Angeles: Chicano Studies Research Center, University of California at Los Angeles, 1986.

Robinson, Cyril D. "Criminal Justice History: Research in Progress in the United States." *Criminal Justice History* 3 (1982): 97–124.

———. "The Mayor and the Police—the Political Role of Police in Society." In *Police Forces in History,* edited by George Mosse, 277–315. Beverly Hills: Sage Publications, 1975.

Romo, Ricardo. *East Los Angeles: History of a Barrio.* Austin: University of Texas Press, 1983.

Rosales, F. Arturo. *Chicano! A History of the Mexican American Civil Rights Movement.* Houston: Arte Público Press, 1996.

Rowen, James. "Quick Triggers in New Mexico." *Nation* (1972): 781–783.

Rubinstein, Jonathan. *City Police.* New York: Farrar, Straus, and Giroux, 1973.

Ruiz, Manuel, Jr. "Latin-American Juvenile Delinquency in Los Angeles: Bomb or Bubble!" *Crime Prevention Digest* 1 (December 1942).

Ruiz, Vicki L. *Cannery Women, Cannery Lives: Mexican Women, Unionization and the California Food Processing Industry, 1930–1950.* Albuquerque: University of New Mexico Press, 1987.

———. *From Out of the Shadows: Mexican Women in Twentieth Century America.* New York: Oxford University Press, 1998.

———. " 'Star Struck': Acculturation, Adolescence, and the Mexican American Woman." In *Building with Our Hands,* edited by Adela de la Torre and Beartríz M. Pesquera, 109–129. Berkeley and Los Angeles: University of California Press, 1993.

Sacks, Harvey. "Notes on Police Assessment of Moral Character." In *Policing: A View from the Street,* edited by Peter K. Manning and John Van Maanen, 167–202. New York: Random House, 1978.

Samora, Julián, Joe Bernal, and Albert Peña. *Gunpowder Justice: A Reassessment of the Texas Rangers.* Notre Dame, Ind.: University of Notre Dame Press, 1979.

Sánchez, George I. "Pachucos in the Making." *Common Ground* (fall 1943): 13–20.

Sánchez, George J. *Becoming Mexican American: Ethnicity, Culture and Identity in Chicano Los Angeles, 1900–1945.* New York: Oxford University Press, 1993.

———. "Reading Reginald Denny: The Politics of Whiteness in the Late Twentieth Century." *American Quarterly* 47 (September 1995): 388–394.

Servín, Manuel P. *The Mexican Americans: An Awakening Minority.* Beverly Hills, Calif.: Glencoe Press, 1970.

Singleton, Gregory. *Religion in the City of Angels: American Protestant Culture and Urbanization, Los Angeles, 1850–1930.* Ann Arbor, Mich.: UMI Press, 1979.

Skerry, Peter. *Mexican Americans: The Ambivalent Minority*. New York: Free Press, 1993.

Skolnick, Jerome H. *Justice without Trial: Law Enforcement in a Democratic Society*. New York: Macmillan College Publishing, 1994.

———. "The Police in the Urban Ghetto." In *The Ambivalent Force: Perspectives on the Police*, edited by Arthur Niederhoffer and Abraham S. Blumberg, 223–238. San Francisco: Rinehart Press, 1973.

Slotkin, Richard. *Gunfighter Nation: The Myth of the Frontier in Twentieth-Century America*. New York: Harper Perennial, 1992.

Steffensmeier, Darrell J., Alvin S. Rosenthal, and Constance Shehan. "World War II and Its Effect on the Sex Differential in Arrests: An Empirical Test of the Sex-Role Equality and Crime Proposition." *Sociological Quarterly* 21 (summer 1980): 403–416.

Stimson, Grace Heilman. *Rise of the Labor Movement in Los Angeles*. Berkeley and Los Angeles: University of California Press, 1955.

Stone, Calvin P. "A Comparative Study of 399 Inmates of the Indiana Reformatory and 653 Men of the United States Army." *Journal of Criminal Law and Criminology* 12 (August 1921): 238–257.

Sutherland, Edwin H., and Donald R. Cressey. *Principles of Criminology*. 7th ed. Philadelphia: J. B. Lippincott, 1966.

Taft, Clinton J. *Fifteen Years on Freedom's Front*. Los Angeles: American Civil Liberties Union, 1939.

Taylor, Henry Louis, Jr. "The Hidden Face of Racism." *American Quarterly* 47 (September 1995): 395–408.

Taylor, Paul S. "Crime and the Foreign Born: The Problem of the Mexican." In *The Mexican American and the Law*, edited by Carlos E. Cortés, 199–243. New York: Arno Press, 1974.

Teneyuca, Emma, and Homer Brooks. "The Mexican Question in the Southwest." *Communist* (March 1939): 257–268.

Tuck, Ruth D. "Behind the Zoot Suit Riots." *Survey Graphic* 32 (August 1943): 818–820.

Vigil, James Diego. *Barrio Gangs: Street Life and Identity in Southern California*. Austin: University of Texas Press, 1988.

Walker, Samuel E. *A Critical History of Police Reform: The Emergence of Professionalism*. Lexington, Mass.: Lexington Books, 1977.

———. "The Origins of the American Police-Community Relations Movement: The 1940s." *Criminal Justice History* 1 (1980): 225–246.

Wallenberg, Charles. "Working on El Traque: The Pacific Electric Strike of 1903." In *The Chicano*, edited by Norris Hundley Jr. Santa Barbara: Clio Books, 1975.

Warnshuis, Paul Livingstone. "Crime and Criminal Justice among the Mexicans of Illinois." In *The Mexican American and the Law*, edited by Carlos E. Cortés, 266–329. New York: Arno Press, 1974.

Weber, Devra Ann. "The Organizing of Mexicano Agricultural Workers: Imperial Valley and Los Angeles, an Oral History Approach." *Aztlán, International Journal of Chicano Studies Research* 3 (fall 1972): 307–347.

Weinberg, Albert K. *Manifest Destiny: A Study in Nationalist Expansionism in American History.* Baltimore: Johns Hopkins University Press, 1935.

Westley, William A. *Violence and the Police: A Sociological Study of Law, Custom, and Morality.* Cambridge: MIT Press, 1970.

Whitten, Woodrow C. "Criminal Syndicalism and the Law in California: 1919–1927." *Transactions of the American Philosophical Society,* n.s., 59, pt. 2 (March 1969).

Williams, William E. "A Tragic Vision of Black Problems." *American Quarterly* 47 (September 1995): 409–415.

Willis, Clark. "Success Record of Delinquent Boys in Relation to Intelligence." *Journal of Delinquency* 5 (September 1920): 174–182.

Wilson, James Q. *Varieties of Police Behavior: The Management of Law and Order in Eight Communities.* Cambridge: Harvard University Press, 1978.

Womack, John, Jr. *Zapata and the Mexican Revolution.* New York: Vintage Books, 1968.

Index

Compositor:	Binghamton Valley Composition, Inc.
Text:	10/13 Sabon
Display:	Sabon